PI Jl 29.9.92

AF901126

New Directions in English Language Corpora

Topics in English Linguistics
9

Editors

Jan Svartvik
Herman Wekker

Mouton de Gruyter
Berlin · New York

New Directions in English Language Corpora

Methodology, Results, Software Developments

Edited by

Gerhard Leitner

Mouton de Gruyter
Berlin · New York 1992

Mouton de Gruyter (formerly Mouton, The Hague)
is a Division of Walter de Gruyter & Co., Berlin.

Ⓞ Printed on acid-free paper which falls within the guidelines of the ANSI to ensure permanence and durability.

Library of Congress Cataloging in Publication Data

New directions in English language corpora : methodology, results, software developments / edited by Gerhard Leitner.
p. cm. — (Topics in English linguistics ; 9)
Includes bibliographical references and index.
ISBN 3-11-013201-X (acid-free paper)
1. English language — Research — Data processing.
2. English language — Discourse analysis — Data processing.
3. Computational linguistics. I. Leitner, Gerhard. II. Series.
PE1074.5.N48 1992
420′.285 — dc20 92-26798
CIP

Die Deutsche Bibliothek — Cataloging in Publication Data

New directions in English language corpora : methodology, results, software developments / ed. by Gerhard Leitner. — Berlin ; New York : Mouton de Gruyter, 1992
(Topics in English linguistics ; Bd. 9)
ISBN 3-11-013201-X
NE: Leitner, Gerhard; GT

© Copyright 1992 by Walter de Gruyter & Co., D-1000 Berlin 30.
All rights reserved, including those of translation into foreign languages. No part of this book may be reproduced or transmitted in any form or by any means, electronic or mechanical, including photocopy, recording, or any information storage and retrieval system, without permission in writing from the publisher.
Typesetting and printing: Arthur Collignon GmbH, Berlin.
Binding: Lüderitz & Bauer, Berlin.
Printed in Germany.

Preface

The corpus-based study of English, as of other languages, has a long tradition, powerfully continued by the researchers and research teams from all over the world who group around the *International Computer Archive of Modern English* (ICAME). ICAME, with its annual meetings (cf. S. Johansson and A.-B. Stenström 1990) and *ICAME Journal*, celebrated its tenth anniversary in Bergen, Norway, where it provided, as usual, "the forum for a wide range of computational corpus linguistic work on English conducted right across the world" (Souter 1990: 14). The new decade began in 1990 in Berlin at a moment that could not have been more appropriate. The wall had come down, eastern European countries began to open up – and it was thus possible for researchers and interested scholars from these parts of the world to attend the conference and to learn from the experiences and results of corpus linguistic work.

The present volume contains a selection of revised papers from the Berlin meeting.[1] It is grouped around three main themes. Firstly, corpus design and text encoding. As the construction of large-scale corpora in the order of many million words becomes less of a problem and more of an ordinary research and teaching commodity, the methodology of corpus design raises new problems and is interesting in the context of English as a world language. English, as is well-known, has potentially quite different manifestations within the native English world and in second language countries. Any corpus that is designed to be used, or is also used, for comparative purposes must be sensitive to both "local" and "global" needs. Methodological problems of corpus design are discussed in the papers by Peter de Haan, Jeremy Clear, Gerhard Leitner, John Kirk, and Christian Mair. These papers look at the differences between native and second language countries, the contrast between "traditional" forms of English and pidgins and creoles, and the spoken and written dimensions. Lou Burnard gives a progress report on the work of the Text Encoding Initiative's attempt to make corpora comparable in their material, physical shape.

The second theme centres around the application of corpus-based analyses to the design and development of software for automated natural language analysis that is suitable for purposes outside corpus linguistics proper. Corpus linguistics thus increasingly feeds back into communication science as such. The papers by Nancy Belmore, Willem de Meijs, Sylvia Janssen, Steve Fligelstone, Geoffrey Sampson, Stephen Sutton and Anthony

McEnery focus on a variety of problems, such as automated semantic analysis of lexemes and texts, parsing, information retrieval and tagging.

The last theme of the present volume continues the more traditional concern of corpus linguistics, *viz.* the description of the English language proper. But here again new directions come to the fore, directions that link that dimension to that of the future large-scale corpora. Thus a comparative research orientation comes out very strongly in the papers by Christer Geisler, Edgar Schneider, Kay Wikberg, and S. V. Shastri. The problems involved in the study of historical periods of English, when it was barely as standardized as it is today, form the focus of Geoff Barnbrook's paper. His results have their uses in the analysis of contemporary varieties, such as pidgins and creoles. The papers by Gerry Knowles, Antoinette Renouf, Hilde Hasselgård, Göran Kjellmer, and Jacques Noël are on a single variety, British English. They also raise new dimensions: how do we construct future reference materials that lead the learner not only to "grammatical" but also to "native-like" utterances, how can one make use of corpus studies in translation, how is the gap between lexis and grammar overcome, etc.

New Dimensions in English Language Corpora thus illustrates the orientations of English corpus linguistics in *ICAME*'s second decade. And, given the international standing of its members, it is not hard to foresee that they will shape research and applications in English linguistics.

Note

1. The editor is grateful to the numerous organizations which supported in many ways the 11th ICAME conference in Berlin. These are in particular the German Research Foundation (DFG), IBM Stifterverband within the Stifterverband für die Deutsche Wissenschaft, IBM, Siemens, the British Council, the German Academic Exchange Service, as well as the Ministry of Higher Education in Berlin and the Freie Universität Berlin. Without their help and constant support that conference would not have been as successful as it was.

References

ICAME Journal. Ed. Stig Johansson University of Oslo, Norway.

Johansson, Stig — Anna-Brita Stenström (eds.)
1991 *English computer corpora*. Berlin: Mouton de Gruyter.

Souter, Clive
1990 "Corpus linguistics: The state of the science. The 10th ICAME conference, June 1–4th, Bergen", *CCE Newsletter* 4(1/2): 1–15.

Contents

Part I
Corpus design and text encoding

The optimum corpus sample size?

Pieter de Haan

1. Introduction

Numerous corpus studies have been carried out in the past two to three decades, many of them on the standard corpora of American and British English (Brown and LOB), both consisting of 500 samples of 2000 words each. One element that has so far not been given much attention is the possible effect of the size of the corpus samples on the research results. As the corpora were assumed to represent a broad cross-section of English, and the focus originally was mainly on frequency and distribution of lexical items, the samples were considered to be sufficiently large to yield reliable results.

More recently corpus linguists' interest has gone beyond the lexical level to the level of syntactic description. The compilation of corpora, in the mean time, has continued very much in the style of the first two corpora, implying that they still usually consist of samples of 2000 words.[1] The question arises whether samples of 2000 words are sufficiently large to yield reliable information on the frequency and distribution of syntactic structures.

Experience with samples of 20,000 words has shown that on the whole these are sufficiently large to yield statistically reliable results on frequency and distribution (cf. e. g. De Haan 1989: 50–51), but even they are sometimes too small, especially when complex interactions are studied (cf. e. g. De Haan–Van Hout 1986: 89), simply because the number of observations yielded is too small. The conclusion seems to be that the suitability of the sample depends on the specific study that is undertaken, and that there is no such thing as the best, or optimum, sample size as such.

2. Frequency tables and sample size

This can be demonstrated by comparing the figures yielded in two entirely different research projects, one of them designed to study the distribution of the most frequent prepositions in the LOB corpus (cf. Mindt – Weber 1989), the other being part of a larger project (cf. Aarts *et al.* to appear), which aims at describing the frequency and distribution of the major syntactic structures that are found in the Nijmegen corpus (cf. De Haan 1984: 134). In Mindt – Weber (1989: 233) it is shown that a mere ten prepositions are used in 86.9% of all the prepositional phrases, whereas it takes another 87 prepositions to account for the remaining 13.1%. In Table 1 the ten most frequent prepositions in the LOB corpus are presented in a decreasing order, together with the ten most frequent prepositions in the written part of the Nijmegen corpus.[2]

Table 1. The ten most frequent prepositions in LOB and Nijmegen

	LOB (Cf. Mindt & Weber 1989)		Nijmegen		
	frequency	cum. %	frequency	cum. %	
of	35287	28.6	of	3300	27.5
in	20250	45.0	in	2055	44.6
to	10876	53.8	to	1050	53.4
for	8738	60.9	with	669	59.0
with	7170	66.7	for	640	64.3
on	6251	71.8	by	563	69.0
by	5724	76.4	at	495	73.1
at	5473	80.8	on	477	77.1
from	4672	84.6	from	418	80.6
as	2804	86.9	as	342	83.4

A comparison of the two sets of data in Table 1 shows that there are very few differences between the two corpora as far as the frequency and distribution of prepositions are concerned. Not only is it exactly the same ten prepositions that occur in both tables, but the relative distribution of these ten is also virtually the same. Considering that the Nijmegen corpus is roughly one eighth the size of LOB, we can see that the frequency of these prepositions is not exactly the same in relative terms: the number of prepositions is relatively smaller in the Nijmegen corpus than in LOB. This is at least partly due to the fact that in the Nijmegen corpus multi-word prepositions have been coded separately and are, consequently, not included in Table 1.[3] Nevertheless, it would seem that for the study of the frequency and distribution of these prepositions either corpus could be used.

Moreover, when we consider the composition of the two corpora we can say, from a statistical point of view, that both corpora are suitable for the study of the frequency and distribution of these prepositions. For the LOB corpus is composed of 500 samples of 2000 words each, whereas the written part of the Nijmegen corpus consists of 6 samples of 20,000 words each. For a relatively simple statistical test on the distribution of the prepositions over the various samples, such as a chi-square test, to be reliable, the number of observations (= occurrences) of the phenomenon studied must be sufficiently large in each sample. It is generally accepted that chi-square tests are no longer reliable when the minimum expected cell frequency (= the number of expected observations of a single variable, such as, in this case, a certain preposition in a single sample) is lower than five.[4]

Looking at the ten most frequent prepositions in the LOB corpus we see that the preposition at the bottom of the table (*as*) occurs 2804 times. Assuming that it is more or less evenly distributed over the various samples[5] we may expect it to occur 2804/500 = 5.6 times in each sample, which can be regarded as statistically sufficient. Making the same assumption for the Nijmegen corpus we may expect the least frequent preposition in this table to occur 342/6 = 57 times.[6] For the study of these prepositions the samples in the Nijmegen corpus might therefore be considered to be unduly large.

However, when we want to study a syntactic category like the noun phrase, and more specifically its frequency and distribution in relation to its realisation, which is a highly detailed study, we see that the size of the samples plays a far more crucial role.

Consider Table 2, which lists the 22 most frequent noun phrase structures that are found in the Nijmegen corpus as a whole.[7] In all, the table contains a little under 90 different structures. In Table 2 the most frequent ones are presented together with their frequencies in decreasing order. The reason why only the 22 most frequent structures are included in Table 2 is precisely the point that was raised above. The 23rd structure in the table (in decreasing order) occurs 29 times. Considering the composition of the written part of the Nijmegen corpus (6 × 20,000 words), there is no way in which the minimum expected cell frequency for that particular structure could be at least 5 in each of the samples, for

Table 2. The 22 most frequent noun phrase structures in the Nijmegen corpus, in decreasing order

HD	31896
DET HD	5736
DET HD POM	2557
DET PREM HD	2131
PREM HD	1810
HD POM	1603
DET PREM HD POM	1119
PREM HD POM	440
A B	387
JOIN COOR JOIN	322
DET PREM PREM HD	231
PREM PREM HD	215
DET HD POM POM	180
DET PREM PREM HD POM	109
DET DET HD	75
HD POM POM	74
DET PREM HD POM POM	73
PREM PREM HD POM	72
JOIN COOR JOIN COOR JOIN	55
PREM DET HD	38
A LIM XB	35
DET DET HD POM	35

$6 \times 5 = 30$. In other words, there will be at least one sample in which this structure cannot be expected to occur at least five times. This means that figures on the distribution of that particular structure over samples cannot be regarded as statistically reliable. The two least frequent structures that do occur in the table in Table 2 both occur 35 times. Under the assumption that they are evenly distributed over the corpus samples we might expect to find them at least 5 times in each sample, which would mean that the outcome of statistical tests would be reliable.

If we were to draw up a similar table on the basis of samples of 2000 words, however, we might, on average, expect them to occur about ten times less often. This, in turn, would mean that the "cut-off point" for statistical reliability would be found at the dotted line, leaving no more than 10 different structures in the table. Although they are the major noun phrase structures, including appositive structures (A B) and coordinated structures (JOIN COOR JOIN), we see that a number of linguistically interesting structures are no longer present, most notably all the cases of multiple pre- or postmodification. At this stage the researcher has to make the decision whether to be satisfied with this incomplete table, or to specify less detail, e. g. by collapsing more than one structure into one single category. In this particular case it might be decided to collapse the structures DET PREM HD, DET PREM PREM HD and PREM DET HD into one category DET PREM HD, in which DET means any number of determiners, PREM any number of premodifiers, and DET PREM at least one determiner and at least one premodifier in any order.[8] A third option would be to collect new corpus data, using samples that are larger than 2000 words, for studies like this, which go beyond more general levels of syntactic description.

3. The experiment

In order to assess the impact of a reduction of corpus samples of 20,000 words to samples of smaller size (2000, 5000, 10,000 and 15,000 words) on the study of a particular syntactic phenomenon we decided to concentrate on one sample in the Nijmegen corpus and actually reduce it.[9]

3.1. Dividing the sample into smaller stretches

The first step was to find a proper way of dividing the sample into ten stretches of equal length.[10] At the same time we had to consider whether it might be better to select ten stretches of 2000 words worth of sentences at random from the sample than to select ten consecutive stretches of 2000 words of running text. In either case we had to gain insight into the distribution of sentence length in the sample. If a random selection was preferred it had to be decided whether, for instance, it would be sufficient to take sentences 1, 11, 21, 31 ... together as one collection, sentences 2, 12, 22, 32 ... as another, sentences 3, 13, 23, 33 ... as a third, and so on. This could only be done if all the sentences in each of the collections created in this way on average turned out to be of average length. If, on the other hand, stretches of 2000 words worth of running text were to be taken, we still had to know the length of each sentence in order to work out where to make the divisions.

We decided to concentrate on stretches of running text first, and leave making any comparisons between running text and randomised text for another project (cf. Schils – De Haan, to appear). Figure 1 shows the average sentence length in the ten consecutive stretches of 2000 words in this sample. It is taken from *The Bloody Wood*, a crime fiction novel. Figure 1 suggests that sentence length is not a randomly distributed

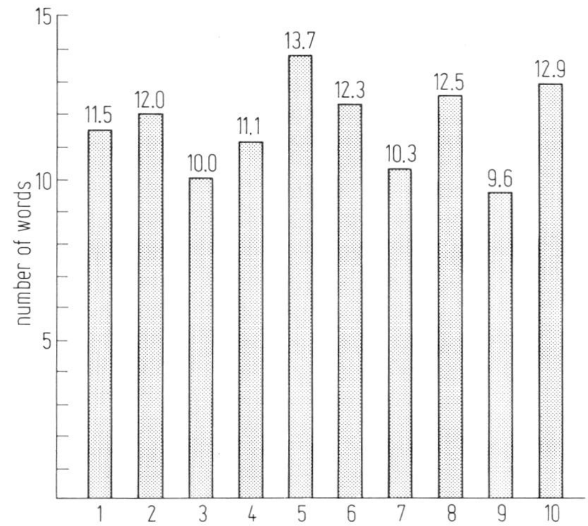

Figure 1. The Bloody Wood – average sentence lengths in ten consecutive stretches of 2000 words

variable in this sample. It should be noted that the sample has not been taken from either the beginning or the end of the book, but from the middle (the 20,000 word sample actually starts on page 37), so that no conclusions can be drawn from this as to the existence of any specific characteristics of the introductory or the final part of this novel. Still, we can observe a good deal of variation in the distribution of sentence length over the various stretches.

3.2. Sentence type

We also looked at the proportion of dialogue sentences in the various stretches. Figure 2 shows that the distribution of dialogue sentences in the samples is by no means random, either. A comparison between Figure 1 and Figure 2 suggests that those stretches that feature many dialogue sentences (most notably the third one) are also made up of shorter sentences on average. Alternatively, the stretches with the longest

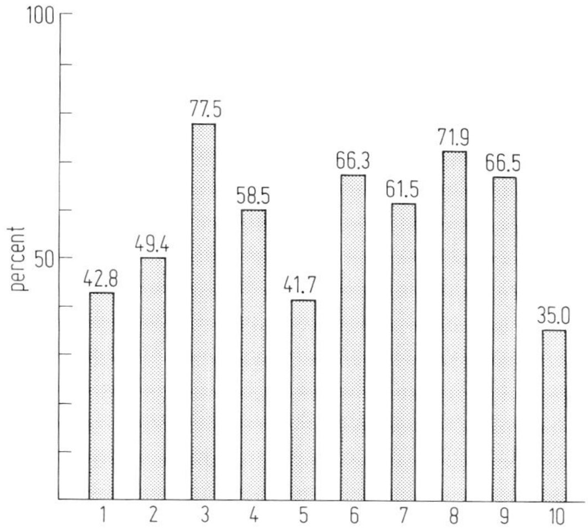

Figure 2. The Bloody Wood – proportion of dialogue sentences in ten consecutive stretches of 2000 words

sentences on average (notably the fifth one) are the ones with the fewest dialogue sentences. This, in turn, may lead to the conclusion that dialogue sentences are, on average, shorter than nondialogue sentences, which is indeed what we found. We were interested to see how this came about.

3.3. Sentence pattern

In order to establish the precise nature of the relation between sentence length and sentence type we looked at the sentence patterns (= the sequence of constituents on the level of the sentence) that were present in all the sentences of the ten stretches in relation to dialogue and nondialogue sentences. Figure 3 shows the nine most frequent sentence patterns that were found in the overall 20,000 word sample, distributed over dialogue and nondialogue sentences, and in an overall decreasing frequency of occurrence. Among them, they cover about 35% of the sentence patterns found. In all, no fewer than 300 different sentence patterns were found in the overall sample. Three things should be noted here:

1. The term "sentence pattern" in this context implies that e. g. SVC means exactly what it says: a subject followed by a verb, which is itself

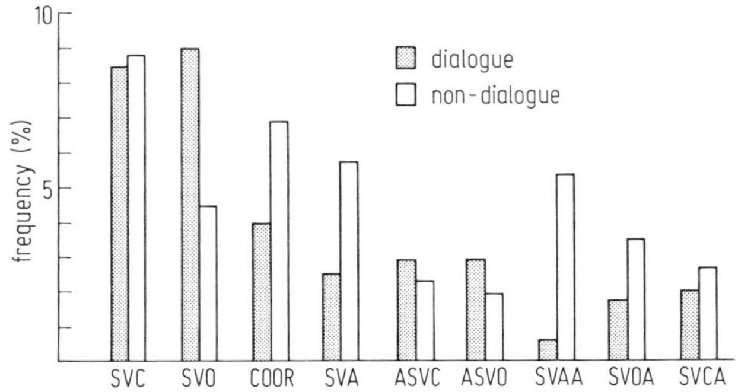

Figure 3. The Bloody Wood – distribution of the nine most frequent sentence patterns in dialogue and nondialogue sentences

followed by a complement. No optional constituents are included. No allowance is made for any possible permutation of the order of the constituents.

2. The pattern COOR stands for "coordination on sentence level", i. e. what is called a compound sentence by Quirk et al. (1985: 987).
3. The least frequent of the patterns in Figure 5 constitutes the "cut-off point" for statistical reliability in the subsequent statistical analyses: the distribution of the next lower structure on the list could not be statistically accounted for.

Figure 3 shows that the sentence patterns are not randomly distributed over dialogue and nondialogue sentences. The chi-square tests are highly significant, and the standardised residuals point especially to the patterns SVO (very frequent occurrence in the dialogue sentences) and SVAA (very frequent occurrence in the nondialogue sentences).

Next, we looked at the distribution of these patterns over short and long sentences. This is shown in Figure 4. Again, the distribution of the sentence patterns over short and long sentences is by no means random: the chi-square test is highly significant and points especially to the patterns SVC / SVO / SVA (frequent in short sentences) and COOR / ASVO (frequent in the long sentences). The division of sentence lengths into two classes (one up to nine words, one longer than nine words) is not entirely arbitrary: it divides all the sentences in the sample into two groups with roughly the same number of sentences. This was done in order to provide a better guarantee that the cells in the subsequent analyses would not be empty (it can be observed that the pattern SVAA

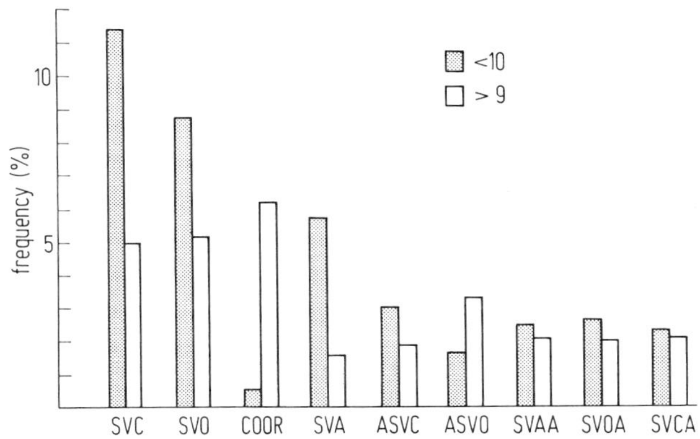

Figure 4. The Bloody Wood — distribution of the nine most frequent sentence patterns by sentence length

occurs very infrequently among the short sentences). The presence of too many empty cells makes the interpretation of statistical analyses less reliable. Moreover, if we had distinguished more length classes (which we might easily have done) it would have made the subsequent statistical analysis too complex, seeing that there were already nine different sentence patterns in the analysis.

3.4. Loglinear analysis of the data

In order to assess the relationships holding among the three variable features (sentence type, i. e. dialogue vs. nondialogue; sentence length; sentence pattern) we carried out a loglinear analysis (cf. De Haan — Van Hout 1986: 83—93; 1988: 9—21) of a three-way contingency table in which these three variables were present. This analysis of the data of the 20,000 word sample showed us that there is a significant relationship between the sentence pattern and the sentence type. There is also a significant relationship between the sentence pattern and the length of the sentence. Contrary to what we had found earlier, however, no significant relationship was found between the sentence length and the sentence type.

This means that our earlier conclusion, that dialogue sentences are shorter than nondialogue sentences, needs to be revised in the sense that there is only an indirect relationship between these two variables: dialogue favours certain sentence patterns, notably relatively simple ones; these patterns occur in short sentences; therefore dialogue sentences tend to be short, on average. After all, it stands to reason that in order to develop a simple pattern fewer words are needed than when a more complex pattern is developed.[11]

The loglinear analysis of the three-way table pointed to five significant effects (i. e. effects that were not only significant in the two-way crosstabulations, but which remained significant even in the three-way interaction table):

1. The pattern SVO is found especially in dialogue sentences;
2. The pattern SVAA is found especially in nondialogue sentences;
3. The pattern SVC is found especially in short sentences;
4. Coordinated sentences are long;
5. The pattern SVA is found especially in short sentences.

3.5. Crosstabulations of the data in the smaller stretches

The analyses so far provided us with a means of assessing the impact of a reduction of the sample size. For while we were gaining insight into the sequence of sentence lengths in the 20,000 word sample, we also studied the interaction of the three variables discussed above. We now proceeded to repeat the original series of two-way crosstabulations for each of the ten stretches of 2000 words, in order to find out how the five significant effects that we had established in the loglinear analysis were significantly represented in them. The results are shown in Figure 5.

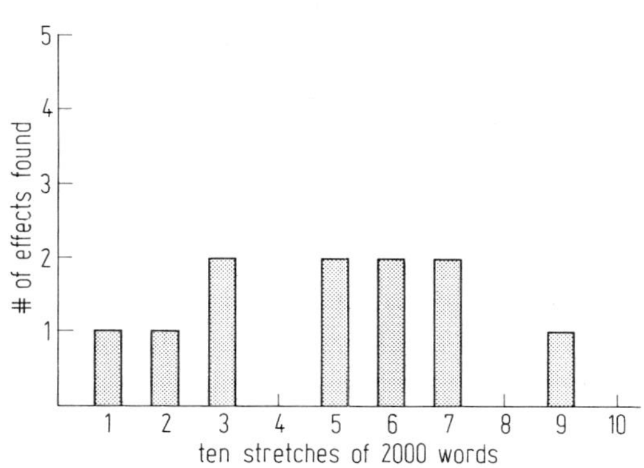

Figure 5. The Bloody Wood — the number of significant effects found in ten consecutive stretches of 2000 words

Figure 5 clearly shows that none of the 2000 word stretches contain as many significant effects as the original sample. Four of them show two effects, three only one, while three do not show any significant effect at all. Figure 6 shows how often the five effects individually are found in the ten stretches.

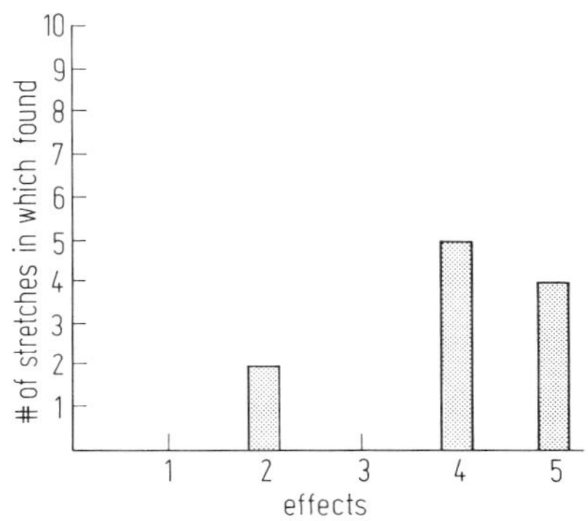

Figure 6. The Bloody Wood — distribution of the significant effects in ten consecutive stretches of 2000 words

It can be seen that two of them are not significant in any of the ten stretches, while the most widespread one in the overall sample (effect #4, which is not even the most interesting of them) is significant in not more than five of the ten stretches. There are possibly two reasons for this observation. In the first place the limited size of the ten stretches, implying a limited number of observations, poses restrictions on the number of effects for which a significant distribution can be determined. In the second place, we had already observed great variation in the number of dialogue sentences in each of the ten stretches, which will undoubtedly have an effect on the presence of specific sentence patterns and, through those, on sentence lengths.

The figures improved when the crosstabulations were repeated for larger stretches of running text. Figure 7 shows how the five effects distinguished in the loglinear analysis were significantly present in four consecutive stretches of 5000 words. All of these stretches show at least two effects significantly, while one of them even shows all five effects. At the same time it can, however, be seen that there are still great differences between two consecutive stretches. In Figure 8 it is shown how often each of the five effects occur in the four stretches of 5000 words.

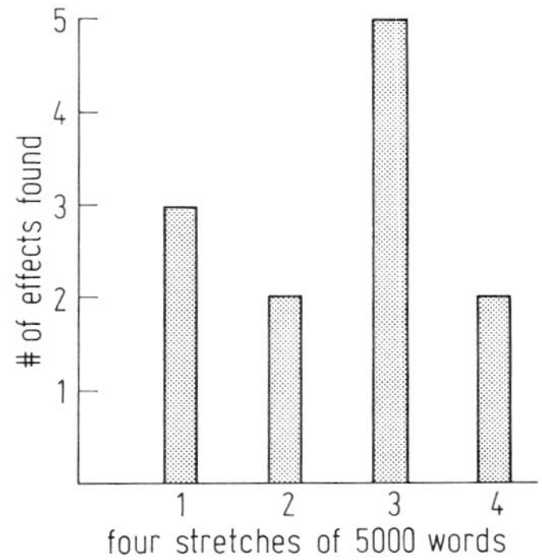

Figure 7. The Bloody Wood – the number of significant effects found in four consecutive stretches of 5000 words

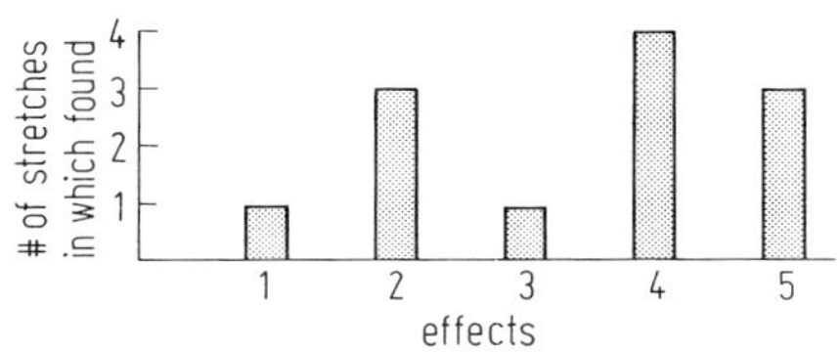

Figure 8. The Bloody Wood – distribution of the significant effects in four consecutive stretches of 5000 words

Effects # 1 and # 3 each now occur in one stretch of words. Apparently these effects are less strong than the other effects, which occur in at least three stretches of words. Effect # 4 is now found throughout the original sample.

To complete the picture, the crosstabulations were carried out on two consecutive stretches of 10,000 words and two stretches of 15,000 words, which partly overlapped, in the sense that one covered the first 15,000 words of the original sample, and the other the last 15,000 words, an overlap of 10,000 words. The results of the crosstabulations of the data in the two stretches of 10,000 words are shown in Figures 9 and 10. Figure 9 shows that each of the two stretches has four of the effects on a significant level, which is actually not a complete improvement on the previous crosstabulation. Not only is it not the same four effects that are found in the two stretches (so that they are still considerably different: they share only three effects), but, as Figure 7 shows, there is one 5000 word stretch that had all five effects on a significant level. Figure 10 shows that effects # 3 and # 5 are found in only one of the two stretches.

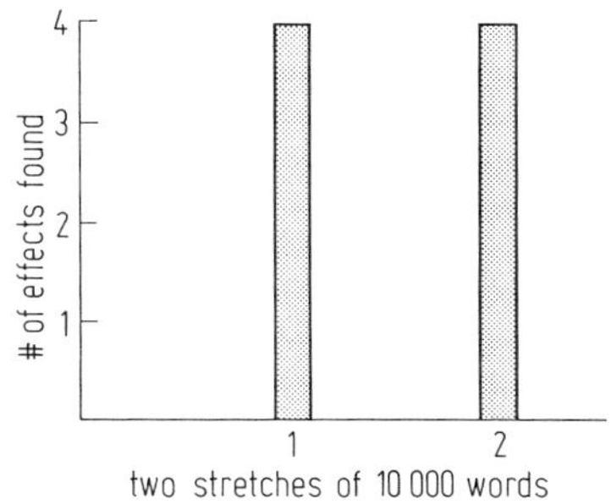

Figure 9. The Bloody Wood — the number of significant effects found in two consecutive stretches of 10,000 words

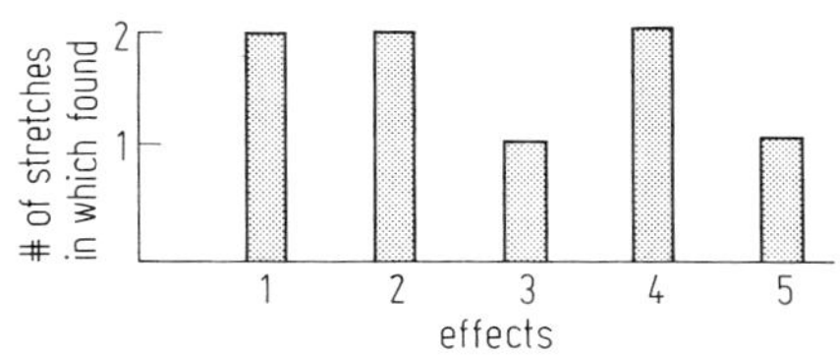

Figure 10. The Bloody Wood — distribution of the significant effects in two consecutive stretches of 10,000 words

Since neither stretch shows all five effects significantly, this must mean that they are not both found in the same stretch. The crosstabulations on the two stretches of 15,000 words did not improve the results of those for the stretches of 10,000 words: neither stretch showed the five effects significantly.

The preceeding discussion shows that even 15,000 words are not sufficient to establish the interaction discussed in section 3.4 in this particular sample to the same extent. Whether all this necessarily means that our original sample of 20,000 words is large enough to establish the full extent of this interaction in the entire text (which is roughly two and a half times as long as the sample) is a question that cannot as yet be answered.[12]

3.6. Further research on language variation

Ultimately we want to be able to use the study of samples of any size to make comparisons between texts representing different categories or authors. Figure 11 shows the distribution of the ten most frequent sen-

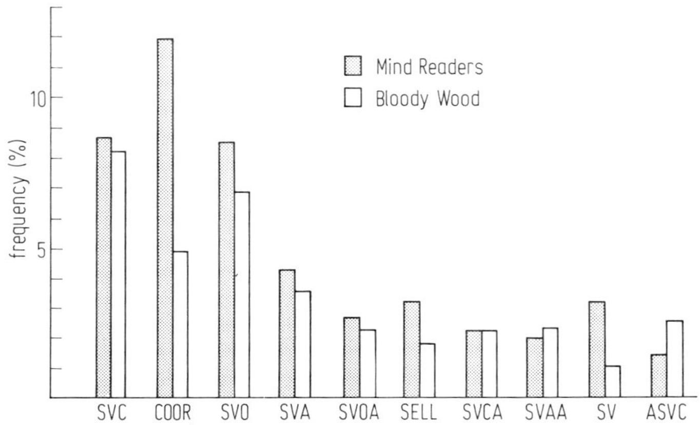

Figure 11. Distribution of the ten most frequent sentence patterns in *The Bloody Wood* and *The Mind Readers*

tence patterns in two samples of 20,000 words: *The Bloody Wood* and *The Mind Readers*, another crime fiction text, by a different author. The sentence patterns are presented from left to right in a decreasing order of frequency, based on the total figures of the two combined samples. It can be seen that the two authors do not distribute the various patterns in the same way: an obvious example is coordination on sentence level, which is clearly done more often in *The Mind Readers*. The chi-square test indicates that this score is highly significant. When the same crosstabulation was carried out another 25 times on smaller stretches, viz. in all the possible combinations of 5 stretches of 2000 words taken from *The Bloody Wood* and five stretches taken from *The Mind Readers* (in all $5 \times 5 = 25$ different comparisons) only seven of these crosstabulations showed a significant score for the coordination pattern, which suggests that if a comparison between these two texts is made on the basis of randomly selected stretches of 2000 words there is only a 28% chance that this difference can be statistically shown.

4. Conclusion

The discussion in this article has shown that there are studies that can quite adequately be undertaken on the basis of relatively small samples.

These may include comparative studies, provided that the number of observations on which the conclusions are based are large enough. There are, however, certainly also studies that can only be successfully carried out on the basis of larger samples. This is not necessarily only related to the number of observations, but also to the nature of the phenomenon studied. This would appear to be especially true for the study of complex interactions, which requires more sophisticated statistical techniques.

Another aspect of corpus sampling, which was hinted at in section 3.1, is the fact that frequency and distribution studies are carried out on them as if they were random samples (i. e. random collections of sentences which are, in principle, unrelated). The comparison of the study of various aspects of sentences in a sample of running text with that of sentences in a randomised sample (i. e. a sample in which the sentences have been placed in a random order) may well point to a number of characteristics that have hitherto not been noticed. We have, for instance, found (cf. Schils – De Haan, to appear) that the sequence of sentences with specific lengths is not arbitrary, but that within texts specific passages can be isolated with characteristic sequences of sentence lengths. We have also found that this particular aspect of sequences of sentences plays a more important role in fiction texts than in non-fiction texts.

In Schils – De Haan (to appear) an attempt is made at developing a model which aims at assessing the effect(s) of running text. This model would not only concentrate on the sequence of sentence lengths, but would also take such syntactic characteristics into account as sentence patterns in consecutive sentences; the presence or absence of adverbials, and if so, how these are distributed over the available positions in the sentence; inversion of subject and verb; etc. Ultimately we hope to arrive at a model that can make explicit claims about the syntactic nature of various passages in running text.

Notes

1. An obvious exception to this practice, of course, has been the Survey of English Usage (SEU), and the computerized version of the spoken part of SEU, the London-Lund Corpus (LLC), which consists of samples of 5,000 words.
2. I would like to thank Hans van Halteren for providing me with the material that enabled me to do the statistics on the Nijmegen corpus for this and the following figures.
3. This means that combinations like *in addition to* or *in spite of* etc., which will have raised the scores for *in*, *of*, and *to* in the LOB corpus, do not add to the scores for these single prepositions in the Nijmegen corpus.

4. The chi-square statistic option in SPSS-X will actually say how many cells in the crosstabulation have expected cell frequencies < 5 (= lower than five).
5. As I do not have figures on distribution over the samples in LOB I have not been able to verify this.
6. Actually, I have looked into this and found that for this particular preposition (*as*) the minimum expected cell frequency was 28, which was well above the statistically acceptable minimum of 5. It does, however, indicate that the assumption that this preposition is evenly distributed over all the corpus samples cannot be maintained. The actually observed cell frequency of this preposition in this particular corpus sample was 9, pointing to a significantly low frequency.
7. I do not have similar figures for any of the other corpora, so this point of the discussion is purely theoretical.
8. For a general survey study this might be considered a perfectly acceptable strategy (cf. Aarts *et al.* to appear). For detailed studies one may wonder whether it is desirable to distinguish categories that comprise this amount of variation.
9. I am extremely grateful to Erik Schils for his willingness to collaborate with me on this.
10. As I wish to reserve the word sample in this article for the original collection of 20,000 words of running text, I will use the word stretch to refer to a smaller collection of words, whether running or randomized, taken from that text.
11. This is, of course, only partly true. It might well be the case, for instance, that a sentence with a relatively simple sentence patterns turns out to have an object noun phrase which is highly complex and which would therefore make the sentence rather long. For a discussion of simple vs. complex noun phrases in fiction and non-fiction cf. De Haan (1987).
12. A comparison of samples of various sizes with an entire text should be carried out to provide further insight in the nature of sampling irrespective of sample size.

References

Aarts, Jan — Pieter de Haan — Hans van Halteren — Nelleke Oostdijk
to appear *Structure frequency counts of modern English.*

Aarts, Jan — Willem Meijs (eds.)
1984 *Corpus linguistics. Recent developments in the use of computer corpora in English language research.* (Costerus. New Series 45.) Amsterdam: Rodopi.
1986 *Corpus linguistics II. New studies in the analysis and exploitation of computer corpora.* (Costerus. New Series 47.) Amsterdam: Rodopi.

de Haan, Pieter
1984 "Problem-oriented tagging of English corpus data", in: Jan Aarts — Willem Meijs (eds.), 123—142.
1987 "Exploring the Linguistic Database: Noun phrase complexity and language variation", in: Willem Meijs (ed.), 151—165.
1989 *Postmodifying clauses in the English noun phrase. A corpus-based study.* (Language and Computers: Studies in Practical Linguistics 3.) Amsterdam: Rodopi.

de Haan, Pieter — Roeland van Hout
1986 "Statistics and corpus analysis: A loglinear analysis of syntactic constraints on postmodifying clauses", in: Jan Aarts — Willem Meijs (eds.), 79—98.

1988 "Syntactic features of relative clauses in text corpora", *Dutch Working Papers in English Language and Linguistics* 2: 1–18.

Meijs, Willem (ed.)
1987 *Corpus linguistics and beyond. Proceedings of the seventh international conference on English language research on computerized corpora.* (Costerus. New Series 59.) Amsterdam: Rodopi.

Mindt, Dieter – Christel Weber
1989 "Prepositions in American and British English", *World Englishes* 8: 229–238.

Quirk, Randolph – Sidney Greenbaum – Geoffrey Leech – Jan Svartvik
1985 *A comprehensive grammar of the English language.* London: Longman.

Schils, Erik – Pieter de Haan
to appear "Statistical analysis of running text".

Corpus sampling

Jeremy Clear

1. The sampling problem

In building a natural language corpus one would like ideally to adhere to the theoretical principles of statistical sampling and inference. Unfortunately the standard approaches to statistical sampling that I have encountered are hardly applicable to the problems raised by a language corpus. First, the phenomenon to be sampled (say, British English) is poorly defined. Textbooks on statistical methods almost always focus on clearly defined populations (e. g. the set of children under 5 years of age in Britain, or the annual output of widgets from a particular widget manufacturing plant). Second, there is no obvious unit of language which is to be sampled and which can be used to define the population. We may sample words or sentences or "texts" among other things. If we sample words (more specifically, *tokens*) then it is not clear how the concept of word-frequency (i. e. frequency of *types*) can be fitted into the theoretical model of a target population of values. Third, the sheer size of the population ensures that any attempt to account for the difficulty of setting up a sampling frame by gathering ever larger samples will not of itself advance our state of knowledge significantly – given current and foreseeable resources, it will always be possible to demonstrate that some feature of the population is not adequately represented in the sample. Defining the population to be sampled is a difficult task, but one which is necessary if data drawn from the corpus sample are to be used to make generalisations about language beyond the sample. This difficulty may account partly for the reaction against corpus-based linguistics during the Chomsky-dominated decades of the 1960s and 1970s. Introspection and intuition are not subject to brutal comparison with the facts of language performance.

Despite these difficulties, some practical basis for progress can be established. An approach suggested by Woods, Fletcher and Hughes (1986: 55) is to accept the results of each study as though any sampling had been carried out in the theoretically "correct" way.

> If these results are interesting then is time enough to question how the sample was obtained and whether this is likely to have a bearing on the validity of the conclusions reached. ... However, this imposes on researchers the inescapable duty of describing carefully how their experimental material – including subjects – was actually obtained. It is good practice to attempt to foresee some of the objections that might be made about the quality of that material and either attempt to forestall criticism or admit openly to any serious defects.

In corpus linguistics such a pragmatic approach seems to me the only course of action. The remainder of this paper deals with the attempt to foresee and forestall criticism of the quality of the experimental material and the collection method.

1.2. Evaluating the evidence

The Collins Cobuild project at Birmingham University has, from its inception, adopted a strong position concerning the analysis of results obtained from a corpus sample. Despite a long tradition of empirical, descriptive linguistic study, it is still necessary in 1990 to proselytize about the value of a corpus of authentic, natural language data. Concluding his introduction to the recent *Cobuild English Grammar*, Sinclair (1990: xi) stresses this point and, giving four corpus examples of the phrasal verb *break out*, writes:

> The independence of real examples is their strength. They are carefully selected instances of good usage. A set of real examples may show, collectively, aspects of the language that are not obvious individually. ... Note that it is bad things that break out, not good ones. Any such points emerging from a set of constructed examples could not, of course, be trusted.

This point, hardly more than a footnote to the Cobuild Grammar, seems to me to be crucial to the new age of corpus-based language study. It should, perhaps, be pointed out that the "trust" which is required from the user of the grammar is not much different from that which is demanded by all such reference works, whether compiled from corpus evidence or not. The user must have faith in the ability of the lexicographers or grammarians to analyse and evaluate their data rigorously and fairly. To put it bluntly, why should the user take these four selected examples (taken from a selection of authentic texts) as a true indicator of the behaviour of the phrasal verb *break out*? Were there examples in the corpus of good things breaking out which the grammarian chose to ignore or explain away as "creative" or "humorous" uses? The user is being asked to trust the corpus and additionally to trust the analysts of the corpus and compilers of the grammar.

Of course, in many areas of scientific and social scientific study, information is disseminated to an audience of non-experts on the assumption that the experts have done their best and are to be trusted – economic and financial statistics, weather reports, census data, exam results. In corpus linguistics the possibility and effects of experimental error are often overstated: indeed, good scientific estimation of the possibility and scale of experimental error is seldom carried out at all. As a simple check on the example given by Sinclair to support the claim for trustworthiness, I compared the occurrences of the phrasal verb *break out* in two separate samples of authentic modern English that I have been collecting at Oxford. One sample (of 3.5M words) is composed of 6 books, 3 magazines, 6 national and regional newspapers, radio news broadcasts, lectures, meetings, business letters and proceedings of a public inquiry. The other is 6M words taken from the *Wall Street Journal* in summer-autumn of last year. Not surprisingly the evidence confirmed overwhelmingly what is noted by the Cobuild Grammar: that only bad things break out. There is one odd example:

(1) Treachery, murder and morris-dancing break out in all their full horror...

but this appears to be a humorous exploitation of the underlying principle.

It may be, however, that the samples are *biassed* in some way. Indeed the sampling problem is precisely that a corpus is inevitably biassed in some respects. There is always the possibility that all three samples (the Birmingham Collection, the *Wall Street Journal* sample, and the mixed Oxford pilot corpus) have either missed a whole category of English text in which *break out* occurs with good things as its subject or due to chance have not captured any such examples. I judge this possibility to be low enough to be disregarded and with every new text that is added to these corpora and with every new corpus that is created this possibility decreases.

This evaluation of the evidence has to be made continually. The 3.5M words of Oxford's pilot corpus contain no instances of *it's* + personal pronoun in the object case. Clearly, this evidence is not strong enough to allow me to claim that this construction does not occur in English. It is a major problem for the compilers of corpus-based language reference works to know when to trust the data and when to suspect it. Although increasing the size of the corpus will always improve the situation, we cannot say that the evidence will support strong claims about the nature of the language as a whole once the corpus reaches a particular size threshold. If we suspect the corpus of bias, we can hypothesize about the nature of the bias and seek to correct it. In the example here, it may be that the *it's me* construction occurs only in particular informal speech situations (so my intuition tells me) and the corpus sample we have at present may not contain enough casual speech to illustrate it. Conversely, it may be that the construction is very rare. The difficulty of drawing firm conclusions in this case underlines the methodological point made by Wood, Fletcher and Hughes: that researchers should question how the sample was obtained and assess whether this is likely to have a bearing on the validity of the conclusions reached.

1.3. Production and reception

When a corpus is being set up as a sample with the intention that observation of the sample will allow us to make generalizations about language, then the relationship between the sample and the target population is very important. In a well-planned statistical study, the distributional characteristics of items included in the sample should match those of the target population as far as these can be determined. If we focus for a moment on word frequency in British English, we can pose some questions about the target population which we may want to answer by observation of our corpus sample. "What is the likelihood that a native speaker has encountered this word recently?" This question is framed in terms of the *reception* of language input. An alternative but related query is "what is the likelihood that a native speaker has used this word recently?" This looks at the issue of word frequency from the point of view of the *production* of language output. Ideally, the population of, say, British English in the period 1980–1990, would be defined in terms of the total language production, since this would take account of all the millions who constitute the speech community. But to sample this in any comprehensive way is clearly impossible and the second question will be difficult if not impossible to answer by corpus sampling. Figure 1 indicates my rough estimate of the make-up of the totality of English language production. The vast majority of the English speakers do not write for publication nor speak to an audience. Figure 2 gives a crude indication of my estimate of the relative proportions of text type cate-

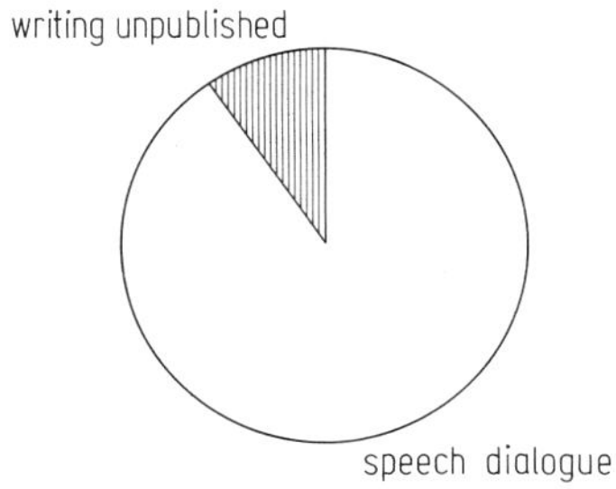

Figure 1. Language production

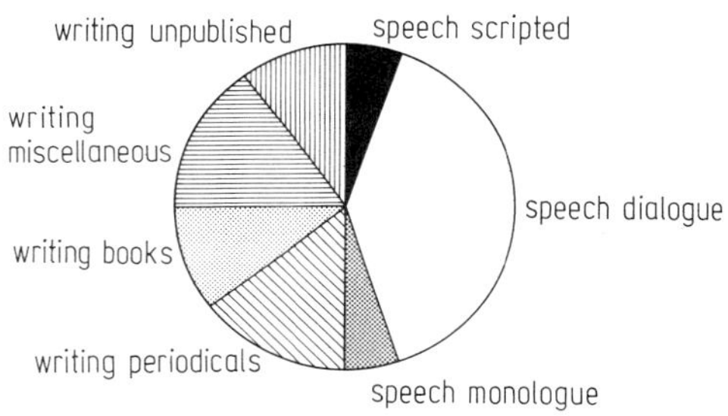

Figure 2. Language reception

gories which make up the totality of language reception. Defining the population in terms of language reception assigns tremendous weight to a tiny proportion of the writers and speakers whose language output is received by a very wide audience through the media. If we assume however that the linguistic differences between language production and language reception are not sufficiently large to be significant for the purposes of building a corpus of general English, then the answer to our first question above will serve as a fairly close approximation to the answer to our second question. At a detailed level, this is obviously an oversimplification: most linguists would reject the suggestion that the language of the daily tabloid newspapers (though they may have a very wide reception) can be taken to represent the language (performance) of an individual member of the speech community. Nevertheless the language of the tabloid newpapers is consumed by a significant number of people in Britain and the inclusion of samples of this type of language can surely be justified on these grounds alone. Similarly it seems likely that private undirected conversation will constitute a large proportion not only of language reception but also of production. Indeed, I suspect that for many within the community of British English speakers, writing (certainly any extended composition) is a rare language activity. Judged on either of these scales, private conversation merits inclusion as a significant component of a representative general language corpus. The achievement of this goal is hampered not only by practical considerations of data capture, but also by the ethical objections concerning surreptitious recording.

A further complication arises with respect to the regional and diachronic aspects of language description. Language that is published or broadcast will account for a significant proportion of the language that is received by speakers of British English, and some proportion of this transmitted material will be remote in time or region. US English, Australian English (e. g. the TV serial *Neighbours*), Shakespeare and Dickens are all likely to be received in some measure by the people of Britain today. A synchronic corpus of British English clearly should not contain any significant proportion either of other varieties or of other periods, something which would be inevitable if we were to sample only on the basis of language reception.

To summarize, we can define the language to be sampled in terms of language production (many producers, few receivers) and language reception (few producers, many receivers). Production is likely to be greatly influenced by reception, but technically only production defines the language variety under investigation. Collection of a representative sample of total language production is not feasible, however. The compiler of a general language corpus will have to evaluate text samples on the basis of *both* reception and production.

1.4. A corpus for a purpose

In the classical textbook examples of statistical methodology, there is a small number of very specific questions to which the researcher seeks answers based upon the sampling of a statistical population. In corpus linguistics, however, the large commitment of cost and time involved in the compilation of a corpus sample makes it desirable to use the material as a basic resource for a wide range of varied linguistic studies. One must bear in mind constantly that the corpus may not be the most appropriate sample for all the studies which one might like to carry out. The more specific the purpose we have in mind for a corpus, the better directed will be our data gathering.

The Oxford Corpus is being assembled in order to serve the needs of compilers and editors of English language reference works which will assist both native-speakers and foreign learners. The primary purpose of this corpus is to provide information in the following areas:

- the *currency* of words and senses of words, etc.
- *frequency*, especially the relative frequency of different senses of polysemous words
- *grammatical/syntactic patterning* of individual lexical items
- *noun and adjective classes*
- *complementation* (optional or obligatory)
- *collocation* (fixed, narrow, open)
- raw material for the selection of natural and helpful *examples* of usage
- comparing *British* and *American English* (and to a lesser extent other forms of English)
- *register* (especially written vs. spoken English) and *appropriacy*
- the appearance of *new words* and *senses* in the language.

2. Some guiding principles

I propose some guiding principles or axioms upon which to base corpus building. These are quite informal and are intended to provide some kind of intuitive tests against which any corpus can be evaluated.

P1: The notion of a "core" of language is useful. Patrick Hanks has talked of language which is "central and typical" and I believe this to be a valid concept. Within applied linguistics there is wide recognition of a core vocabulary (Carter 1987: 33–44), however loosely delimited, and we can extend this idea to all levels of language use. I take it that there is a consensus-based tendency towards a norm of language use and that there is a shared core of English within the vast community of native speakers. Of course, social factors lead individuals and groups to use marked forms or to establish local norms (dialect, jargon, register variation), but these can in turn be absorbed into the "central and typical". The transfer of what were once highly specialised peripheral terms into the common stock of English is well documented *(use your loaf, in the offing, hoist by his own petard)*. Corpus building should begin by tackling the central and typical. Common-sense and critical discussion will be our only guides in the early stages of this process. It will take a great deal of detailed research to demonstrate categorically that national daily newspapers are representative of this core language, but I hope that linguists and lexicographers will not need too much persuading to adopt this as a working hypothesis.

P2: The corpus may be a sample corpus or a monitor corpus. A sample corpus is one which is fixed at a particular size and usually contains relatively short samples, while a monitor corpus is open-ended and consists of complete texts. The Brown and LOB corpora are good examples of sample corpora. Sidney Greenbaum at the Survey of English Usage is currently co-ordinating a concerted effort towards building representative sample corpora, each of 1M words, for a range of national English varieties. There are no good examples of a monitor corpus. John Sinclair at Birmingham is working towards the achievement of an open-ended corpus which grows in a motivated and controlled way. The American ACL Data Collection Initiative tends towards the monitor corpus principle, but the acquisition of texts is only very loosely controlled at present. The sheer bulk of text which is typically included in a monitor corpus leads to the adoption of a different methodology for its acquisition and processing than is appropriate for sample corpora. Typically, the sample corpus is made up of strictly controlled samples of fixed size and from a narrowly specified time period. The sample corpus, being of limited size, can be manually pre-coded to a high level of sophistication and accuracy. The emphasis for the monitor corpus is on size (and the consequent improvement in statistical value) and on computational procedures for annotating and classifying the texts, since detailed manual coding would be quite impractical. This sample/monitor distinction is one based very much on practice rather than theory, since it is quite reasonable to envisage a corpus which is very large and which is open-ended, but which is founded on rigorous sampling principles, encoding and annotation. The problem is to find the compromise between size on the one hand and the amount of detailed specification (with the consequent increases in cost and time) on the other.

P3: The definition of a "text type" should be fairly clear and objective. The relationship between a "text type" and the linguistic features it manifests is not well understood. A literate native speaker of English may have strong intuitions concerning the categorization of texts, based on experience of reading and listening. The trades of publishing and bookselling have a long history and have established a set of convenient labels to refer to different types of printed matter. This intuitive classification needs to be supported with theoretically motivated criteria for distinguishing one text type from another. I do not think, however, that a rigorous and comprehensive taxonomy of text types can be achieved. A text is a very complex socio-linguistic artefact and the corpus builder can only hope to bring some sort of order to the chaos of written and spoken discourse.

P4: The definition of "text types" should distinguish internal criteria from external. This distinction between external and internal criteria is not always made, but I believe it is of particular importance for constructing a corpus for linguistic analysis. The internal criteria are those which are essentially *linguistic:* for example, to classify a text as formal/informal is to classify it according to its linguistic characteristics (lexis/diction and syntax). External criteria are those which are essentially *nonlinguistic:* for example, to classify a text according to the sex of the author is clearly an external classification. Of course, the internal criteria are not independent of the external ones and the interrelation between them is one of the areas of study for which a corpus is of primary value. In general, external criteria can be determined without reading the text in question, thereby ensuring that no linguistic judgements are being made. The problem here is that since external (social and contextual) factors are assumed to condition linguistic behaviour then some criteria seem to be both external and internal. The formal/informal distinction can be made externally on the basis of knowledge about the mode of communication (written/spoken), the topic and the social roles of addresser and addressee. In cases such as this, I suggest that the terminology is adopted to avoid confusion. We may classify a text in external terms – roles of participants, mode, topic – and we may *expect* that certain internal characteristics will be evident. A corpus selected entirely on internal criteria would yield no information about the relation between language and its context of situation. A corpus selected entirely on external criteria would be liable to miss significant variation among texts since its categories are not motivated by textual (but by contextual) factors.

P5: The corpus will help us to discover new aspects of language use and will provide evidence to confirm (or refute) provisionial hypotheses. In this respect the corpus fulfils a different role from a directed programme of citation gathering. The corpus collection therefore should not be constrained to include only material which is expected to furnish evidence for particular linguistic phenomena. This point relates to my distinction between internal and external criteria for selection. The danger of selecting texts because they exemplify certain linguistic features (that is by internal criteria) is that the corpus will become simply a reflection of the lexicographers' or linguists' prior assumptions about the nature of language use.

P6: Decisions concerning corpus quality and quantity should be based whenever possible on assessment of existing corpus resources. This is a methodological point. There is an immediate need to set up new and large text repositories, which are widely available and which can be subject to scrutiny by different researchers. The goal of establishing a valuable corpus can best be achieved by gathering text, studying and evaluating it, refining our definitions and schemes, and then gathering more text in the light of our increased awareness. I believe that there is some justification for collecting text on the assumption that it will be valuable in one way or another. The immediate value is that we can process these data, present them to those who have a need for corpus material, and start the cycle of text acquisition, review, feedback and refinement. I see no reason why the corpus collection should not evolve while the detailed specifications concerning sampling, size, composition, etc. are developed in the light of experience. The LOB and Brown corpora provided hundreds of corpus linguists with a common base of authentic text and allowed subsequent corpus building efforts to advance not only through the greater power of the computational hardware and software but by a better understanding of language in performance.

3. Concluding remarks

Until we have the benefit of results drawn from substantially more research into the statistics of natural language and sampling strategies, there is very little to guide the corpus linguist in setting up a sample of language as the basis of linguistic study. The technology for handling text on computer will continue to improve rapidly and allow larger samples to be gathered and analysed. The importance of the overall size of the corpus upon which claims about a language are based cannot be ignored – more is definitely better. But now that the prospect opens up of collecting enormous quantities of text, much of it already in machine-readable form, the corpus linguist must justify the sampling strategy.

Corpus linguists need better statistical models for their work than have been employed hitherto. Even a simple word frequency listing drawn from a corpus must be interpreted with considerable caution if false and misleading conclusions are to be avoided. We must remind ourselves constantly that when we publish the results of our observations from a corpus the linguistic statements are merely statements about our sample and *not* about the population from which the sample was drawn. Our assessment of the hidden linguistic "facts" is based on estimates whose reliability must be kept under constant scrutiny.

References

Carter, Ronald
1987 *Vocabulary.* London: Allen and Unwin.
Sinclair, John
1990 "Introduction" to *Collins Cobuild English Grammar.* London: Collins.
Woods, Anthony – Paul Fletcher – Arthur Hughes
1986 *Statistics in language studies.* Cambridge: Cambridge University Press.

International Corpus of English: Corpus design — problems and suggested solutions[1]

Gerhard Leitner

0. Summary

This paper addresses the issue whether the tradition established by such corpora as Brown, Lancaster—Oslo—Bergen, and Survey of English Usage, of which the *International Corpus of English* is a part, can be adapted to the study of English worldwide and that of the new national varieties. The differences that accumulate on the pragmatic and discoursal levels, over and above those found in lexis and morphosyntax, do not seem to be catered for adequately at the moment. The following modifications to the structure of the *International Corpus of English* may be worthy of consideration:

(1) A top-down approach to communication (domain-communicative event-text(-sentences)) complementing the bottom-up one;
(2) Collection of full-text/discourse samples;
(3) Corpus division into:
  (a) core and periphery corpus,
  (b) main and monitor corpus.
(4) Collection of sociolinguistic data on speakers, texts, etc.

With these modifications the issue of the nature of English, *viz.* whether it is one system or a set of overlapping, differing, codes would be treated as an empirical issue.[2] Points (1) to (3) are meant to take care of that in particular. Point (4) is strategic, and specifically useful in corpus linguistics in that it is necessary to collect data that are alike across *all* varieties in a core corpus, those that differ (on the code level) in a periphery corpus.

The implementation of these ideas is both a matter of corpus design and of on-going corpus management. My arguments concerning the current *International Corpus of English* consensus are based mainly on *ICE Newsletters* 3 and 4. *ICE Newsletter* 6 incorporates substantial modifications that emerged from three sources, *viz.* a paper by Schmied (1989), an earlier version of this one (Leitner 1991 b), and a variety of comments sent to S. Greenbaum.

This paper begins with a statement and explication of the empirical dilemma that must be resolved by any corpus linguistic study. Section 2 follows with an outline of the corpus tradition that the *International Corpus of English* broadly endorses. Section 3 surveys the key characteristics of the *International Corpus of English* and the problems it faces. It concludes that its current position is not entirely adequate. In section 4 I outline an alternative approach whose possible implementation is discussed in the final section. It will, however, be clear that a number of issues remain open and require further research. This goes in particular for a clear taxonomy of texts and the number of texts to be collected.

1. World English and varieties of English worldwide: the empirical dilemma

That English is the most widely used language of the world with the largest number of users who require it as a first, a second or a foreign language for a variety of purposes,[3] that numerous Englishes have been developing — these are all well-known facts. Many facets of the current nature of English in many parts of the world have been investigated. It has been shown that nativization, the main process that results in the "new" Englishes, has altered the forms and structures of English. But there are, as yet, few substantial descriptions of these 'new' varieties,[4] a fact that Quirk (1988) rightly emphasizes in his critical discussion of the implications of Kachru's "sacred cows". Very few 'hard' facts have been established so far that allow one to draw far-reaching conclusions on the nature of English today.

There are two, only partially complementary, ways of looking at the issue of the nature of English. The first assumes that most features are valid globally. It is close to the so-called core and periphery view of English that has been endorsed in most international reference materials of English. Peter Strevens, who is one of the most ardent advocates of that position, explains this in these terms:

> Standard English dialect (...) has no local base. On the contrary, it is accepted throughout the English-using world. And it is spoken with any accent. There are remarkably few varieties of grammar in Standard English, whether the writer comes from Britain or Ghana or Canada or Hongkong

> or India or the U.S. There are a number of varieties ... but they are quickly learned or rarely cause more than momentary hesitations. (1985)

The core is (largely) identical with an assumed standard of English worldwide, the small peripheries signal features of nativization.

B. Kachru has put forward the alternative view. According to him, English is best characterized in terms of three overlapping circles, *viz.* the inner, the outer and the extended circle. The inner circle comprises mother tongue forms of English, the outer one second language English, and the extended one foreign language English. Since the circles overlap, they share many features, but there is a growing body of differences. Those can be found on all linguistic levels but they are increasingly visible on the textual, discoursal and interactional ones (cf. Y. Kachru 1985). It is for that reason that the possible complementariness of the two views may *soon* dissolve and require a redefinition. Let me illustrate that this may indeed be so.

I was once talking to a senior Pakistani linguist and in what seemed to me an on-going chat he said to me "Have I your permission to leave, Sir?" I was puzzled and said, "Of course you have." This was not exactly the "right" answer. What he meant was something like: 'It's been nice talking to you.' In terms of conversational analysis his remark was a 'pre-closing statement', not a question, and what I should have done was to reciprocate accordingly. A long editorial commentary in the Hindustan Times, entitled "Fly in the ointment", complains about the injustice of the Indian capital gains tax laws. The text discusses the case of an Indian couple who got themselves entangled in the "tax trap". The following passage which describes the solution to the couple's quarrel about the best way of securing their wealth is interesting for its use of tenses (Leitner forthc.):

(i) (a) Argument and counter-argument, until his wife had said, "If you ask me, it's gold. Now you are free to do what you like." (b) With that finale Mr Mehta's choice was limited to one. (c) The very next day he had gone to the market and bought four pieces of jewelry ... (d) In the last 10 years these were lying in the safe deposit vault of his bank ...

In native English (i) (c) would be in the simple past to indicate a step forward in the narrative, (i) (d) in the present perfect progressive to indicate current relevance. However, tense use may not necessarily count as errors. It may be related to a semantic distinction not available in Anglo-American English, i. e. between remote and recent past. The past perfect indicates remote, the simple past recent past; the use of the present perfect is not entirely clear. This kind of analysis has also been suggested by Y. Kachru in a different case (1985) and confirmed to me by numerous speakers of Bengali, Hindi, and other Indian languages. It suggests a semantic differentiation despite the identity of form.[5]

I close with an example from a mother tongue variety of English. Political language in America, in particular amongst the Republicans, is heavily influenced by religious rhetorical devices, as could be seen during the 1988 conventions.

Such examples illustrate that the controversy between the two competing metaphors of English must be extended beyond (the uncontroversial areas of) lexis and morphosyntax. Its resolution, however, also depends on the way language is conceptualized, i. e. as merely a morphosyntactic system or a communicative code that is used to pursue one's goals. Any attempt to study world English and English worldwide should be as unbiassed with regard to either metaphor as possible.

These issues, obviously, involve a number of further questions that need to be addressed. Thus, it is important to know precisely the areas of greater or lesser stability and change; to study the linguistic and text-linguistic parameters. It is necessary also to investigate the language-external, social, regional, ethnic, or other determinants of change and/or stability (cf. section 3.2. below).

While the study of these questions appears to be relatively straightforward if individual varieties are studied, they become rather complex in a project on the nature of English worldwide, which is bound to be comparative. Such an endeavour is faced with a basic empirical dilemma that crystallizes in a clash between the consideration of *global* and *local* requirements:

(A) textual parameters must apply (with minor modifications) to the overall corpus to guarantee its homogeneity and permit quantified *comparative* statements across individual constituent corpora;
(B) textual parameters must be true for each individual variety, i. e. allow quantified *descriptive* statements.

Both requirements are in potential conflict since there may be dimensions of differences that cannot be captured by a (very general) cross-cultural set of parameters. While requirement (A) may argue for one set of parameters, (B) may suggest another.

It is obviously arguable if such a balance can ever be found. Görlach (pers. communication) argues that comparative corpora are rarely insightful for more than a few linguistic features (cp. also Leitner 1991 a).

In a similar line, Algeo (pers. communication) argues that the fundamental distinction between institutionalized and noninstitutionalized varieties should be applied strictly. That distinction cuts across the mother tongue/second language dichotomy since not all mother tongues are also institutionalized. Cases in point are Falkland Island English, South African English (of British descendents); even Canadian English is arguable. But no second language variety is (as yet fully) institutionalized. Little or noninstitutionalized varieties, he concludes, "will never be comparable to those varieties that have institutionalized norms. There will inescapably be a chance factor in the samples of those varieties – they will not represent the variety authentically, because there is no institutionalized norm for them to represent." But he adds, more positively, that an agreement on "rather specific text types" may be a way towards a pragmatic compromise. While one may be sympathetic to that proposal, it is hard to see that even fully institutionalized varieties, like American English, could be represented adequately in both their written and spoken forms. As a chance factor seems to be inevitable anyway, one might be more positive of the outcomes of comparative corpora.

Let me now discuss methodological and other issues that arise out of the conflict between global and local needs. I will focus on the question if, and to what extent, the current structure of the *International Corpus of English* project can be made sensitive to that dilemma.

2. The tradition of English language corpora and the *International Corpus of English*

The tradition of English language corpora has been established by such general purpose corpora (Leitner – Schäfer 1989) as the American English Brown Corpus, British English Lancaster-Oslo-Bergen Corpus, and the British English Survey of English Usage. These corpora have continued earlier trends in empirical linguistics (Leitner 1989 a), they have enriched our knowledge of the structure of Anglo-American English, and they provide a yardstick for current and future research. But most importantly, they have helped to shape a view of English as a (largely) unitary system worldwide, *viz.* the so-called core and periphery view (Quirk *et al.* 1985). Since the *International Corpus of English* (still) largely follows Brown-Lancaster-Oslo-Bergen-Survey of English Usage's research lines, it is useful at this point to outline the major corpus design features.

Description and comparison have played a central role from the beginning. True, the Brown corpus was only meant to *describe* (educated, written) American English, but the immediately following Lancaster-Oslo-Bergen Corpus was to allow *comparative* statements. The compilers of Brown and Lancaster-Oslo-Bergen were well aware of the fact that description and comparison were potentially conflicting goals[6] and they suggested methods that should guarantee comparability. Four features are particularly relevant in this respect.

Firstly, both corpora followed exactly the same method of text compilation. They adhered to, for instance, the tenet of exact synchronicity, accepted quantitative statements in accord with beliefs about the nature of language and the possibilities of hardware, etc. Secondly, many of the presuppositions about Anglo-American societies were, and could legitimately be, taken for granted. Thus, the socio-political and technological structure of Anglo-American societies were largely identical (contrasting sharply with that in former British and American colonies). A high degree of industrialization and urbanization had led to a high degree of language standardization. Language was stratified horizontally (i. e. regionally) and vertically (i. e. socially). The corpora were to focus on the top, the so-called educated, end of vertical stratification. Thirdly, one did not, and perhaps did not need to, worry about non-mother-tongue users (e. g. "Aboriginal forms of English", "migrant English"). Nonnative speakers could be marginalized linguistically. Fourthly, corpus compilation could rely on extrinsic, social categories which helped to define the notion of "educated speech", "standard language", etc. The homogeneity of the corpora was guaranteed by the homogeneity of the population sampled and not by the language samples. In fact, it was one of the empirical issues to find out to what degree social and linguistic categories were related.

Finally, data were sampled according to a hierarchy of categories that was to guarantee the overall representativeness of the corpus (cf. Table 1). That hierarchy was based primarily on linguistic, communicative, considerations. Language-external, social categories played a marginal role, but can be seen in such categories as 'miscellaneous' (a collection of texts from diverse areas). The number of texts to be collected for each category reflected their assumed communicative weight, the overall size of the corpus reflected the possibilities and limitations of computer hardware. While textual categories, thus, played a crucial role in compilation, interest in their linguistic impact was only taxonomic. Subsequent corpus analyses confined themselves to quantitative statements about the distribution of lexical, collocational and grammatical patterns across text categories, neglecting such topics as topic development, cohesion, and the like.

Brown and Lancaster-Oslo-Bergen were restricted to the written mode. But the need for spoken corpora had been much felt earlier and, when the Survey of English Usage was begun about 30 years ago, it meant a major step forward in the study of "real English". Naturally, the taxonomy had to be altered to allow for the mode of speech. The principal basis was no longer that between fictional and nonfictional texts, but mode of speech, i. e. spoken, written, and "as spoken" (i. e. written for oral delivery). The nonfiction/fiction distinction was demoted to a subcategory of the written mode. The changes did not amount to radical departure from Brown-Lancaster-Oslo-Bergen practice.

A number of tenets of structuralism on both sides of the Atlantic, British descriptivism, and (to some extent) generativism supported these decisions. There was, for instance, the interest in a corpus and in performance data as a source of evidence in the first place.[7] The system and structure of language were seen as residing in lexis and morphosyntax. In line with the state of linguistic research, semantics, pragmatics, text and discourse linguistics were quite beyond theories and research interests, as was the relationship of language and society.

Such research interests, however, are not necessarily precluded from these corpora, as can be seen from the numerous studies which have established the usefulness of this taxonomy (Biber 1988). But the question remains if that tradition can be extended to cover the range of varieties to be studied by the *International Corpus of English.*

3. The *International Corpus of English*: design and problems

The development of the *International Corpus of English* (cf. *ICE Newsletters*) and the current consensus will form the basis of the subsequent discussion.

3.1. Design: range of data, corpus structure, immediate research interests

The *International Corpus of English* aims to cover all types of varieties of English, *viz.*:[8]

(1) Mother tongue varieties: British, Scottish, Irish, American, Australian and New Zealand English;
(2) Second language varieties: Indian English, East and West African English, Hong Kong, Jamaica, the Philippines, and Singapore; East Africa consists of three subcorpora, i. e. sections on Kenya, Tanzania, and Zambia;
(3) Foreign language English: communication between second language and foreign language users of English;
(4) Translations into English (mainly from European languages);
(5) Teaching-English-as-a-foreign-language materials.

For each individual variety a constituent corpus will be set up on the basis of similar criteria, see below. While each constituent corpus is to be used for the description of the variety it represents, the fifteen-odd corpora together will constitute the overall international corpus that is to permit comparative statements. The criteria of corpus compilation are as follows:

(1) Corpus size: 1+ million words, divided into 500 texts of (roughly) 2,000 words each.
(2) Population: adults (18+ years), who received formal education through the medium of English up to high (secondary school). (This requirement is particularly important in second language contexts but appears inapplicable for the teaching English as a foreign language corpus.)
(3) Manner of sampling: nonrandom, based on an intersubjective consensus and practical criteria (cf, (5) below).
(4) Period of sampling: 1990 – 1993.
(5) Principles of sample collection: as with all corpora, the language total is conceived of as composed of hierarchically ordered sets of communicative contexts in which verbal communicative acts take place.

Since principle (5) is amongst the most crucial ones for the balance between the global and local, variety-specific requirements, it is useful to elaborate on the current structure of the corpus briefly here; cf. Table 1.[9]

Note that the *International Corpus of English* follows the *Survey of English Usage* lines more than Brown and Lancaster-Oslo-Bergen: the *International Corpus of English* starts with mode of speech as the highest level. The spoken component has two more levels before it reaches the level of specific text types from which samples are taken. Firstly, the number of (active) participants in a speech event, i. e. dialogue (i. e. at least two active participants), and monologue. The presence or absence of a (passive) audience is ignored but is implicit as an influencing factor in the next parameter which looks at the social character of the speech event. It is divided into two polar types, namely the private and the public. Public implies the (potential) presence of a wider audience. A list of text types follows that could count as prototypes of these category clusters or, to put it somewhat differently, reflect the respective "paths" down the hierarchy of categories. To give an example. A committee meeting would realize the path (up) "public-dialogue-spoken".

The scripted component is organized much more simply: there is only one intervening level between the notion of scripted and text types, *viz.* the distinction between dialogue and monologue. The written component is the one with the greatest number of differentiations. The first distinction concerns the nature of writing, i. e. whether something is printed or nonprinted. While the latter section jumps right into text types, the former is subdivided further. Printed is divided into the categories informational, persuasional, administrative, instructional, and imaginative. The subsequent differentiations differ again: informational is divided into learned, popular, and press news reports; persuasion divides into press editorials; administrative into government documents; instructional into skills and hobbies; and, finally, imaginative into fiction. In other words, a text on technology would realize the cluster of features or the path "learned/informational/printed/written".

The taxonomy does make allowances for special features of non-Anglo-American varieties. For instance, Jan Svartvik suggested (in discussion) that a text type such as "parliamentary debate" may not be available in all parts of the English-using world and one will have to look for comparable types. Also, adult, educated speakers need not have a university degree but may count as educated speakers on other grounds. Decisions are left to individual research teams.

Principles (1), (2), and (5) are closest to the Brown-Lancaster-Oslo-Bergen-Survey of English Usage tradition although it would be wrong to infer that (1), for instance, is meant to guarantee diachronic comparability with the earlier corpora. Principles (3) and (4) deviate somewhat for practical reasons and (4), because the tenet of synchronicity is no longer taken too narrowly.

Let me now investigate what problems arise if this structure is used for nonnative varieties of English.

Table 1. ICE consensus (according to *ICE Newsletter* 6)

Verbal Com'ion (500)	SPO (250)	DIA (180)	PRI (100)		face-to-face conv. (90) dist. conversations (10)
			PUB (80)		class lessons (30) broadcasts (R/TV) – interviews (20) – discussions (10) parliamentary debates (10) legal cross-examinations (10)
		MON	PUB		spontan. commentaries (e. g. sports, ceremonial events) (20) unscripted speeces (e. g. lectures, political, legal) (30) demonstrations (e. g. science, cookery) (10)
	SCR (50)	MON (50)			broadcasts (R/TV) – news (10) – stories (10) – talks (20) not broadcast – speeches (10)
	WRI (200)	NPR (50)			student untimed essays (10) student exam essays (10) social letters (15) business letters (15)
		PRI (150)	INFO (40)	LRN	humanities (10) social sciences (10) natural sciences (10) technology (10)
			INFO (40)	POP	humanities (10) social sciences (10) natural sciences (10) technology (10)
			INFO (20)	REP	press news reports (20)
			INSTR (20)		administrative, regulatory (10) skills, hobbies (10)
			PERSUASIVE (10)		press editorials (10)
			CREATIVE (20)		stories, novels (20)

3.2. The challenges of English worldwide

A number of design features are uncontroversial. For instance, principles (1), (3) and (4), *viz.* corpus size, manner of text compilation, and dates of compilation, seem sound as far as they go. Fifteen one-million word corpora will amount to an overall corpus size of around fifteen million words, a figure that will pose enough problems for computation and grammatical analysis. The manner and dates of compilation are largely dictated by practical considerations. Random sampling in Brown-Lancaster-Oslo-Bergen-Survey of English Usage has not been shown, as far as I know, to lead to better results than nonrandom sampling, and exceptions have always been made for practical purposes, so it seems justified not to insist on it.[10] The tenet of synchronicity has been given up in sociolinguistics many years ago but it is, no doubt, necessary for a corpus project like the *International Corpus of English* to define a rough reference period.

It is principles (2) and (5), i. e. the population to be sampled and the text taxonomy, that bear most crucially on the interpretation of the results and may enhance or minimize the intended representativeness of each constituent corpus and that of the entire corpus.[11] They give rise to four more specific questions that need to be clarified:

(1) The taxonomy of text categories and their hierarchical order in light of the current position of text and discourse linguistics and the reality of language use in second language societies (principle (5));
(2) The possible implications of language-external factors, such as the socio-political and economic type of country, the stage of technological development (principle (2));
(3) The assumptions on who counts as an educated speaker, what is educated speech, and what are the relevant socioeconomic parameters (principle (2));
(4) The consideration of current and forseeable research interests and practices (general issue).

Question (1) will be discussed presently, (2) and (3) in section 3.2.2. from the perspective of the nature of English as a language system (or not). More specific aspects will be taken up in section 3.3. (4) is more pragmatic and can be dealt with briefly here. It concerns the question if the current position of the *International Corpus of English* takes sufficient account of what researchers are already doing, or will be doing in the foreseeable future, with corpora like the *International Corpus of English*.

3.2.1. Category types and hierarchical order

A look at Table 1 shows that the categories are heterogeneous, ordered unsystematically, and not applied consistently to all category "paths".[12] The further "down" a path one goes, the less stringent the taxonomy becomes. The scripted section, for instance, omits the private/public dimension that is available in the spoken. It could be stipulated, redundantly, that scripted implies public. The relationship of the nonprinted/printed dimension under written to the private/public dimension is left implicit. It should be made clear that printed implies public and non-printed can be either private or public. Thus, social letters are either private or public; business letters are always public.

Some categories have correlates in different paths, and this is left unaccounted for. For instance, "written-printed-persuasion-press editorials" is related to "spoken-public-(spontaneous)-commentary" or to 'scripted-commentary'. A "spoken-public-broadcast discussion" on, for instance, the subject of linguistics could correspond to "written-printed-informational-learned (or popular)-humanities" on the same subject. Similarly "informational: press news reports" and scripted "news" belong together; they only differ in terms of mode and degrees of preparedness.

For some categories no text types are mentioned at all. This goes in particular for "written/printed/informational/learned/popular". All that is mentioned is scientific disciplines. The notion of informational may stipulate reports but also arguments, etc.

It certainly is desirable to develop a schema that brings out more clearly the different nature of categories and their interrelations and is based on a more stringently definable taxonomy. Such a schema needs to be multidimensional so as to allow computer access from a variety of features or clusters of features. This will be attempted in section 4.1.

3.2.2. Language-external parameters of variation

Questions (2) and (3) in section 3.2., *viz.* the types of countries and the notion of educated *English* speaker, provide further dimensions of differentiation (cf. Moag 1982; B. Kachru 1989). Let me mention four, i. e. the question of native speaker base, the functional restrictions of English, the socio-geographic space that it occupies, and, finally, age-grading.

(1) In second language contexts and in those like the Caribbean where educated English coexists with daughter varieties of English (see Mair, this volume) there are very few genuine mother tongue speakers who use

English (almost) exclusively. English is used as a second, *additional* language or a language of wider communication, in addition to one or more dominant other languages or to creole English.[13] Code switching is for all intents and purposes an essential characteristic of people's communicative competence (appearing more frequently in speech than in printed/public writing).

In order to describe the educated spectrum of speech, one cannot, therefore, rely exclusively on the extrinsic definition that is valid in native environments. On the contrary, the setting up of a correlation between educated person, educated English-using person, and educated English will be part of the outcome of research. It is, therefore, necessary to collect detailed information on speakers/writers (e. g. sex, age, education, ethnic and linguistic background; Schmied 1989) and to include more (educated) persons' English speech than may turn out to be acceptable as educated English later.

(2) Outside the small minority of mother tongue users, who could, but don't, use English for all purposes (given the multilingual environment), the use of English clusters in certain areas of intra- and international communication. These clusters can be described in terms of Fishman's concept of domain.

The *International Corpus of English* ideally covers all domains[14] but not all of them will be equally relevant in second language countries and in foreign language environments. The following domains are mentioned frequently in connection with these varieties: (higher) education, mass media, government and political life, economy including the very important subdomain of business, law, (Christian) religion (to some extent), creative writing, and tourism (which could be seen as belonging to leisure). Social life is rarely mentioned as an important domain, although it cannot be disregarded because of the prestige attached to it.

In other words, while the weightings attached to the number of texts to be collected of each type (cf. *ICE Newsletter* 3 and 6), may reflect a native context, they do not necessarily hold for other types of English.[15] Note in passing that language competence may also vary according to domain of language use.

(3) Truly native English occurs in mainly urbanized and industrialized societies like Great Britain, the United States, or Australia. Second language English on the other hand can be found in either countries like Singapore or Hong Kong that have changed recently from Third World status to advanced industrial-economic centres or, alternatively, in mainly

agrarian, industrializing countries like India, Pakistan, Kenya, etc. They still rely heavily on agricultural production and small-scale businesses and industries.

This difference has important consequences. For one, in the former type of country English will cover the entire range of communicative events. It will in particular be found in all regions, i. e. in urban and rural environments. In the latter type, English will be restricted to (larger) urban centres and disappear the smaller the locality is. Secondly, given that there is a division of labour between urban centres and rural areas, it follows that English will be used more, or exclusively, in certain professional and social circles than in others. It is well-known, for instance, that English is used (in India) at management level (down to perhaps middle management level) in business companies but hardly on the shop floor. To put it briefly, English is the language of engineering science but not of machine production; it is the language of veterinary science but not of the vet!

The third point is related to these two. The advanced state of technology in industrialized countries like America, Great Britain, Singapore, or Australia makes technology-based communication, like distant conversations or messages by telephone, telephone answering systems, FAX and electronic mail, a matter of life. To omit them from a corpus would be foolhardy. But one will be hard put to find them (or in good quality) in India, Pakistan or Tanzania. And it would be equally foolhardy to gather the few instances that one may find.

(4) Age-grading in language use has been the topic of much sociolinguistic research. It is equally important in second language contexts where, however, it seems peculiarly related to external political developments that bear upon the structure and development of the education system.

It appears (from India) that three age groups should be distinguished, i. e. the older generation (50+ years), which was (largely) educated under a colonial system or shortly after, the younger generation that began their studies when it emerged, from around 1960, that English was unlikely to "go" and received stronger political backing, and, finally, the middle generation.

In sum, one must reckon with the possibility of substantial differences between varieties of English to emerge from the socio-economic and other features of language use that the *International Corpus of English* currently is hard put to account for. And, moreover, the *International Corpus of*

English still applies the terminology of westernized societies to the study of English worldwide (Cheshire 1991).

Let me now move on the show how a modified consensus can be developed to provide a more adequate basis for the descriptive and comparative research goals.

4. A modified corpus structure

It follows from the observations made above that a more adequate balance between the global and the local requirements is called for. This will make it necessary (i) to treat varieties as potential codes, and not as just as morphosyntactic systems; (ii) to be sensitive to the text, the discourse, and the entire interaction; (iii) to be open to sociolinguistic, interactional parameters; (iv) to show the boundaries of a (limited) general purpose corpus and suggest links with (future) special purpose corpora that will deal with more specific topics, as the structure of class lessons or "radio interviews".

This can be done if the following design features are adopted:

(1) a top-down approach to communication, i. e. one that starts with broad social categories and moves down to sentence, via text types;
(2) a division of each variety corpus into a core and a periphery component;
(3) a distinction between a main and monitor corpus.

There will be other essential modifications, related to the choice of domains to be studied and the number of text samples to be collected in each domain. Let me outline what these three decisions imply and go into the question how (and if) they can be implemented in section 5.

4.1. A top-down approach

A top-down approach to communication can handle three kinds of problems. For one, it can cope with problems regarding the taxonomy and hierarchy of categories. Secondly, it can deal explicitly with the issue of the nature of English and the speaker/writer-related differences (section 3.1). And, lastly, it can explicate the limitations of a general

Table 2. Three hierarchical levels

Extralinguistic, social facts:	set of domains
Inside a domain:	communicative events
Structure of communication:	text linguistic structure

purpose corpus and specify where special purpose corpora are called for.[16]

Such an approach is based on a three-layer hierarchy that relates "broad" social categories to "narrow" linguistic ones. It draws on Fishman's macro-sociolinguistics and Hymes' ethnography of speaking (for levels 1 and 2) on the one hand and on Graustein – Thiele's (1987) and Werlich's (1976) text linguistic systems (for levels 2 and 3) on the other. Cf. Table 2 for a summary outline.

Data are initially organized on the basis of language domains (Fishman 1974; but see also Bell 1991 for media taxonomic details). These are defined as large-scale socio-communicative environments that (co-)determine their own specific socio-communicative norms and the choice of language (or variety). Aspects of functional restriction of English, of variation related to degrees of competence, the choice between English and other native languages, and of nativization can be discussed on this level.

On the second level domains are specified according to major communicative events. These are potential loci where particular time- and place-bound acts of communication occur. Relevant parameters are: temporal and spatial setting, domain-specific context, geographic area of communicatioin, topic, gender, ethnic and language background of participants. To give some examples: a classroom lesson on social science in an urban/rural area in an English-medium school; a commentary in a national daily paper on sports, but as part of the commentary section, from the editor; a public debate on human rights (= social/political sciences) between speakers of different language backgrounds in a national conference centre; a television interview between different language speakers on constitutional matters; etc.

The third layer looks at the textual and linguistic structure of language/communication proper in terms of text linguistic categories. On this level data need to be organized in terms of a broad taxonomy of text types. One will have such categories as descriptive, narrative, expositary, and argumentative text forms with their (broad) subcategories, *viz.* report, comment, news story, etc.[17]

Practical experience with such a three-layer scheme shows that decisions are far from easy in many cases, so that these layers must be understood as standing in a scalar relationship. It would appear that ultimately a feature-type of categorization will emerge that, with the aid of artificial intelligence systems, will permit complex cross-classifications and yet be based on insightful features (Leitner 1991b).

4.2. Core and periphery corpus

The core and periphery distinction is useful to cater for the fact that there may not be a unique cross-culturally valid set of parameters. As I have shown above, the fact that English may consist of different codes (and not of a common core and a regionally variable periphery) makes it necessary to account for the common features in one way, and the different ones in another.

There are two ways of conceptualizing that situation. One might, firstly, think of a *static*, i. e. stable, core and of static sets of peripheries. Those text types (including their "path" from the social top to the text typical bottom) that are common to all varieties go into the core corpus, those that are (more) specific to some only, like distanced conversation and dictation, religion, etc., go into the periphery corpus. The underlying assumption is that there is a large enough set of categories that are common across all types of Englishes so that a comparative analysis provides insights into the structure and working of English.

In view of the realities of the use(s) of English in the types of countries studied it may, however, be necessary to follow the second, *dynamic*, view of the core and peripheries. Taking two extreme cases for illustrative purposes, i. e. (urban) American English and (small-town) Tanzanian or Indian English, there may not emerge a sufficiently large set of categories that is equally telling. It may emerge that national, second language varieties, which are not identical with urban entities like Hong Kong and Singapore, share more features between them than they do with native varieties and urban centres like Singapore. Within each cluster, regionally closely related entities may have more in common than if they are enriched by more distant entities. For example, varieties of English in South Asia, i. e. Pakistan, India, Sri Lanka, Bangladesh, may share more features and rely on a larger common core (corpus) than if they are enriched by varieties of English in West Africa.

If this seems a plausible hypothesis, then one should opt for a *dynamic* concept of the core/periphery corpus components. This would allow to remain maximally flexible and to modify the core whenever this is desirable for a particular comparative purpose: one could either enrich, impoverish, or alter the core at the stage of corpus analysis and data interpretation.[18]

4.3. Main and monitor corpus

This distinction is set up along the lines of COBUILD and is meant to account for the fact that, whatever taxonomy one sets up, it will be difficult to gather enough data to allow subsequent text-sensitive and sociolinguistic micro-analyses along the lines of a Labovian paradigm (see also de Haan, this vol.).

If, for instance, one includes, as I have suggested, sociolinguistically relevant parameters, such as gender, age, socio-educational background, ethnicity, first language(s), one would ultimately like to use them for quantified statements. This will normally be impossible since – to give one example – for a particular text type, say report in a particular domain (e. g. education) and communicative context (class lesson), only 10 text samples can be chosen. Within this limit, one will hardly be able to study the parameters of gender and age. Ten text samples will not be sufficient to quantify sociolinguistically-determined variation.

In other words, the *International Corpus of English* (even in its modified description) will be, and must be, limited. But, what can be done, should be done and this is (i) to make explicit the limitations imposed on the (monitor) corpus, and (ii) to gather further data for later, more specific analyses (as part of the main corpus).

5. A realistic approach to corpus design and the *International Corpus of English*

Let me now discuss if, and how, these proposals can be implemented without throwing out completely the current consensus. To do this it will be useful to probe to what extent the current consensus already contains elements mentioned above.

5.1. A three-layered corpus

A look at the overall structure of the *International Corpus of English* (*ICE Newsletter* 6) shows that the distinctions between different layers of a variety-specific corpus, i. e. core/periphery and monitor/main corpus, have been incorporated, following Leitner (1989 b and forthcoming). The *International Corpus of English* is now better able to cater for unforeseen differences between varieties (i. e. the conflict between requirements [A] and [B] in section 1 above and, partially, for (subsequent) sociolinguistically-oriented research. It will, however, be necessary to gather more data than just one million words, presumably in the order of 1.5 million words, and to go for full, rather than truncated texts, wherever possible.[19]

5.2. Explicating and revising the categories and their paths

In order to work out a practical approach to a new structure, I will explicate the *current* consensus.

Table 3 reformulates the category list in Table 1 but also makes explicit those categories that relate to the notions of domain, subdomain, etc. These are marked by "⟨,⟩". Brackets, i. e. "(,)" are used when elements can easily be inferred.

Table 3 consists of four columns, with the large left one adhering most narrowly to Table 1. Note here the extension of the paths SPO – MON by the categories ⟨PUB⟩ and ⟨DIR⟩; of SCR by ⟨MON⟩ and ⟨PUB⟩; of WRI by ⟨MON⟩; and, finally, of WRI – ⟨MON⟩ – PRN by ⟨DIS⟩.

Columns two and three are derived from the approach outlined. It will be immediately clear, for instance, that the notion of classroom lesson implies the domain of EDUCATION, the subdomain of HIGHER or MIDDLE (i. e. secondary), and the text type "lesson".

Table 3 reveals gaps that are sometimes indicated by dots. If one looks at the top line that attempts to spell out the type of category dealt with below and compares it with information in the right-hand column, even more problems emerge. The notion of broadcasts, for instance, suggests a systematic category distinction between mediated and nonmediated communications. Thus, all texts in the domain of Mass Media are mediated, and that, incidentally, would include WRI – MON – PRN. Others, such as speeches at funerals, letters between individuals, would be non – mediated. The notions spontaneous, unscripted, and (un-)timed that occur in conjunction with commentaries, speeches, and student essays

Table 3.

MODE NO	SOCIAL SETTING	SPATIAL SETTING	COM'IVE GOAL	STYLE APPROACH	DOMAIN	SUB-DOMAIN	TEXT TYPES
		DIR			(HOME)	…	conversations
					(HOME)	…	
	PRI –	DIS					conversations
DIA –	PUB –	(DIR)			(MASS MED)	⟨R/TV⟩	discussion, interviews
		(DIS)			(EDUC)	(MID/HIGH)	lessons
					(GOVT)	⟨PARLT⟩	debates
					⟨LAW⟩	(COURT)	cross-examinations
SPO							
MON.–	⟨PUB⟩ –	(DIR)			(⟨SPORTS..⟩)	(……)	– (spont.) commentaries
					…	…	(unscript.) speeches
							⟨e. g. lectures; political,
					…	…	legal presentations;
					…	…	demonstrations (e. g. science,
							cookery)⟩
SCR. ⟨MON⟩	(PUB)				(MASS MED)	⟨R/TV⟩	news, stories, talks
					…		speeches
	NPR –	(DIS)			(EDUC)	(HIGH)	(untimed) student essays
							(⟨timed⟩) student ⟨exam⟩ essays
					(HOME)	…	⟨social⟩ letters
					⟨BUSINESS⟩	…	letters
				LRN	(SCIENCE)	⟨HUMAN⟩	…
						⟨SOCIAL⟩	…
						⟨NATURAL⟩	…
						⟨TECHNOL⟩	…
			INF –				
				POP	(SCIENCE)	⟨HUMAN⟩	…
						⟨SOCIAL⟩	…
						⟨NATURAL⟩	…
						⟨TECHNOL⟩	…
WRI (MON) –				REP	(MASS MED)	⟨PRESS⟩	news reports
			INS		??	??	administrative (texts)
	PRN –	(DIS) –					regulatory (texts)
					(LEISURE)	⟨SKILLS⟩	…
						⟨HOBBIES⟩	…
			PER		(MASS MED)	⟨PRESS⟩	editorials
			CRE		CREATIVE	⟨PRESS⟩	stories, novels

Table 4. Categories in version of Table 3

(1)	SITUATIONAL PARAMETERS	
	Mode of speech:	spo, scr, wri
	Number of participants in event:	mon, dia
	Social setting among particip.:	pri, pub (print, non-print)
	Spatial setting among particip.:	dir, dis
(2)	SPEAKER-RELATED PARAMETERS	
	Communicative goal:	information, instruction, persuasion, creative presentation
	Style, approach to audience:	learned, popular, reportage (unclear category)
(3)	SOCIAL PARAMETERS	
	Domain:	home, mass media, sports, education, business, science, leisure, government
	Sub-domain:	R/TV, press, parliament, high/mid education, humanities, social sciences, natural sciences, technology, skills, hobbies
(4)	TEXT TYPES (G: *Textsorte*)	conversation, debate, interview, lesson, cross-examination, commentary, lecture, speech, presentation, demonstration, talks, news, stories, essays, letters, reports, editorials, novels

respectively seem to form a cluster relating to (un-)preparedness in style. They will, however, overlap with the distinctions between learned and popular.

The categories "reportage" and "creative" (writing) have nothing to do whatsoever with the path they are assigned to. The first one refers to a particular type of mass media program format that, normally includes quite distinct input elements; the latter requires its own (and new) path, i. e. (non)fictional. Note, in passing, that reportages can increasingly be found also in the print media (Leitner 1991b). Such changes can easily be incorporated into an improved version of the list of text types.

The types and the hierarchy of categories that Table 3 is based are summarizes in Table 4: It is clear that the sequence of parameters in table 4, i. e. from (1) to (4), is unconvincing and that the sequence (3),

Table 5.

DOMAIN	SUB-DOMAIN 1 (explicated)	SUB-DOMAIN 2 (explicated)	TEXT TYPE (G: Texttyp) (left open)	CROSS-REFER-ENCE	TEXT TYPE (G: Textsorte) sp = spoken sc = scripted wr = written	QUANTITIES OF TEXT TO BE COLLECTED				
						ACC. TO NEWS-LETTER 6 (= indicates max. no.)	ACCORDING TO DOMAIN			
							TOTAL	WRI	SCR	SPO
HOME		(open)			Sp: conv.	(90+10)	115	100	0	15
					(face/face; distanced)	(15)				
					Wr: letters					
LEISURE	SKILLS	(open)		see $	Sp: demonstrations	(10−)	30> × >10	0/10	0/10	10
	HOBBIES			see O	Sc: speeches	(10−)				
	(TRAVEL)				Wr: ⟨open⟩	(10)				
	(LIVING)				(instructional)					
SPORTS	SEASONAL	(open)		see +	Sp: commentaries	(20−)	20> × >0	0/20	0	0
	INTERNA-TIONAL/				(spontaneous)					
	NATIONAL									
EDUCA-TION	TERTIARY	school educ.			Sp: lessons (class)	(30)	90> × >50	30/60	0/10	20
	SECONDARY	univ./college		see +	Sp: lectures	(30−)				
	IN-SERVICE			see O	Sc: speeches	(10−)				
	ADULT				Wr: essays by students free/examination	(10+10)				
SCIENCE	HUMANITIES	philosophy		see $	Sp: demonstrations	(10−)	100> × >80	0/10	0/10	80
	NATURAL	linguistics		see O	Sc: speeches	(10−)				
	SOCIAL	literature			Wr: ⟨4 discipl.⟩ (learned)	(4×10)				
	TECHNOLOGY	computing			Wr: ⟨4 discipl.⟩ (popular)	(4×10)				

Table 5. continued

DOMAIN	SUB-DOMAIN 1 (explicated)	SUB-DOMAIN 2 (explicated)	TEXT TYPE (G: Texttyp) (left open)	CROSS-REFER-ENCE	TEXT TYPE (G: Textsorte) sp = spoken sc = scripted wr = written	QUANTITIES OF TEXT TO BE COLLECTED				
						ACC. TO NEWS-LETTER 6 (= indicates max. no.)	ACCORDING TO DOMAIN			
							TOTAL	WRI	SCR	SPO
BUSINESS	PRODUCTION/						25 > × > 15	0	0	15/
	SALE	(open)			Wr: letters	(15)				25
	IN/EXTERNAL									
	TRADE			see *	Wr: ⟨administrative, regulatory⟩					
GOVT/	NATIONAL/	parliament			Sp: debates (parliamentary)	(10)	50 > × > 10	10/40	0/30	0/10
ADMIN.	REGIONAL/			see +	Sp: political speeches	(30–)				
	LOCAL				Sc: speeches					
	AREA OF			see *	Wr: ⟨adminstrative, regulatory (instructional)	(10–)				
	GOVNT.									
	INSTITUTION									
LAW	AREA OF LAW	court			Sp: cross-examination	(10)	40 > × > 10	10/40	0	0
	COURT	(pro-cedure)		see +	(court)	(30–)				
					Sp: speeches (legal)					
				see +	Sp: commentaries (ceremonial)	(20–)	120 > × > 100	30/50	40	30
MASS.-MED.	RADIO	(open)			Sp: discussions, interviews	(20 + 10)	120 > × > 100	30/50	40	30
	TV				Sc: news, stories, talks	(10 + 10 + 20)				
	PRESS				Wr: news reports (vague)	(20)				
	BOOKS				Wr: editorials (persuasive)	(10)				

(1), (2), and (4) would be more logical and in line with a top-down approach. That this can indeed be done is shown in Table 5 where the relevant parts of table 3 are reorganized in a domain basis.

Table 5 is organized in three major blocks. On the left side we find the corpus structure according to the notion of domain and two lower levels of subdomains. The domain of sports, for instance, can be (as one conceivable analysis) divided into seasonal sports (summer/winter) and national/international sports on the first sublevel before it is spelt out as skiing, wrestling, cycling on the second sublevel. The second block spells out the organization based on textual categories. The first column, left open, will have to refer to higher level abstractions found in Werlich (1976) and Graustein – Thiele (1987). The third column (G: *Textsorten*) uses the categories of table 4 and *ICE Newsletter* 6. The middle column is used to indicate where *Newsletter* 6 allows multiple domain assignment. For instance, demonstrations may come from the domain of leisure (i. e. cookery) or science. The third block represents the quantities suggested in *ICE Newsletter* 6. The first column here gives the figures in *ICE Newsletter* 6. The second one, which takes note of possible multiple domain assignment, gives the ranges according to the domain, the last one spells out figures according to mode of speech.

5.3. Revision and extension of the consensus

It should be clear by now that the current *International Corpus of English* position already contains the essential elements of the type of approach outlined in section 4. It is not necessary, then, to throw it out and replace it by something new but to reformulate and extend it, where necessary. Table 6 presents such an attempt.

Let me comment on Table 6. The list of social parameters is based on the domains and subdomains mentioned frequently in macro-sociolinguistics and the literature on varieties of English. The proximity to Fishman (1974) and Fishman – Cooper – Conrad (1977) should be clear.

A problem arises with the domains of mass media, government and law which are normally treated as domains like any other domain. But unlike other domains, e. g. economy or science (with their particular subdomains), they are totally unspecified with regard to the range of areas they deal with. Newspapers report on politics, leisure, home, economy, science, etc. Parliaments and governments equally cover the whole range of social life, as does law. It seems that they could be treated as

Table 6. Revised top-down version of the hierarchy

(1) SOCIAL PARAMETERS	
Domain:	home, leisure, mass media, sports, government (including politics), economy (including business), religion, science, arts
Subdomain: (levels to be defined within each domain),	e. g. government would cover parliament, government proper, administration etc.;[1] leisure would include skills, hobbies; arts comprises painting, music, dance, etc.
Locale of interaction:	home, office, public area, church, classroom, etc. regular place of domain vs. non-regular place
(2) SITUATIONAL PARAMETERS	
Mode of speech:	spoken, written, scripted, spoken-to-be-written
Number of (potentially active) participants:	mon, dia (including one or more than one author in written and spoken-to-be-written communications)
Participant-related information:	age group, sex, other languages, education, social class, ethnicity, caste, role, status, etc.
Social setting:	pri-pub cline (print-non-print distinction incorporated into pri-pub cline)
Spatial setting:	dir, dis (of potentially active/ participants); if pub, then mediated or not through mass medium to an audience,[a]
(3) INTERACTION-RELATED PARAMETERS	
Communicative goal:	information, persuasion, instruction, etc. (speech act theory)
Style, approach to audience:	formal-informal cline,[b] prepared-unprepared cline[c]

continued overleaf

Table 6. continued

(4) TEXT TYPES (G: *Texttyp*)	
Text types:	narrative, argumentative, expository, etc. (Werlich 1976; Graustein – Thiele 1987)
Text type exemplars: (G: *Textsorte*)	interview, conversation, commentary, presentation, essays, letters, editorials
Topics (main):	(will interconnect with domains and subdomains, but include also, e. g. 'unspecified'
Relation to reality:	fiction,[d] non-fiction

Notes:

[1] These would have to be further specified according to national government, state government, local government

[a] Note that all books (on science, etc.) belong to the mediated category;

[b] It is unclear how the relevant learned-popular distinction relates to this cline;

[c] This parameter subsumes the notion of (un-)scriptedness, (un-)timedness, (non-)spontaneity;

[d] Fiction subsumes the notion of creative writing and speaking.

higher domains than all others or, preferably, as domains, which are unspecific with regard to topics etc. This option necessitates the distinction between domains and reported domains (Leitner 1991 b).

Situational parameters apply to communicative events. Note here that the category of mode of speech must be enriched by the category spoken-to-be-written (SWR) to account for interviews, debates etc. done by a print media for the sole purpose of printed publication. Also, number of (potentially active) participants must be extended to the written mode. One frequently finds, for instance, texts in mass media under a single heading that came from different writers (like letters-to-the-editor) or news agencies (like "In Brief" etc.). The distinction between independent and composite text will be useful here (Leitner 1991 b).

Participant-related information must specify the usual sociolinguistic information (cf. Schmied 1989), but also role and status in a given event. With print media it will usually be difficult to gather all relevant facts and often they are condensed into a news agency source.

With regard to social setting, it is necessary to stipulate that all public events may or may not be mediated through a mass medium (including books and periodicals to an audience). The print/nonprint distinction, which is really a cline,[20] should be related to that between private and public. All printed texts are (redundantly) public, nonprinted ones may, but need not, be.

Given that public events may or may not be mediated, it follows that the category of spatial settings relates to the setting of potentially active participants. For instance, a debate at a table in a lecture theatre is marked as direct, whether it takes place in a university, in a television studio or is reprinted in a newspaper. The axis to a wider (passive) audience is covered by marking it as plus or minus mediated. In the first case, i. e. in a university lecture hall, it would be [-mediated], in the two other cases as [+mediated].

Interaction-related parameters comprise the communicative goal(s) of the (potentially active) participant(s), i. e. speakers and/or writers, and the approach used to address the partners and/or the intended audience under the constraints of time and place in a given setting.

The category of text types subsumes the German notions of *Texttyp* and *Textsorte*, which could perhaps be renamed as text type and text type exemplar. Thus, a (radio) commentary on an ongoing sports event would represent the text type narrative and the text type exemplar of reporting. A (press) editorial illustrates the text type argumentative and the exemplar editorial. A reportage on TV, radio or in a magazine will normally consist of narrative, expository and argumentative text segments. Since most concrete texts are composites of different text types, more research will be necessary.

Note in passing that the category of relation to reality, which from a literary point of view, is not unproblematical, reintroduces the old fiction/nonfiction distinction in Brown – Lancaster – Oslo – Bergen – Survey of English Usage. A radio or television story will be marked as fiction, a sports commentary as non-fiction.

By following this approach, we will be able to account for the fact that the domain of science, like any other, can take concrete shape in multiple ways: as a demonstration in a university (captured by locale of interaction), a lecture at a public forum, a discussion on television, a paper in a scientific journal, a column in the science page of a paper, etc. All of these manifestation will be similar in some ways (e. g. lexis) but different in others (spoken vs. written-printed dimension, science page vs. scientific periodical etc.).

Table 6 can be translated into tree diagrams like Tables 1 and 3, i. e. by starting with categories close to language, or like 5 and 6, i. e. by starting from the social level. Since the categories are to apply to all texts (with certain exceptions) any type of category can ideally be taken as primary in a relational network.

How can these proposals be implemented?

5.4. Implementing the revision

One could obviously take a *maximalist* and a *minimalist position.* The maximalist position would be that a complete framework must be developed *before* any work can start. This would imply the danger that corpus research is postponed indefinitely since it will be difficult to devise such a schema that is agreeable to everybody and that is unassailable. The minimalist position would seek compromises and ask at what stage of research a particular decision needs to be taken. This is what I would suggest.

It would seem that the proposals can be (partly) implemented fairly easily if the following facts are borne in mind:

(1) Even the current *International Corpus of English* consensus makes reference to the three levels of analysis I postulated; cf. Tables 1 and 3. So the type of approach suggested is only in need of explication and refinement, as I have shown.

(2) A distinction can be made between *corpus compilation* (a data selection activity) and *corpus processing* and *corpus data interpretation* (which happens later).

If this is done, not all questions need by addressed immediately; some can wait until a clearer picture arises. For instance, an immediate issue would be to agree on a practical typology of texts (higher level typology) and a provisional path hierarchy (cf. Table 5). As for the notions of communicative contexts and domains, some decisions should be straightforward and uncontroversial. There is a set of cross-culturally important domains, i. e. politics (and administration), education, science, mass media, law, creative writing (drama, fiction), arts, and economy. Others are valid for some societies more than for others. This goes, for instance, for education (English-medium) and tourism in second language countries, and religion in native English countries. Texts that presuppose particular technological developments, like the distanced/direct parameter, are specific to some speech communities but not to others.

Other decisions can wait, e. g. the development of a precise hierarchy inside domains, a greater specification of text types, and the categorization of speaker/writer-related features. Differences will emerge as, for instance, English will not cover all levels of interaction inside (English-using) domains. As mentioned earlier, in many countries English is the language of engineering science but not of the workshop etc. This specification can be left to the requirements as one collects data on the one hand, and data analysis at the end. What needs to be done, however, is to gather (and keep for retrieval) as much information as possible. Finally, it could be left till rather late to indicate more precisely the limits of the *International Corpus of English* as a General Purpose Corpus and the loci where Special Purpose Corpora are called for.

In other words, by exploiting what is already contained in the current consensus and careful corpus monitoring and management, the main implications of these proposals should be accounted for.

Notes

1. Thanks are due to S. Greenbaum, J. Algeo, C. Meyer, M. Fee, M. Görlach, and N. S. Shastri for valuable comments. While I have taken note of them in general, I have kept to my original design wherever I felt this to be necessary. So I bear alone the responsibility of shortcomings.
2. The distinction between "system" and code here will become clearer later. Let me say here that it takes up the controversy between a conception of language as a morpho-syntactic system and its exploitation in discourse, as a code.
3. Cf. a recent discussion by B. Kachru (1989).
4. Australian, New Zealand, Canadian, and Singaporean English are exceptions to this generalization.
5. Similar deviations have been reported on Nigerian English, where, under the influence of L1s, tense marking is optional.
6. Suffice it to say that structuralist linguistics, which was the theoretical background of early corpus work, would have allowed different, language-specific approaches to corpus design.
7. There is no need to emphasize that transformational grammar did not support that view. But corpus data are increasingly discussed in generative literature.
8. As a result of compilation and processing, essential research tools for descriptive, applied, and computational linguistics are to be provided. In particular, tagged and parsed versions of the corpora, word and collocational concordances, frequency and lemmatized dictionnaries, etc. will be made available. They will be of use in the production of *variety-specific* and *international* reference materials, computer software, etc. It is hoped too that the corpus will allow for more specific research interests (e. g. in text, discourse analysis and on sociolinguistics) by specifying the boundaries of the corpus and making clear where the database needs to be enriched with specially collected language samples.
9. As to perceived weight, which is an important category, a minimum of 10 texts have to be collected in each category.

10. Nonrandom sampling has, however, been an important consideration in the Labovian paradigm and may prove to be necessary in some cases. However, it may not be the nonrandomness of a particular speech event that counts, but a random distribution of speech event types.
11. Note in passing that varieties of the British Isles are clearly overrepresented. Four corpora are to be set up. In contrast, there are only one for the United States, one for South Asia, etc.
12. Note that there is a considerable improvement from *ICE Newsletter* 3 to 6. For instance, the path "written – printed – administrative – government documents" has now been replaced by "written/printed – instructional – administrative/regulatory".
13. But even the minority of native speakers may differ vastly in their individual competence and show linguistic features similar to second language users.
14. This is only true by implication, as I will show below. The current position (see Table 1) does allow the researcher to collect, for instance, a conversation (spoken/dialogue/public) in a bar (domain social life), a business company (domain occupation), a church (domain religion), etc. But by allowing so much freedom of choice, it also gives too much leeway since one must assume that there are substantial differences also.
15. Note in that context that important changes have already been made in *Newsletter* 6.
16. As will be become clearer in section 5, it will hardly be possible to devise *a priori* a neat and unassailable top-down approach that could provide the basis for the structure of a corpus – even social and political scientists might find this a daunting task. It will, therefore, be sounder to take it as a reference measure, not as a yardstick and to aim at a pragmatic agreement on the domains and subdomains that should be studied.
17. This modification will also affect quantitative stipulations for the *International Corpus of English*. Because of the necessity of collecting full text samples, there is no guarantee that a particular text will have only 2,000 words or that the entire corpus will be limited to 1 million words. In order to deviate minimally from the current consensus, one could suggest that texts may exceed the stipulated size by 5%, i. e. texts may have up to 2,100 words; the corpus could be as much as 1,050,000 words. It must be left to statisticians to work out the implied problems of weighting.
18. I would think that the dynamic concept will turn out to be more appropriate than the static concept embodied in Leitner (1989 b; forthcoming).
19. Note here that the Brown – Lancaster – Oslo – Bergen – Survey of English Usage practice of going for relatively long texts so as to avoid composite texts must be rejected.
20. Note here publications in book format, photocopied manuscripts for wider circulation and typed or handwritten letters.

References

Baumgardner, Robert (ed.)
forthc. *Proceedings of "English in South Asia" conference*, Islamabad, Pakistan, Jan 4 – 10, 1989.

Bell, Allan
1991 *The language of news media.* Oxford: Blackwell.

Biber, Douglas
1988 *Variation across speech and writing.* Cambridge: Cambridge University Press.

Cheshire, Jenny
1991 "Introduction: Sociolinguistics and English around the world", in: J. Cheshire (ed.), *English around the World*, 1–12. Cambridge: Cambridge University Press.

Fishman, Joshua
1974 "The sociology of language", in: Thomas Sebeok (ed.), *Current trends in linguistics*, vol. 12(3). The Hague: Mouton.

Fishman, Joshua – Robert Cooper – Andrew Conrad (eds.)
1977 *The spread of English.* Rowley, Mass.: Newbury House.

Graustein, Gottfried – Wolfgang Thiele
1987 *Properties of English texts.* Leipzig: Enzyklopädie.

ICE Newsletter. Ed. Sidney Greenbaum.
University College, London.

Kachru, Braj
1989 "Teaching world Englishes", *Spelt Newsletter* 4(3): 3–8.

Kachru, Braj (ed.)
1982 *The other tongue. English across cultures.* Oxford: Pergamon Press.

Kachru, Yamuna
1985 "Discourse analysis. Non-native Englishes and second language acquisition research", *World Englishes* 4(2): 223–232.

Leitner, Gerhard
1989a *BBC English und Englisch lernen mit der BBC.* München: Langenscheidt.
1989b "Corpus design – problems and suggested solutions". MS (sent to members of the *International Corpus of English*).
1991a "The *Kolhapur Corpus of Indian English* – Intravarietal description and/or intervarietal comparison", in: S. Johansson – A. Stenström (eds.), *English computer corpora.* Berlin: Mouton de Gruyter, 114–124.
1991b "*International Corpus of English* – working with the text encoding initiative's guidelines", *CCE Newsletter* 5(1/2): 31–46.
forthc. English in South Asia: Bad, different or new?" [Paper given at the International conference on English in South Asia, Islamabad (Pakistan), Jan. 4–10, 1989].

Leitner, Gerhard – Uwe Schäfer
1989 "Reflections on corpus linguistics – the 9th ICAME conference in Birmingham, England", *CCE Newsletter* 3(1): 2–16.

Moag, Rodney
1982 "English as a foreign, second, native, and basal language: A new taxonomy of English-using societies", in: J. Pride (ed.), *New Englishes*, 11–50. Rowley, Mass: Newbury House.

Quirk, Randolph – Sidney Greenbaum – Geofrey Leech – Jan Svartvik
1985 *A comprehensive grammar of the English language.* London: Longman.

Quirk, R.
1988 "The question of standards in the international use of English", in: P. Lowenberg (ed.), *Language spread and language policy: issues, implications, and case studies*, 229–241. Washington D. C.: Georgetown University Press.

Schmied, Josef
1989 "Text categorization according to use and user and the *International Corpus of English*", *CCE Newsletter* 3(2): 13–29.

Werlich, Egon
1976 *A text grammar of English*. Heidelberg: Quelle und Meyer.

The Northern Ireland Transcribed Corpus of Speech

John M. Kirk

1. Northern Ireland Transcribed Corpus of Speech

This paper reports on the Northern Ireland Transcribed Corpus of Speech (hereafter "TCS"). This corpus was created between June 1989 and July 1990 with the primary support of an Economic and Social Research Council grant, but also with the support of the Tape-Recorded Survey of Hiberno-English Speech (hereafter "TRS") and the Ulster Folk and Transport Museum, where the TRS taperecordings are now stored.[1]

The corpus is based on the TRS taperecordings for Northern Ireland. The 38 localities are represented in Map 1. At each locality, three age groups were recorded: children, middle-aged people, and the elderly. The recordings are of "unscripted conversation" (Barry 1981: 27) (see below, section 2) and were made between 1973 and 1980 (cf. TRS "locality information sheets", now in the Ulster Folk and Transport Museum). The methodology of the TRS is described prospectively in Barry (1981).

The corpus textfile consists of 41,215 lines and has 240,322 informant word tokens (representing 8762 word types). If fieldworker utterances are included, then the corpus contains over 300,000 words (cf. Kirk 1991: Vol 1). A random example of the corpus, recorded of an elderly informant in Ballygawley (Locality 25) is given in the Appendix.

In the transcription, the following conventions have been used:

[...] enclose fieldworker utterances and locality names

(...) denote missing syllables, either those which can be identified, and those which can not.

⟨...⟩ denote editorial codes (so-called cocoa references), with regard to:

⟨L L00⟩	locality
⟨A A00.0⟩	TRS locality number
⟨R R2:00.0⟩	tape side and location
⟨I JK01⟩	informant and turn number
⟨FW CG⟩	fieldworker

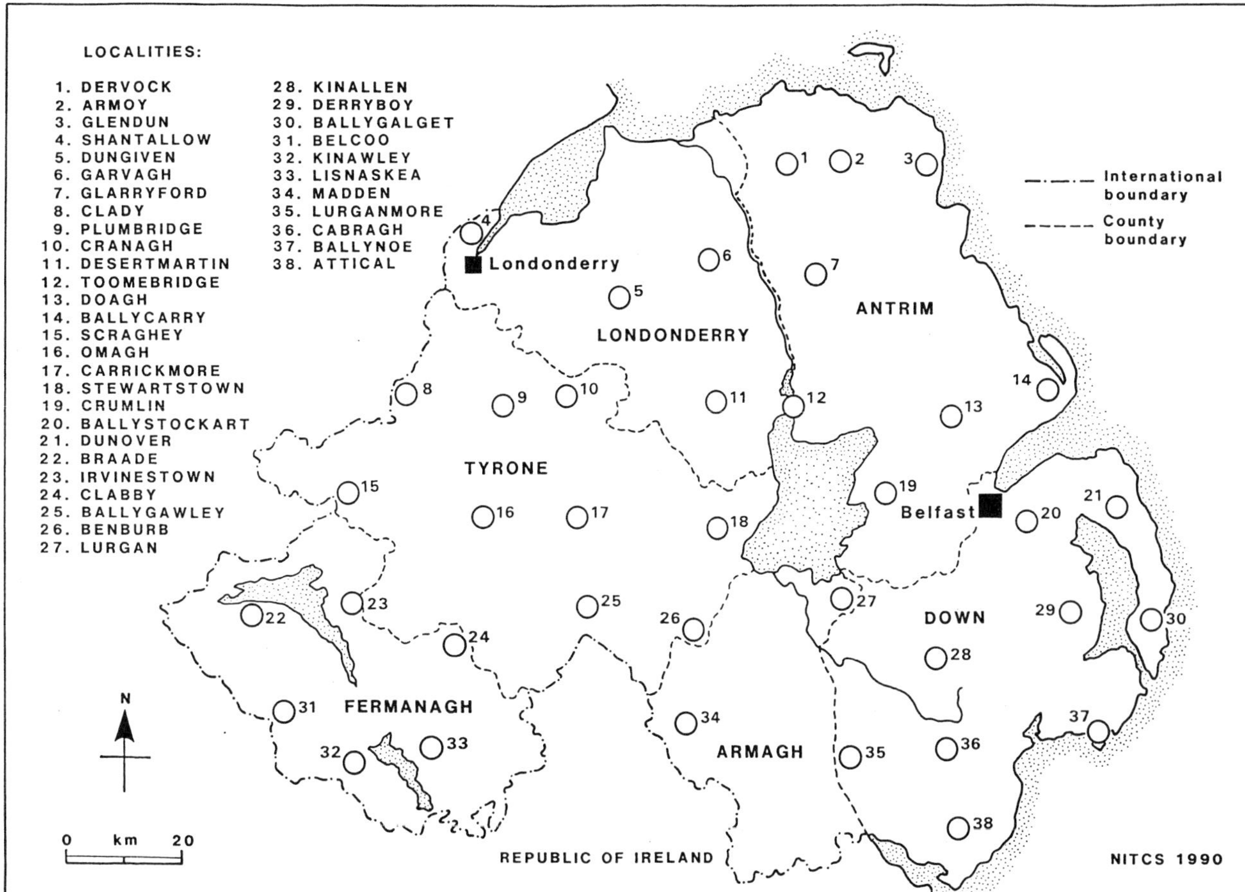

Map 1. Localities represented in the Northern Ireland Transcribed Corpus of Speech

{...}	editorial comments, with regard to:	
	{indistinct}	indistinct untranscribable utterances
	{pause}	pauses
	{laughter}	paralinguistic features
	{Alodia}	uncertain or unidentified referents
	{yotten}	unconfirmed words
...	simultaneous speech	

A preliminary version of the corpus was available in July 1990. A revised, now definitive, version was produced in June 1991.

2. TCS as discourse

It is suggested by Barry (1981) that the TRS unscripted material, upon which the TCS is based, and which constitutes the exchanges between fieldworker and informant, amounts to "conversation". This claim is worth closer examination. To the description of traditional dialect material not elicited by a questionnaire, I wish to apply the insights of recent developments in discourse analysis.

A model of conversation is proposed by Oreström (1982). Oreström suggests that conversation is private (rather than public); is casual and spontaneous (i. e. not scripted or premeditated); and is not institutionalised (i. e. uses an informal setting, but where turn order, length, aim, and topic are not specified in advance); moreover, Oreström suggests that there is a focus on the interaction; a freedom to introduce new topics; a frequent use of intimacy signals (such as tag questions); and a frequent use of listener responses. To these features, Oreström adds those features once proposed by Crystal – Davy (1969): the inexplicitness of the language; the frequent incompleteness of many utterances; a common personal background between the speakers; the randomness of the subject-matter; a general lack of planning; and the use of hesitation features.

The absence of most of these features seriously challenges the claim that the "unscripted conversations" of the TCS are indeed "conversations". To make an assessment, a number of variables are invoked: speaker variables, topic variables, functional variables, and the speech-act status of the exchanges.

2.1. Speaker variables

In the TCS, the speakers (fieldworkers and informants, without exception) are strangers. Moreover, they have come together for a purpose and for the performance of roles of which both parties are conscious. In most cases, the exchanges take place between one fieldworker and one informant. Usually, the fieldworker holds the power, controls the exchange, sets the agenda, and chooses the topics. The informants were selected locally by the fieldworkers as "genuine natives of the the locality" and assumed to be people "who have speech considered typical of the area" (Barry 1981: 31), presumably speakers whose language retained large quantities of approvable conservative usage. Further research might show how "good" these speakers actually were.

There are several departures from this simple model of speaker variables. One fieldworker had an RP-accent. Moreover, the fieldworker proved to be both misinformed and highly opinionated. As a result, considerable time is taken up with the informant's "correction" of the fieldworker's information or of mistaken assumptions, especially about ways of life of which she is evidently ignorant. These recordings serve to reinforce the long accepted principle that much better fieldwork is done by insiders than by outsiders. A second fieldworker played the fatal card of talking about language academically, thus losing her informant completely. A further fieldworker, who was possibly the best, had the habit of asking several good questions all at once, with the effect that the elicitation of potentially good information was lost. Although the use of children produced the least rewarding exchanges, they appear to have been the hardest to elicit; in their attempts to overcome this, several fieldworkers resort to a frequent use of *yes-no* questions, which, although answered, provide a remarkably low yield of information and especially of dialect. One fieldworker, who chose to elicit the conversational material by discussing the survey's locality information sheet, came over as "authoritarian" by acknowledging his informants' responses as being usually "right" or "correct".

The exchanges, nevertheless, display some commendable techniques. It seems clear from the recordings that where the fieldworker used dialect forms, the informant cooperatively followed, but in some cases not until then. It was as if the fieldworker had first to validate the use of dialect. Conspicuous examples are the use of the local second person plural pronoun *youse* or the alveolar nasal realisations of *-ing* forms. Moreover, it appeared to help with the fluency of the exchanges if the fieldworker's own accent displayed a strong local colouring, with which the informant could identify both regionally and socially.

Two recordings are worth especial mention. On one occasion, there was one fieldworker but two informants. As a result, the informants ended up talking to each other and becoming much less self-conscious. They had a common ground not shared by either with the fieldworker, and as a result this common ground was available for query, discussion, and access. This single recording most closely approximates "conversation" or "naturally occurring speech", with the fieldworker adopting a "fly-on-the-wall" approach and somewhat overcoming the observer's paradox. In a second recording, the fieldworker flounders, and the recording is only saved by the informant who reverses the roles and begins to interview the fieldworker. As the fieldworker was an American, she was of obvious exotic interest to a talkative Ulster farmer. In the end, what began disastrously turned out to be much better "conversation" as the two parties attempted to create a new common ground.

Finally, it emerges from the tapes again and again just how positive and constructive a role the fieldworker can play, distinguishing those localities which align themselves with the project's original expectations from those which do not.

2.2. Function variables

Following Oreström's criteria, typical conversation need have no other function than social interaction. With the TRS taperecordings, however, the talk had a function which was clear at least to the fieldworkers if not – or only in part – to the informants. By means of response-eliciting questions about certain topics, the aim was the recording itself. These recordings show that fieldworkers regularly display their power and control over the situation.

2.3. Topic variables

For the fieldworker, the recordings had not only a function but they had also to deal with certain topics. These had generally to do with patterns of life earlier this century and with changes in society; in particular, there are many accounts of processes and activities (such as cutting turf, ploughing a field with a horse), of pastimes and games, of schooling, of employment (or its shortage), of calendar customs (such as hallowe'en), and of the sightings of phantoms or ghosts.

2.4. Speech-act status

While there are inevitably exchanges which relate to the immediate situation of the recording, much of the material can be described as reports, accounts or descriptions usually of events or activities of the past, or as anecdotes and personal reminiscences especially of people, places and events.

2.5. Conclusion

Few of Oreström's criteria for conversation are to be found in the corpus material, and it is therefore not helpful to think of the material as "conversation". The exchanges are formal and public. In sociolinguistic terms, they constitute "formal speech" (Trudgill 1974: 110). The field-worker has a purpose and a goal, and directs the exchanges in that direction. Through his cooperation in these exchanges, the informant appears to surrender his speech rights characteristic of a partner in typical conversation.

3. Publications

Four publications arise from the basic material of the corpus: the textfile, a wordlist, an index, and a concordance.

The textfile is described above and exemplified in Appendix 1 (cf. Kirk 1991, Vol 1).

The wordlist is a simple alphabetical list of the corpus's 8762 word types together with an indication of frequency (cf. Kirk 1991, Vol. 2).

The index is a second alphabetical list of the corpus's 9820 word types but which lists the location of each type's tokens in terms of a binary reference. The reference states first the locality number, then the speaker turn number. In this way, a user should not have any difficulty in retracing the original context for any word (cf. Kirk 1991, Vol. 3).

The concordance is a third type of word list. Every token of each type is listed in the centre of separate lines, surrounded by the word's immediately preceding and immediately following contexts of some 50 letters, so that an indication is given of the word's immediately collocational and syntactic context. With each type, the tokens are organised alphabetically in terms of the immediately following word, and within that, chronologically by locality (cf. Kirk 1991, vol. 4).

All four publications are available in machine-readable form from the Economic and Social Research Council's Data Archive (University of Essex, Colchester, C04 4SQ). Certain written application formalities are required, and details are available from the Archive.

In addition, bound paper copies of the volumes and of their parts will be available for consultation within the School of English at the Queen's University of Belfast and at the Ulster Folk and Transport Museum. Requests to purchase hard copies may be made to the author.

Appendix

Northern Ireland Transcribed Corpus of Speech, Vol. 1: *Textfile*

Here is a random example of the corpus, recorded of an elderly informant in Ballygawley (locality 25):

{FW CG⟩ [And youse had football as well?]

⟨I PH21⟩ Well, it was football, but it was, it wasn't like the {LAUGHS} football that's now.

⟨FW CG⟩ [How was it different?]

⟨I PH22⟩ Och, they didn't know, they didn't know how to play football, quite different from now, you see ... no, no.

⟨FW CG⟩ [It would be rougher?]

⟨I PH23⟩ Och, it was rougher, surely, and there was no rules for it. And they would fall out at it sometimes {LAUGHS}, and it was a matter, in some games, hit the man as quick as {LAUGHS} ... That was the kind of football [I know, I know], not like now at all [aye] ... ah, no.

⟨FW CG⟩ [And the houses were mostly thatched were they?]

⟨I PH24⟩ The what?

⟨FW CG⟩ [The houses, they were thatched roofs on them?]

⟨I PH 25⟩ They were, there was a world of them thatched, a world of them. There would be, ah, there was, there was, there wouldn't, mightn't be twenty houses in a hundred houses in the country thatched, eh, slated.

⟨FW CG⟩ [Ahah, what kind of thatch did they use round this part?]
⟨I PH26⟩ They always used oatstraw [ah], or wheatstraw. They preferred it. Any place that they had thatching to do, eh, they knew they had thatching to do, in the summer they would put in a ru(le), half a rule of wheat [ahah], and that was great straw, and then they would get that lashed in the wintertime, get them m(illed), get a grou(nd) [aye], milled into flour [mm]. Well, that was good. Well, in some cases, if they were hard hit, they might mow rushes and tie them up into (INDISTINCT) thatch, but they were of no importance.
⟨FW CG⟩ [And was there men went round thatching? Thatchers?]
⟨I PH27⟩ Yes, there was men same as shoemakers. And they, at this time, there was shoemakers all through the country, and if you had a family, you went before the winter come, and you made a deal with that man, till when he would come [mm], and stay in the house, and sort the shoes, and repair shoes, and make shoes for the winter months. There was no, well, there was some, surely, but the country was full of them, towns was full of them too.
⟨FW CG⟩ [And tailors?]
⟨I PH 28⟩ The tailors, there was tailors through the country just the same as there are. There's a tailor up there now, but his trade gets out of business altogether, and the shoemaking is out of business altogether. There's the, the shoes now, the weight of the shoes, well, there's some, the weight of the shoes is all foreign. And you know what all this foreign stuff is, all of it, no, no. There's nothing made now to last [no], to wear long [different times]. Lock of months, and something in a style ...

Note

1. I am most grateful to the Economic and Social Research Council for its grant (ref. no. R000221091); to Michael Barry for his permission to use the TRS material; to the Ulster Folk and Transport Museum (in particular to Clifford Harkness) for making copies of the TRS material available; to the School of English for making available accommodation and the necessary equipment; to Antoinette Renouf and especially to Alex Collier of the University of Birmingham's Research and Development Unit for English Language Studies for their generous assistance with the production of the preliminary versions of the wordlist, index and concordance; to Gillian Alexander for her cartography; to Ray Gregg, George Munroe, and Tony Sheehan, for assistance and advice with computing; and to Michael Montgomery and Colin Neilands for encouragement and advice.
My greatest debts are to Susanne West, who prepared the first draft of the transcription with commendable efficiency and unfailing cheerfulness, and to Stephen Gibson, for his invaluable assistance in the preparation of the final draft.

References

Barry, Michael V.
1981 "The methodology of the tape-recorded survey of Hiberno-English speech", in: M. V. Barry (ed.) *Aspects of the English dialects in Ireland.* Belfast: The Queen's University of Belfast, Institute of Irish Studies.

Crystal, David – Derek Davy
1969 *Investigating English style.* London: Longman.

Kirk, John, M.
1991 *Northern Ireland Transcribed Corpus of Speech.* Vol. 1 (with S. West and S. Gibson): *Textfile* (in 2 parts); Vol. 2: *Wordlist;* Vol. 3: *Index*; Vol. 4: *Concordance* (in 9 parts). Colchester: Economic and Social Research Council Data Archive, University of Essex, Colchester.

Oreström, Bengt
1982 *Turn-taking in English conversation.* Lund Studies in English, Vol. 66. Lund: CWK Gleerup.

Trudgill, Peter
1974 *Sociolinguistics.* Harmondsworth: Penguin.

Problems in the compilation of a corpus of standard Caribbean English: A pilot study

Christian Mair

1. Introduction

Most of the research on language in the Caribbean has in the past been devoted to the structural and sociolinguistic description of the various Creoles in the region – justifiably so in view of past neglect. By comparison, very little is known about educated English usage, as, in the words of Pauline Christie, "serious research into the formal spoken and written English of educated persons in the region, roughly defined here as those who completed at least seven years of secondary education and/or have had professional training, has so far been concerned only with the area of lexis" (1989: 247). In view of this, the planned compilation of a corpus of educated/standard Caribbean English as part of the International Corpus of English ("ICE" – for information on the project see Greenbaum 1988 and Leitner, this volume) is a timely undertaking. In several papers circulated informally members of the various ICE teams have pointed out the need to place the project on a secure sociolinguistic basis before the actual collection of material for the individual corpora starts. This discussion, although fruitful, has had a theoretical bias so far, and it is, therefore, useful at this point to tackle some of the problems involved in an empirical pilot study.

Since the use of English in the Creole-speaking communities of the Anglophone Caribbean provides an interesting borderline case between the standard situations of English being used as a native language and English being used as a second or official language, I have analysed my private collection of Jamaican texts which I have been using for teaching purposes in courses on English as a World Language with a view to corpus development. I have focussed on news reports and editorials, two written genres which will be part of any "Caribbean" sub-corpus of ICE, and on phone-in broadcasts as an easily accessible form of (relatively) spontaneous spoken language.

2. What is standard Caribbean English?

In a paper intended as a discussion of a specific set of empirical data, I do not want to linger longer than necessary over theoretical issues, but it is clear that the compilers of the "Caribbean" component of ICE will have to make conscious decisions on issues which can be solved by appealing to a societal consensus in areas in which English is more securely established as the native language of the population.[1]

To ask the most fundamental question first: should we assume that there is a "Caribbean English", the educated variety of which could be targeted for documentation in the proposed ICE corpus, or is educated standard English in Jamaica different enough from its counterparts in, say, Belize or Guyana to warrant description as an independent national variety? Pauline Christie, who herself lists some intra-regional differences in Caribbean English usage (1989: 251–253), nevertheless argues that local varieties of educated English are united by "an extensive core of agreement, especially with regard to syntax" (1989: 245) and concludes that

> despite an extensive common core particularly at the syntactic level, Caribbean English is not identical with internationally recognized varieties of English. The main concern here has been with the fact that the distinguishing features can no longer be officially ignored since, not only are they becoming more and more common in the formal usage of persons from all levels of Caribbean society, but they have also coincided with a change of attitude, especially on the part of young people, towards the traditional model, British English. Similar changes have been occurring in other spheres of activity and they can all be traced to the growth of regional identity which has involved the re-examination of old values and a search for new standards. The point has been made, however, that official recognition of Caribbean English as a variety in its own right need not mean rejection of those traditional varieties which are relevant for those users who must establish and maintain contacts with the outside world. (1989: 262)

Similarly, Robert LePage writes that

> in spite of all [the] parameters of difference defining the multidmensional space, there is no doubt that the Creole-English-speaking Caribbean, from Guyana and Panama to Belize on the mainland and from Trinidad to the Leewards to Jamaica in the Antilles, constituted one cultural area whose educated varieties of English, each one marked by the peculiarities of the particular territory, were focused by institutions such as broadcasting, the colonial civil service, interisland travel, and the University of the West

> Indies, and by the common cultural heritage expressed in a large outpouring of fiction and poetry in the postwar years. (1988: 34)

However, a page later LePage hints that "the former focusing agencies may be disintegrating", thus giving rise to separatist linguistic developments in the future. It seems to me that such fears are premature because other forms of regional integration have replaced the links forged in the era of colonialism and the BBC – ranging from the Caribbean Examinations Council, whose potential role as a provider and promoter of local norms of educated usage is studied by Christie, to commercial music and other forms of popular culture. But it is clear that the point LePage raises is of central concern to the ICE project. A wrong assessment of the situation at the time of the collection of the texts for the corpus will have fatal results. If, to mention the three most populous states, educated English in Jamaica, Trinidad and Tobago and Guyana were in fact developing different norms, then lumping these varieties together in a corpus of Caribbean English would be a waste of time because the results from an analysis of such a corpus would not represent any of the three actually emerging standards but create an artificial one that is irrelevant both in prescriptive and descriptive terms.

Financing and resources permitting, the safest way to proceed at present seems to be to collect material from one of the more populous states in the region first and then to see whether the norms emerging from an analysis of the data are valid elsewhere. Alternatively, a pan-Caribbean corpus could be systematically vetted for intra-regional variation as it is being compiled, for example through the collation of the results obtained from all material and those obtained for material from individual territories. (Needless to say, such a comparison ceases to be statistically reliable with small samples of text.) Quite likely, the extent of intra-regional variation will vary from text-type to text-type for sometimes rather mundane reasons. If, for example, most of the regional sports coverage in the press is from the Caribbean News Agency (CANA), then variation is bound to be less important here than in editorials, where no such standardising agency is available.

Whatever policy is eventually adopted, however, it is clear that the corpus will document an emerging rather than an established standard.[2] While in the United States compliance with a British standard is not expected (or *vice versa*), this is not necessarily so in the Caribbean. As long as *de facto* local norms of educated speech and writing are not codified and explicitly accepted by the majority of speakers, the two major external standards of English will continue to play a role, as models consciously or unconsciously followed for their prestige value in domains as different as advertising for quality-consumer goods and school-teaching.

3. A note on methodology

A word of caution is in order here concerning the results of the present study. First of all, it is not clear whether the corpus investigated was large enough. In order to test the validity of the results reported here, I analysed a matching set of data. While the categories of deviation to be observed were broadly similar, the relative frequencies of individual types still differed considerably, which suggests that the present corpus is a typical though not yet statistically representative sample.

The second problem is the manual analysis of the corpus. The human analyst records what strikes him as unusual but frequently fails to keep track of the regular instances. What for example is the significance of an admittedly considerable number of instances of proximity concord when – in educated Jamaican English just as in any other educated variety – grammatical concord continues to be the overwhelming statistical norm? It is here – in the systematic and controlled comparison of usage in matching corpora – that the ICE project will make possible real advances in scholarship. Corpora with grammatical and word-class tagging would be ideal, but much information could be gained even from plain lexical concordances. Thus, high-frequency auxiliaries such as *is* or *has* are marked for concord, so that even a simple KWIC ("key-word in context") display of the data from the various corpora would allow interesting grammatical comparisons across varieties. So the following remarks stand as a collection of potentially interesting local usages, worth investigating with more sophisticated linguistic research tools which will, hopefully, be available soon.

4. The language of Jamaican daily papers and periodicals

The guidelines for compilers of ICE sub-corpora (*ICE Newsletter* 6, January 1990) recommend the inclusion of 40,000 words of press news reports and half that amount of editorial text. A survey of this amount of text from the pages of the *Daily Gleaner*, the Jamaican paper of record, the *Daily Star* and the *Jamaica Record*, two other daily publications, shows that such a division into reportage and comment is indispensable. Divergence from the linguistic and rhetorical norms of international standard English tends to be far more conspicuous in editorial writing than in reportage. An additional problem with sampling reportage is that most international news is lightly edited material supplied by external sources such as AP and Reuter. In view of this, compilers might want to restrict the collection to locally written reports of local news.

An interesting discourse-level feature in all papers is the use of Creole in verbatim quotations. To vary the Fishman-Hymes dictum, one might ask: "Who is reported as speaking Creole to whom on what occasion?" and answer that, broadly speaking, the uneducated lower classes are depicted as speaking Creole, while the educated and powerful use English. Thus, the complaint of an unruly member of a local amateur soccer team will be quoted as: "Dem ah tief, dem tief wi out" (S 26/8 – 14), while "concerned businessmen" debate how best the "creeping devaluation of the dollar could be halted or reversed" (G 5/9 – 6).[3] It goes without saying that the reader will be confronted with the most diverse mixtures of standard English and Creole in such verbatim quotations – probably a true reflection of sociolinguistic reality – and that no consistent norms have developed for scripting the essentially spoken medium of Creole.[4] However, quotation practices are not solely guided by journalists' desire for speech realism but by complex additional stylistic conventions. Creole denotes humour, hence its use in cartoons by politicians that would elsewhere be quoted in standard English,[5] whereas standard English stands for seriousness. On the ceremonious occasion of his 105th birthday Mr. Ezekiel Feurtado of Basin Hill, Islington, St. Mary, is depicted as saying: "I hardly feel any pain and I am as fit as a fiddle" (G 5/9 – 10). Commenting on the large number of injuries due to knife-fights, a nurse from the Kingston Public Hospital says the situation "is severe, [a] great strain on manpower and hospital facilities. Most of the time the patients have to be given injections in addition to dressing. It is a great strain and it doesn't have to be", and then goes on "Man caan just cut op man so"

(G 28/8 – 1). Here the writer standardises those passages of the nurse's statement which contain factual information but leaves the last sentence unchanged in order to preserve its emotional impact on the reader. (This is assuming that the switch from English to Creole was not part of the nurse's original utterance.)

These and similar verbatim quotations show that the Creole should not be treated as an invisible substrate in the description of standard English in Jamaica, its role restricted to accounting for speakers' involuntary deviations from international English. Rather than be trapped in circular reasoning and define standard English as the Creole-free passages of the spoken and written texts under study, one should recognise the Creole for what it is even in the most educated and formal varieties of English in Jamaica, namely a visible presence – as proverbial lore ("one one coco full basket"), as a highly effective rhetorical device or as the only appropriate response in specific communicative situations:

> Mr. Charles [government minister responsible for ICAS, the newly introduced international call authorisation system] at one point implored the forum to be patient and to give the system a chance.
> Mr. Charles: Bear with it (ICAS).
> A customer hissed his teeth loudly.
> Mr. Charles: You can suck you teeth 'till you dead.
> During the question-and-answer section, a question raised was: "What would happen if the system doesn't work? Is there a cut off point?" (G 25/8 – 12)

To *suck one's teeth*, according to the *Dictionary of Jamaican English*, (Cassidy – LePage 1980) means "to make a sound of annoyance, displeasure, ill-nature, or disrespect by sucking air audibly through the teeth and over the tongue", and no matter how formal the context, there is only one appropriate way of responding to the locally typical gesture for showing contempt, namely answering back in Creole.

Sometimes, it seems that variation in the speech of persons quoted does not reflect any actual shift in register on the part of the speakers themselves (*vide* the nurse's comment above) but is employed to create a subtle emotive bias in news-stories. I take as my example a four-column story titled "Bailey: My son was murdered" (R 4/9 – 4), in which an ex-policeman complains about the shooting of his son by former colleagues. He is depicted as saying, "From what I understand and saw for myself my son was murdered and I want this case to reach the hands of the Commissioner of Police, for him to look into the matter and have swift and proper investigations conducted." He then goes on to tell of an incident in which one of his ex-colleagues threatened his son's life, "Him tell mi sey him ago mek mi go dung a Madden go look pan mi son and after what has happened now I have taken that threat very seriously." All the remaining verbatim quotations of the distraught father are in standard English. Creole comes up twice more, when a witness to the shooting is reported as saying "Every time police murder youth an then sey a shootout" and when the father's former colleagues in the station charge that "Him a lead a demonstration against the police." Remember that the father's only "slip" into the Creole occurs when he reports the policeman's threat against his son's life, and it is clear that Creole here serves as a linguistic marker for the bad guys (even if in this case they happen to be on the police force) and the lazy bystander – with the reporter consciously or unconsciously reinforcing a traditionally widespread negative view of the Creole.

It is among the politically progressive sections of the educated public and in literary writing that the use of Creole as a stylistic device has in recent years been taken to new heights, without – it is important to add – preserving the Creole's traditional associations with "rudeness" (to be taken here in its full Jamaican sense – see *Dictionary of Jamaican English*) (Cassidy – LePage 1980) and humour. Compare the following editorial from *Sistren* Magazine (Vol II, no 1, 1989), titled "Sistren out deh!":

> Time come and we gaan again! It's been years since Sistren did a Caribbean tour, so to make up for it, we've bitten off a huge chunk – nine countries in ten weeks beginning April 19 and going through to the end of June! So, you can imagine the planning and the preparation; the hustle and the bustle, that has marked the office for the past few weeks. And what with the new play, Buss Out! (see review on p. 21), we have been very busy indeed.
>
> Now when Sistren tour, dem caan jus' tour so. In 'nuff meetings, apart from rehearsals and the normal day-to-day ones that keep the business going, all involved have been learning about the history and geography of the region and the specific countries to be visited. They've also been preparing themselves for any cultural differences they may encounter, and familiarising themselves with the background and work of the various host groups.
>
> It's a particularly significant tour coming as it does in a period of great activity among women in the individual countries as well as regionally. We shall all be learning a great deal from it. (page 2)

In its standard passages, the text shows a secure command of the niceties of the British English tense and aspect system, down to the *shall*-form for the future continuous tense, which would be felt to be quaint elsewhere in the Anglophone Western hemisphere. On the sociolinguistic criteria proposed so far for the design of ICE sub-corpora, such texts would have to be considered for inclusion in the corpus despite their Creole embellishments.

However, 60,000 words of newsprint, even if stored in computer-readable and easily accessible form, is not the ideal basis for research on the role of code-switching and code-mixing in the speech and writing of educated Jamaicans. Product-oriented corpus-analysis cannot replace process-oriented participant observation and sociolinguistic fieldwork as a method of study for this purpose. What the corpus can do, however, is to provide data on a variety of lexical and syntactic features which strike a reader familiar with British and US papers only. I will single out a few instances for discussion and try to point out ways in which a completed corpus could contribute to research.

a) Subject-verb concord

The most obvious difference between the grammatical norms of international English and the English of Jamaican newspapers is the greater role played in the latter by what Quirk *et al.* (1985: 755) call "proximity concord." Proximity concord occasionally overrides grammatical and notional concord in sentences such as – Quirk's examples – *No one except his own supporters agree with him* or *A good knowledge of English, Russian and French are required for this position* (neither of which is, incidentally, considered fully acceptable by the authors). Quirk *et al.* note that the principle of proximity comes into play "mainly in unplanned discourse" and that "in writing it will be corrected to grammatical concord if it is noticed" (1985: 757).

In my pilot study I do not aim at statistically representative analysis of the newspaper texts studied, but uncorrected instances of the proximity principle in action clearly are the most frequent grammatical peculiarity to be observed in the texts. I have collected dozens of examples, some of which follow below:

(1) *Dormitories, classrooms, the library and resource centre and multi-purpose building is to be renovated.* (G 5/9-2)
(2) *The area around both piers have silted up.* (G 5/9-3)
(3) *The condition of the roads have made worse an already bad transportation system.* (5/9-11)
(4) *Presentation of awards were made by Mr. Stewart...* (G 5/9-14)

(5) *Zinc meant for Hurricane Gilbert victims have been seen being distributed in Lauriston and other areas.* (R 4/9-2)
(6) *At that time one or two prints of the film is dispatched...* (R 4/9-10)
(7) *...the massacre of human lives that occur daily on the roads of Jamaica...* (S 26/8-1)
(8) *The talent in all the required disciplines are available.* (G 25/8-6)
(9) *The fight against injustice, socio-economic oppression, slavery and exploitation were long, brutal and cruel.* (G 25/8-7)

There are also examples in which the principle of notional concord has been extended further than is usual in international English:

(10) *31 awards has been to children...* (G 5/9-14) [i. e. 'a total of 31 awards']
(11) *But their practice game results to date suggests otherwise.* (R 4/9-12) ['their success as evinced in the practice game results']
(12) *...to remind the public that incidents which alarm was the basis on which a State of Emergency was called in 1976.* (G 25/8-3) ['the paragraph in the law on incidents which alarm (authorities)']
(13) *This special educational facilities provides pre-schoolers with the opportunity to develop their learning potential.* (G 25/8-28, advertisement) ['this educational regimen'; note the singular demonstrative present even in the original]

Other instances of lacking concord are more difficult to account for in terms of the rules laid down for international English by Quirk *et al.* Individual examples may be typographical errors, but the cumulative evidence points to the existence of a trend worth linguistic attention:

(14) *But now this area has been forgotten and road-work material lie in waste along the wayside.* (G 31/8-7)
(15) *...regardless of the cards that fate deal us...* (G 5/9-6)
(16) *Vacancy exist at United Protection Ltd. for men of good character.* [...] *The best rate per hour in the industry are guaranteed.* (G 5/9-16; classified advertisement)
(17) *Lowered pressure after damage to the water system make fire fighting difficult.* (G 5/9-21)
(18) *Bailey said that since the* Jamaica Record *carried the story about the killing he have been shunned by his colleagues who charged that "him a lead demonstration against police".* (R 4/9-2)
(19) *Remember opportunity shake hands only with the prepared.* (R 4/9-15)
(20) *Why were equipment by local engineers rejected?* (G 25/8-12)

(21) *Samaranch oppose life bans for first-time doping offenders.* (R 4/9-13)

(22) *Here a happy customer receive his prize* (G 25/8-33; caption in a photo advertisement)

(23) *Members of the family* [...] *charged that Barrett, who reside in Buff Bay, Portland, is demanding $ 20,000 before handing over the body.* (R 4/9-4)

In fact, the large number of such examples calls into question the usefulness of describing the data within the framework of international English concord rules, that is as a strengthening of two subsidiary factors (i. e. the proximity principle and notional concord) at the expense of a basically intact grammatical concord rule. It could be that the feeling for concord itself is being eroded by a persistent tendency to take over invariant verbs and unmarked plural forms from the Creole even in educated usage.[6] With examples like (2) – *The area around both piers have silted up* – the issue is impossible to decide. *Have* could be accounted for both as proximity concord with *piers* and as an invariant verb form derived from the Creole; the converse constellation – singular noun phrase triggering proximity concord and verb marked for third person – as in:

(24) *Incomplete investigations by the police has forced another postponement.* (G 5/9-3)

(25) *The external trade results of the first half of the year continues to deteriorate alarmingly.* (G 28/8-2; statement by Government Minister)

cannot be explained as direct grammatical interference from Creole and requires an explanation in terms of standard English concord rules. However, unambiguous examples of this type are rare; most of them contain morphologically irregular verbs like *be* and *have* or can be explained as instances of very broadly understood notional concord, or even as hypercorrect use of the third-person singular forms, which also occurs independently:

(26) *Wrongdoers with assistance from persons within government departments continues with their illegal practices.* (R 4/9-2)

The usefulness of even a relatively small computer-readable corpus of Caribbean English in the present connection is, I think, obvious. It would make it possible to determine the frequency of "deviant" concord in educated Jamaican usage and would help in choosing between rival explanatory theories. Most importantly, the results of the analysis of the corpus would help in the formulation of realistic prescriptive guidelines to be promoted in the schools and universities of the region – for example by deciding the question of whether proximity concord should continue to be proscribed in future – as Christie (1989: 249) seems to recommend in a brief comment – or whether it should be regarded as a permissible deviation from international norms in the local educated standard.

b) Tense and aspect

A reading of the newspapers also reveals some interesting divergences from international English tense and aspect usage. A computerised corpus will show whether or not these are systematic enough to posit an independent local norm. As complex tense and aspect forms contain auxiliaries or sequences of auxiliaries, the majority of them should be easy to extract even from a corpus without grammatical tagging. Alongside examples which correspond to international English norms for present perfect usage, one also encounters the following type – present, preferably the present continuous, being used for present perfect (or past for past perfect):

(27) *For 100 years everyone knows...* [that Benjamins Vanilla is the best] (*Flair Magazine*, G 28/8-5)

(28) *He mentioned a process which is being widely-used* [sic] *since 1987...* (G 31/8-19)

(29) *HOW TERRIBLE: This is one of the overfilled pit toilets which has an offensive stench emanating from it, at the Jacques Road housing units. The ex-Stadium dwellers are the occupants of this scheme, since they were removed from the National Stadium in April 1989.* (G 5/9-1, photo caption)

(30) *Since March 1989 we are suffering the most frequent unscheduled power cuts.* (G 31/8-7, letter to the editor)

(31) *Up to that time they were being used for cargo service.* (G 5/9-3)

Shields (1989: 50–51), who briefly comments on this phenomenon, regards it as interference from the tense-aspect system of the Creole. As the following examples show, there may be a general tendency to overuse the continuous aspect:

(32) *...he had been told by the Manager of the Holiday Inn in Montego Bay that they cannot take all the bookings and have had to be turning away people from now.* (G 28/8-3)[7]

(33) *Because rents are high, teachers have had to be doubling up and sharing with persons who they normally would not want to room with.* (G 28/8-3)

Gratuitous use of *being* in nonfinite clauses should be analysed in the same context:

(34) *The Clarendon Parish Council wants a full report to be submitted at its September 11 meeting on the state of a pig farm being operated by Mr. John Plummer in Race Course.* (G 31/8-13)

(35) *Julian Bond, the American civil rights leader, who arrived in Jamaica yesterday on a one-week visit. He will be guest speaker tonight at a fund-raising dinner being put on by the JLP's Clarendon Central Constituency.* (G 31/8-3, photo caption)

Other peculiarities of tense/aspect usage – such as the occasional use of infinitives (e. g. *like*) for preterite forms, or corresponding hypercorrect forms, e. g. *strucked* or *struck* (R 4/9-13) – should be interpreted against the background of Creole phonology and grammar. Spellings such as *close-door discussions* (G 5/9-1), *the mix-bag of buildings* (G 25/8-6), *their inexperience opponents* (G 25/8-15), or – to give some corresponding hypercorrections – *an annual lost of $70 million* (G 25/8-12), *their only lost* (DG 5/9-14), *matured single lady* (G 31/8-20) would seem to argue for the primacy of the phonetic factor, i. e. a tendency to avoid certain word-final consonant clusters. The use of *know* for *knew* (e. g. in S 26/8-11), on the other hand, calls for a grammatical explanation – substrate-influenced use of the unmarked verb with past-time reference. Quite likely, both factors may even be at work simultaneously in some cases. One particularly convoluted instance of the interaction of phonetics, grammar and meaning – unfortunately not involving a verb from – is *A air dryer was found beside his body* (R 4/9-1), where the dropping of the aitch and the absence of the required form of the indefinite article make unexpected semantic sense, because after all it is hot air which is used to dry the wet hair.

c) Complementation of verbs

This is a particularly difficult area to discuss, because acceptability judgements often differ even among speakers of international English, for example because contextually admissible metaphorical interpretations may render acceptable what on a literal reading would be rejected. Nevertheless, patterns of verb complementation are among the most salient grammatical features of the emerging Jamaican standard:

(36) *...anyone who purchases furniture or appliances that value over $500 has a chance to enter the raffle draw.* (G 25/8-34)

At the time Jamaica was beginning to be colonised by the British (i. e. the mid-seventeenth century), this use of the verb *value* was already obsolescent in England (see OED, *value*, III.8b). However, it is not really necessary to trace such forms back to archaic English usage. At any point in the history of the language, they could have arisen from the Creole substrate, which freely allows conversion from verbs to nouns (and *vice versa*) and has a morphologically unmarked passive. In evaluating the evidence, one faces the usual problems of having to decide whether an instance of unusual verb complementation is due to a typographical error, e. g. omission of a preposition, or whether one is dealing with a genuine linguistic datum:

(37) *The MP took note the very poor conditions* [sic] *of the road.* (G 31/8-12)

(38) *Are you looking a job?* (G 25/8-20, classified advertisement)

Firmly established throughout the Caribbean is the transitive use of *care* (Christie 1989: 249), as exemplified in:

(39) *Care your book, care your school – that's the best way to keep your cool! A message from Kool Kat and Desnoes & Geddes Sof* [sic, as trademark] *Drinks.* (G 25/8-28)

The greatest problems arise in the analysis of examples involving sentential complementation, where it is notoriously difficult to disentangle logic and syntax. An accidental anacoluthon or instance of sloppy thinking or bad writing is clearly not a distinctive feature of Caribbean English. One probably should not make too much of cases like the following:

(40) *The talent in all the required disciplines are available through Jamaicans to do it, and help is out there.* (G 25/8-6)

But the general question of whether the distribution of *ing*-clauses and infinitival clauses differs from international English is certainly worth pursuing, and – to judge from the material analysed here – a one-million word corpus of Caribbean English would no doubt provide a fair amount of pertinent data:

(41) *How many people would refuse buying U.S. dollars at J$4 to US $1 from a ganja man?* (G 31/8-2)

(42) *Many people have lost their lives to go from one place to another* [during a hurricane]. (G 5/9-21)

A computer-readable corpus will make it easier to decide whether such usages are exceptional even by Jamaican standards, or whether they reflect a local norm diverging from international English. Another recurrent phenomenon in my material is the inversion of subject and predicate in indirect questions. It is found both in other varieties and in older stages of the language, but proscribed in the present-day international standard:

(43) [The young women] *have no idea what they are getting themselves into or what exactly is a beauty contest.* (G 25/8-7)

d) Prepositions

Expanded functional load borne by certain prepositions is a feature of the emergent Jamaican standard already noted by Shields (1989: 48–49). My material contains many instances of preposition usage unusual or absent in British and American English. No systematic trends emerge, however, and I hesitate to draw conclusions at this point, except to say that here is probably the area where a computer-readable corpus would be most helpful, as even a simple lexical search would yield hundreds of tokens of a given preposition.

One example will suffice to illustrate the kind of phenomenon one is dealing with. Alongside *employed by* and *employed with* one encounters *employed to:*

(44) *NOTICE: This is to notify the public that Messrs. Robert Wright and Patrick Brown otherwise called "The Dread" are no longer employed to the company and are therefore not allowed to transact any business on their behalf. Sgd. Management Tenderflake Donut Co.* (1988) Ltd. (G 5/9-14)

This use of *employed to* is not at all rare and recalls phrases such as *indentured to* or *apprenticed to* with their overtones of a paternalistic and pre-capitalistic mode of economic organisation.

e) Articles

One frequently finds definite, indefinite or zero-articles used in ways not easily reconciled with the relevant international English norms. Compare, for instance, the definite article preceding proper names in the following example:

(45) *The court was told that on January 5, the Yellowman* [pseudonym of popular musician] *chased the Angelita Marshall around her house with a knife.* (S 26/8-1)

Both British and American English would require *in a draw* in the following example:

(46) ... [only if] *the final game today between Trinidad and Tobago and Barbados ends in draw.* (G 25/8-15)

Considering the near complete absence of articles in basilectal Creole, writers' occasional insecurity in the use of *the* or *a(n)* does not come as a surprise, but it is only rarely that deviations from international English norms are frequent and systematic enough to speak of a local norm in educated English usage. The closest one comes to such a norm is the omission of the definite article in phrases such as *at right, at left, at centre, at right/left background. Society* is an abstract noun in its sense of 'people in general' in British English; in Jamaican English it is frequently treated like a concrete collective noun and preceded by the definite article.

5. The language of phone-in radio programmes

JBC (Jamaican Broadcasting Corporation) and RJR (Radio Jamaica), the two major radio stations in the country, both have very popular lunchtime call-in programmes. These are of interest to the linguist as easily accessible samples of unrehearsed speech from the presenters and their studio guests – both normally members of the educated elite – and by members of the public from a variety of educational backgrounds.

For the purposes of the proposed corpus of standard Jamaican English these phone-in programmes constitute interesting but "messy" data, not only because – as Nikolaus Coupland has pointed out in a statement circulated among ICE collaborators – they are an ill-defined genre from a textlinguistic/discourse analytical point of view but also because they lay bare immediately the precarious status of the analytical construct "standard/educated Jamaican English" at the basis of ICE. The major problem is not calls by people unwilling or unable to express themselves in standard English, as such calls could easily be edited out. Generally speaking, one gets the impression that the presenters, guests and many of the callers acknowledge the standard as the existing norm in broadcasting and largely conform to it in practice. Nevertheless, it is difficult to find even a few minutes' worth of Creole-free text, and it is not so much involuntary lapses into the Creole which are responsible for this but the conscious or at least systematic use of the Creole as a stylistic device.

If a writer intends to represent the Creole in a written text, he or she will use nonstandard spellings, but no such cues are available in recorded speech. Very often a particular feature of a text allows two interpretations, one consistent with the phonology and grammar of the educated Jamaican standard, and one consistent with the Creole. For example, the loss of the past tense morphemes in verbs such as *looked, hanged*, etc. could be a phonetically conditioned simplification of word-final consonant clusters in rapid standard speech, or be due to a tendency to use the invariant verb forms of the Creole even in formal speech. It is, of course, easy to classify [luk] referring to past time as an invariant verb form if the same speaker uses other invariant verb forms which are not phonologically conditioned, or that it is an instance of cluster simplification if the speaker's tense system is otherwise intact, but such consistency is rare as speakers rapidly shift styles and registers or just simply do not produce the required diagnostic sets of forms. To give the flavour of radio conversation at the standard end of the "continuum",[8] I present the following extract from a call revolving around the problems of small cultivators in Jamaica (RJR Hotline, 29 August 1989; passages focussed on in the analysis are given in boldface:

Host: *...it's not so much that the land doesn't necessarily belong to them – we know there's a fair amount of land capturing going on in Jamaica which is simply another form of stealing – but on the other hand most of the land tenure problems is not that land does not belong to people who claim to own the land – is that they cannot show a legal title – largely because they have not gone through the process for instance in the business of wills to make sure that that title is properly established you know* ***grandfather James dead and im lef dat piece of square under the pear tree up dere to Jimmy***

[...]

Caller: *well you see coming back to the point*

Host: *mhm*

Caller: *the government should set up a programme to assist the small farmer*

Host: *but the* [cough] *the government successive governments in Jamaica have been setting up programmes to assist the small farmer* ***from the devil was a boy***

Host: *but aren't there educational programmes – I was talking to Mr. Courtney Fletcher last week and he tells me that the taxpayers of this country are subsidising the JAS to the extent of about one hundred and fifty million dollars a month and what Mr. Fletcher tells me is that this helps the JAS to educate* ***the farmer*** *and to do field work and to help* ***the farmer to come together*** *and to have meetings and exchange ideas and all the rest of it...*

This rough-and-ready transcription is not meant to do justice to the recorded data. Features of accent and prosody are not indicated at all although they would be essential in a sociolinguistic analysis of the data.[9] But even so the short passage illustrates three situations in which code-switching and mixing typically occurs. There is, first, the direct quotation of folk speech – familiar from newspapers – then the occasional deliberate inclusion of a folksy turn of phrase to make for a comfortably informal atmosphere in a talk otherwise conducted in standard English and, finally, the unplanned merger of the two expressive codes we have in the last paragraph. In accordance with standard English grammar, *the farmer* starts out being used as a generic singular and a few sentences later ends up as an unmarked plural, as it is difficult to picture the generic-singular farmer having a meeting with himself.

One finds the occasional instance of a caller quoting himself or herself, but in a different register:

> *...to be honest with you if they started to explain to me the technicalities of communicating between here and the world and using fibre optics and this and that you know my* [noise] *would be saying* ***yes yes sound good sound good sound good – you follow me*** (RJR Hotline, 29 August 1989)

Linguistic etiquette also seems to demand that the host meet a Creole caller half-way when there is a problem in understanding:

Host: *o. k. it's now twenty to twelve hello*
Caller: *hello*
Host: *mhm you're on Hotline – go ahead – go ahead*
Caller: *the road want to fix*
Host: *which road*
Caller: *the road want to fix*
Host: ***which road wants to fix***

Caller: *hm*
Host: *stop listening to your radio – just listen to me on your telephone – tell me which road it is that you want fixed – hello* [call disconnected] *all right let's try another one*

(RJR Hotline, 29 August 1989)

Note that, by retaining the third-person singular *-s*, the host remains a cut above the caller. In a desire to accommodate callers, some presenters give up standard English for extended passages. In the following stretch of discourse, technical terms of the standard such as *deduction* are paraphrased for the benefit of the listener, subject and verb are not inverted in some questions, and invariant verbs are in free variation with third-person singular forms:

Host: *hold on hold on hold on hold on don't be like the last caller that* ***don't want to hear nothing*** *– hold on and listen now – now* ***you have a paper*** *which shows how much were the deductions – how much they took out of your grandfather's pay –* ***you have a paper*** *that* ***show*** *how much they took out of your grandfather's pay [...] no no you could have some paper but it* ***don't be*** *quite the right paper – does it have anything in it which* ***say*** *your grandfather whatever is his name paid the following amount to NHD – do you have a paper like that*

(RJR Hotline, 4 September 1989)

The real challenge to a compiler of a corpus of standard Jamaican English, however, is not such isolated switches taking place for identifiable reasons but continuous variation of register. Take the following example, from the same presenter making a passionate plea for integrity in the administration of building-stamp and hurricane relief programmes. (The most expressive and dynamic plane of variation, phonetics and prosody, is again lost in transcription.):

Host: [the real difficulty with that programme is] *that people who could turn their hand and do it really should not be getting any building* ***stamp*** *at this stage – it should be people who are in absolute dire need and necessity – I cannot go any further because – with respect – if people have shown their initiative and have been able to build up their house then we should thank them for not being a burden on the public purse now because at this stage that cannot be changed for money I mean people should say I have been able to build up my house I don't need it and let the building* ***stamp*** *be given to* ***somebody who really don't*** *have anything*

Caller: *I understood it thank you*
Host: *okay [...] and the programme was supposed to be for those who were absolutely needy and don't see the first of it if I were in charge — and that is why nobody put me in charge — I'd have* ***stop[ped]*** *the whole thing and* ***I done*** *the whole thing — but you see I'm not a politician I'm not elected to rule over anybody because to me it is an embarrassment now — one year later you know —* ***we fighting*** *over zinc and* ***we still seeing*** *we don't get* ***stamp*** *till we get black and the house* ***done repair*** *— it was supposed to have been for the* ***needy needy needy needy needy needy*** *but now I don't know —* ***dem now waan de money instead — well mi nah know*** *— that's why I don't run things — — Hotline hallo — hallo — hallo Hotline — hallo*
Caller: *hallo — good morning*
Host: *good morning ma'am — how are you today*
Caller: *not too bad*
Host: *okay what's your — what do you want to talk about*

(RJR Hotline, 4 September 1989)

This is definitely not international standard English. Nor is it likely to be accepted as Jamaican standard by local speakers. But the text was produced by an educated speaker in the relatively public and formal context of a radio programme, and one may well ask whether the concept of the educated standard the compilers of ICE seem to have in mind is adequate to a description of spoken data from the Anglophone Caribbean.

6. Conclusion

A Caribbean ICE sub-corpus devoted to the description of educated English usage in the region will stimulate research in precisely the area in which it is most needed at present. The corpus will yield some interesting lexical data. A lexical concordance listing Creole word forms will also provide indirect access to macro-structural textual features such as style shifting. The most valuable findings, however, are to be expected in the area of morphosyntax, where statistically reliable data on the more frequent morphological and syntactic features of the variety may ultimately contribute towards the development of a realistic and socially accepted prescriptive norm of educated usage. Whether, outside specific text-types such as news broadcasts or formal oratory, "standard English" is a relevant concept in the description of spoken language in the region is a question which remains to be addressed in further research.

Notes

1. Official language and educational policies, and probably also the self-description of the majority of speakers, suggest that, with minor exceptions such as St. Lucia and Dominica with their French Creoles, the territories of the Commonwealth Caribbean are "English-speaking" and that, by implication, the Creole languages are dialects of English suitable only for use in specific informal communicative domains. However, the expert opinion of many linguists is different. In a recent paper Pauline Christie, for example, comes close to arguing that English is a foreign language for most of the population of the supposedly "Anglophone" Caribbean. Hubert Devonish explores the consequences of such a stance for future social policy and argues that, in the interest of popular participation in local affairs, international English should be phased out as the standard language of the "Anglophone" Caribbean and be replaced by standardised varieties of Creole languages spoken by the majority of the population (see Devonish 1986).
2. Cf. Shields (1989: 42), who writes: "The exercise of defining StE [Standard English] in Jamaica from the point of view of the user is an interesting one. It underscores the existence of dual standards: the one acknowledged traditionally and reflecting metropolitan norms, the other, actually emergent, promulgated in the writing and speech of the majority of prominent, educated Jamaicans. The discrepancies, though important, are for the most part, undocumented."
3. R is short for the *Jamaica Record*, S for the *Daily Star* and G for the *Daily* or *Sunday Gleaner*. Then follows the date of publication of the issue quoted (all either August or September 1989), and after the hyphen the page number.
4. On the inconsistency and illogicality of the existing writing conventions see Hellinger (1986).
5. Also compare the following bit of decidedly non-serious political reportage: "We hear there was one grand shouting match at the Hope Road house where the important ones got together for their weekly meetings. Seems a senior minister of Government was trying to tell one of his bragadocious [*sic*] colleagues that 'is not so this t'ing go' and that 'him running up him mouth too much and him can't bite the hand that feed him.' The Minister being scolded got mad and screamed at his colleague..." (*Flair Magazine*, G 28/8-16).
6. Unmarked plural noun phrases are attested in non-subject position or as subjects with past-tense verbs other than *to be*, i. e. in positions where the problem of subject-verb concord does not arise:
   "She [the local magistrate] questioned Casey's story [that] the constable had fired so many shot at him but had missed..." (G 25/8-24)
   "...accessories, beautiful carpets for motor vehicles, vinyls and material for making cover for trucks and pick-up." (G 31/8-11, advert)
   "These voucher showed that several person had benefitted." (R 4/9-2)

There are also the expected instances of hypercorrection:
"Care must be shown to those elderlies..." (R 4/9-3).

7. This example illustrates a further phenomenon worth closer study, namely a widespread disregard for international English sequence-of-tense rules in indirect speech.
8. In their attempts to come to terms with multilingual or multidialectal communities, linguists have come up with a variety of theoretical constructs, none of which seems to be entirely satisfactory for the description of the complex sociolinguistic reality of the Creole-speaking societies of the Caribbean. These are clearly not "bilingual" or even "diglossic" (in Ferguson's sense), because standard English and the Creole are not two distinct language systems co-existing side by side but (relatively) insulated against each other. DeCamp (1971) proposed the concept of the post-Creole continuum, to allow for gradient yet systematic transitions between the Creole and the standard. The "continuum" in its turn has been rejected as too rigid by LePage – Tabouret-Keller (1985), who in their description of Caribbean societies focus not so much on the Creole languages themselves as on the speakers' "acts of identity" conveyed through linguistic choices and alignments, and by Romaine (1988). This criticism notwithstanding, the continuum-model is probably still the received one in current linguistic literature (cf., e. g., Rickford 1986).
9. For example, speakers differ with regard to whether they cultivate British-like, American-like or local accents in their standard English. The stereotypes associated with these various accents in a Jamaican context come out most clearly in radio advertising, where accent may serve to "style" the image of the products promoted. Rate of delivery is an important trigger for phonetic, phonological and morphophonemic processes.

References

Cassidy, Frederic G. – Robert B. LePage
1980 *Dictionary of Jamaican English.* (2nd edition) Cambridge: Cambridge University Press.

Christie, Pauline
1989 "Questions of standards and intra-regional differences in Caribbean examinations", in: Ofelia Garcia – Ricardo Otheguy (eds.), 243–262.

DeCamp, David
1971 "Towards a generative analysis of a post-Creole speech continuum", in: Dell Hymes (ed.), 349–379.

Devonish, Hubert
1986 *Language and liberation: Creole language politics in the Caribbean.* London: Karia.

Garcia, Ofelia – Richardo Otheguy (eds.)
1989 *English across cultures, cultures across English: A reader in cross-cultural communication.* Berlin: Mouton – de Gruyter.

Görlach, Manfred – John Holm (eds.)
1986 *Varieties of English around the world 8: Focus on the Caribbean.* Amsterdam: Benjamins.

Greenbaum, Sidney
1988 "A proposal for an international computerized corpus of English", *World Englishes* 7: 315.

Hellinger, Marlis
1986 "On writing English-related Creoles in the Caribbean", in: Manfred Görlach – John Holm (eds.), 53–70.
Hymes, Dell (ed.)
1971 *Pidginisation and creolisation of languages.* Cambridge: Cambridge University Press.
LePage, Robert B.
1988 "Some premises concerning the standardisation of languages, with special reference to Caribbean Creole English", *International Journal of the Sociology of Language* 71: 25–36.
LePage, Robert B. – Andrée Tabouret-Keller
1985 *Acts of identity: Creole-based approaches to language and ethnicity.* Cambridge: Cambridge University Press.
Quirk, Randolph – Sidney Greenbaum – Geoffrey Leech – Jan Svartvik
1985 *A grammar of contemporary English.* London: Longman.
Rickford, John R.
1986 *Dimensions of a creole continuum.* Stanford: Stanford University Press.
Romaine, Suzanne
1988 *Pidgin and creole languages.* London: Longman.
Shields, Kathryn
1989 "Standard English in Jamaica: A case of competing models", *English World-Wide* 10: 41–53.

The Text Encoding Initiative: A progress report

Lou Burnard

The first public draft of the Text Encoding Initiative's *Guidelines for the Encoding and Interchange of Machine-Readable Texts* (TEI P1) is now available. Parts of the *Guidelines* were presented in preliminary form in June 1990 at the annual conferences of the ACH/ALLC in Siegen (Germany) and of the ACL in Pittsburgh (USA). The first full publication of the *Guidelines* took place in August of the same year, marking the end of the first phase of the TEI's work. At the time of writing, over 500 copies of the *Draft Guidelines* have already been distributed for comment to interested scholars, researchers, librarians and computing specialists around the world. This article begins by briefly describing the background to the TEI itself and summarizing the current content of its published *Guidelines*. Some aspects of particular relevance in corpus linguistics are then discussed in more detail, and an outline of the work plan for the remaining two years of the project is given.

1. The TEI

The Text Encoding Initiative (TEI) arose out of a planning conference convened by the Association for Computers and the Humanities (ACH) at Poughkeepsie, New York, in November 1987. It is a major international research project, sponsored jointly by the ACH, the Association for Computational Linguistics (ACL), and the Association for Literary and Linguistic Computing (ALLC), with the further participation of numerous other organizations and learned societies, and funded by the US National Endowment for the Humanities, DG XIII of the Commission of the European Community, the Canadian Social Science and Humanities Research Council and the Andrew W Mellon Foundation.

Its task is to develop and disseminate a clearly defined format for the interchange of machine-readable texts among researchers, so as to allow easier and more efficient sharing of resources for textual computing and natural language processing. In addition, the TEI has taken on the task of making recommendations about which textual features should be distinguished when encoding texts from scratch, to help ensure that the resulting text can be maximally useful to the research community. The current *Guidelines* thus have two closely related goals: a "how" defining a format for text interchange among researchers and a "what" recommending specific practices in the encoding of new texts.

The availability of an international standard for the description of encoding schemes (the Standard Generalized Markup Language – SGML; ISO 8879, 1986) and its increasing recognition within both the commercial and academic text processing communities encourages the belief that this effort at standardization may succeed where previous ones have failed. SGML provides a simple method of text encoding which consistently distinguishes markup from the content of the text being marked up. It allows texts of any kind to be marked up as an ordered hierarchy of typed objects and is designed to be independent of both hardware or software environments and of the application to which encoded texts are to be put.

During its first two year cycle, the work of the TEI was done within four working committees, with membership drawn from a broad cross section of the international scholarly community. One committee, with expertise in librarianship and archive management, concerned itself with problems of text documentation and produced detailed recommendations for the in-file encoding of cataloguing information about the electronic text itself, its source and the relationship between the two. A second committee, with technical expertise in formal language theory and in SGML itself, produced recommendations about how SGML should best be used and addressed the problems of conversion between the TEI and other encoding schemes.

As a first attempt to divide up the daunting task of producing recommendations for the immense variety of textual features which scholarship might need to encode, a distinction was made between textual features conventionally represented by typographic or other visible means on the one hand, and those which could be identified only by some analytic or interpretative act on the other. The former features were the responsibility of the Text Representation Committee, which produced a set of recommendations on ways of dealing with diverse character sets and laid ground rules for the encoding of textual features common to most types of continuous prose text, as well as exploring some specific types of (largely, but not exclusively, literary) texts.

For the latter, the initial focus was on linguistic analysis, since it was felt that this would provide the best basis for any more specialised analytic or interpretive efforts in the future. Members of this committee, most of whom had considerable expertise in computational and theoretical linguistics, developed a number of powerful theory-independent mechanisms for the encoding of analytic features in SGML, represented as tree structures or as parallel (but aligned) levels of analysis. A subgroup of this committee also worked on defining a standard for monolingual dictionaries.

The task of co-ordinating the work of the four committees, and combining their drafts into the initial publication is carried out by two editors, one European and one American. The project as a whole is managed by a steering committee, with two representatives from each of the three sponsoring organisations. An Advisory Board, with representatives from 15 major learned and professional societies, endorsed the initial work plan at its first meeting in February 1989, and will also (all being well) endorse the final document when it is available in June of 1992.

2. The *Guidelines* – draft 1

It should be stressed that the first draft of the *Guidelines*, despite its weighty appearance (nearly 300 pages of closely printed A4), is very much a discussion paper and far from being complete or definitive. At least one and probably two interim drafts will be produced over the next two years, as described further below. Some characteristics of the TEI approach are however already discernible which are unlikely to change. One is a focus on the encoding of the content of text, rather than its appearance, which is also a characteristic of SGML. Another is the rigorous application of Occam's razor: the TEI approach to the immense variety of text types in the real world is to attempt to define a comparatively small number of features which all texts share, and to allow for these to be used in combination with user-definable sets of more specialised features.

The current draft has eight main sections, which are briefly summarised below.

Chapter 1 outlines the purpose and scope of the TEI scheme. As outlined above, its main goals are both to facilitate data interchange and to provide guidance for those creating new texts. The desiderata of simplicity, clarity, formal rigour, sufficient power for research purposes, conformance to international standards, and independence of software, hardware or application alike are stressed.

Chapter 2, recognising that SGML is not yet widely understood within the TEI community, provides a gentle introduction to the basic concepts of SGML. It also contains some more technical information about the ways in which the TEI scheme uses the standard.

Chapter 3 addresses the problems of character encoding and translation in a world dominated by the rival claims of ASCII and EBCDIC. If the goal is to provide machine-independent support for all writing systems of all languages, these problems are far from trivial. The specific recommendations made are that only a subset of the ISO-646 character set (sometimes known as ASCII) can currently be relied on for data interchange, and that this should be extended either by using the entity reference mechanism provided by SGML or by using transliteration schemes. It proposes a powerful but economical way of documenting such transliteration schemes by a formal Writing System Declaration.

Chapter 4 contains recommendations for in-file documentation of electronic texts adequate to the bibliographic needs of researchers, data archivists and librarians. It recommends that a special header be added to each file to perform a function analogous to that of the title page of a non-electronic text, and proposes sets of tags for information about the file itself, the source from which it was derived and how it was encoded.

Chapter 5, the largest chapter, attempts to define general purpose structural and non-structural tags for continuous prose texts. It embodies a view of text as a hierarchic structure, divided into front, body and back matter, within which neutrally-named subdivisions may be tagged, down to a level corresponding with paragraphs, or other segments. It also allows for 'phrase level tags' to identify nonstructural units contained arbitrarily within the lowest level of structural tags, and proposes tagging schemes for such features as notes, names, abbreviations, numbers, foreign or emphasised phrases, cross references, and hypertextual links. Other sections discuss ways of encoding textual variation and critical apparatus and of recording the rendering of arbitrary textual fragments within this overall framework. There is also some discussion of different ways of maintaining multiple referencing schemes within the same text.

Finally, it contains some initial proposals for low-level structured items (termed "crystals") which can be contained by, or between, structural tags, such as lists, citations, formulae, figures and tables.

Chapter 6 outlines a number of theory-independent mechanisms for representing all kinds of linguistic analyses of running text. It is probably the most daunting chapter for the non-specialist reader, though much of its contents are of very wide relevance. It argues that most, if not all, linguistic analyses can be represented as bundles of named, value-bearing, "feature structures", which may be nested and grouped into sets or lists. It proposes ways of supporting multiple and independently aligned analyses, chiefly by means of the ID/IDREF pointer mechanism native to SGML. It also contains some tagsets for such commonly occurring formalisms as tree structures and parts of speech.

Chapter 7 considers in more detail particular aspects of some specific types of text. The text-types discussed in this draft are: language corpora and collections; verse, drama, and narrative; dictionaries; and office documents. In each case, an overview of the problems specific to these types of discourse is given, with some preliminary proposals for tags appropriate to them. This chapter is one that will be considerably revised and extended over the coming months, as its initial proposals are firmed up and as its scope is extended to other types of text.

Chapter 8 outlines a method by which the current *Guidelines* may be modified and extended, largely by introducing indirection into the Document Type Definitions (the formal SGML specifications for the TEI encoding scheme). Extension and modification of the TEI proposals is an important design goal, since this is both expected and intended, and the final form of the *Guidelines* will facilitate it.

Preliminary versions of a number of technical appendixes are provided in the current draft. These include annotated examples, illustrating the application of the TEI encoding scheme to a wide range of texts, formal SGML document type declarations (DTDs) for all the tags and groups of tags defined in the TEI scheme, and code pages for some commonly used character sets. Later drafts will extend and improve these initial versions considerably, and will also contain an alphabetical reference section with a summary of each tag, its attributes, its usage, and an example of its use, as well as full Writing System Declarations for a range of commonly used alphabets.

3. The encoding of linguistic corpora

To define a method of encoding large (or not so large) language corpora was a prime objective of the first cycle of the TEI. While the current proposals are far from complete, and will be refined considerably in the second cycle, particularly with respect to corpora of spoken language, and some specific text types such as newspapers and magazines, the general shape of the recommendations is already adequate for many purposes. This paper concludes with a discussion of some of the principal recommendations, with special reference to the problems of encoding linguistic corpora.

3.1. The TEI header

Every TEI-conformant text is composed of two parts: a header, containing the bibliographic and descriptive information proposed by chapter 3 of the *Guidelines*, and the text itself. A corpus is simply a large number of such texts, which, because it is regarded as a single unit, may itself have a header. All the information which is common across the whole corpus – the encoding principles, the category definitions, the editorial policy and so forth – can be defined once for all in the header to the corpus, with only individual variations from those general principles being defined in the headers to the individual texts. Every header has the same basic three-part structure. First comes a file description section, in which the electronic text itself is documented and described from a bibliographic perspective. Here are recorded such matters as a name by which the text should be cited, the people or institutions responsible for its creation and the nature of their responsibilities, the agency by which it is published or otherwise made available, and the source from which it was taken. The second major subdivision of the header is concerned with the way in which the text has been encoded. Such matters as normalisation and other aspects of editorial practice are defined here, as are statements of the selection principles underlying the corpus construction, the reference system used within it and any codebook or similar category definition list. The third part of the header is concerned with the history of a particular version of the text, and contains entries recording revisions and changes within it.

The header file thus contains most of the information one might need to identify a corpus as a bibliographic entity and also much of the information one would need to determine its usability for some analytic purpose. It thus serves a function analogous to that of the title page and front matter in a printed volume. It also serves as a repository for definitions which will be used by other headers which are subordinate to it. A list of category definitions may be included, or a set of declarations for the (possibly different) conventions used for such aspects as editorial policy, selection procedure etc. The headers of individual texts within the corpus can then specify which of these declarations apply by reference to the code specified in the corpus header.

3.2. Reference systems and segmentation

Existing language corpora have always placed great importance on the ability to provide referencing information within the body of the text. When traditional concordances are produced, it is essential to be able to locate individual word occurrences within the source text, by giving references to text, page or line numbers etc. The usual method of doing this has been to segment the text for reference purposes into arbitrary units, roughly corresponding with printed lines or, frequently, 80 column cards, associating a reference number with each one. For linguistic purposes, segmentation into other units, such as syntactic sentences, may be more important, but has often been regarded as subordinate. The need to maintain these two parallel (and essentially incompatible) segmentations of the text has led to many difficulties.

Because of its reliance on SGML, the TEI offers a wide range of segmentation facilities. In SGML, text is not regarded as a single sequence of bytes arbitrarily divided into 80-byte chunks, but as an ordered hierarchy of content objects. A corpus is divided into texts, texts into front, body and back matter. The body may be divided hierarchically into segments, each of which may be given a name and a hierarchic level. SGML allows a segment to be treated as a whole unit, irrespective of size: thus it becomes possible to process a whole chapter, paragraph, or sentence, as a single unit. A processor can determine for any such unit its name (e. g. "chapter"), its hierarchic position (e. g. within "part") and also its ordinal position (e. g. second chapter within the enclosing part). Finally, an identifier may be associated with any such unit to provide a unique key (its number or name). The TEI recommendations in fact provide for two such identifiers for any tagged element within a text: one, the ID attribute, which is constrained to be unique within the whole corpus, and the other, the N attribute, which need not be.

It is probably worth noting that the need for a reference scheme relating an electronic text to its non-electronic source is greatly reduced when (as is increasingly the case) the text is being manipulated and consulted exclusively by electronic means. An interactive browsing system in which individual word occurrences may be displayed within a variable amount of context does away with the need for many of the complex indexing required in printed concordances, from which access to the original source may be hard to track. In continuous prose texts, the need to retain original lineation seems increasingly dubious, quite apart from the tendentious nature of many of the decisions its use implies (treatment of end of line hyphenation being one notable case).

If, however, segmentation which cuts across the natural hierarchic segmentation of text is felt to be essential, the TEI recommendations propose two methods: one, technically preferable but expensive in processing and somewhat rebarbative in appearance, is to represent the alternative segmentation in the same way as the more natural one, using an optional feature of the SGML standard called CONCUR. The other, simpler but technically less elegant, is to use what the *Guidelines* call "milestone" tags to represent boundary points within one of the hierarchies. As a simple example, consider pages and paragraphs in a printed text: because paragraphs may both span pages and be contained within pages they cannot be fitted into the same hierarchic structure. The CONCUR solution would require the definition of two hierarchies, one for the pages, the other for the paragraphs. The "milestone" solution requires that only one hierarchy be defined. If this is based on paragraphs, the point at which page breaks occur may be tagged by using an empty tag called "page.break" simply to mark the boundary. An application program can then determine which page a particular paragraph belongs to by counting the page.breaks. Note however that the semantics of this solution depend on knowledge external to that provided by the encoding scheme itself – it is a matter of arbitrary decision whether the first page break in a text comes before the first paragraph or after the last part of the text on page 1! One possible compromise solution is simply to include only approximate pagination information, for example by recording the page number at which a paragraph begins as part of its identifier.

3.3. Free floatinng elements

Many textual elements which need to be distinguished for purposes of analysis are not bound to any particular position in a hierarchy. Such elements as block quotations, quoted phrases, direct speech, passages or phrases in foreign languages, headings or captions, abbreviations, proper names and the like may occur at almost any point in a text. The TEI recommendations provide for the tagging of all of these, and many others, in such a way that particular analyses may ignore or select them. It should be stressed that the intention is to suggest ways in which distinctions amongst these various elements should be encoded where this is desired, not to require that these distinctions should necessarily be made.

3.4. The question of rendition

A recurrent issue when existing printed or written texts are converted into machine readable form is the extent to which the electronic form should seek to mimic the appearance of the original from which it is derived. This assumes particular importance when very large quantities of text are to be encoded, or when existing bodies of electronic text are to be standardised, because it is generally simpler and cheaper to capture a subset of the presentational features of a text (its format, punctuation etc.) than it is to determine and encode the underlying textual features which those aspects convey to the reader. On this issue, as others, the *Guidelines* attempt to be eclectic, but, as the preceding discussion indicates, their overall tenor is to favour descriptive over presentational markup. Their guiding principle has been the observation that the more accurately an encoding reflects functional distinctions between individual textual components the more generally useful it is likely to be. Thus, the *Guidelines* facilitate the encoding of textual features such as quotation, direct speech, proper name etc. and place less emphasis on the encoding of such matters as changes of type face or size, use of particular punctuation marks etc. In this prioritisation, it is believed, they reflect the requirements of the majority of scholars. Nevertheless, recognising that descriptive markup of this kind may be inappropriate or economically infeasible in some cases, the *Guidelines* also provide suggestions for presentational markup. Where the appearance of some structurally identifiable component (such as a heading for example) is considered of importance, a RENDITION attribute may be attached to the appropriate tag. Where the exact function of some textual component which is presentationally distinct cannot be determined, a neutral tag such as HIGHLIGHTED may be used, again with a RENDITION attribute to specify more exactly its appearance.

In the same spirit, the *Guidelines* recommend a range of ways of encoding passages using quotation marks. Where direct speech is intended, and felt to be essential to distinguish, specific tags to handle both the speech itself and narrative intrusions within it are proposed. Specific tags are also proposed for quotations not necessarily signalled by quotation marks. And finally, where the function of quotation marks in a text cannot be determined, whether on pragmatic or theoretical grounds, it is also possible simply to record their presence with a neutral Q.MARK tag.

4. The future

Standards cannot be imposed. They must be achieved by consensus, which can only be achieved by the widest consultation, and the most tolerant eclecticism. There is an obvious risk that, in endeavouring to please all, the TEI may end by pleasing no-one. There is an equally obvious risk that its recommendations will be regarded as ideals, as a perfection to which mere mortals cannot afford to aspire. To counter those risks the only practical course is to ensure that the *Guidelines* are widely read and discussed, that criticism and reaction are taken heed of, and that their precepts are widely tested. By making the *Guidelines* available now, in an admittedly incomplete state, it is hoped to stimulate the widest possible discussion of their proposals. Incomplete as they are, it is believed that they contain a good basis for extension, and that the basic approach they advocate is a sound one. Three methods are proposed by which the academic community as a whole can participate in the task of putting this claim to the test.

Firstly, individual scholars are encouraged to read and report on the usability of the current draft of *Guidelines*, which is being distributed free of charge. Secondly, individual research projects, engaged in the creation of large textual resources, may become Affiliated Projects of the TEI and attempt to put its recommendations into practice. Affiliated Projects, once approved by the TEI's Steering Committee, will be given access to internal drafts of the Initiative and may have a major role in shaping the content of final *Guidelines*. Thirdly, specialist working groups will be set up to help in the task of drafting extensions to the *Guidelines*. The TEI has limited funds to help in the setting up of such specialist groups and is currently actively seeking volunteers with specialist knowledge to extend the coverage of the *Guidelines*.

Over the next two years, by drawing on the expertise of specialist working groups and the experience of the affiliated projects, the scope and depth of the current draft *Guidelines* should be extended considerably. Feedback from these and from individual respondents will be acted on to refine the current proposals. The publication of the draft *Guidelines* is thus only the first step in a process of consultation which will continue for many months to come.

References

International Organisation for Standardisation: Information Processing – Text and Office Systems
1986 *Standard Generalized Markup Language* (*SMGL*). (ISO 8879.) Geneva.

Sperberg-McQueen, C. M. – Lou Burnard (eds.)
1990 *Guidelines for the encoding and interchange of machine-readable texts*. (TEI P1.) Chicago–Oxford: ACH-ALLC-ACL Text Encoding Initiative.

Part II
Automated syntactic and semantic text analysis

Pinpointing problematic tagging decisions

Nancy Belmore

1. Introduction

Linguistics over the years has seen the ascent and subsequent decline of numerous theories or research paradigms. Throughout that time the major data have been native-speaker intuitions and introspection. While undoubtedly important, both in suggesting new approaches and in providing examples and counter-examples, any theory whose lowest-level hypotheses are not empirically testable on statistically adequate samples, and thus falsifiable, is not, properly speaking, a scientific theory at all.

Those who pioneered the development of corpora and those who have developed more and more sophisticated programs for their automatic analysis have made it feasible to test hypotheses against representative samples and to use analytic techniques which can be exactly replicated. Both rely on advances in computer technology which, as Clear (1987: 61) has noted, have liberated the study of language.

In this respect, linguistics is no different from any other science: fundamental advances have invariably required new tools for collecting data and new tools for analyzing them. Thus, "Corpus and computer change fundamentally the nature of research in linguistics. The need to solve a problem which is not of one's own choosing leads to the discarding of cherished orthodox views in favor of new ideas ... In this way it is possible to replace received opinion with hard knowledge." (Knowles – Lawrence 1987: 148).

2. Purpose

The research described here builds on the contributions of those linguists who recognized the role of computer and corpus in arriving at genuine theories 30 years ago. The immediate aim is an objective comparison of two different tagging systems, the tagging program (Greene – Rubin 1971) and manual tagging (Francis – Kutera 1979) used to tag the Brown corpus and the CLAWS1 programs (Garside 1987; Marshall 1987) which were used to tag the Lancaster-Oslo-Bergen corpus (hereafter LOB). What are the exact differences between the two tagging systems? In which linguistic contexts do they make a different tagging decision? The assumption is that pinpointing problematic tagging decisions will prove invaluable in arriving at a word classification system which will be adequate for natural language understanding systems (Belmore 1987 and 1988).

To achieve an objective comparison of the two tagging systems, new micro-computer versions of the Brown corpus are in preparation and new techniques for analyzing them have been developed (Belmore 1990 and 1991). These techniques should make it much simpler than before to test hypotheses against representative samples and thus to place less reliance on intuition and introspection.

3. The problem

The first step in achieving an objective comparison of the two systems, tagging the Brown corpus with CLAWS1, is described in Belmore 1991. In that paper I noted, "The most important task remaining is to set up a database in which to record the tagging decisions for each word in the corpus" (Belmore 1991: 81). This paper describes the procedures that have been developed to achieve this.

The first task in setting up the required database is to insure that only genuine differences between Brown as tagged at Brown University (hereafter BBR) and Brown as tagged by CLAWS1 (hereafter BCL1) will be recorded. The numerous pseudo-differences between the two tagging systems must therefore be eliminated.

One of the most important pseudo-differences is that BCL1 appears to have a greater number of words than BBR. For example, *can't* in BCL1 is split into two words, *can* and *n't*, and each half of the split entry has its own tag, "MD" (modal) and "XNOT" (not). In BBR *can't* is not split. Instead, it is assigned the merged tag "MD*" ("MD", modal and "*", not). Another discrepancy in the number of words arises because CLAWS1 retains and tags a number of marks of punctuation which were stripped from the Brown corpus before it was tagged.

There are also differences in the apparent number of sentences. In BBR, e. g., a semi-colon is a sentence closer while in BCL1 it is not. In BCL1 each number in a numbered list is treated as a separate sentence but in BBR the number is a part of the sentence it designates.

In addition, there are a number of tag equivalents or aliases in the two systems as well as different meta-symbols. As noted, the tag "*" in BBR is equivalent to the tag "XNOT" in BCL1. "/O" indicates an abbreviation in BCL1 while in BBR a period at the end of the word indicates an abbreviation; a dash in BCL1 is coded "*-"; in BBR it is coded "--".

Another pseudo-difference arises because BBR affixes comments directly to a tag while BCL1 puts such information in a separate field. Thus, if a word is part of a headline, BBR will indicate this by hyphenating the tag and adding the abbreviation "HL" (headline). On other occasions, however, the comment in a BBR hyphenated tag actually corresponds to a BCL1 tag. "FW" (foreign word), e. g., is an annotation in BBR but a tag in BCL1.

Table 1 illustrates some of these pseudo-differences.

The problem is to create a relational database in which the distinctions that do make a difference are the only ones which are recorded. In other words, the two tagged corpora must be brought into phase so that they have an equal number of words and an equal number of sentences and the entries must be normalized. The same abbreviation must be used to designate the same tag; meta-symbols must be the same and hyphenated comments in BBR must be stripped so that only the tag is left. Any differences that remain will then be genuine differences.

4. Procedures

Using the Fourth Dimension database management system and programming language (hereafter 4D) and, to a lesser extent, MindWrite, a word processor with sophisticated searching and editing capabilities (both are described in Belmore 1990 and 1991), I have developed automated procedures to edit and process the original BBR and BCL1 text files. The ultimate relational database will only record the normalized corpus and tagging decisions. It should be noted that BBR assigns only one tag and so does the final program in CLAWS1. However, the penultimate

Table 1. Some records from the original Brown corpus as tagged at Brown (BBR) and from that same corpus as tagged by CLAWS1 (BCL1)
Note that in BBR *can't* is treated as a single word and assigned the tag "MD*" ("MD", modal, and "*", not). BCL1 splits the word into *can* and *n't*. Examples 1 and 2 illustrate some of the aliases in the two systems: "XNOT" (not) is equivalent to "*". "\0" indicates an abbreviation in BCL1 (\0Feb) while in BBR a period indicates an abbreviation (*FEB.); a dash in BBR is represented by "--" while in BCL1 it is represented by "*-". Examples 2 and 3 show that in BBR comments are affixed to the tag, e. g., -HL, which means that the word is part of a headline, while in BCL1 they are either not included or are placed in a separate field as in Example 3. In BCL1, split entries like *can't* and lines of hyphens between sentences cause BBR and BCL1 to be out of phase. Such apparent differences must be eliminated before it is possible to compare the two tagging systems.

Example 1,BBR			
CAN'T	MD*	A03134009E1	
Example 1,BCL1			
A03 1340100 can	>		02 MD
A03 1340101 n't	<		02 XNOT
Example 2,BBR			
*WASHINGTON	NP-HL	A03075001E1	
,	, -HL	A03075002E1	
*FEB.	NP-HL	A03075003E1	
9	CD-HL	A03075004E1	
--	--	A03075005E1	
Example 2,BCL1			
A03 0750012 --			
A03 0750020 washington			54 NN
A03 0750021 ,			01 ,
A03 0750030 \0Feb	\0		02 NR
A03 0750040 9			10 CD
A03 0750042 *-			01 *-
Example 3,BBR			
OUTLAYS	NNS-HL	A03096009E1	
WOULD	MD-HL	A03096010E1	
INCREASE	VB-HL	A03096011E1	
Example 3,BCL1			
A03 0961012 --			
A03 0961020 outlays		H	56 NNS
A03 0961030 would		H	02 MD
A03 0961040 increase		H	02 VB

CLAWS1 program sometimes assigns more than one tag, each with an associated probability. For my purposes, this is the more interesting output, and it is therefore the one which is being imported into the database.

4.1. Processing BBR

Importing BBR into 4D is fairly simple since it just has three fields: the word, the tag and the identifier as shown in the examples in Table 1. Once imported it does need some "prettying up". At the time the Brown corpus was keyed in, the character set available had only upper-case letters. "True" upper-case letters were preceded by an asterisk. Upper-case letters must therefore be converted to lower-case except when preceded by an asterisk while letters preceded by an asterisk must be kept in upper-case and the asterisk removed.

The major complication is to get BBR in phase with BCL1. Table 2 is a sample from the BBR file showing how it looks after running a program to split words like *can't* and merged tags like MD*. Two new fields have been added to each record, New Record, which is assigned the value 1, if it is in fact a new record (otherwise it has the default value 0) and Word Number, which is the same as the BCL1 number for the corresponding word. In the future I will restore the punctuation which BBR stripped. This time I just deleted it from BCL1.

4.2. Processing BCL1

Editing and processing BCL1 is somewhat more complicated. From the original file imported into 4D two new files were created, a word file and a tag file. A comments file will be added later. So that they can be linked to all other files, the records in both files include the word number. The word file also includes the sentence number in which each word occurs.

CLAWS1 makes it easy to find sentence boundaries. As shown in Table 1, each sentence is preceded by a line of hyphens. The program which creates the word file uses these to identify each sentence and add a sentence number. The line of hyphens is then deleted. After their deletion, BBR and BCL1 are in phase. Table 3 shows an extract from the BCL1 word file; Table 4, an extract from the first BCL1 tag file. They

Table 2. An extract from BBR after it has been imported into the 4D database
A program has split entries like *can't* (see words 1001 and 1002) and assigned a separate tag to each. The BCL1 tag "XNOT" has replaced the BBR tag "*". The 1 in the new record field (word 1002) shows that this "word" has been added. All letters which were lower-case in the original documents from which the corpus was compiled have been restored to lower-case and word numbers have been added. The word number will be used to relate the information in this file to information in the other files in the database.

BBR Word	BBR Tag	BBR ID	New Record	Word #
going	VBG	A03134002E1	0	994
into	IN	A03134003E1	0	995
medicine	NN	A03134004E1	0	996
and	CC	A03134005E1	0	997
dentistry	NN	A03134006E1	0	998
because	CS	A03134007E1	0	999
they	PPSS	A03134008E1	0	1000
can	MD	A03134009E1	0	1001
n't	XNOT	A03134009E1	1	1002
afford	VB	A03134010E1	0	1003
the	AT	A03134011E1	0	1004
schooling	VBG	A03135001E1	0	1005
costs	NNS	A03135002E1	0	1006
.	.	A03135003E1	0	1007

Table 3. An extract from the BCL1 word file which corresponds to the extract from BBR which is shown in Table 2
Sentence numbers have been added to the records in this file.

BCL1 ID	BCL1 Word	Word #	Sentence #
A031340030	going	994	51
A031340040	into	995	51
A031340050	medicine	996	51
A031340060	and	997	51
A031340070	dentistry	998	51
A031340080	because	999	51
A031340090	they	1000	51
A031340100	can	1001	51
A031340101	n't	1002	51
A031340110	afford	1003	51
A031340120	the	1004	51
A031350020	schooling	1005	51
A031350030	costs	1006	51
A031350031	.	1007	51

Table 4. An extract from the BCL1 tag file, corresponding to the BBR and BCL1 word files shown in Tables 2 and 3
When CLAWS1 assigns more than one tag, it surrounds the first tag with brackets, adds a probability and sometimes a so-called rarity marker, either "@" (less than 10%) or "%" (less than 1%). A slash indicates the boundary between tags.

BCL1 ID	BCL1 Tags	Word #
A031340030	[NN@]/ 60 VBG/ 36 JJ%/ 4	994
A031340040	IN	995
A031340050	NN	996
A031340060	CC	997
A031340070	NN	998
A031340080	CS	999
A031340090	PP3AS	1000
A031340100	MD	1001
A031340101	XNOT	1002
A031340110	VB	1003
A031340120	ATI	1004
A031350020	[NN]/ 63 VBG/ 37	1005
A031350030	NNS	1006
A031350031	.	1007

Table 5. An extract from the BCL1 tag file generated from the tag file illustrated in Table 4
Each tag is now a separate record and the rarity marker, if any, is in a separate field.

Word #	Tag	Rank Order	Probability	Rarity
994	NN	1	60	@
994	VBG	2	36	
994	JJ	3	4	%
995	IN	1	100	
996	NN	1	100	
997	CC	1	100	
998	NN	1	100	
999	CS	1	100	
1000	PP3AS	1	100	
1001	MD	1	100	
1002	XNOT	1	100	
1003	VB	1	100	
1004	ATI	1	100	
1005	NN	1	63	
1005	VBG	2	37	
1006	NNS	1	100	
1007	.	1	100	

are the tags which CLAWS1 assigned to the words shown in Table 3, and correspond to the BBR words in Table 2.

As shown in Table 4, when CLAWS1 assigns more than one tag, the first choice is surrounded by brackets and each choice is followed by a "/" and a number indicating the probability that that tag is the correct tag. If a tag is rare (a probability of less than 10%), "@" is affixed to the tag; if even rarer (less than 1%), a "%" is affixed to the tag.

I therefore needed to write a program to create a new file in which each tag is a separate record, from which rarity markers, slashes and brackets have been deleted and which places the rarity marker, if any, in a separate field. Each word in the BCL1 word file can now be linked to the tag(s) which CLAWS1 assigned to that word. Table 5 shows an extract from the new tag file. The records displayed correspond to the records displayed in Tables 2 through 4.

4.3. Pinpointing differences between the two tagging systems

With BBR and BCL1 normalized and in phase, it is at last possible to relate the BBR file, the BCL1 word file and the new BCL1 tag file so that information from all three can be accessed from any one of them and displayed however one would like. Using 4D's powerful search capability, subsets can be selected which meet particular criteria. To pinpoint problematic tagging decisions, e. g., a subset of all words in which the BBR tag differs from the BCL1 tag, if there is only one, or the first choice, if there are several, can be selected. Subsets of this subset can then be generated, e. g., all words to which CLAWS1 assigned multiple tags but none of the tags corresponds to the BBR tag.

Table 6 shows one way of displaying information from the database. It reveals that in most cases the BBR tag and the BCL1 tag are the same. The differences, it seems to me, are the kind of differences which would occur if two different linguists were asked to tag such words independently.

5. Conclusion

So far I have worked with 2000 word samples and there is considerable further work before the database reaches an optimal form. As Table 6 shows, I have not yet stripped all of the comments affixed to BBR tags.

Table 6. A display from the 4D database, illustrating the first computer comparison of grammatical taggings of a corpus ever made
Note that BBR's tag for *as* is "CS" (subordinating conjunction) but BCL1 prefers "IN" (preposition) or "QL" (qualifier). Also *expected* shows differences: "VBN" (past participle) versus "JJ" (adjective). Such tagging problems may be identified and researched by using 4D's search capabilities. The relevant sentences can be called forth by the researcher as in this actual desktop view.

Word #	BBR Word	BBR Tag	BCL1 Tags	BCL1 Probability
1349	reaction	NN-HL	NN	100
1350	as	CS-HL	IN	41
			QL	39
			CS	20
1351	expected	VBN-HL	JJ	57
			VBN	43
			VBD	1
1352	congressional	JJ	JJ	100
1353	reaction	NN	NN	100
1354	to	IN	IN	100
1355	the	AT	ATI	100
1356	message	NN	NN	100
1357	was	BEDZ	BEDZ	100
1358	along	IN	RI	99
			IN	1
1359	expected	VBN	VBD	54
			VBN	41
			JJ	5
1360	lines	NNS	NNS	100

Nor have I regularized all aliases. There is still some redundancy and ultimately the original Brown and LOB IDs should be removed. As with the tagging of the untagged Brown corpus (Belmore 1990), my procedure has been to test each step on small samples. This has permitted determining the adequacy of each step and how well it can be integrated with the next step.

As the work progresses, the automated techniques which have been developed will be applied to successively larger samples until their adequacy seems assured and ultimately to the entire one-million-word corpus. The results will be two tagged Brown corpora, an edited version of the original corpus as tagged at Brown University, and a second version tagged by CLAWS1. The database will include the normalized version of the corpus described here and the associated tags and comments.

This will meet my own immediate goal, the use of completely objective procedures to arrive at a word classification system which will be adequate for natural language understanding systems. My hope, however, is that such procedures can make a contribution which goes beyond the immediate objective. By demonstrating that they can be used to determine the exact consequences of different theoretical approaches, the results could suggest new higher-level theories and new standards for evaluating any linguistic theory. This, it seems to me, has been an unstated aim all long of all of us who have chosen to work in corpus linguistics.

Acknowledgments

The research described here has been partially supported by the Social Sciences and Humanities Research Council of Canada, to whom grateful acknowledgment is made.

List of Software

4th Dimension
ACIUS
Suite 495, 20300 Stevens Creek Blvd.
Cupertino, California 95014
Canadian distributor of 4th Dimension:
Agoratech Canada, Inc.
6 Blainville Ouest
Ste.-Thérèse, Québec, Canada J7E 1W9

MindWrite
DeltaPoint (formerly Access Technology, Inc.)
Suite B1, 2 Harris Court
Monterey, California 93940-2483

References

Aarts, Jan — Willem Meijs (eds.)
1990 *Theory and practice in corpus linguistics.* Amsterdam: Rodopi.
Belmore, Nancy
1987 "A pilot study of the application of corpus linguistics to the specification of word classes for language understanding systems", in: Willem Meijs (ed.), 141—150.
1988 "The use of tagged corpora in defining informationally relevant word classes", in: Merja Kytö — Ossi Ihalainen — Matti Rissanen (eds.), 71—82.
1990 "Working with Brown and LOB on a microcomputer", in: Jan Aarts — Willem Meijs (eds.), 27—44.
1991 "Tagging BROWN with the LOB tagging suite", *ICAME Journal* 15: 63—86.
Clear, Jeremy
1987 "Computing", in: J. M. Sinclair (ed.), 41—61.

Francis, W. Nelson — Henry Kučera
1964 Manual of information to accompany a standard sample of present-day edited American English, for use with digital computers. [Unpublished manual, Department of Linguistics, Brown University.]
[1971] [Revised.]
[1979] [Revised and augmented.]
Garside, Roger
1987 "The CLAWS word-tagging system", in: Roger Garside — Geoffrey Leech — Geoffrey Sampson (eds.), 30—41.
Garside, Roger — Geoffrey Leech — Geoffrey Sampson (eds.)
1987 *The computational analysis of English: A corpus-based approach.* London: Longman.
Greene, Barbara B. — Gerald M. Rubin
1971 Automatic grammatical tagging of English. [Unpublished manual, Department of Linguistics, Brown University.]
Knowles, Gerry — Lita Lawrence
1987 "Automatic intonation assignment", in: Roger Garside — Geoffrey Leech — Geoffrey Sampson (eds.), 139—148.
Kytö, Merja — Ossi Ihalainen — Matti Rissanen (eds.)
1988 *Corpus linguistics, hard and soft.* Amsterdam: Rodopi.
Marshall, Ian
1987 "Tag selection using probabilistic methods", in: Roger Garside — Geoffrey Leech — Geoffrey Sampson (eds.), 42—56.
Meijs, Willem (ed.)
1987 *Corpus linguistics and beyond.* Amsterdam: Rodopi.
Sinclair, John M. (ed.)
1987 *Looking up: An account of the COBUILD project in lexical computing and the development of the Collins COBUILD English language dictionary.* London: Collins ELT.

Inferences and lexical relations

Willem Meijs

1. Introduction

This paper presents some ideas based on work that we have been engaged on in three projects: LINKS, LEXALIZA, and ACQUILEX: What linguistically relevant insights are emerging from the results, and how can we organize and systematize these results further, for instance with a view to possible utilization in the semantic interpretation and disambiguation of corpus-data and in NLP-contexts generally? My account here is not a systematic statement of specific, stated goals of these projects, but rather a personal assessment of some of the prospects arising from them.

Experimental evidence suggests that certain kinds of inferences are automatically created in human information-processing. I shall argue that a good monolingual dictionary is a reasonable guide to the knowledge that comes with people's general vocabulary and that such inferences can often be related to dictionary-like knowledge. The phenomenon known as semantic "priming" in studies of lexical access points in the same direction. If we assume that our mental lexicon is (among other things) semantically organized, inferencing can be explained in terms of automatic semantic "activation-spreading". This assumption is compatible with neurophysiological evidence as well as with functional grammar views that a great deal of what is normally called "world-knowledge" is verbally coded in much the same way in which such knowledge is represented in dictionary definitions. I shall illustrate this by reference to findings in the LINKS in the Lexicon project, arguing in effect that knowledge-activation crucially involves the "horizontal" and "vertical" links that we are charting out in that project.

To me, the notion of lexical relations essentially involves the question: how are words, or, more precisely, word senses related to each other? In practical terms this comes down to asking: given the kind of data that we are working on in the projects mentioned, how can we organize them in such a way that we can relate the word-senses in ways that are both in accordance with our theoretical insights and existing empirical evidence, and which are useful for possible further applications? Basically, I feel we are now in a position in which some of the ideas presented rather speculatively in Meijs (1988, 1989) can be made more precise, and perhaps to some extent be realized.

The outline for this paper is as follows: first I shall present some examples of inferences and show how these could be traced from chains of dictionary-definitions, as suggested in Meijs (1988, 1989). Moving on to some ideas about relational reasoning in functional logic put forward in Dik (1989 a), I shall show that in everyday language truth-conditional assumptions are sometimes bypassed. This leads to a consideration of the kind of "naive semantics" which Dahlgren (1988) and others take to be more appropriate than a strict truth-conditional theory to explain actual language-use. The semantic relations and taxonomies that people normally go by, they claim, are likewise not as neat and orderd as most theories assume: they are more reminiscent of the "tangled hierarchies" which Amsler (1980) laid bare in the taxonomies that emerge from his analysis of the Merriam-Webster dictionary, and those we have found in LDOCE (Procter 1978).

To make use of the networks of semantic relations that are hidden in the interconnections between word-senses in dictionaries, disambiguation of the words used in the definitions in essential, i. e. it must be unambiguously clear in which sense any word is being used in a dictionary definition. Given the enormous amounts of data that we are dealing with here, such disambiguation is a formidable job. However, as Vossen (1991) points out, a number of heuristic strategies may be employed to do this semi-automatically. Once this has been done, the kind of "collative semantic analysis" developed by Fass (1989) for a limited "toy" lexicon may be extended to one of a more realistic size by the incorporation of systematized dictionary-data. There are parallels here with the sketch of a computational lexicon outlined in Dik (1989 b), but a note of warning about the complexity of the task seems in order.

2. Inferencing

Dik (1986 a) argues that knowledge representation structures take the form of underlying predications as developed in Functional Grammar (henceforth FG). The lexical knowledge that goes into such underlying predications is derived from the meaning definitions contained in the lexicon. Following Dik (1978) it is assumed that these meaning-definitions in turn are organized in an economical, stepwise fashion, rather along the lines of what Dik calls 'standard dictionary practice'. Dik (1986a, 1986b, 1987a, 1987b) present various detailed examples of how an integrated FG model of linguistic interpretation along such lines can deal with various puzzles of interpretation, including inferences.

Inferences often involve reference to items that are not actually present in a text but that are "understood", "implied" in some sense. Thus when we hear or read the sentence

(1) *Catherine kissed George.*

then we may infer that Catherine touched George, more specifically that she touched George with her lips. (Whether we actually always make such inferences is another matter – see below, section 3). Hence sentences like

(2)a. *Catherine kissed George, but she didn't touch him.*

or:

(2)b. *Catherine kissed George, but not with her lips.*

are contradictory under normal truth-conditional assumptions. Similarly if the message is that

(3) *Catherine punched George on the nose.*[1]

we know (or can infer) that, while only one body-part is explicitly mentioned in the text (*viz.* George's nose), another body-part (i. e. Catherine's fist) was also involved in the action.

The availability of a computerized dictionary provides an interesting opportunity to trace such inferences. The dictionary concerned (LDOCE) was of course not set up along FG lines, but it is certainly a very rich source of information, including a great deal of the kind required in the FG model. Our aim in the LINKS project was to make all of the information optimally accessible, and to the extent in which this could be done in a way which is compatible with FG, we felt, so much the better. Voogt–van Zutphen (1987, 1989) show that many syntactic aspects of predicate-frames can indeed be derived in a straightforward way from the dictionary, while Vossen (1989) shows that it may be possible to organize much of the essential semantic information in the form of a systematic data-base. Using the special files and search programs developed in the two projects I have tried to establish how much of the information necessary for the inferences going with *kiss* in our grammatically coded "Definition Corpus" could indeed be found in the dictionary. The computer-tape entry for *kiss* reads as follows:

> 7899 – ....-....h....c 181977 **kiss** v ul UL to I0T0 touch N0V0 with I0 the D0 lips NS as R0C0 a D0 sign N0V0 of I0 love N0V0 or C0 as R0C0 a D0 greeting VG

Notice that the "h" here indicates that the subject of *kiss* must be "human" (an Agent, presumably), and that the object must be "c", i. e. "concrete (non-abstract) – animate or inanimate". Following the "vertical links" via the definition-kernel *(touch)* we can "decompose" the action in a stepwise fashion:

> 15480 – ....-....h....5 344835 **touch** v ul UL to I0T0 feel V0 with I0 a D0 part N0 of I0 the D0 body N0 , LT esp M0 . LT the D0 hands VJNS or C0 fingers NS

The "h" (for human subject) here ties in with that in the information for *kiss* itself. Following the "Instrument-trail", fairly unambiguously marked by the *with*-phrase, we arrive at the entry for *lip*:

> 20507 – mdza-....5..... 191129 **lip** n ul UL one D0P0 of I0 the D0 edges NS of I0 the D0 mouth N0 where R0C0 the D0 skin N0 is BJ delicate A0 and C0 rather R0Z0 red A

Via the entry for *mouth* we arrive at *(part of) the body* and this again reinforces the reference to the Instrument-phrase 'with a part of the body' in the definition of *touch.*

Dik (1986 a) contains a detailed analysis of how an integrated FG model of linguistic interpretation might account for A's reply in the following text-fragment being accepted as a coherent reaction to S's remarks:

(4) S: *John's wife is pregnant. The baby is due in August. If it is a boy, Mary would like to call him after me.*
A: *Well, "Peter Parker" doesn't sound too bad.*

Dik gives the following predicate-frames and meaning definitions for *pregnant, due*, and *baby*:

(5) $pregnant_{A}$ $(x_1: \langle\text{female}\rangle(x_1)) =_{\text{def}}$
Prosp $\text{have}_{v}(x_1)$ $(\text{i}x_i: \text{child}_{N}(x_i))$

(6) $due_{A}(x_1)(x_2)_{\text{Temp}} =_{\text{def}}$
$\text{expect}_{v}(\text{G}x_i)(x_3: |\text{arrive}_{v}(x_1)(x_2)_{\text{Temp}}|(x_3))$

(7) $baby_{N}(x_1: \langle\text{child}\rangle\ (x_1)) =_{\text{def}}$ recently $\text{born}_{A}(x_1))$

Looking now whether, and to what extent, the lexical knowledge as found in LDOCE going with some of the words in this passage might help to explain part of the inference-pattern, it turns out that the "jump" from *pregnant* to *baby* is not quite so straight forward in LDOCE as in the above FG definitions. LDOCE does not define *pregnant* in terms of 'a woman going to have a child', as in the FG definition (in which *Prosp* stands for *Prospective*, which is described as an "aspectual operator"), but in terms of 'a woman having an unborn child in the body'. However, it might still be possible to establish the link with *baby*, via the word *child* which occurs in its definition (as in that of *pregnant*):

> 1835 – ....-....h..... 018091 **baby** n ul UL a D0 very R0 young A0 **child** N0, LT esp M0 . LT one D0P0 who P0 has HJ not R0 learnt VD to I0T0 speak V

From there on it is probably plain sailing, given the fact that one of the meanings of *due* is given as 'expected', and seeing that one of the definitions of *expect* is:

> 5184 – ....-..i.....y. 117553 **expect** v ul UL be expecting a **baby** EXPR also R0 infml & euph META be expecting EXPR (LT of I0 a D0 **woman** N0) LT to I0T0 be B0 **pregnant** A01XX (LT carrying VG a D0 **child** N0 in I0 her D0 body N0) L

I have emphasized various words in these definitions (bold print) to show that together they exhibit a rich pattern of interconnections. There are also links with other words which figure prominently in Dik's account, such as:

> 6947 – ....-....h....h 155182 **have** v ul UL to I0T0 **give** V0 **birth** N0 to I0T
> 451 – mdzg-....h..... 013680 **arrive** v ul UL (LT of I0 a D0 **baby** N0) LT to I0T0 be B0 **born** A0

3. Inferencing and priming: psycholinguistic evidence

It seems clear that inferences such as those discussed in the preceding section follow lexical patterns related to those underlying the so-called "priming" phenomenon amply documented in psycholinguistc experimental research. Basically, what the experimental evidence shows is that during text-processing incoming data are constantly being checked for consistency against the data contained in long-term memory and against the results of what has been processed before, and that this takes place at all levels and in an interactive fashion, down from elementary signal level via the morphological, syntactic and semantic level through to higher pragmatic organizational levels. This means that at any time during text-comprehension there is a process of anticipatory activation going on which is immediate and automatic, often wide-ranging and yet directed, the direction being determined by the preceding context in the widest sense, and on many different levels. The anticipatory character of this spreading activation process involves strategies favouring a default interpretation of incoming data as being compatible with what is known already. On the syntactic level, for instance, this means that there will be facilitation (i. e. the processing will be faster) for part-of-speech assignment for the next incoming item if it fits in with the syntactic analysis (or analyses) developed up till then. On the semantic level there will be facilitation for words related in some sense to items that have been processed before; pragmatically there will be facilitation for items typically associated with the overall kind of situation which the discourse concerned seems to be about etc. Perhaps, therefore, the ongoing process can best be described in terms of a continual word-by-word alternation between "short-listing" and "final selection" (cf. Hudson 1979).

The experimental findings in the semantic sphere underline the immediate and automatic character of semantic activation-spreading (cf. e. g. Marslen-Wilson – Welsh 1978; Marslen-Wilson – Tyler – Seidenberg 1978), as well as its directedness, thus supporting the short-listing / final-selection scheme, with preceding context as the operative principle. To give just two examples: Foss – Ross (1983) demonstrate that word-recognition is facilitated if the meaning of the word can be integrated easily in the semantic representation of the preceding sentence-context. Schwanenflugel – Shoben (1985) provide evidence that high sentence constraint leads to a very narrow scope of facilitation so that only highly expected completions are facilitated. Unexpected words appearing in such sentences do not experience facilitation and may even demonstrate inhibition when readers' expectations for particular words are high. In contrast, low constraint sentences yield a very broad scope of facilitation so that even unexpected words are facilitated, this amount of facilitation being generally low, however.

While semantic activation-spreading is direct in the sense of immediate in time, in another sense it is often indirect. Thus Potter – Faulconer (1979) suggest that contextualization of word-meaning is primarily controlled by the conceptually most relevant elements, not necessarily by the immediately preceding words. Tabossi (1982) argues that it is primarily the main verb which controls contextualized meaning-activation during sentence-processing. In fact the "control" may come from words that are not visibly present, but implied by the context. Tabossi (1985) points to the fact that different meaning-aspects of a word like *piano*, for instance being heavy and producing musical sounds, may be differentially activated depending on the sentence in which it occurs (e. g. *The man lifted the piano* versus *The man tuned the piano*). Similarly Sharkey – Mitchell (1985) provide evidence that prior presentation of a script context (rather than simply related words, like *nurse* to prime *doctor* or vice versa) significantly facilitates recognition of words fitting into such a context.

Some authors (e. g. Garrod – Sanford 1985, Sanford 1987) stress the fact that inferencing, too, is automatic and immediate. However, not all inferences that could possibly be made are in fact made. Thus van Dijk – Kintsch (1983) make a distinction between "bridging" and "elaborative" inferences. Bridging inferences are ones that must be made during text comprehension; i. e. they are required for the coherence of the text. Verification for such implicit inferences typically does not require more time than verification on the basis of explicit statements in the text. Elaborative inferences, on the other hand, are not necessary prerequisites for text-comprehension; they "occur when the reader uses his or her knowledge about the topic under discussion to fill in additional detail not mentioned in the text or establish connections between what is being read and related items of knowledge."

A distinction which plays an important role here is that between expert and nonexpert knowledge. Thus Spilich *et al.* (1979) show that expert and nonexpert knowledge levels influence information processing. On the whole the experimental findings (Noordman – Vonk – Kempff 1984; Kempff forthcoming) suggest that people do make inferences when the discourse concerns everyday nonexpert subjects. Vonk – Noordman – Kempff (1984) and Vonk – Noordman (forthcoming) conclude that in a normal reading situation, no inferences are made which would constitute expansion of the reader's knowledge, but only inferences which constitute activation of already existing knowledge. Readers without expert knowledge about a particular domain, do not make inferences going beyond their nonexpert knowledge.

As far as everyday reasoning and logic are concerned it is important to realize that people often make inferences that are obviously prompted by the given discourse but which are not necessarily correct from a strictly logical point of view. Sanford (1987) puts a great deal of emphasis on this point. The experimental evidence he refers to clearly shows that often people just do not consider other possibilities than the one most clearly suggested in a given discourse. He quotes the following example:

(8) *The Southern General Hospital is extremely large and well-equipped. It takes all the head injuries in the West of Scotland. Late last night, a small boy was admitted following a car accident in which his father was killed....*

Sanford comments (1987: 85): "*Of course* it doesn't follow that the boy had a head injury, at least not logically. Yet, unless assumptions of this sort are made, text comprehension would soon grind to a halt. It is clearly necessary to distinguish between pragmatic inferences made while reading discourse and logical, deductively valid inferences made in more analytic reasoning." Rather than formal logical rules, people usually apply everyday sensible rules – which may produce performance that looks like logic – in situations that they experimence as pragmatically and socially relevant. With Johnson-Laird (1983), Sanford therefore argues that we should beware of "the doctrine of mental logic".

Everyday language thus doesn't always adhere too strictly to truth-conditional logicalities. For instance, one can say *the two cars were chasing each other at full speed*, without meaning to imply that car A chased B *and* that car B chased car A. Similarly, one can say *the explosions followed each other in quick succession*, without meaning to suggest that each explosion followed every other explosion. As Sanfort points out, everyday logic ("commonsense reasoning") sometimes simply falls short of the standards of logic in the truth-conditional sense.

4. Lexical relations

We may regard a good monolingual dictionary as a linear, alphabetically ordered representation of the passive and active vocabulary of normal, educated speakers of the language. There is of course ample evidence (including the kind of empirical psycholinguistic evidence discussed in the previous section) to suggest that a language user's mental lexicon is not, or not primarily, organized in this way, as a long list of isolated elements. Rather, the mental lexicon forms a coherent, tightly-knit whole, whose elements are somehow intricately related to one another along a number of different dimensions: phonological, morphological, orthographical etc. One of the most basic organizing dimensions, however, is no doubt the semantic-conceptual one, as witness word-association and semantic priming tests: words activate, "call up", other words that are related to them in meaning. A dictionary in machine-readable form in principle allows one to waive the alphabetical ordering of the printed book, and study its inherent semantic-conceptual organization. And this is exactly what we have tried to do in our work on LDOCE.

The meaning-representations of the words in a dictionary can be regarded as a kind of lexical knowledge-bank which constitutes a specific linguistic representation of (a large part) of our knowledge of the world. The Functional Grammar view (as expressed, for instance, in Dik 1989 a) is that all of our knowledge is either perceptual or conceptual, and to the extent in which it is conceptual it is at the same time linguistic. Such a view is compatible with the well-documented phenomenon that different cultures cut up reality in different ways, and that such differences are reflected in the meanings of the words in the respective languages. One effect of this is the well-known fact that it is sometimes impossible or very difficult to translate some concepts from one language (culture) to another – "'defining meaning' is a language-internal affair", as Dik (1989: 86) puts it. For this reason, among others, FG – which constitutes an important point of orientation in our research – rejects abstract semantic features to represent word-meanings. Instead, in the FG approach conceptual knowledge is claimed to be stored in the form of basic predicates. One consequence of this is that the same piece of knowledge may in fact be stored in different ways – i. e. in different predicates.

Dictionaries show similar differences: different dictionaries seldom describe the conceptual content of one and the same entry in precisely the same combination of words. Nonetheless, as regards the overall underlying interdependence of the concepts defined there tends to be a wide-ranging congruence. In view of the shared cultural and linguistic anchoring it is highly unlikely that one dictionary will classify a particular word (or rather the concept it labels) under the category "birds", while another dictionary marks it as belonging to the category "fish" (for instance). The shared anchoring leads to classifications and taxonomies which show a great deal of overlap and congruence, even though the predicates actually employed in the wordings of the definitions may vary considerably.

Since we are now able to look at (machine-readable) dictionaries from this semantic-organizational angle, some obvious questions suggest themselves: which words "belong together"; how can we characterize the groupings that emerge; what is the nature of the links that connect them? The answers resulting from investigations of these questions are coined in terms of the various ways in which man's attempts to classify the world around and within him can be described: thesauruses, taxonomies, semantic fields, hierarchies, networks, graphs etc. Not many dictionaries indicate semantic relations of this kind explicitly and systematically. The machine-readable LDOCE is an exception in this respect. Its "subject-field codes" (not present in the printed version) indicate the semantic field to which the senses of a lexical item belongs: zoology, botany, sports, religion, architecture etc. Although there is a sub-field layer for most main fields, the codes taken together do not form a clear hierarchical structure, and they have been rather unevenly and not very consistently applied. Still, as Janssen (1990) shows, they provide very valuable information which, especially in certain specific domains – law, sports, food, for instance – can be used to guide automatic semantic disambiguation procedures.

Where explicit semantic-field markers are absent, taxonomic structure has to be derived from information that is implicit in other parts of the dictionary-entries, especially the definitions. Amsler (1980, 1981) constitute pioneering enterprises to lay bare, in a semi-automatic fashion, the taxonomic hierarchies implicit in the Merriam-Webster *New Pocket Dictionary*. One of Amsler's important findings is that the taxonomies that emerge from his investigation are not so neat and strictly hierarchical; hence he calls them "tangled hierarchies". Consider the cluster of "group" concept nodes (from Amsler 1980) represented in Figure 1.

In the "LINKS" project (Meijs 1986, 1988, 1989; Vossen – den Broeder – Meijs 1988, Vossen – Meijs – den Broeder 1989), similarly tangled relationships were found to obtain in the top-nodes of the noun-taxonomies emerging from a study of the definitions in LDOCE. Consider Figure 2 (from Vossen 1991: 120). Vossen points out that there are some striking inconsistencies in these LDOCE-derived networks:

a. There are some "islands" in the network of concepts that are circularly defined and that are not related to the main network, e. g. "creature" and "animal"; "vessel", "boat" and "ship".
b. Some concepts which one might expect to be closely related are not. According to LDOCE "person" is more closely related to "plant" than to "animal". Something similar holds for "aeroplane" and "plane" on the one hand, and "rocket", "aircraft" and "jet" on the other.

c. Because more or less the same concept is sometimes paraphrased in different ways (e. g. "material", "matter" and "substance", or "aeroplane", "plane" and "aircraft"), some apparent relations between words in the network may in reality be redundant.

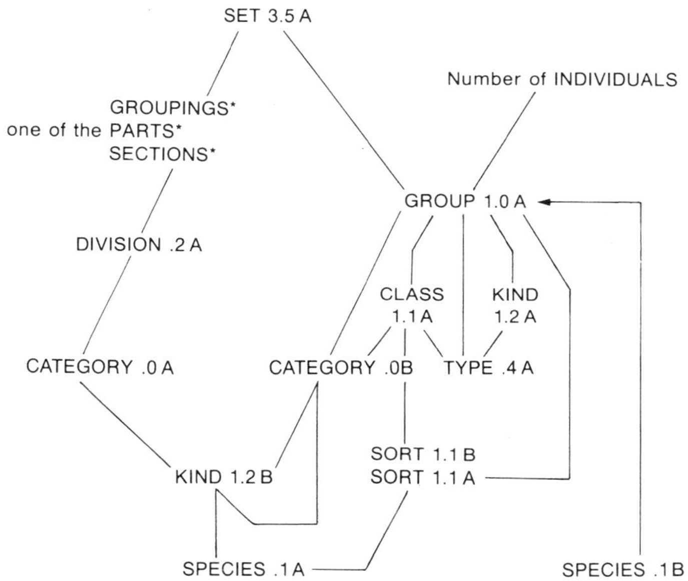

Figure 1. Tangled hierarchy of 'group' concepts (from Amsler 1980)

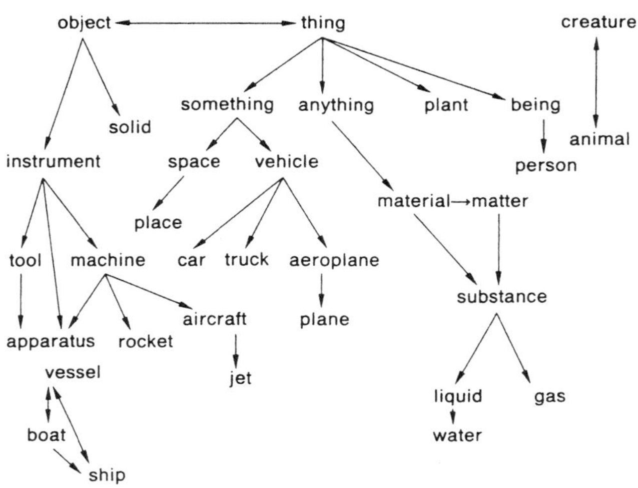

Figure 2. Top-level hyponomies in LDOCE (from Vossen 1991: 120)

Vossen suggests that the problem may be not all that serious, because most of the inconsistencies occur towards the top of the hierarchies, which means that they can be amended manually in a relatively simple way.

Taxonomic and hierarchical relationships are very important for the development of reliable logico-semantic interpretation procedures in NLP. A key notion here is that of "hyponymy". Clarity about hyponymy relations is important for handling things like entailment, inferences etc. Dik (1989 b) develops a truth-conditional approach to what he calls relational reasoning in Functional Logic in which hyponymy plays a central role. Dik distinguishes three kinds of hyponymy:

d. lexical hyponymy	(rose) (flower)
e. hyponymy through predicate formation	(tea rose) (rose)
f. hyponymy through term formation	(red rose) (rose)

As far as dictionaries are concerned, (d) is of course central. Still, (e) and (f) are also relevant: compounding occurs both in dictionary entries and in definitions. Dik points out that relative adjectives (*big, small, long* etc.) need special attention. Thus *I saw a big flea* entails *I saw a flea*, but not *I saw something big*: relative adjectives require reference to some norm, which must somehow be coded in the lexicon. (Presumably the LDOCE definition, which refers to 'more than *average* size' for *big* is not very helpful here).

Another important aspect is the nature of the relationship: (in)transitive, (a)symmetrical etc. Thus verbs like *precede, follow* etc., which must be marked for "order" in the lexicon, denote a transitive relations: if A precedes B and B precedes C, then it follows that A precedes C. Words in this class may have a converse relation with each other, with logical consequences: if A precedes B, then B follows A. As pointed out above, however, in connection with the example of the cars chasing each other, everyday language doesn't always adhere too strictly to such truth-conditional logicalities. This aspect of normal language use is given special prominence in the so-called "naive semantics" approach to knowledge representation (Dahlgren 1988; Dahlgren – McDowell 1989). The concepts and categories that people use are often vague, gradient and intermingled; they are not like scientific concepts, and hence often not truth-conditional in the usual sense. That communication between speakers of the same language is by and large successful is due to the fact that they are "anchored in the real world", in which there are some real, stable classes of objects, states, events etc.

Apart from the usual things, word-meanings in this approach are also associated with a large number of characteristics along various dimensions, such as typical behaviour, social status and function, characteristic tools, instruments and other paraphernalia (books, briefcases, gowns, and wigs for lawyers, judges etc.), as well as common assumptions about character traits, such as ambition, articulateness, cleverness, educational background etc.

Knowledge-representation in the naive semantics framework thus does not aim to reduce everything to abstract primitives, but tries to represent the intertwined conceptualizations and categorizations people associate with word meanings. The cognitive model developed along these lines is based on empirical observation of constraints governing selection restrictions in the use of a large number of verbs, psychological studies of classification, and philosophical studies of epistemology. The result, which is claimed to reflect "the naive ontology embodied in English", is a so-called directed acyclic graph rather than a binary tree, which means that its nodes can have more than two subordinate nodes, and that it allows cross-classification. Apart from more traditional distinctions, this ontology gives prominence to notions such as SENTIENT, NATURAL, SOCIAL, SELF-MOVING, GOAL, ACHIEVEMENT etc. The naive semantic relations and taxonomies proposed by Dahlgren are thus not as neat and ordered as most theories assume: they are more like the "tangled hierarchies" from Amsler (1980) and Vossen (1991).

Essentially, the approach developed by Fass (1989), as embodied in his Meta5 grammar, is an attempt to utilize the full range of semantic relations connecting the sense descriptions in the lexicon, by means of "collation" (combination) procedures which can trace these connections via the genus and differentiae information stored in the lexical entries. The sense frames are in the form of Prolog list structures associated with word senses, pairing arcs and nodes: the arcs contain the genus information, and the nodes the differentiae, and both of these themselves again comprise (combinations of) word senses, with their own associated sense frames, so that by tracing these links in the collating process, one can traverse the semantic network of senses. The nodes further contain information to guide the semantic disambiguation process, such as functional and structural information for nouns, preferences and assertions for adjectives and adverbs, and case-frames for verbs. Figure 3 contains examples of sense frames for an adjective (a), a noun (b) and a verb (c) from Fass (1989).[2]

```
sf(male1,
  [[arcs,
    [[superproperty, sex1],
     [property, male1]]],
   [node 1,
    [[preference, organism1],
     [assertion,
      [[sex1, male1]]]]]]]).
```

a.

```
sf(crook1,
  [[arcs,
    [[supertype, criminal1]]],
   [node0,
    [[it1, steal1, valuables1]]]]).
```

b.

```
sf(eat1,
  [[arcs,
    [supertype,[ingest1, expend1]]]],
   [node2,
    [[agent,
      [preference, animal1]],
     [object,
      [preference, drink1]]]]]).
```

c.

Figure 3. (From Fass 1989)

Via the collating procedures, the Meta5 grammar attempts to find the best sense-matches for the words that are being combined syntactically. The Meta5 framework is especially interesting in that, in addition to "normal readings", the grammar also allows various metonymic readings, such as Producer for Product *(He bought a Ford)*, Controller for Controlled *(Nixon bombed Hanoi)*, and Object for User *(The buses are on strike)* – for details see the article, which describes in some detail how the system decides on the most likely reading of the sentence *Mary drank the glasses*. Metonymy is something that is also represented to some extent in the LDOCE material, albeit indirectly, by (sometimes fairly systematic) sequences of literal and extended senses within entries. Wilks *et al.* (1989) point out that for a full-scale lexicon of this kind, the LDOCE-material would have to be analysed in a way that would yield clear genus and differentiae information, something which, they assert, is as yet "beyond the abilities of the best current extraction techniques".[3]

The redundancy-rules in Dik's (1989 c) model of a computational FG lexicon are somewhat similar in effect to Fass' collating rules. Thus their application to *sailor* and *kick* results in frames like the following, which can be regarded as statements of selection restrictions for the words concerned:

(9) predn([sailor, [hum,masc,anim,concr,vert]]).
(10) predv([kick,[act,dyn,contr], [[[anim],t,[ag]],[[concr],t,[go]]]]).

Thus Dik claims that restrictions such as these will allow (11 a) and (11 b), while excluding (12 a) and (12 b):

(11) a. *The sailor kicked the boy.*
b. *The sailor kicked the book.*
(12) a. **The sailor kicked the city.* (*city* not concrete)
b. **The book kicked the boy.* (*book* not animate)

It is doubtful, actually, whether LDOCE-derived information would be helpful to reject (12 a) for example, since the first sense of *city* is in fact concrete ('a usu. large and important group of houses, buildings, etc. ...'), while the second is animate and collective ('all the people who live in such a place'). An even more important complicating factor however (but one which any serious attempt to use realistic lexical data would have to face) is the fact that every word may have a number of senses. Thus there are 6 senses for *boy*, 7 senses for *kick*, and 2 senses for *city* in LDOCE, bringing the number of theoretically possible readings for *the boy kicked the city* (or *the city kicked the boy*) to $6 \times 7 \times 2 = 84$!

Clearly, then, to make use of the networks of semantic relations that are hidden in the interconnections between word-senses in dictionaries, disambiguation of the words used in the definitions is essential, i. e. it must be unambiguously clear in which sense any word is being used in a dictionary definition. For LDOCE various researchers are working on this kind of disambiguation (cf. Wilks *et al.* 1989; Vossen 1991). Given the daunting amounts of data to be dealt with, such disambiguation is a formidable job.[4] However, as Vossen (1991) points out, a number of heuristic strategies may be employed to do this semi-automatically. Once this definition disambiguation process has been completed, it might be possible, for example, to extend Fass's kind of "collative semantic analysis" – which so far works only for a limited "toy" lexicon containing 460 word senses – to one of a more realistic size by the incorporation of systematized dictionary-data.

In the "LINKS" project this disambiguation has now been completed manually for the most central and most frequently used words, and the results have been incorporated in "DEVIL", a prototype "chain-scanning" system which can relate definitions upwards and downwards in the semantic network (cf. Vossen – Serail 1990), while taking account of the further complications caused by various recurrent special structures: "PART OF" relations, cross-category references (N > V, A > N etc.)

via nominalizations etc. – cf. Vossen 1989, forthc.; Vossen – Meijs – den Broeder 1989. In the DEVIL system, which can be consulted on-line or in batch-mode, we can now for the first time get a detailed overview of the taxonomic relationships embodied in the definitions in LDOCE (and in other dictionaries, such as the Van Dale Dutch-Dutch and Dutch-English dictionaries that are going to be "DEVILized" in the ACQUILEX context).

By way of illustration Figure 4 (from Vossen forthc.) shows how a large portion of the abstract nouns in LDOCE "hangs together" taxonomically, via their definitions. This tree diagram shows part of the top of the abstract noun taxonomy in terms of the number of times a particular word functions as the (syntactic) kernel of the definition of an abstract noun entry, plus some examples of branches further down. Notice that towards the top most of these are typically what we call "shunters", i. e. they are themselves general, semantically relatively empty words, which function as pointers to the verbs and adjectives in the post-modifying phrase (usually a nominalized predicate of some kind: "the condition of being ambiguous", "an act of gasping", "something which annoys", etc.).

In the version of the DEVIL system now being developed we are charting out all these trails, allowing shifts back and forth between nominal, verbal and adjectival taxonomies as required, and catering for a wide range of query-types relevant to inferential logic and knowledge-handling generally, such as:

- Which category of items (activities, events, states etc.) is X an instance of?
- Which items (events, states) exhaustively or typically constitute exemplifications of category X?
- What kind of item (etc.) is X a part of?
- What are typically parts of which X is composed?
- What are the activities (functions, states etc.) typically associated with items of category X, specified for case role (Agent, Instrument etc.)?
- What are the categories of items typically associated with activities (etc.) of category X, specified for case role?

We will not rest until we can let DEVIL infer for us what it was that Catherine used to kiss George with.

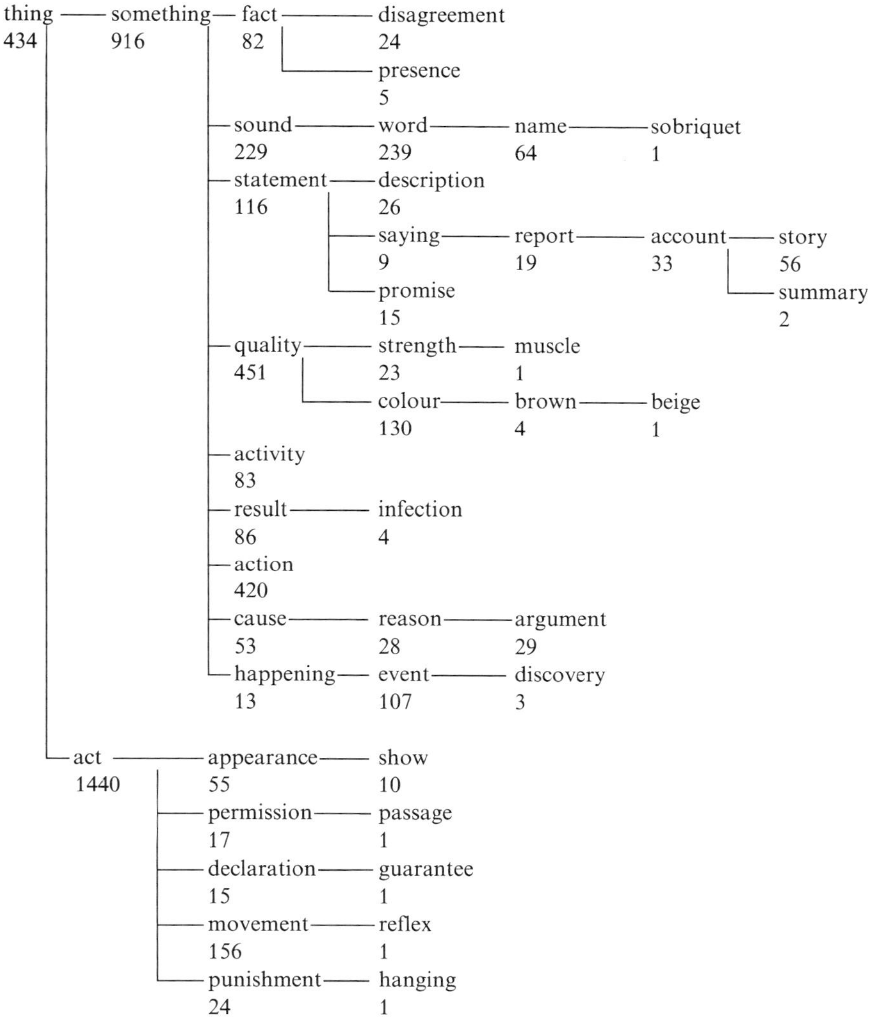

Figure 4. Part of the top of the abstract-noun taxonomy in LDOCE.

Notes

1. In all these cases I am of course assuming "normal world" readings; as Gerhard Leitner points out in a comment, there are special contexts in which these inferences need not always hold: ballet, films, dancing, for instance, or in cases where what is really meant is something like 'wave a kiss', 'blow a kiss' etc.
2. Why the entry for *eat* should have *drink* as preferred object is not clear to me. Perhaps there is an error here, and (3 c) is in fact meant to be the sense frame for the verb *drink*.

3. Developments in MRD-research are moving at an accelerating pace, however. The "LINKS" project has meanwhile yielded syntactic parses for all Noun, Verb and Adjective definitions in LDOCE, which may well be able to supply the kind of information Wilks *et al.* (1989) require.
4. The task is alleviated somewhat by the fact that LDOCE uses a controlled vocabulary for its definitions and examples. However, since these are all common words, they are also ones that tend to have relatively many senses. The job is further complicated by the fact that the defining vocabulary also contains many complex words derived from the controlled vocabulary.

References

Amsler, R. A.

1980 *The structure of the Merriam-Webster pocket dictionary*, Doctoral Thesis, University of Texas at Austin.

1981 "A taxonomy for English nouns and verbs", in: *Proceedings of the 19th annual meeting of the Association for Computational Linguistics*, Stanford, California, 133–138.

Boguraev, B. — E. Briscoe (eds.)

1989 *Computational lexicography for natural language processing*. London—New York: Longman.

Dahlgren, K.

1988 *Naive semantics for natural language understanding*, Boston: Kluwer Academic Press.

Dahlgren, K. — J. McDowell

1989 "Knowledge representation for commonsense reasoning with text", *Computational Linguistics* 15/3: 149–170.

van Dijk, T. A. — W. Kintsch

1983 *Strategies of discourse comprehension*, New York: Academic Press.

Dik, S. C.

1978 *Stepwise lexical decomposition*. Lisse: Peter de Ridder Press.

1986 a Linguistically motivated knowledge representation. [Paper read at the International Symposium on Language and Artificial Intelligence, Kyoto.]

1986 b "Lexicon en syntaxis in Functionele Grammatica", *GLOT* 9/1–2: 15–27.

1987 a "Functional Grammar and its potential computer applications", in: W. J. Meijs (ed.), *Corpus linguistics and beyond*. Amsterdam: Rodopi 253–269.

1987 b *Functional Grammar computational model of the natural language user: A research program*. Amsterdam: IFOTT.

1989 a *The theory of Functional Grammar. Part I: the structure of the clause*. Dordrecht: Foris.

1989 b "Relational reasoning in functional logic", in: J. Connolly — S. C. Dik (eds.) *Functional Grammar and the computer*, Dordrecht: Foris, 273–288.

1989 c *The lexicon in a computational Functional Grammar*, Amsterdam: General Linguistics Institute, Amsterdam University.

Fass, D.

1989 "An account of coherence, semantic relations, metonymy, and lexical ambiguity resolution", in: S. L. Small — G. W. Cottrell — M. K. Tanenhaus (eds.) *Lexical ambiguity resolution*. San Mateo, California: Morgan Kaufmann.

Foss, D. J. – J. R. Ross
1983 "Great expectations: Context effects during sentence processing", in: G. B. Flores d'Arcais – R. J. Jarvella (eds.), *The process of language understanding*, London: John Wiley and Sons.
Garrod, S. – A. J. Sanford
1985 "On the real-time character of interpretation during reading", *Language and Cognitive Processes* 1: 43–61.
Hudson, P. T. W.
1979 "The short-list and double deadline model for word-recognition". [Colloquium, Dept. of Psychology, MIT, November 1979.]
Janssen, Sylvia G.
1990 "Automatic sense disambiguation with LDOCE: Enriching syntactically analyzed corpora with semantic data", in: J. Aarts – W. J. Meijs (eds.), *Theory and practice in corpus linguistics*. Amsterdam: Rodopi, 105–135.
Johnson-Laird, P. N.
1983 *Mental models*. Cambridge: Cambridge University Press.
Kempff, H. J.
forthc. *Inference processes in reading*. PhD. Dissertation.
Marslen-Wilson, W. D. – L. K. Tyler – M. S. Seidenberg
1978 "Sentence processing and the clause boundary", in: W. J. M. Levelt – G. B. Flores d'Arcais (eds.), *Studies in the perception of language*. London: Wiley.
Marslen-Wilson, W. D. – A. Welsh
1978 "Processing interactions and lexical access during word-recognition in continuous speech", *Cognitive Psychology* 10: 29–63.
Meijs, Willem J.
1986 "Links in the lexicon: The dictionary as a corpus", *ICAME News* 10: 26–28.
1988 "Knowledge-activation in a large lexical data-base: Problems and prospects in the LINKS-project", *Amsterdam Papers in English (APE)* No. I. Amsterdam: Amsterdam University English Department, 101–123.
1989 "Spreading the word: Knowledge-activation a functional perspective", in: J. Connolly – S. Dik (eds) *Functional Grammar and the computer*. Dodrecht: Foris, 201–215.
Noordman, L. G. M. – W. Vonk – H. J. Kempff
1984 "Does knowledge control inference processes?", *Paper 26* (Tagung experimentell arbeitender Psychologen.) Nürnberg.
Potter, M. C. – B. A. Faulconer
1979 "Understanding noun-phrases", *Journal of Verbal Learning and Verbal Behavior* 18: 509–521.
Procter, P. (ed)
1978 *Longman dictionary of contemporary English*. Harlow: Longman.
Sanford, A. J.
1987 *The mind of man. Models of human understanding*. Brighton: Harvester Press.
Schwanenflugel, P. J. – E. J. Shoben
1985 "The influence of sentence constraint on the scope of facilitation for upcoming words", *Journal of Memory and Language* 24: 232–252.
Sharkey, N. E. – D. C. Mitchell
1985 "Word recognition in a functional context: The use of scripts in reading", *Journal of Memory and Language* 24: 253–270.

Spilich, G. J. — G. T. Vesonder — H. L. Chiesi — J. F. Voss
1979 "Text processing and domain-related information for individuals with high and low domain knowledge", *Journal of Verbal Learning and Verbal Behavior* 18: 275—290.

Tabossi, P.
1982 "Sentential context and the interpretation of unambiguous words", *Quarterly Journal of Experimental Psychology* 34A: 79—90.
1985 "Interpreting unambiguous words during sentence comprehension", in: G. Hoppenbrouwers — P. Seuren — A. Weyters (eds.), *Meaning and the lexicon*. Dordrecht: Foris, 245—250.

Vonk, W. — L. G. M. Noordman — H. J. Kempff
1984 "Tekstbegrip en inferenties: word tijdens het lezen meer begrepen dan wat er staat?", in: A. J. W. M. Thomassen — L. G. M. Noordman — P. A. T. M. Eling (eds.), *Het Leesproces*. Lisse: Swets and Zeitlinger, 261—274.

Vonk, W. — L. G. M. Noordman
in press "On the control of inference in text understanding", in: D. A. Balota — G. B. Flores d'Arcais — K. Rayner (eds.), *Comprehension processes in reading*. Hillsdale N. J.: Lawrence Erlbaum.

Voogt-van Zutphen, H. J.
1987 *Constructing an F. G. lexicon on the basis of LDOCE*. (*Working Papers in Functional Grammar* No. 24.) Amsterdam: Dept. of Linguistics, University of Amsterdam.
1989 "Towards a lexicon of Functional Grammar", in: J. Connolly — S. Dik (eds.), *Functional Grammar and the computer*. Dordrecht: Foris, 151—176.

Vossen, Piek
1989 "The structure of lexical knowledge as envisaged in the LINKS-project", in: J. Connolly — S. Dik (eds.) *Functional grammar and the computer*. Dordrecht: Foris, 177—199.
1991 "Polysemy and vagueness of meaning descriptions in the *Longman dictionary of contemporary English*", in: Stig Johanson — Anna-Brita Stenström (eds.), English computer corpora. Selected papers and research guide. Berlin—New York: Mouton de Gruyter, 105—123.
forthc. "The end of the chain: Where does decomposition of lexical knowledge lead us eventually?", to appear in: *Proceedings of the 4th conference on Functional Grammar, June 1990, Copenhagen* [provisional title].

Vossen, Piek — M. den Broeder — Willem J. Meijs
1988 "The LINKS project: building a semantic database for linguistic applications", in: M. Kytö — O. Ihalainen — M. Rissanen (eds.), *Corpus linguistics, hard and soft: Proceedings of the eighth international conference on English language research on computerized corpora*, Amsterdam: Rodopi, 279—293.

Vossen, Piek — Willem Meijs — M. den Broeder
1989 "Meaning and structure in dictionary definitions", in: B. Boguraev — T. Briscoe (eds.), 171—192.

Vossen, P. — I. Serail
1990 *DEVIL: A taxonomy-browser for decomposition via the lexicon*. (ACQUILEX Working Paper, Amsterdam University.)

Wilks, Y. — D. Fass — C. Guo — J. McDonald — T. Plate — B. Slator
1989 "A tractable machine dictionary as a resource for computational semantics", in: B. Boguraev — E. Briscoe (eds.), 193—228.

Tracing cohesive relations in corpora samples using dictionary data

Sylvia Janssen

1. Introduction

Corpora are interesting testbeds for linguists in several respects. They offer empirical data on syntactic, semantic and pragmatic structure. The search for specific occurrences is often hampered, however, by the raw form in which they are presented. While syntactic taggers have made swift progress over the past decade, semantic and pragmatic information is still difficult to extract since such data are never overtly marked. The task of tagging corpora semantically clearly has a first priority. Semantic tagging is here understood to be the assignment of correct senses to all the (syntactically tagged) content words of a given corpus sample. This is also known as sense disambiguation. This paper looks at the potential of MRD (Machine Readable Dictionary) data, in particular the semantic data, in view of one specific NLP (Natural Language Processing) task, that of sense assignment.

1.1 Theoretical background

Words in any given (coherent) piece of text are often felt to fit together, not only structurally but also lexically. This is generally known as *cohesion* in linguistic literature (especially Halliday – Hasan 1976). Because certain words typically co-occur (either as loose items or in a collocation), they reinforce (or aid) each other's interpretation. This reinforcement has also been extensively studied within the field of psycholinguistics and is there known as "priming". Thus, in the sentence:

(1) *This tennis tournament is played on a clay court*

the words *court* and *tennis* (among other words) "cohere" (in Hallidayan terms) or, in psycholinguistic theory, the word *tennis* "primes" the 'sport' interpretation of the word *court*. Though looked at from different perspectives, the two theories (linguistic and psycholinguistic) more or less explain the "reinforcement" phenomenon in the same way. Now, assuming that co-occurring words indeed are likely to have something in common, i. e. share parts of their meaning representation, this is considered as a major pointer to the resolution of lexical ambiguity in a given piece of text. Halliday and Hasan have defined two classes of lexical cohesion: "reiteration" and "collocation". Reiteration is subdivided into four types:

(2) a. same word
  b. synonym or near-synonym
  c. hyperonym/hyponym
  d. general word

The second class of lexical cohesion, that of collocation, is not clearly defined but illustrated by a number of examples such as {candle..., flame..., flicker} where it is stated that these words form a collocation. While this classification is certainly a useful one, no mention is made of any parallelism between syntactic dependencies and lexical semantic relations. If, however, the tracing of lexical cohesion is not to be guided by syntactic relations between words, any word can in principle cohere with any other word in the text. Yet it is clear that in a verb phrase, the arguments and the verb are more likely to cohere than, say, the arguments and the head of a noun phrase in the previous sentence. Cohesion beyond syntactic boundaries should be subject to proximity, i. e. to the number of intervening words between two words that cohere. The further words sharing a possible cohesive tie are apart, the less "tight" or effective the cohesion becomes. It seems sensible, therefore, to trace coherence within syntactic dependencies or between words that are within reasonable distance of each other, before venturing across this local context.

1.2. Using MRD data to uncover lexical cohesion

Now that it has been established that lexical cohesion is exhibited by either reiteration or collocation, first and foremost within some syntactic dependency, we wish to turn our attention to the semantic data present in a machine readable dictionary (LDOCE). Previous work on automatic sense disambiguation has never involved exploitation of an extensive MRD. Lexicons are drawn up by hand, providing structured, exhaustive syntactic, semantic and sometimes pragmatic data for each sense to be discriminated. While some attempts have been made at the application of subject field codes in an ambiguity resolution task (Black 1988), the full potential of semantic data present in a large, computerised dictionary has never been explored for sense discrimination purposes.

Since lexical cohesion is the process of interlinking words in context lexically, we wished to find out whether the meaning representations of a machine readable dictionary would lend themselves towards this mapping process. In other words, does an MRD (in this case LDOCE = the *Longman's Dictionary of Contemporary English*) provide sufficient data to lexically disambiguate the senses it distinguishes in a given (domain-restricted) corpus sample? Secondly, can these data be extracted from the dictionary in an automatic (or semi-automatic) way? Clearly, if the latter fails, there is no point in exploiting a machine readable dictionary for this purpose since we then have to revert to manual lexicon building after all. While tracing semantic cohesion is a means to disambiguate senses in texts, it is not our aim to uncover *all* the cohesive ties which a given text displays. So instead of defining all the necessary lexical input we may want to use in the process of lexical analysis, we decided to look at what LDOCE had to offer.

1.3. Exploiting dictionary data

Each sense in LDOCE is defined by means of a wealth of semantic (and syntactic) information. The LINKS project (Vossen – den Broeder – Meijs 1988) was set up to gain more systematic access to the semantic data, and this was done by means of a syntactic parse of the meaning definitions. Next, the genus terms were extracted and represented in a taxonomy of the nominal and verbal entries through a recursive look-up method (the DEVIL system – see also Meijs forthc.). Thus, the taxonomy provides information about the type of genus (co-ordinated, compound, and semantic class such as ISA, group-of, etc.) and its immediate hyperonym and hyponym. This results in the following type of chain:

(3)	*Entry word*	*genus term*
	bun	cake
	cake	food
	food	substance
	substance	material
	material	anything

(Vossen – Serail 1990)

The output of the LINKS project is a useful source of information for the recognition of Hallidayan reiteration. Taking the above example, we can represent the taxonomic information about *bun* as follows:

(4) cake is a hyperonym of bun (reiteration type c)
food is a general word referring to bun (reiteration type d)

Two simple rules may be constructed:

(5) word X is related to word Y through reiteration type c if word X is the immediate descendant of word Y (or Y of X) in the taxonomy

And similarly:

(6) X and Y share reiteration relation type d (general word) if the two nodes are linked vertically with one or more intervening nodes.

Synonyms and near-synonyms (reiteration type b) are overtly marked in the dictionary and share the same node in the taxonomy. Finally, the first type of reiteration is that of repetition and obviously no taxonomic or dictionary data need to be consulted to recognise this lexical relation provided that the reiterated word is meant in the same sense of course.

The following coordinated noun phrases (extracted from the LOB corpus) each illustrate one of the Hallidayan types of reiteration which, in principle, should be derivable from a taxonomic representation:

intricacy and complexity (near synonyms)[1]
stillbirths and deaths (hyponym/hyperonym)
her aunt and uncle (synonyms – gender alternates)
peers and peeresses (synonyms – gender alternates)
night and day (antonyms)[2]
pilot and co-pilot (near synonyms)
mothers and children (? mutually dependent, i. e. no mothers without children and vice versa)

I was unable to extract a coordinated noun phrase in which the nouns shared a "general word" relation. Presumably, a "general word" relation does not typically occur in a coordinated phrase, but rather across sentences. In one sentence, a concept *milkman* may be introduced and in a subsequent sentence, he may be referred to as *this person* (anaphoric reference).

Though authentic, these NPs represent rather eclectic examples. While reiteration certainly is a valid lexical cohesive relation, it is much less frequent than the second Hallidayan type of lexical cohesion, that of "collocation". Take the following coordinated noun phrases (also taken from LOB):

(7) a. *all ports and airports*
b. *the President and Premier*
c. *piano and chamber music*
d. *government and state housing*
e. *grief and anger*

All the noun pairs are lexically, or better, conceptually related and come under the poorly defined "collocation" category. While mutually reinforcing as result of shared meaning, these nouns can not be related (and, therefore, disambiguated) by means of taxonomic information. We need to look for other properties of these words which narrow them down to unique concepts. What other dictionary data can we exploit in this respect? Roughly speaking, LDOCE has subject field codes, box codes, meaning definitions and the example phrases. In addition, the meaning definition of adjectives are often preceded by what I shall refer to as "lexical restrictions" as in:

(8) a. *straight*[3] (of the face) not laughing...
b. *red* (of wine) a dark purple colour

Verbal meaning definitions may also include one or two lexical restrictions for their respective arguments as in:

(9) a. *to mop up* to remove (unwanted liquid, dirt, etc.) with...
b. *to shoplift* to take (goods) from a shop without...

These restrictions were clearly not designed for generation, as is illustrated in the following example:

(10) *fractious* (of an animal) difficult to control

where while it would be appropriate to refer to a dog as being fractious, it seems odd to characterise one's tortoise as a "fractious tortoise". If, however, *fractious tortoise* were to crop up in a given text, the adjective-noun combination would be treated as a valid one because the restrictions are satisfied. Note that the restrictions may be interpreted as nodes in a taxonomy such that all items subsumed by e. g. the concept *wine* (that is, all the types of wine) may freely combine with the predicate *red.*

Lexical restrictions are mostly collocation-specific restrictions, often narrowing down the scope of the selection restriction, which is represented in the "box code". The selection restriction for *red* in the *of wine* example is 'L' (liquid). Wine is indeed a specific type of liquid. Sometimes, the lexical restriction is the same as the selection restriction as in:

(11) 'H' – *travelled* (of a person) experienced in travel

where 'of a person' and 'H' (= human) convey the same restriction value.

The subject field codes have proven their value in my past work on topic retrieval and sense priming (Janssen 1990). The codes can aid the disambiguation process in creating conceptual links both between words of the same syntactic category and a different syntactic category. In

(12) *a close vowel*

both *close* and *vowel* are, in one of their respective senses, coded as 'LNZP' (= linguistics, subfield phonology/phonetics). A shared subject field code is a strong indication of a correct match.

The subject field code sometimes coincides with the lexical restriction:

(13) 'EQ' *unshod* (of a horse) not having had horseshoes fitted

'EQ' is the code for 'equestrian', and a horse is the prototypical animal coming under this class.

1.4. Disambiguating *rich*

To illustrate the potential of the lexical and selection restrictions and the subject field codes, a dry run of the disambiguation of the adjective *rich* is carried out in this section. It must be stressed that while the disambiguation is here carried out for illustrative ends exclusively on the basis of information pertaining to the adjective and noun only, any sense disambiguation system should take a larger context into account to arrive at a valid resolution of an ambiguous item.

LDOCE lists nine senses for *rich*, two of which form part of a fixed expression (*that's rich* and *the rich and poor*), and two of which can only occur in predicative position. This leaves us with the following five senses to be discriminated:

(14) *rich*
1 H[4] (of a person) wealthy; possessing a lot of money or property
3 C (of possessions) costly, valuable, and beautiful
4 FO/E (of food) containing a lot of cream, sugar, eggs, etc.
5 N (of land) good for growing plants in
6 4 (of a sound or colour) deep, strong, and beautiful

With these pieces of information, it was attempted to disambiguate *rich* in a number of adjective-noun combinations (all drawn from LOB). Seven of these combinations are worked out below.

(15)a. *rich parsonage* [house (RLAC/N]
b. *rich actress* [actor (THON/F)]

c. *rich Londoners* [- - -]
d. *rich mahogany* [tree (PM/P), wood (FRZW/S), colour (CO/T)]
e. *rich grass* [plant (PM/P), land (S), plant (P), person (SOZC/H), cannabis (DG/S)]
f. *rich variety* [state (T), group (T), type (T), theatre (TH/T)]
g. *rich fertility* [condition (MDZB/T)[5]

In the first example, *rich parsonage*, a match can only be achieved by means of a selection restriction, *viz.* 'N', resulting in the fifth sense of *rich*. There is no connection, however, between the lexical restriction 'land' and the noun 'house'. A *rich actress* is straightforward; sense 1 of *rich* is applicable, both in terms of the selection restriction 'H' and the lexical restriction (an actor is a type of person). In the third example, the entry for *Londoners* is missing in the dictionary, so no match can be searched for. In *rich mahogany*, the lexical restriction is satisfied ('sound' maps onto 'of a sound or colour'), but there is a clash of selection restrictions once again. In the fifth noun phrase, we see an interesting case of ambiguity which can only be resolved by reverting to the broader context. *Rich* here is either meant in sense 5 ('N' is subsumed by 'S' since 'S' is solid, movable or unmovable unspecified) or sense 1, since both 'H' and 'person' match. In *rich variety* and *rich fertility*, no match could be found due to the fact that LDOCE apparently has not foreseen a possible combination with an abstract noun.

What we have seen here is an attempt to resolve lexical ambiguity by mapping dictionary data between co-occurring adjectives and nouns. The basic rule is: find a maximum score of matches. This is a process in which a large number of simple computations is carried out. While in our view this process should be guided by knowledge of previously processed text, the computational process remains the same. It is one where available data are checked against the current and the previous input to the system. Weights must be balanced against different types of data, largely depending on the contextual information available.

What can we conclude from this dry run of sense disambiguation? A number of things. Firstly, that not all of the data are reliable in its current format. We would not want any system to reject or, for that matter, accept any senses on the basis of incorrect or missing data. Secondly, ambiguity cannot always be solved locally, i. e. a broader context has to be taken into consideration. Since both the selection restrictions and the lexical restrictions function within a syntactic dependency, other data must be consulted to be able to extend beyond these boundaries.

1.5 Deriving knowledge other than genus information

As has already been stated, a conceptual link between two words that are not syntactically bound may be established on the basis of the subject field code. These relations would come under the "collocation" type of lexical cohesion. Information conveyed by the meaning definitions other than the genus terms can also be highly useful but, unfortunately, this is not very transparent. The information contained in the definitions not only provides "core" information, they also give peripheral details. By this I mean that apart from describing the entry word in terms of taxonomic phrasing (a type of, is a, etc.), the definition often provides "functional" (or "world knowledge") details. Thus, of a *jailer* it is not only said that this is a kind of person, it is also stated what his task is:

(16) *jailer* a person, esp. a man, who is in charge of a prison or prisoners
(17) *butcher* a person who kills animals for food or one who sells meat

Habitats of people and animals are frequently given:

(18) *Nereid* (in Ancient Greek literature) a young nature goddess (NYMPH) living in the sea
(19) *squatter* a person who lives in an empty building...

The manner in which something is carried out:

(20) *live with* to line in the same house as (someone of the opposite sex), like a married person

The tool used:

(21) *ink in* to complete with ink

Once this information is overtly marked in our lexicon, it may be applied in the process of sense resolution. It would help us, for example, to create a link between *butcher* and *chicken* and thus establish the correct sense of *chicken* (the 'meat' sense and not, e. g. the 'coward' sense) through knowledge of the fact that a butcher sells meat, and that *chicken* in one of its senses is 'the *meat* of a young hen...'. Attempts are currently undertaken to enrich the DEVIL database with more refined information, and it is expected that such detailed "peripheral" information will prove to be a useful and rich source for a system designed to disambiguate words by tracing the lexical and conceptual overlap that exists between them.

Appendix

Selection restrictions:

H	=	human
T	=	abstract
C	=	concrete
E	=	solid or liquid
N	=	not movable
4	=	physical qualities
F	=	female
P	=	plant
S	=	solid

Subject field codes:

FO	=	food
RLAC	=	religion
THON	=	theatre + occupations
PM	=	plant names
FRZW	=	types of wood
CO	=	colour
SOZC	=	criminology
DG	=	drugs
MDZB	=	biology

Notes

1. This is by no means easy to establish; both nouns are described as 'the state of being intricate/complex', and it is only at the adjectival meaning definition that cohesion is found; both are described as '...difficult to understand'.
2. Two antonymous words may intensify each other's interpretation as much as two synonyms may, yet they cannot be looked upon as 'reiterative' in the Hallidayan sense.
3. Entry word is always underlined, lexical restriction is bracketed.
4. Codes are explained in the appendix.
5. The square brackets contain the senses of the noun, where appropriate followed by a subject field code (in capitals) and a selection restriction (after the slash). All the codes are explained in the appendix.

References

Black, E.
1988 "An experiment in computational discrimination of English word senses", *IBM Journal of Research and Development* 32: 185–193.

Halliday, M. A. K. – R. Hasan
1976 *Cohesion in English*. Longman.

Janssen, Sylvia G.
1990 "Automatic sense disambiguation with LDOCE: Enriching syntactically analyzed corpora with semantic data", in: J. Aarts — W. Meijs (ed.) *Theory and practice in corpus linguistics.* Amsterdam: Rodopi, 105—135.

Meijs, W. J.
1992 "Inferences and lexical relations", this volume, 123—142.

Vossen, Piek — M. den Broeder — Willem Meijs
1988 "The LINKS project: building a semantic database for linguistic applications", in: M. Kytö — O. Ihalainen — M. Rissanen (eds.), *Corpus linguistics, hard and soft: Proceedings of the eighth international conference on English language research on computerized corpora.* Amsterdam: Rodopi, 279—293.

Vossen, P. — I. Serail
1990 *DEVIL: A taxonomy browser for decomposition via the lexicon.* (ACQUILEX Working Paper, Amsterdam University.)

Developing a scheme for annotating text to show anaphoric relations[1]

Steve Fligelstone

Abstract

The development of a scheme for showing anaphoric relations in text is described. The scheme has been developed in order to facilitate efficient encoding of electronically stored corpus material. The scheme encompasses a level of detail which has been found to be manageable in the context of machine-aided corpus analysis by humans. A task-orientated editor and other associated software are used in the implementation of the scheme. Some examples of the annotation are presented.

1. Introduction

The purpose of this paper is to give an insight into some work which has been carried out recently at Lancaster on developing the means to create an annotated corpus with readily utilisable information concerning a range of anaphoric and cohesive relationships within the text samples which make up the corpus.

This paper focuses largely on the context within which the scheme was developed and on some of the problems posed by the task. A more complete description of the scheme itself can be found in Fligelstone (1990).

It is important to view this work in the context of Lancaster's "Grammar Factory" (see Leech – Garside 1991), in order to appreciate the way in which the scheme has been developed. Various factors may impinge upon the task of developing a scheme of encoding, and the resulting scheme will reflect the relative priority given to those factors. One such factor will be the pursuit of informational precision, the need for the various codes to be translatable into distinct definitions, and for the avoidance, where possible, of two different encodings of the same information. Another factor will be the greater or lesser concern with detail and exhaustiveness. But a factor which played a salient role in our project was the need to develop a set of conventions which could be applied consistently and efficiently in a "production line" setting. The significance of this point should become clearer in the account which follows.

2. Developing the scheme

Our task began when we were asked by our IBM partners in the USA to consider ways of developing an anaphorically tagged treebank. Originally, we took the view that this should be a (relatively) simple matter of resolving third person pronouns and a selection of substitute forms which could be said to have antecedents in the text.

However, subsequent discussion and experimentation led to our seeking to incorporate further aspects of cohesion within the scheme, so long as this did not conflict with our overall objective of fast input.[2] The original coding scheme was a simple device in which pronouns were related to antecedents by co-indexing the two, and by using a directional marker to indicate whether the proform was anaphoric or cataphoric, where this could be determined:[3]

> On Monday (1 the company 1) reported higher fourth quarter earnings, raised <REF=1 its dividend and announced plans for a 3-for-2 stock.

Thus the presence of a bracketed item and a directional item can be seen as signalling the presence of a "tie" in the sense of Halliday–Hasan (1976). As an extension of this, by using the same index number for all coreferring nonpronominal items, we were able to use the notation to encode whole chains of coreference. The following extract is marked up only in connection with the references to Ronald Reagan:

> (2 Former California Gov. Ronald Reagan 2) reported today <REF=2 he raised more than $7 million in 1979 for <REF=2 his campaign for the 1980 Republican presidential nomination. That total puts (2 Reagan 2) in second place behind John B. Connally among presidential campaign fund-raisers. (2 Reagan 2) raised $4,418,826 in private contributions during the last quarter of 1979...

We then embarked on the task of moving from a pronoun resolution mark-up to a fuller, but inevitably still restricted, anaphora mark-up.

An altogether positive consequence of the "grammar factory" context was that it meant we could develop the scheme with direct reference to the abilities and habits demonstrated by our analysts, who were already engaged on the project as syntactic analysts.[4] Each time we thought of including another type of information within the scheme, we could try out our ideas directly by asking people to apply the conventions on randomly selected text samples, and if necessary, we could modify our proposals in the light of their performance and experience.

This means that the birth of our scheme has followed a somewhat different course to that of Lancaster's syntactic treebanks (see e. g. Sampson 1987). That work began by working out the details of a scheme, which basically entailed writing a grammar, and then continued with the attempt to marshal the human resources which would enable the scheme to be implemented. Only then was it discovered that this goal was virtually unattainable and that some fairly major surgery would have to be carried out on the scheme itself. In this venture we were able to develop the scheme incrementally. One consequence of this is that the data we have used as a development resource for both the analysts and the conventions will be fully consistent with material to be annotated in the long run. Although some retrospective amendment of the early data will probably be required, we do not expect to have to launch a completely revised "mark 2" scheme, leaving us with a rather small "mark 1 corpus" on our hands. Nonetheless, there is, of course, still an element of conjecture in this view.

Over a period of several months a range of conventions were introduced, some of which were subsequently dropped because they proved too problematic. These new conventions encompassed such features of text as recoverable ellipsis, indirect definite NP anaphors (with "implied" antecedents), and some kinds of metatextual reference. More information about these conventions is given in section 4, below.

3. Developing the software

One of the first things we had to confront was that this project raised a great many so-called "human factors" issues. We could not simply adapt our existing software for parsing and manual word-tag correction, as these did not allow sufficient scope for the analyst to move around the text, back-tracking where necessary. Furthermore, there is considerable scope for making errors in applying the conventions in this scheme. To begin with, the symbol-set is open ended, even though it is rule-governed, because of the use of a numerical index to denote identity. It was apparent that using an available text-editor to compose and input individual items of mark-up would be an inadequate approach. (In the very early days, we had little choice but to do this, and, apart from the errors, the process was, not surprisingly, very time-consuming.) Another apparent reason for errors, though not directly software-related, was that because cohesion is not confined to intrasentential relationships, the analyst must retain a greater quantity of the text within his or her active memory than is the case with parsing. It was a simple "human factors" equation of "more load leads to more errors". Thus, in designing the software for this project, we sought from the outset to achieve maximum economy of effort so far as retention of numbers and other such intellectual trivia were concerned, so that the analyst's mental resources would be free to concentrate on the sense and cohesion of the text.

The software which we have developed to add the annotation into the corpus is a "task-orientated" X Windows-based interactive editor, the code for which has been written by Roger Garside of the Computing Department, Lancaster University. At present it runs on a Sun SPARC-station. It allows the user to move around a block of text, displaying circa 20 lines at a time. The user can use a mouse to mark any segment of text (the word "it" or the phrase "these people", for example) to which s/he wishes to add some labelling. Although the input file may contain word-tags and constituent bracketing, only the raw text is normally displayed. If necessary, the analyst can "zoom in" on part of the text, displaying the full grammatical mark-up. This is done, for example, when an ellipsis marker is being inserted, in order that its position within the syntactic structure can be indicated precisely. Apart from the text window, there are two primary windows which are always displayed. The first of these contains a set of "command buttons", which, for the most part, refer specifically to categories of anaphora which are recognised as being within the scope of our scheme. For example, one button says "coreference" which in fact refers to a nonpronominal coreferring NP, rather than a coreferring pronoun such as *he*. Another "button" bears the term "subst. form". One button, called simply "new", is used to create a new index number for an item in the text, enabling other items to be co-indexed with it. The editor does not make use of general purpose commands such as "insert". Rather, clicking on one of these buttons sets up what may be termed an "insertion routine" geared specifically to the linguistic phenomenon just identified by the analyst. The second additional window contains a list of items which have been identified, roughly speaking: an "antecedent list". At some point in the insertion routine for an anaphor, the analyst will be required to identify the antecedent. This is done by clicking on the appropriate item in that list (which may be scrolled). This means, of course, that an anaphor cannot be marked at all until its antecedent has been indexed. The input software thus has the following characteristics:

– The retention of numbers is taken over by the machine. The analyst never keys in a number.
– The analyst's control of the notation is carried out at the functional or conceptual level, rather than in terms of the characters which make up the symbols.

The purpose of the basic editing session is not to produce the final mark-up as such, but to capture enough information from the analyst to enable the final mark-up to be produced, after a degree of automatic post-processing. This last-stage program has not been implemented yet, but some of its functions are clear:

– It will re-shuffle the numerical indexing so that it follows a textual sequence. Without this procedure, use of index numbers will appear erratic, since the sequence of numbers will simply reflect the order in which the analyst identified items for marking.
– A set of rules are applied to enable greater economy in the marking of coreference for identical proper nouns. The analyst uses these rules to save time, the program will use these rules to expand the mark-up to cover all proper noun coreferences.

The degree of explicitness required for the final mark-up is a question still to be resolved. For example, it has yet to be decided whether some features should be marked on all first and second person pronouns. At any rate, the analysts are required only to mark enough detail to allow a post-processing program to make the mark-up "verbose" if required. For example:

> Now, (3 dear reader 3), cast <REF=3[P] your mind back if <REF=3 you will a couple of issues to column in which I informed <REF=3 you that...

The first *you* anaphor is marked as a "primary reference", but the succeeding *you*s are left unmarked for that feature. Only if the value for that feature changed would we bother to mark it. This assumption of a current value for a particular feature only applies, of course, in relation to a cluster of similar pronouns which are marked as having the same referents. Eventually, this post-processing stage will also include a set of error checking procedures.

4. An outline of the scheme

4.1. Basic features

This section contains no more than an outline of some of the major conventions, and a few minor ones, in order to convey the flavour of the scheme as a whole.

As already noted, a coreferring pronoun will point to its antecedent (if one can be found). A distinction is made between substitute forms and central (coreferring) pronouns. This may at first seem an unnecessary distinction to make, but the cohesive function of a pronoun cannot always be deduced from its form. This is, of course, particularly true of the words *that* and *those*, and strong possessive pronouns such as *ours* and *his* will frequently corefer simultaneously with two kinds of antecedent, corresponding to the questions "whose?" and "what?". It therefore seems desirable that our mark-up should avoid ambiguity be encoding these referential links as instances of two kinds of relationship. It may also be pointed out that our working definition of "substitution" has been made rather broader than is conventionally the case, and covers many examples which might arguably be considered cases of ellipsis.

Coreference:

> It followed (4 fires in the downtown area that destroyed a number of business, stores and apartments 4). Many of <REF=4 those were declared of suspicious origin.

Substitution:

> According to sources, federal nuclear regulators might want (4 more changes 4) than <SUBS=4 those recommended by the company.

> Davidson sought to donate $25 to (4 a taxpayer group 4). Finding <SUBS=4 none, he...

We also encode a number of "pro-verbs" such as *do* and *do so* as instances of substitution:

> Virginia Attorney General Marshal Coleman told the justices he felt state courts had the Gannet ruling in mind in upholding the trial judge's decision (5 to close the murder trial 5) when asked to <SUBS=5:2 do so by the defendant.

(Note: In this last example, the colon and the following "2" signify a compound proform consisting of 2 elements.)

In fact virtually all of the annotations are based on the same basic device of signifying a tie by means of "antecedent" and "pointer". There is some use made of pointers which do not have antecedents i. e. they point somewhere else than to another place in the text, but this aspect of the scheme is fairly restricted in the interests of economy.

Ellipsis is shown thus:

> There are nine categories in PGA Tour statistical service. Assists isn't (6 among them 6). If it were <ELLIP=6, Ben Crenshaw...

A definite NP "anaphor" for which there is no direct antecedent, but rather an implied one, is marked as follows:

> In (7 the "Love Triangle" case 7), <IMP=7(8 the defendant 8) was called to give evidence today

A noun for which it is possible to infer an *of* complement as a means of making its reference explicit takes this variation:

> ...from the hospital cost bill considered by (9 the House 9) last year. The failure of that bill has led <OF=9(10 many members 10) to predict that hospital cost containment is a dead issue.

What is encoded here is that "many members" (10) can be understood as an abbreviation for "many members of the House". This device is often used to show the reference of a non-numerical quantitative expression, and for words like *picture* and *result*.

The two categories of IMP and OF are at least partially the result of an observation about what can be readily identified by analysts. Even so, it is not at all obvious that the two categories can always be distinguished. A definite NP, for example, which can be related to a previous

NP by the preposition *of*, and only by the preposition *of* could be seen as belonging to either category, or indeed, both. Where such "grey areas" have arisen, we have striven to lay down strict guidelines, even where this involves apparently arbitrary approaches to some questions. In the case of a definite "OF" NP, we decided that these should be categorised as OF rather than IMP. The reason was that since the IMP category is designed primarily to gather data on definite NPs, whilst being nonspecific about how the two NPs are related, inclusion in that category would sacrifice the information about the "OF-ness" of the NP. On the other hand, if we encode the NP as belonging to the OF category, it would be a simple procedure, should the need arise, to locate all the definite NPs in that category and create a "supercategory" of definite NPs, however they had been originally encoded. In other words, we opted for the solution which was most profitable in information-gathering terms. E. g.:

> They playfully dove into (11 the Intracoastal Waterway 11). Miles struck his head on <OF=11(12 the bottom 12), resulting in a broken neck and partial paralysis.

An additional device for adding detail in specifying certain relationships (i. e. those which involve a central pronoun) is the inclusion of "features":

(a) (13 Kelly 13) fielded reporters' questions for more than half an hour. "Did <REF=13[Ss] you ever take a bribe?" he was asked.
(b) That's because he believes ><[g] you cannot tell people the truth.
(c) One figure, incidentally, which ><14[S] you might find useful for tax purposes...

In example (a), above, the feature [s] shows *you* to be singular in this case, and the uppercase 'S' shows that *you* is a "secondary reference" – i. e. not the reader of the text, but a character (Kelly) quoted within it. In example (b) the use of *you* is generic, and in the third example, *you* is marked as a primary reference, that is to say, a reference to a reader/listener of the text and not some character mentioned within it.

4.2. Uncertainty

It would be foolish to expect or to pretend that an analysis of anaphoric relationships within "real" texts can always be clear-cut and uncontroversial. We have used the device of at times fairly arbitrary legislation to try and remove the uncertainty in cases where typically more than one analysis may suggest itself. But this can only reduce the scale of the problem. It cannot eradicate it. There exist therefore, a variety of ways of showing uncertainty. In the following example, it is the "boundaries" of the antecedent which are uncertain:

> ?(15 Carter has warned the Soviets that if they do not withdraw their troops from Afghanistan by Feb. 20, he would recommend a boycott. 15)? <REF=15 That means the huge contacts that...

Encoding uncertainty does not serve merely to weaken the data. It also gives us a way of recovering examples of textual ambiguity. When two numbers are separated by a slash, it indicates that the analyst takes one of the given antecedents to be the intended one, but cannot tell which. For example:

> [Members] called for the dismissal of a representative who acknowledged writing (16 a racial slur against blacks 16) on a news media questionnaire.
>
> [The representative] issued (17 a written apology for his use of certain words... 17)
>
> ?(18 But he indicated he stands by his political views... 18)?
>
> [One member] called (16/17/18 [the offending representative's] statement 16/17/18) "disgraceful" and demanded that...

We simply cannot tell whether "statement" refers to the comments written on the questionnaire, the subsequent apology, or the part thereof which was felt to be tantamount to a repetition of the original misdemeanour. As it turns out, a thorough reading of the text from which this example is drawn does not really help to resolve the ambiguity.

4.3. Exclusions from the scheme

Some things have been introduced into the scheme and subsequently abandoned because it was found that in practice a consistency of approach among analysts, or even by a single analyst, could not be achieved. Two notable examples of this were the generic use of NPs and the directionality of relationships involving NP coreference. It was found that these aspects of texts led not only to a great deal of inconsistency, but also a considerable loss of time through "agonising" on the part of analysts.

Clearly then, the coverage of this scheme is incomplete, for reasons which have been explained. No serious attempt is made to deal with what Halliday and Hasan refer to as "lexical cohesion". Antecedents for comparative expressions are not indicated except where this falls within the scope of the conventions for marking up recoverable ellipsis:

> (19 Jim plays 19) tennis better than <ELLIP=19 football Sam (20 plays tennis 20) better than Jim <ELLIP=20

We would not mark the comparison, for example, in:

> John came round to show off his new car. I prefer mine – It may be older but it's a lot faster.

even though it would be simple to introduce a convention which covered such straightforward examples. There was some evidence, however, that introducing comparatives as a category would lead to "agonising" when examples such as the following were encountered:

> I was driving my car along wishing I could make it go faster.

However, if the partial analysis pays dividends by enabling certain difficult issues to be simply ignored, there is a corresponding disadvantage in that often the analyst is being asked to ignore textual features which are clearly cohesive, and which could be clearly marked if the notation were adequate. There is a tendency in such cases to force things into categories whose criteria they do not quite match. For example, a reference to a football match as "Newport's win on Saturday over a weakened Liverpool team..." does, in a sense, corefer with "Liverpool's surprise defeat at the hands of Newport". But the coreference here can be seen to be of a less than straightforward kind, since the new formulation both introduces and emphasises different aspects of the referent in question than the original formulation. Our category of coreference is not intended to extend to such examples.

In order to try to reinforce the discipline required to keep the data within each category reasonably controlled, we introduced a category for "miscellaneous cohesive ties". "MISC" can be conceived of in two ways. On the one hand, it can be thought of as a "pressure valve" which serves to counteract the "lumping" tendency to which we have referred. However, it can be seen in a more positive light as a means of trawling for interesting but as yet undifferentiated data. This data could be categorised at a later stage if such an exercise were felt to be worthwhile. A preliminary search through the MISCs in our data suggests this may indeed turn out to be the case. Here are some examples of where it has been used:

> Police investigating (21 the killings 21) have so far been unable to establish <MISC=21(22 a motive 22).

Here, "a motive" cannot be categorised as IMP because it is not definite, and it will slip through the net of the OF category because it is, so to speak, a "FOR".

> (23 Local residents 23) said the swirling mass of children were from the nearby Catholic school. <MISC=23(24 Some local citizens 24) also seemed to think an area public school had been let out also.

Again, the inclusion of this item in the MISC category arises directly out of the fact that we neither allow such "subsets" to be marked as simple coreference, nor encode any specific subset category (the latter possible course of action being precisely the sort of innovation which would make the scheme much less manageable).

> Sen. Edward Kennedy, who is demanding ?(25 that President Carter debate him 25)? , thwarted demands for <MISC=25(26 a similar confrontation 26) by Republican opponent...

Comparative expressions using words like *such* and *similar* are prime candidates for inclusion in this catch-all category. One could almost say that, as far as the analyst is concerned, they cry out for marking!

Another pressure valve is the facility for commenting the text. Like MISC, however, the addition of comments has a positive function since it can be a convenient and direct means of communication between the analyst and another member of the team who is responsible for overseeing the work and ensuring that technical problems are ironed out, and omissions or ambiguities in the guidelines rectified.

5. Progress to date

At the time of writing, the team has almost completed the first 100,000 words of material drawn from the U.S. press (see note 2) – material which has previously been parsed. This material has served as our training data, but as previously stated, it will also form part of the eventual corpus, since it will have been subjected to close scrutiny to ensure that it is fully in accordance with whatever version of the scheme we eventually adopt for the compilation of a larger corpus. The question of what size of corpus we will eventually attempt to create is still being considered.

Soon, too, we will turn our attention to creating software with which to implement the "trimming" of data referred to at the end of section 3, and in turn we will consider practical issues of information retrieval (though it should be clear that information retrieval considerations have played a role throughout this work.)

There are now some 100+ pages of internal guidelines being used by the treebankers as a sort of reference manual. This belies the essential simplicity of the scheme in use, but will not surprise those who have persevered with similar types of enterprise in the past. The coherence of the scheme and its underlying principles do however make it relatively easy to internalise these guidelines after a period of training. Use of the editing program itself can be learned in a matter of minutes.

6. Putting the data to use

The original motivation for beginning this work was to investigate the potential for developing a probabilistic anaphor resolver. Clearly, such a device would need to make use of a considerable amount of pre-analysed data, and this work represents the beginnings of such a database.

It should be borne in mind that this annotation is being carried out on text which has already been tagged and parsed. Several million words of such text are already at our disposal, and the amount is likely to keep growing. Over and above direct exploitation as a statistical database, then, the multi-layered nature of this treebank opens up interesting prospects simply for the study of anaphora. The possibility of studying ambiguity was alluded to earlier. It seems possible, too, that focussed studies of the cohesive ties identified within this scheme, though only crudely categorised in the first place, may serve to broaden and deepen our understanding of anaphora in various kinds of text. Indeed, it may be as a database from which data concerning anaphora can be extracted for purposes of scholarly research that this corpus material will ultimately be most useful.

This is not the place to undertake a survey of theories of anaphora or of attempts to develop anaphora resolution devices. A good such survey (and much else besides) can be found in Carter (1987). Another useful source is Hirst (1981). A point which may, however, be made is that the material in our corpus is of the kind which, arguably, should be considered suitable as a testbed for any kind of automatic resolution device, whether probabilistic or not. Of course, it is possible to imagine that some researchers will argue that this data would be "unfair" to their limited domain devices, but we take the view that the trend in NLP must be towards "robust" analysers, and for that, the availability of authentic, albeit suitably prepared, test material is essential.

One interesting area of exploitation worth mentioning in particular has been identified by researchers in the field of speech synthesis (Campbell and Wichmann, personal communications). The question arises whether prosody can be shown to have a predictable relationship with cohesive ties, and whether such a relationship can be used to improve algorithms for speech synthesis. Such work can begin on the basis of the type of annotated data we are producing. Looking further into the future, this kind of knowledge may eventually play an important part in the development of speech comprehension systems.

7. Conclusion

Although the classification of anaphora we have adopted is derived, albeit crudely, from that of Halliday and Hasan, considerable leeway has been allowed in developing operational definitions (of substitution, for example) which are widely at variance with any popular theories. The point has often been made that annotated corpora should endeavour to be theory-neutral, and this in spite of the fact that most scholars would agree this to be an unattainable objective (see e. g. SALT 1990: 24). The real viewpoint being expressed, of course, is that the information in an annotated corpus should not be of such a theory-specific nature that it is of little or no interest to researchers who do not share the theoretical assumptions of the corpus-creators. It is with this consideration in mind that we have felt it useful to adopt this fairly coarse-grained scheme. Together with the syntactic and word-grammatical information in the corpus, we feel the information we are encoding offers considerable benefits to those researching in the field of anaphora who want to base their studies and experimentation on observed data.

Appendix 1. Summary of the Conventions

The elements of the notation

A system of numbered bracketing is used to mark a section of text. The relationship between that item and another is expressed by means of the notation on the other item. In effect, plain numbered brackets indicate antecedents, to which one or more anaphoric items may point. However, two items which are numbered and bracketed identically are assumed to be coreferences. In the case of such (non-pronominal) NP-coreference no attempt is made to analyse one NP as the antecedent and one as the anaphor.

> (1 Feodor Federenko 1), a former Nazi death camp guard, has asked the U.S. Supreme Court to allow <REF=1 him to retain <REF=1 his American citizenship, (2 the Hartford Courant 2) reported Monday. (2 The Newspaper 2) said (1 Federenko 1), 72, is appealing a ruling handed down...

A range of symbols is used to link an item to its antecedent. These symbols are made up of a number of elements which enable more or less information about the relationship to be encoded. These symbols may consist of up to 4 elements:

1. Direction
2. Type of relationship/reference
3. Identification of antecedent(s)
4. Additional features

In addition, the boundaries of the referring item are encoded, but this is not regarded as part of the symbol itself, since it does not convey any information about the nature of the relationship.

Not all combinations of elements are allowed. The possible combinations are controlled by the editing program which acts an an interface between the analyst and the text to be annotated – this program will be described in a future report.

The following synopsis of the elements is followed by a description of the symbols which may be used in conjunction with each relationship type.

Direction

<	anaphoric
>	cataphoric
?< >	nondirectional or ambiguous directionality
> <	not endophoric

Relationship types

REF=	central (coreferring) pronoun
SUBS=	substitution form
ELLIP=	ellipsis
IMP=	indirect anaphor
OF=	NP with inferrable *of*-complement
MISC=	miscellaneous cohesion
{{... ...}	NP predication (copular relationship)
MTR	metatextual reference

Identification of antecedents

n	antecedent is last occurrence of item marked *n*
n,o,p...	multiple antecedents: *n,o,p...*
?*n*	antecedent is probably item *n*
n/o	antecedent is either *n* or *o*
n/o,p	antecedents are either *n* or *o*, and *p*

Features

[s]	singular
[p]	plural
[g]	generic
[S]	secondary reference

[P]	primary reference
[x]	exclusive of addressee(s)
[i]	inclusive of addressee(s)

Features can, where appropriate, be bundled together (eg: [Ss] for a singular *you* in quoted speech). [S] and [P] are mutually exclusive, as are [s], [p] and [g], and [x] and [i].

These "features" can be seen as a shorthand way of representing feature/value pairs from a notional scheme:

reference (specific, generic)
number (singular, plural, no number)
addressee (included, not included)
level (primary, secondary)

The feature symbols could then be interpreted thus:

[s]	(reference|specific) (number|singular)
[p]	(reference|specific) (number|plural)
[g]	(reference|generic) (number|no number)
[S]	(level|secondary)
[P]	(level|primary)
[x]	(addressee|excluded)
[i]	(addressee|included)

A question mark preceding a feature indicates a degree of uncertainty. An additional feature [diff] is marked on certain problematic pronouns.

Appendix 2. Examples of annotation

The examples used throughout this document have been only partially annotated in order to let the relationships under discussion stand out. The following examples are of text marked up fully according to the scheme. A paper which gives extra details about the scheme and which gives longer examples of marked-up text is available from UCREL (see Fligelstone 1990).

Example 1 (from Spoken English Corpus)

(1 The deputy leader of (2 the Labour-controlled Liverpool Council 2) 1) , {{1 Mr. Derek Hatton 1} , has said any of (3 <REF=1 his town hall staff 3) who (4 cooperate with (5 the district auditor 5) 4)

faced the threat of suspension. Yesterday, <MISC=3(6 two senior officials who 'd <SUBS=4:3 done just that 6) were sent home, pending an investigation. (5 The auditors 5) were called in immediately after (2 the council 2) agreed to a nine per cent rates increase to fund spending beyond Government limits. (1 Mr. Hatton 1) said last night <REF=1 he did'nt know?(7 whether <MISC=3,6(8 officers 8) were obliged by law to cooperate with (5 the district auditor 5) 7)? <REF=1 He added: " <REF=1[S] I 'm not bothered about <REF=7 that ".

Example 2 (from Spoken English Corpus)

(1 One person 1) (2 was 2) killed late last night and (3 five <SUBS=1 others 3) <ELLIP=2 injured, when (4<REF=1, 3 their car 4) was involved in (5 a collision with (6 a train 6) at (7 an automatic level crossing near (8 Romsey in Hampshire 8) 7) 5). Kevin Bocquet of BBC Radio Solent has been to (7 the scene of (5 the crash 5) 7).

[Change of speaker: Kevin Bocquet]

(5 The accident 5) happened in the village of East Dean near (8 Romsey 8). (6 A freight train 6) which had just left (9 Southamton 9) on <REF=6 its way to Liverpool collided with (4 a saloon car 4) on (7 an unmanned half barrier crossing 7).

(4 The car 4) was shunted about twenty yards up <MISC=7(10 the track 10). (11 One of (1, 3 the passengers 1, 3) 11), who was less seriously injured than <MISC=1, 3(12 <REF=11 his companions 12), raised the alarm, and (13 two doctors 13), who happened to be driving through <MISC=8(14 the area 14), both stopped and did what <REF=13 they could to help <MISC=1,3(15 the injured 15). (15 The survivors from (4 the car 4) 15) were all taken to (9 Southampton 9) General Hospital. The (6 train 6) driver wasn't injured, and there were no passengers on (6 the train 6).

Notes

1. Grateful acknowledgement is given to IBM Yorktown Heights, USA, for their continued interest in, and support for, Lancaster's work on annotated corpora in general, and this work in particular.
2. The original scheme for pronoun reference was devised by Geoff Leech of the Linguistics Department, Lancaster University, who has been a source of valuable advice in the development of later versions of the scheme. The impetus for the more complex analysis

came above all from Ezra Black of IBM, Yorktown Heights, who maintains an active interest in the project. Both should be considered as co-authors of the scheme.

3. Most of the examples in this paper are taken (some in amended form) from the IBM-Lancaster "AP Corpus", consisting of some one million words of parsed and tagged 1970s American press material form the Associated Press news agency. The extended examples shown in appendix 2 are taken from the Spoken English Corpus (SEC), developed by the Department of Linguistics and Modern English Language, Lancaster University, Great Britain, and the Speech Research Group, IBM UK Scientific Centre, Winchester (see Taylor – Knowles 1988).
4. The team during the period described in this paper consisted of: Simon Botley, Liz Eyes, Jean Forrest and Janice Hurst.

References

Carter, David
1987 *Interpreting anaphors in natural language texts.* Chichester: Ellis Horwood.

Fligelstone, Steven D.
1990 *A description of the conventions used in the Lancaster Anaphoric Treebank Scheme.* Lancaster: Department of Linguistics and Modern English Language, Lancaster University.

Halliday, Michael A. K. – Ruqaiya Hasan
1976 *Cohesion in English.* London: Longman.

Hirst, Graeme
1981 *Anaphora in natural language understanding – A survey.* Berlin: Springer Verlag.

Leech, Geoffrey – Roger Garside
1991 "Running a Grammar Factory: the production of syntactically analysed corpora or 'treebanks'", in: Stig Johansson – Anna-Brita Stenström (eds.), *English computer corpora: Selected papers and research guide.* Berlin: Mouton de Gruyter, 15–32.

Quirk, Randolph – Sidney Greenbaum – Geoffrey Leech – Jan Svartvik
1985 *A comprehensive grammar of the English language.* London: Longman.

SALT
1990 *Proceedings of a workshop on corpus resources, 3–4 January 1990, Wadham College Oxford.* London: Department of Trade and Industry – Speech and Language Technology Club.

Sampson, Geoffrey
1987 "The Grammatical Database and Parsing Scheme", in: Roger Garside – Geoffrey Leech – Geoffrey Sampson (eds), *The computational analysis of English: A corpus-based approach.* London: Longman.

Taylor, Lita – Gerry Knowles
1988 *Manual of information to accompany the SEC Corpus.* Lancaster: Department of Linguistics and Modern English Language, Lancaster University.

SUSANNE – A deeply analysed corpus of American English

Geoffrey Sampson

This paper discusses an analysed corpus currently being produced by my research team at the University of Leeds. By "analysed corpus" I mean a sample of natural language annotated not just with grammatical classification of individual words, as in the case of a "tagged corpus", but with codes showing the grammatical structures and perhaps the semantic properties of the material at the levels of phrase, clause, and sentence, normally in terms of some sort of labelled-tree notation. Analysed corpora have diverse uses. For my own group they are important as a source of grammatical statistics for probability-based automatic natural language analysis techniques, such as our APRIL system which parses by stochastic optimization (see e. g. Sampson – Haigh – Atwell 1989). But analysed corpora are relevant also to very different fields. Hard information about relative frequencies of various grammatical patterns in authentic usage has obvious potential relevance for syllabus design in language teaching, for instance; and research such as that of Douglas Biber (e. g. Biber – Finegan 1989) has shown how new insights into the history of language and intellectual life can be derived from such data.

There exist at present several publicly-available analysed corpora; our own APRIL work has been based up to now on the so-called Lancaster-Leeds Treebank, an analysed subset of the LOB Corpus which I produced in the mid-1980s in consultation with Lancaster colleagues (see Garside – Leech – Sampson 1987: ch. 7). I have surveyed the various analysed corpora I am aware of in Sampson (in press). But all of them have severe limitations. In the first place, because manually analysing authentic language accurately is a highly skilled and very laborious activity, all the analysed corpora are quite small (which is obviously a major drawback for any kind of statistical work). Our own Lancaster-Leeds Treebank is particularly small, at circa 45,000 words; even the largest of these corpora (the "Nijmegen Corpus"; see de Haan 1984) is only about 130,000 words. Furthermore, in several cases the grammatical categories used for the annotations are defined too cursorily to be applied predictably to material exhibiting the immense diversity of authentic language, and the analyses contain a significant proportion of errors or gaps; and not all the corpora are satisfactorily representative (thus the Nijmegen Corpus, though larger than others, contains material from only five authors).

A problem of another kind is that the analytic schemes of all these corpora are, in terms of linguistic theory, relatively "surfacy". The Lancaster-Leeds Treebank does not even classify clause constituents functionally as "subject", "direct object", etc.; it uses exclusively formal categories such as "noun phrase", "adverbial clause". Some of the other analysed corpora do include functional as well as formal labelling for clause constituents, but they pay little or no attention to grammatical "deep structure" or "logical form", where this diverges from surface structure. Work has recently begun in the USA under Mitchell Marcus to produce an analysed corpus that is planned to be far larger than any now existing, but as I understand it the analytic scheme for this will be only skeletal, including just surface tree-structures with less labelling of nodes even than the Lancaster-Leeds Treebank.

From the perspective of natural language processing for information technology, this is a grave limitation (though not at all a surprising one). Many NLP applications require "understanding" of input texts, including logical analysis, not just surface parsing. We would like to extend our own APRIL system to deliver deeper output analyses; as a surface parser it is by now working reasonably well, and we see no reason of principle why its stochastic optimization technique should not be adapted to search for most-plausible logical analyses of inputs as well as most-plausible surface analyses, but this requires a database of logically-analysed material to supply statistics for the construction of an evaluation function. I would assume that many users of analysed corpora for non-IT purposes are also likely to want analyses at other than surface-grammar levels.

It is in order to go some way towards meeting these needs that I have established Project SUSANNE, which is funded by the UK Economic and Social Research Council for the period September 1988 to March 1992. Project SUSANNE employs three researchers, Tim Willis, Nancy Glaister, and Hélène Knight, and has been receiving considerable input also from Robin Haigh, the chief researcher on Project APRIL. SUSANNE stands for "Surface and Underlying Structural Analyses of Naturalistic English". As is always the case, we can hope to go only a few steps beyond what is already available, and in particular Project SUSANNE cannot do much about the size limitations of existing analysed corpora; but its goal is to produce a corpus which is as big as the largest existing ones, analysed in accordance with a significantly deeper and richer scheme of categories than any of them (and with a low incidence of errors). The SUSANNE analytic scheme is to be explicit, detailed, and comprehensive, and the finished corpus will be structured in a fashion making it easy for researchers to use and will be equipped with a comprehensive user manual. Our goal is to construct an analysed corpus that will serve diverse types of "consumer"; in fixing the SUSANNE analytic scheme, we are not consulting only the needs of our own NLP research effort but as far as possible trying to include whatever categories of information are likely to be useful to different linguistic researchers.

To do this from scratch, beginning with unanalysed texts, would require far more resources than are available to us. Instead, our strategy is to begin with the most suitable of the existing analysed corpora and adapt it, by converting the information already in it into a more usable form and by adding new categories of information. For this purpose (I do not say for all purposes) the most suitable corpus is the "Gothenburg Corpus", constructed by Alvar Ellegård and his students and described in Ellegård (1978). The Gothenburg Corpus is a manually-analysed 128,000-word subset of the Brown Corpus of American English, whose annotation scheme goes further in the direction of underlying, logical analysis than that of any of the other existing corpora.

The downside of the Gothenburg analytic scheme is that it is not defined in much detail or applied as consistently as it might be — Ellegård himself points out (1978: 8) that there is a certain incidence of errors, and we can all understand that there are limits to what can be achieved on a project staffed by students rather than salaried professionals. The strengths and weaknesses of the Gothenburg Corpus are reversed in the Lancaster-Leeds Treebank, which is small and annotated with a surfacy scheme, but a scheme that is defined comprehensively and in great detail, easy to work with, and applied with high consistency. What we are doing, therefore, is extending the Lancaster-Leeds analytic scheme so as to embrace all the extra categories of information covered by the Gothenburg scheme (together with some further categories); "debugging" the resulting extended scheme by applying it to the Treebank, whose properties we are familiar with from long experience; and replacing the hard-to-work-with Gothenburg annotations by those of the new scheme — where possible by deriving the new annotations automatically from the old with manual postediting, and otherwise wholly manually. When the SUSANNE Corpus is ready for public distribution it will contain the material of the Gothenburg Corpus reanalysed according to a scheme that is both computationally tractable and a good deal richer than that of any existing corpus. We shall probably also include the material of the Lancaster-Leeds Treebank annotated according to the same new scheme; if so, the SUSANNE Corpus will be bigger, at 173,000 words, than any existing analysed corpus, and will contain a proportion of British as well as American English.

The Lancaster-Leeds Treebank contains short runs of two or three sentences taken from many places throughout the fifteen genre categories of the LOB Corpus. The Gothenburg Corpus on the other hand contains the whole of sixteen "texts" from each of the Brown genres A, G, J, and N. These genres exemplify each of the four broad genre-groupings established by Hofland and Johansson (1982: 27), so in its own way the Gothenburg Corpus also offers representative coverage; the fact that it includes complete 2000-word "texts" has obvious advantages for some kinds of logical analysis, e. g. reference indexing in connexion with anaphora.

As already said, the Gothenburg Corpus is the only corpus known to me that includes a serious attempt to indicate underlying grammatical structure: it has notations to mark "moved" or "deleted" constituents, to use the terminology of transformational grammar. Nevertheless, although the Gothenburg Corpus has been on offer to any researcher wishing to use it since 1978, I believe I was the first person outside Gothenburg ever to ask for a copy. This neglect is understandable, in view of the fact that its format could not by any stretch of imagination be called user-friendly. In order to explain what we are doing with it, I must explain how the Gothenburg Corpus is organized, and my exposition will necessarily focus on a number of aspects which are less than ideal – since these are the aspects which our project has to put most work into. However, let me say emphatically that my intent here is certainly not to pillory the Gothenburg Corpus. My decision to choose it rather than any alternative as the basis for Project SUSANNE was taken because I believed that, despite its faults, the Gothenburg Corpus was potentially the most valuable analysed corpus extant; I have not regretted that decision. Any complex research product contains faults, and I should be very sorry if my need in this paper to dwell on the faults of the Gothenburg Corpus suggested that I have a low opinion of it. On the contrary, it is clear to me that the Gothenburg Corpus is the repository of a large amount of very useful linguistic information of many categories. If the eventual SUSANNE Corpus yields the benefits to linguistic research that we hope it will, the credit will be due at least as much to Alvar Ellegård and his Gothenburg collaborators as to my team at Leeds.

The Corpus as received from Gothenburg consists of a single long file in a one-word-per-line format. Figure 1 displays a section from near the beginning of the file, part of the analysis of Brown text A01. One surprising (but trivial) initial problem was that the records (lines) of the Corpus are in a jumbled order. Compare Figure 1 with Figure 2, which shows an interim state of the same section of the Corpus as at halfway through Project SUSANNE: the first full sentence shown reads *However, the jury said it believes "these two offices should be combined to achieve greater efficiency and reduce the cost of administration"*. (with the words in field 7 of Figure 2 interspersed with codes beginning with slashes that identify clauses). In Figure 1 the corresponding words are in the sequence *"these two offices should be combined to achieve greater efficiency and reduce the cost of administration", the jury said. However, it believes*. There is no apparent reason for this re-ordering, which plays no part in the way the Gothenburg Corpus indicates grammatical structure; but since the records are equipped with consecutive numbers corresponding to their correct ordering, this was trivial to restore. Another problem was that the original Brown text is represented in Gothenburg (in columns 13 ff. of Figure 1) in an all-capital format and stripped of most punctuation marks, but my team replaced this with the fuller orthographic information in the original Brown Corpus by running the Gothenburg tape against the "Bergen I" version of Brown.

In order to understand how the Gothenburg Corpus represents grammatical structure, it will be convenient to consider the sample from text G12 shown in Figure 3, which exemplifies a stage of our processing of the original tape after the problems just identified had been sorted out, and the fields of each line had been clearly visually separated and organized into a convenient sequence, but little more had been done: Figure 3 represents a much earlier stage of our work than Figure 2. In Figure 3, field 1 contains a code identifying each record uniquely, divided by underline characters into Brown text number, sentence number, and word number (our word numbering is normally incremented in tens so that, for instance, hyphenated words can be divided up and punctuation marks given separate records as appropriate – at this stage we had already split off enclitics such as apostrophe-*s* and given these records of their own). Field 2 shows the original Brown line number. Field 6 contains a wordtag (for Ellegård's wordtag-set, see Appendix B of Garside – Leech – Sampson 1987). The grammatical analysis proper is shown in fields 3, 4, and 5.

FILE: ELLEGBIT OCPTEXT B1 LEEDS UNIVERSITY COMPUTING SERVICE VM/SP4 CMS

000007000198TOPICS	A010180ZDF1	K2	NS
000007000199AMONG	A010180ZDF1	EP	P
000007000200THEM	A010180ZDF1	E	RS
000007000201THE	A010180ZDF1	K1	T
000007000202ATLANTA	A010180ZDF1	K21	C
000007000203AND	A010180ZDF1	Y	Y
000007000204FULTON	A010180ZDF1	K22	C
000007000205COUNTY	A010180ZDF1	K2	N
000007000206PURCHASING	A010190ZDF1	K3	VG
000007000207DEPARTMENTS	A010190ZDF1	K	NS
000007000208/RDF11	A010190ZDF1	K4/	
000008000232MERGER	*A010210ZDL1	S	N
000008000233PROPOSED	A010210ZDL1	4V1	VN
000009000242THESE	*A010220PDF111	1 S1	ES
000009000243TWO	A010220PDF111	1 S2	L
000009000244OFFICES	A010220PDF111	1 S	NS
000009000245SHOULD	A010220PDF111	1 V	MD
000009000246BE	A010220PDF111	1 V1	B
000009000247COMBINED	A010220PDF111	1 V11	VN
000009000248/PDJ1111	A010220PDF111	1 E/	
000009000253/PDJ1112	*A010220PDF111	2 E/	
000009000249TO	*A010220PDJ1111	VP	U
000009000250ACHIEVE	A010220PDJ1111	V	V
000009000251GREATER	A010220PDJ1111	01	JR
000009000252EFFICIENCY	A010220PDJ1111	0	N
000009000254AND	*A010220PDJ1112	Y	Y
000009000255REDUCE	A010230PDJ1112	V	V
000009000256THE	A010230PDJ1112	01	T
000009000257COST	A010230PDJ1112	0	N
000009000258OF	A010230PDJ1112	02P	P
000009000259ADMINISTRATION	A010230PDJ1112	402	N
000009000234/ZDF11	*A010210ZDF1	1 0/	
000009000236THE	*A010210ZDF1	2 S1	T
000009000237JURY	A010210ZDF1	2 S	N
000009000238SAID	A010210ZDF1	2 V	VD
000009000235HOWEVER	*A010210ZDF11	1 E	A
000009000239IT	*A010210ZDF11	2 S	R
000009000240BELIEVES	A010210ZDF11	2 V	V
000009000241/PDF111	A010220ZDF11	2 0/	
000010000260/ZDF11	*A010230ZDF1	1 0/	
000010000265THE	*A010240ZDF1	2 S1	T
000010000266JURY	A010240ZDF1	2 S	N
000010000267SAID	A010240ZDF1	2 V	VD
000010000261THE	*A010230ZDF11	1 S1	T
000010000262CITY	A010230ZDF11	1 S2	N
000010000263PURCHASING	A010230ZDF11	1 S3	VG
000010000264DEPARTMENT	A010240ZDF11	1 S	N
000010000268IS	*A010240ZDF11	2 V	B
000010000269LACKING	A010240ZDF11	2 V1	VG
000010000270IN	A010240ZDF11	2 EP	P
000010000271EXPERIENCED	A010240ZDF11	2 E1	VN
000010000272CLERICAL	A010240ZDF11	2 E2	J
000010000273PERSONNEL	A010250ZDF11	2 E	N
000010000274AS	A010250ZDF11	2 EQ	Z
000010000275A	A010250ZDF11	2 E1	F

Figure 1.

```
field:  1               2             3        4       5       6         7         8
[]
A01_0070_0301   A01_0200      PDF      112     O2/     <>        /RDF1121
[]
A01_0070_0310   A01_0200      RDF      1121    S       DDQr      which     [Fr[D[]D
]
A01_0070_0320   A01_0200      RDF      1121    V       VV0t      inure     [V[]V]
A01_0070_0330   A01_0200      RDF      1121    KP      IIt       to        [P[]
A01_0070_0340   A01_0200      RDF      1121    K1      AT        the       [N[]
A01_0070_0350   A01_0200      RDF      1121    K2      JJT       best      []
A01_0070_0360   A01_0200      RDF      1121    K       NN1n      interest
[]
A01_0070_0370   A01_0200      RDF      1121    K3P     IO        of        [P[]
A01_0070_0380   A01_0200      RDF      1121    K31     DB2       both      [N[]
A01_0070_0390   A01_0210      RDF      1121    K3      NN2       governments".
[]N]P]N]P]Fr]N]Fn+]Fn&]Fr]N]3]S]
A01_0080_0010   A01_0210      ZDL      1       S       NN1n      #MERGER [Tn[N[]N
]
A01_0080_0020   A01_0210      ZDL      1       V1      VVNv      PROPOSED#
[V[]V]Tn]
A01_0090_0002   A01_0210      ZDF      1       O/      <>        /ZDF11    [S[]
A01_0090_0010   A01_0210      ZDF      11      c       RR        However,
[R[]R]
A01_0090_0020   A01_0210      ZDF      1       S1      AT        the       [N[]
A01_0090_0030   A01_0210      ZDF      1       S       NN1c      jury      []N]
A01_0090_0040   A01_0210      ZDF      1       V       VVDv      said      [V[]V]
A01_0090_0050   A01_0210      ZDF      11      S       PPH1      it        [Fn[N[]N
]
A01_0090_0060   A01_0210      ZDF      11      V       VVZv      believes
[V[]V]
A01_0090_0061   A01_0220      ZDF      11      O/      <>        /PDF111   []
A01_0090_0070   A01_0220      PDF      111     S1      DD2i      "these    [Fn[N[]
A01_0090_0080   A01_0220      PDF      111     S2      MC        two       []
A01_0090_0090   A01_0220      PDF      111     S       NN2       offices   []N]
A01_0090_0100   A01_0220      PDF      111     V       VMd       should    [V[]
A01_0090_0110   A01_0220      PDF      111     V1      VB0       be        []
A01_0090_0120   A01_0220      PDF      111     V11     VVNv      combined
[]V]
A01_0090_0121   A01_0220      PDF      111     c/      <>        /PDJ1111
[]
A01_0090_0130   A01_0220      PDJ      1111    VN      TO        to        [Ti[V[]
A01_0090_0140   A01_0220      PDJ      1111    V       VV0t      achieve   []V]
A01_0090_0150   A01_0220      PDJ      1111    O1      JJR       greater   [N[]
A01_0090_0160   A01_0220      PDJ      1111    O       NN1u      efficiency
[]N]
A01_0090_0161   A01_0220      PDF      111     c/      <>        /PDJ1112
[]
A01_0090_0170   A01_0220      PDJ      1112    Y       CC        and       [Ti+[]
A01_0090_0180   A01_0230      PDJ      1112    V       VV0v      reduce    [V[]V]
A01_0090_0190   A01_0230      PDJ      1112    O1      AT        the       [N[]
A01_0090_0200   A01_0230      PDJ      1112    O       NN1n      cost      []
A01_0090_0210   A01_0230      PDJ      1112    O2P     IO        of        [P[]
A01_0090_0220   A01_0230      PDJ      1112    O2      NNJ1n     administration".
          [N[]N]P]N]Ti+]Ti&]Fn]Fn]S]
A01_0100_0001   A01_0230      <>       <>      <>      <>        <minor-break>
A01_0100_0002   A01_0230      ZDF      1       O/      <>        /ZDF11    []
A01_0100_0010   A01_0230      ZDF      11      S1      AT        The       [S:g1[N[
]
A01_0100_0020   A01_0230      ZDF      11      S2      NNL1c     City      []
A01_0100_0030   A01_0230      ZDF      11      S3      VVGt      Purchasing
[]
A01_0100_0040   A01_0240      ZDF      11      S       NNJ1c     Department,
[]
A01_0100_0050   A01_0240      ZDF      1       S1      AT        the       [Si[N[]
A01_0100_0060   A01_0240      ZDF      1       S       NN1c      jury      []N]
A01_0100_0070   A01_0240      ZDF      1       V       VVDv      said,     [V[]V]
A01_0100_0075   A01_0240      ZDF      1       O/      <>        <o1>      []Si]N]
A01_0100_0080   A01_0240      ZDF      11      V       VBZ       "is       [V[]
A01_0100_0090   A01_0240      ZDF      11      V1      VVGv      lacking   []V]
A01_0100_0100   A01_0240      ZDF      11      rP      II        in        [P[]
A01_0100_0110   A01_0240      ZDF      11      r1      VVNt      experienced
[N[]
A01_0100_0120   A01_0240      ZDF      11      r2      JJ        clerical
```

Figure 2.

field: 1	2	3	4	5	6	7
G12_0560_0220	G12_0710	PDF	211	C	A	previously.
G12_0570_0010	G12_0710	ZQL	1	Y	Y	And
G12_0570_0020	G12_0710	ZQL	1	c	W	why
G12_0570_0030	G12_0710	ZQL	1	M	G	not?
G12_0580_0002	G12_0710	ZDF	1	O/	<>	/ZQF11
G12_0580_0010	G12_0710	ZQF	11	D	W	How,
G12_0580_0020	G12_0710	ZDF	1	S	R	I
G12_0580_0030	G12_0710	ZDF	1	V	VD	asked,
G12_0580_0040	G12_0710	ZQF	11	V	MD	could
G12_0580_0050	G12_0710	ZQF	11	S	N	chaos
G12_0580_0060	G12_0710	ZQF	11	V1	B	be
G12_0580_0070	G12_0710	ZQF	11	V11	VN	admitted
G12_0580_0080	G12_0710	ZQF	11	BP	P	to
G12_0580_0090	G12_0720	ZQF	11	B	N	chaos?
G12_0590_0010	G12_0720	ZQF	1	V	MD	Would
G12_0590_0020	G12_0720	ZQF	1	M	G	not
G12_0590_0030	G12_0720	ZQF	1	S	E	that
G12_0590_0040	G12_0720	ZQF	1	V1	B	be
G12_0590_0050	G12_0720	ZQF	1	H1	T	the
G12_0590_0060	G12_0720	ZQF	1	H	N	end
G12_0590_0070	G12_0720	ZQF	1	H2P	P	of
G12_0590_0080	G12_0720	ZQF	1	H2	N	thinking
G12_0590_0090	G12_0720	ZQF	1	Y	Y	and
G12_0590_0100	G12_0720	ZQF	1	H1	T	the
G12_0590_0110	G12_0720	ZQF	1	H	N	end
G12_0590_0120	G12_0720	ZQF	1	H2P	P	of
G12_0590_0130	G12_0720	ZQF	1	H2	N	art?
G12_0600_0002	G12_0730	ZDF	1	c/	<>	/PDF11
G12_0600_0010	G12_0730	PDF	11	U	Z	If
G12_0600_0020	G12_0730	PDF	11	S	RS	we
G12_0600_0030	G12_0730	PDF	11	V	V	look
G12_0600_0040	G12_0730	PDF	11	KP	P	at
G12_0600_0050	G12_0730	PDF	11	K1	J	recent
G12_0600_0060	G12_0730	PDF	11	K	N	art
G12_0600_0070	G12_0730	ZDF	1	S	RS	we
G12_0600_0080	G12_0730	ZDF	1	V	V	find
G12_0600_0090	G12_0730	ZDF	1	-O	R	it
G12_0600_0091	G12_0730	ZDF	1	-O/	<>	/PDP12
G12_0600_0100	G12_0730	PDP	12	V	VN	preoccupied
G12_0600_0110	G12_0730	PDP	12	EP	P	with
G12_0600_0120	G12_0730	PDP	12	E	N	form.
G12_0610_0010	G12_0740	ZDF	1	S1g	C	Beckett
G12_0610_0011	G12_0740	ZDF	1	S1	GG	<'s
G12_0610_0020	G12_0740	ZDF	1	S2	J	own
G12_0610_0030	G12_0740	ZDF	1	S	N	work
G12_0610_0040	G12_0740	ZDF	1	V	B	is
G12_0610_0050	G12_0740	ZDF	1	H1	F	an
G12_0610_0060	G12_0740	ZDF	1	H	N	example.
G12_0620_0010	G12_0740	ZDF	1	-S	NS	Plays
G12_0620_0011	G12_0740	ZDF	1	S1/	<>	/RDP11
G12_0620_0020	G12_0740	RDP	11	D1	AR	more
G12_0620_0030	G12_0740	RDP	11	D	A	highly
G12_0620_0040	G12_0740	RDP	11	V	VN	formalized
G12_0620_0050	G12_0740	RDP	11	D11Q	Z	than
G12_0620_0060	G12_0750	RDP	11	V+	VG	"Waiting
G12_0620_0070	G12_0750	RDP	11	KP+	P	for
G12_0620_0080	G12_0750	RDP	11	K+	C	Godot",
G12_0620_0081	G12_0750	RDP	11	D11=	<>	<>
G12_0620_0090	G12_0750	RDP	11	H+	N	"Endgame",
G12_0620_0091	G12_0750	RDP	11	D11=	<>	<>
G12_0620_0100	G12_0750	RDP	11	Y	Y	and
G12_0620_0110	G12_0750	RDP	11	H1g+	C	"Krapp
G12_0620_0111	G12_0750	RDP	11	H1+	GG	<'s
G12_0620_0120	G12_0750	RDP	11	H2+	JT	Last
G12_0620_0130	G12_0750	RDP	11	H+	N	Tape"
G12_0620_0131	G12_0750	RDP	11	D11=	<>	<>
G12_0620_0140	G12_0760	ZDF	1	V	MD	would
G12_0620_0150	G12_0760	ZDF	1	V1	B	be
G12_0620_0160	G12_0760	ZDF	1	H	J	hard
G12_0620_0161	G12_0760	ZDF	1	-S/	<>	/PDJ12
G12_0620_0170	G12_0760	PDJ	12	VN	U	to
G12_0620_0180	G12_0760	PDJ	12	V	V	find.
G12_0630_0001	G12_0760	<>	<>	<>	<>	<minor-break>
G12_0630_0002	G12_0760	ZDF	1	S1/	<>	/RDF11
G12_0630_0010	G12_0760	RDF	11	O	W	"What
G12_0630_0020	G12_0760	RDF	11	S	R	I
G12_0630_0030	G12_0760	RDF	11	V	B	am
G12_0630_0040	G12_0760	RDF	11	V1	VG	saying

Figure 3.

The codes in these fields represent a type of grammatical analysis which is a hybrid between Continental dependency structure, in which the head word of a constituent is associated with a nonterminal node from which modifiers slope down to left or right as daughters, and the constituency structure more familiar to English-speaking linguists, which ignores head/modifier relationships and uses trees in which the words of a sentence occur only on leaf nodes, with nonterminal nodes being labelled with symbols for phrase or clause categories. In the Gothenburg system, each main or subordinate clause is represented by a nonterminal node, with the immediate constituents (ICs) of the clause as its daughters – to that extent it follows the constituency model; but the internal structure of constituents other than clauses is represented in the dependency fashion.

There are other unusual features of the analytic scheme: for instance, the scheme does not recognize a separate category of prepositional phrases, treating such constituents instead as noun phrases whose first premodifying element happens to be a preposition. This strikes me as a perfectly reasonable way to analyse English; however, for the sake of agreement with the majority consensus we have decided in producing the SUSANNE Corpus to replace this analysis with one in which preposition and noun phrase are treated as ICs of a separate prepositional phrase constituent.

The hierarchical arrangement of clauses within clauses is represented by the numerical codes in field 4. The main clause of a sentence is normally coded as clause 1; if it contains two subordinate clauses, these will be numbered 11 and 12, and if clause 12 contains a sub-subordinate clause it will be 121, and so on. The formal type of a clause is shown in field 3, in terms of codes defined in Figure 4: e.g. ZDF represents a finite declarative main clause. Field 5 shows the functional role of an IC (whether clause or phrase) within its containing structure. Consider, for instance, the sentence near the top of Figure 3, *How, I asked, could chaos be admitted to chaos?* The main clause, 1, is shown as consisting of three ICs: *I* marked in field 5 as subject (S); *asked* marked as predicate verb (V); and the first record for the sentence, representing the subordinate clause node ZQF11, which is marked as direct object (O) of the main clause. This subordinate clause is shown in turn as having four ICs: *how* as adverbial of manner or degree (D), *could be admitted* as predicate verb group (V), *chaos* as subject (S), and *to chaos* as adverbial of direction (B). Among these constituents, those consisting of more than one word have their internal structure indicated in field 5 by suffixes to the letter representing the head function: thus *be* is labelled V1 as modifier of the V *could*, and *admitted* is labelled V11 as modifier of the V1 *be*. Normally, modifying elements within phrases have their role indicated simply by digits as in these cases, but certain special types of modifier are indicated by letter codes: e. g. the preposition of a prepositional phrase is assigned the function letter P, as in BP for the *to* of *to chaos*.

(In some cases we have found it convenient to replace the Gothenburg code letters with others, shown in Figure 4 in square brackets.)

CLAUSE CONSTITUENT FUNCTIONS

S	subject
O	direct object, non-prepositional
J	indirect object, non-prepositional
K	prepositional object
V	primary predicate verb
A	adverb of place
B	adverb of direction
C	adverb of time
M	adverb of modality
D	adverb of manner and degree
E	other adverb
G	agent of passive
F	existential *there*
P [H]	predicative complement of subject
Q [L]	predicative complement of object
T	vocative
I	interjection
Y	pure co-ordinating conjunction
Z	pure subordinating conjunction
AY [W]	adverbial co-ordinating conjunction
AZ [U]	adverbial subordinating conjunction

CLAUSE TYPES

Z	non-subordinate	D	declarative	F	finite
P	subord. non-relative	Q	interrogative	J	infinitive
R	relative	J	imperative	G	*-ing*
		E	exclamatory	P	*-en*
				L	verbless

PHRASE CONSTITUENT FUNCTIONS

P	preposition (treated as noun modifier)
Q	semipreposition, e. g. *as*, *than*, *like*
P [N]	infinitival to
Q [R]	verbal particle, in e. g. *come on*, *get off*, *clear out*.
X	appositional modifier

WORDTAGS

T	definite article	L	reflexive
F	indefinite article	S	plural (nouns/pronouns)
N	common noun	X	genitive
C	proper noun	D	past tense
X	existential *there*	N	past participle
J	adjective	M	imperative
V	main verb	B	overt subjunctive
M	modal auxiliary	G	*-ing* form
B	*be*	R	comparative
D	*do* (as auxiliary or pro-verb)	T	superlative
H	*have* (as auxiliary)	Note that 3rd person sing.	
L	(cardinal) numeral	verb forms are not marked.	
K	ordinal		
A	adverb		
G	*not*		
P	preposition		
R	personal pronoun (inc. possessive, reflexive)		
W	rel./interrog. pronoun/adjective/adverb (*who which what when where*)		
Q	indefinite pronoun/adjective (*some any one every many much a little*)		
E	demonstrative pronoun/adjective		
Y	co-ordinating conjunction		
Z	subordinating conjunction		
U	infinitival *to*		
I	interjection		
O	problematic/unclassified		

Figure 4.

There are two major problems with this method of indicating structure. First, it is sometimes systematically ambiguous. It is quite possible to get three successive records all belonging to the same clause and containing, in field 5, codes of the form:

XY
XYZ
XY

which shows that the second word modifies either the first or the third word but does not show which. There is no example in Figure 3, but such cases are not uncommon.

Secondly and more seriously, sometimes there is no specific tree structure which the codes can be seen as representing. When I first encountered the Gothenburg Corpus, I supposed that the Gothenburg analysts had done their work by manually drawing labelled trees which they then converted into the linear notation of Figure 3 when entering them at a terminal. As our team's experience grew, however, it became clear that this was not so; the Gothenburg analysts had evidently moved directly from the sentences in the Brown Corpus to the linear grammatical codings of Figure 3, and although most aspects of the coding system were notationally equivalent to labelled tree structures, some aspects were not. One recurring example is the treatment of co-ordination (which admittedly is widely recognized as a problematical phenomenon for formal grammatical analysis). Many grammarians would treat a noun phrase such as *the house and the garden* as a unit having three ICs: [[*the house*] *and* [*the garden*]]. Our Lancaster-Leeds scheme is somewhat idiosyncratic in assimilating coordination to subordination, so that the second and any subsequent conjunct is treated as daughter of the first: [*the house* [*and the garden*]]. The former of these structures would logically be handled in the Gothenburg scheme by representing the conjunction as head and the conjuncts as modifiers, so that if the entire phrase were, say, direct object of its clause then *and* would be coded O in field 5, and *house* and *garden* would be O1 and O2. If the second structure were preferred, then *house* would be O, *garden* O2 (since O1 would be used for *the* before *house*), and the word *and* would be O2Y (using Y to indicate a co-ordinating conjunction as a special-status modifier, akin to P for the preposition of a prepositional phrase). Instead, the Gothenburg Corpus simply codes the words *house, and, garden* in such a construction as O, Y, O, making it difficult to deduce what structure is being attributed to a co-ordination or even, sometimes, which sequence of records is regarded as jointly forming a co-ordination.

Figure 5 shows the structure implied by the Gothenburg codings for one of the longer sentences of Figure 3: *Plays more highly formalized than "Waiting for Godot", "Endgame", and "Krapp's Last Tape" would be hard to find.*

Most of the hierarchical structure of the sentence is unambiguous, but the play titles involve several complications. Because the titles are quoted elements serving a function in the sentence that does not depend on their internal linguistic structure, each title is shown as a subtree whose head corresponds to no word: the device of suffixing equals-sign to the function code in a record having an empty word field, and suffixing plus-signs to the function codes for an adjacent sequence of words, is a Gothenburg device for showing that the word-sequence is jointly fulfilling some function normally fulfilled by a single word. Each title is coded D11, i. e. as a modifier of D1 *more* which in turn modifies D *highly*; as we have seen, the coding Y for *and* does not show how the sequence of titles

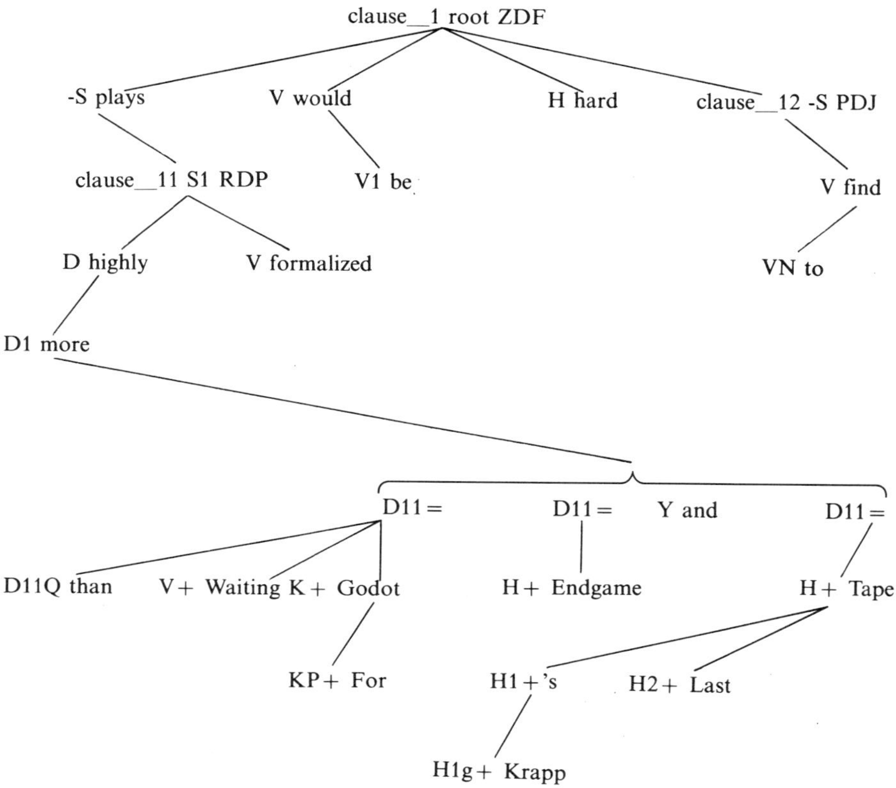

Figure 5.

groups together (hence my use in Figure 5 of a curly brace rather than a clearcut dependency notation). Because formally speaking there is no one constituent comprising the whole coordination, there is no way to show that the word *than* logically premodifies the entire co-ordination; the code D11Q could be taken as modifying any head labelled D11, and a simple algorithm for converting the Gothenburg codes into trees would be likely to attach it just to the first title, as I have shown in Figure 5.

Turning to the higher-level grammatical structure of the example: this is a sentence which exemplifies one of the methods used by the Gothenburg scheme to indicate differences between deep and surface grammatical structures. In the sentence *Plays ... would be hard to find*, the word *plays* is subject of *would be* at the surface, and the subordinate clause *to find* has no specific surface role. In logical structure, on the other hand, the *to find* clause is subject of *would be*, and *plays* is direct object of *find*. This is partly indicated in the Gothenburg notation by the minus signs in field 5 preceding the functional codings for *plays* and for the subordinate clause, which show that these two surface constituents between them in some sense jointly make up the underlying subject. In this case one would have to say, though, that the notation is less than wholly explicit; some other deep/surface grammatical differences are indicated more precisely than this.

Figure 2 represents the extent to which we had processed the Gothenburg tape by early 1990. We had validated the corpus, correcting many "misprints" and codings that were inconsistent with its own norms, and had filled in various short passages present in the original Brown Corpus that for one reason or another were omitted in the Gothenburg tape – this involved working out what the Gothenburg analyses of various constructions would be and adding the corresponding codes to the appropriate fields. Furthermore, we had replaced the Gothenburg wordtags, which were drawn from a rather crude set of about sixty tags, with the much more refined "Lancaster" wordtags (Garside – Leech – Sampson 1987: Appendix B). This was done by using the information in the Gothenburg tags to choose between the alternatives offered for a given text word in an electronic dictionary – a version of Roger Mitton's computer-usable edition of the *Oxford Advanced Learner's Dictionary of Current English* (Mitton 1986) in which Mitton's own wordtags had been replaced by their Lancaster equivalents. In fact the wordtags shown in Figure 2 are more precise than the Lancaster tagset as defined in Garside – Leech – Sampson (1987), since they incorporate further information derived from *OALDCE* but not marked in the Lancaster tagset: e. g. lower-case suffixes "c, u, n" on noun tags marking the noun as countable, uncountable, or either. (The considerable effort we put in to developing this electronic dictionary was justified by the fact that the finished resource serves other important purposes for our research group apart from this retagging exercise.) Field 8 in Figure 2 shows the result of an early version of the software we have developed to extract labelled-tree information automatically from the Gothenburg codings and express it in the labelled-bracket format already adopted for the Lancaster-Leeds Treebank. At the stage represented by Figure 2, only a certain number of surface formal categories were handled, but this work has been taken much further since; at mid-1990 current indications are that a good deal more of the desired target structures can be reconstructed automatically from the Gothenburg codings than we expected earlier, though there will undoubtedly remain some things that have to be done manually.

Meanwhile, we have evolved an extended version of the existing Lancaster-Leeds annotation scheme described in Garside–Leech–Sampson (1987: ch. 7), allowing us to indicate in a clear and consistent fashion the additional categories of grammatical information appropriate to a deeply-parsed corpus. This extended scheme is designed to incorporate (i) all categories of information which the Gothenburg scheme attempts to represent, and (ii) all aspects of deep-structure/surface-structure differences discussed in mainstream grammatical theory (we consulted standard textbooks of transformational grammar such as Burt (1971) and Akmajian–Heny (1975) in order to check that our scheme dealt with logical structure comprehensively). Our use of deep-structure annotations is not intended to imply any partisan position with respect to rival grammatical theories. It seems to me that theoretical conflicts in the area of grammar are principally about the nature of the rules or principles relating logical to surface form in a natural language, and the extent to which those rules or principles differ from one natural language to another, and that rival theorists on the whole agree with one another about the facts of logical grammar. Thus it should be possible to design a notation for English underlying structure which theorists of different camps could each interpret in terms of their own preferred concepts; I believe our annotation scheme to a large extent achieves this.

As an example, I show the sentence of Figure 5 as it would be annotated in our scheme. The elements printed in bold are the new elements belonging to the extended scheme; the annotations in light print are those of the established, surfacy Lancaster-Leeds scheme (it was a cardinal principle in developing the extended scheme that we should not alter any aspects of the existing scheme but only add to it):

> [O [Np:**S1** *Plays* [Tn [R:**h** *more highly* **⟨2⟩**] [Vn *formalized*] [P:**G2** *than* [N&t “ [Tg [Vg *Waiting*] [P:**K** *for Godot*]] ” , “ [Ns–t *Endgame*] ” , [Ns+t *and* “ [G *Krapp 's*] *Last Tape* ”]]]]] [Vb *would be*] [J:**H** *hard*] [Ti:**s** [Vi *to find*] **⟨o1⟩**] .]

A node-label may contain up to three elements: a formal category, a functional role, and an index. The latter two elements are always represented by respectively a single letter and a single digit, and in a label containing a formal category together with a functional role and/or an index the formal category is followed by a colon. Thus in the label Np:S1, Np represents the formal category “plural noun phrase”, S represents the functional role "surface subject", and the index 1 shows that this constituent corresponds to the item ⟨o1⟩ at the end of the structure. The latter item is surrounded by angle rather than square brackets because it is a "trace" rather than a piece of overt wording, and it contains the functional role marker "o" for "underlying direct object". The *find* clause is marked as underlying subject ("s") of the main clause. There are rules specifying which constituents must be assigned a functional role marker; the marker G is used for an item that has been moved into the clause of which it is a surface IC and lacks a specific grammatical role in that clause (for instance the *than* phrase has been extraposed from the adverbial phrase *more highly than...*). In the case of adverbial elements, the role marker classifies their function according to a set of categories akin to Ellegård's "place", "direction", "time", etc. (cf. Figure 4), but we have used Quirk *et al.* (1985) to establish a rather more comprehensive and satisfactory categorization than Ellegård's.

Note that, in our scheme, punctuation marks are treated as parsable items akin to words, and there are rules saying how they fit into parse-trees – for automatic natural language processing some punctuation marks are almost as significant as closed-class words such as *of*. The Gothenburg Corpus ignores punctuation, and in our processing of the Corpus we have not yet detached the punctuation marks from the words to which they are attached orthographically and restructured the parse-trees to accommodate them; this is due to be done shortly.

In the completed SUSANNE Corpus, labelled bracketings such as those of the example above will be split over successive records, as is done with the limited labelled bracketings in field 8 of Figure 2.

One category of information shown in the Gothenburg scheme but not in the above labelled bracketing is the difference between head and modifier ICs of a constituent. Our decision to represent sentences in terms of constituent-structure rather than dependency-structure trees means that heads must be explicitly marked as such; we have not yet chosen a suitable notation for this.

In one respect the notation shown represents a defeat for the original aims of Project SUSANNE. I had supposed when the project began that the most useful way to specify the logical functions of the "complements" of a verb (as opposed to "adjuncts") would be in terms of some version of Fillmorean case theory. I examined various case-sets elaborated by Charles Fillmore and other linguistic theorists, and selected that of Stockwell *et al.* (1973) as suitable for our purposes because it is theoretically non-extreme and is much more fully worked out than any other case theory known to me: the book quoted includes specimen case-frames for about 150 English verbs and predicative adjectives, and it looked as though this should provide a solid basis from which to extrapolate to a consistent case analysis for other verbs and predicative adjectives found in corpus text. Despite very considerable efforts by our team, in the event we were quite unable to make this work. Again and again we found that the existing case-frames gave us no clear precedent, or conflicting precedents, for applying cases to a new verb, or that a verb in Stockwell *et al.*'s list functioned in the corpus in ways that did not seem to be covered by the frames given. Since other versions of case grammar are normally illustrated just by a small number of invented "clear cases", I cannot think that these difficulties would have been solved by rejecting the Stockwell *et al.* system in favour of one of its rivals. It may of course be that we were simply not clever enough in how we went about extending the original case-set specifications to the full range of authentic usage; but I am inclined to conclude that we were attempting the impossible, and I discuss the point here in case it is helpful to others who get involved in similar work. (I do not know whether any researchers had previously tried to apply case theory to authentic corpus material.) To me as to many others it has seemed intuitively right that the logic of clauses ought to be statable in terms of a limited number of complement roles, each one of which is relevant to a high proportion of the thousands of verbs in the language; but in reality there are too many different sorts of verbs, and a particular verb functions in too many different ways, for this to work. In the SUSANNE Corpus we have reverted to the relatively straightforward concepts of surface and underlying subject and object, together with categories of indirect object, prepositional object, and functional classification of adjuncts into place, time, etc.

When we have finished the task of recasting the Gothenburg analyses into the notation sketched here, we aim to add two further categories of information going beyond anything in the existing Gothenburg Corpus or Lancaster-Leeds Treebank, relating to word-sense and to reference relationships.

In the case of word-sense, we plan to equip each open-class word-token in the SUSANNE Corpus (other than proper names) with an annotation identifying its meaning. Obviously this cannot mean spelling out the meaning in terms of some linguistic theory of semantic features; any attempt to do that would undoubtedly lead to a repetition, in spades, of the kinds of problem we encountered with case theory. Instead, we intend to give an identification of the relevant sense among the various senses listed for the word in a standard published dictionary. (We shall probably use for this purpose the *Longman Dictionary of Contemporary English*, since this dictionary is organized in a way that makes the work of identifying and adding the codes relatively convenient.)

As for reference, I undertook when proposing the project to include annotations for each reference-bearing noun phrase or other constituent showing which items co-refer, which would allow the SUSANNE Corpus to be used for anaphora studies. This aspect of the work has since become a lower priority, because the Lancaster group are already producing a corpus with this category of information represented (cf. Steven Fligelstone's paper in this volume). However, it still seems desirable to have available a corpus which includes this type of information for the same texts that are also analysed in the other ways discussed above. Accordingly, if time permits we do intend to include reference annotations in the SUSANNE Corpus. It will clearly be desirable to borrow the well-worked-out annotation scheme developed at Lancaster, rather than inventing an independent scheme.

Let me close on a personal note. I have written about Project SUSANNE as an undertaking which I had initiated and expected to lead to its conclusion – as, until very recently, I did. Unfortunately, the University of Leeds has now decided to run down Linguistics, and is letting me go in October 1990. Accordingly I shall not be directing the latter half of the project; at the time of writing it is not clear whether I shall be in a position to continue contributing as an external consultant. But we are making arrangements to ensure that the project continues; after I leave it will be directed by my colleague Lee Davidson, assisted by Robin Haigh. To date the SUSANNE team's rate of progress has been highly satisfactory. I have every expectation that in 1992 the SUSANNE Corpus will become a publicly-available research tool, and a valuable addition to the computational linguist's armoury of resources.

References

Akmajian, Adrian – Frank Heny
1975 *An introduction to the principles of transformational syntax*. Cambridge, Mass.: MIT Press.

Biber, Douglas – Edward Finegan
1989 "Drift and the evolution of English style: a history of three genres", *Language* 65: 487–517.

Burt, Marina
1971 *From deep to surface structure*. New York: Harper & Row.

Ellegård, Alvar
1978 "The syntactic structure of English texts", *Gothenburg Studies in English* 43.
Garside, Roger — Geoffrey Leech — Geoffrey Sampson (eds.)
1987 *The computational analysis of English: a corpus-based approach.* London: Longman.
Haan, Peter de
1984 "Problem-oriented tagging of English corpus data", in J. Aarts — W. Meijs (eds.), *Corpus Linguistics.* Amsterdam: Rodopi, 123—129.
Hofland, Knut — Stig Johansson
1982 *Word frequencies in British and American English.* London: Longman.
Mitton, R.
1986 "A partial dictionary of English in computer-usable form", *Literary and Linguistic Computing* 1: 214—215.
Quirk, Randolph — Sydney Greenbaum — Geoffrey Leech — Jan Svartvik
1985 *A comprehensive grammar of the English language.* London: Longman.
Sampson, Geoffrey R.
1991 "Analysed corpora of English: a consumer guide", in: Martha Pennington — V. Stevens (eds.), *Computers in applied linguistics: an international perspective.* Clevedon, Avon: Multilingual Matters.
Sampson, G. R. — R. Haigh — E. S. Atwell
1989 "Natural language analysis by stochastic optimization: a progress report on Project APRIL", *Journal of Experimental and Theoretical Artificial Intelligence* 1: 271—287.
Stockwell, Robert P. *et al.*
1973 *The major syntactic structures of English.* New York: Holt Rinehart and Winston.

Information retrieval and corpora

Stephen Sutton and Anthony McEnery

Abstract

Information Retrieval is an area of computer science concerned with retrieving documents and other information bearing items from machine storage. Applications for machine readable corpora require that the information they contain can be accessed. Information Retrieval is of potential use in this task, but is an underdeveloped area within the corpus-linguistics paradigm. This paper seeks to introduce the notion of information and Information Retrieval for linguists. Current technology is reviewed and its shortcomings enumerated. Finally the paper proceeds to outline a path for the development of software tools to aid the processes of information retrieval from corpora, and outlines some of the emergent technologies that may be of use in this task.

1. Introduction

This paper is concerned with examining the potential of applying certain philosophies of Information Retrieval (IR) to corpora and outlining the benefits to be gained.

Conceivably, corpora may contain many forms of information. The scope of this study is restricted purely to written forms, also known as text bases. Further, this paper considers IR in a computational context thus the terms corpus or corpora are intended to refer to machine readable text bases.

2. Information

"Information" is a term fundamental to many areas of study. Unfortunately, however, its use is not always consistent. Before continuing, a distinction must be drawn between common usage in linguistics and computer science. The following brief sections examine the meanings of "information" in Information Theory and Information Processing, consider its role in linguistics and explain the use of the term for the purposes of this paper.

2.1. Information theory

Information Theory was first formally introduced in the nineteen twenties by researchers such as Nyquist and Hartley. It was later extended, providing a firm basis for the field, by the important work of Shannon (Shannon – Weaver 1949). Shannon developed a theory of communication, defining information as a mathematical expression of symbols on a channel and aimed to maximise throughput of information along a telecommunications wire. This work, fundamental in nature and of general scope, proved relevant in both computer science and linguistics and has been widely used as a basis for mathematical models of both written and spoken language (Garside – Leech – Sampson 1987, Niemann – Lang – Sagerer 1988).

2.2. Information processing

Information Processing is typically concerned with the aspects of representation, manipulation and retrieval of information, in the forms of written text, spoken utterances, graphs and images (Salton 1989). Consider in turn the various functions that information processing entails, commencing with information representation. The representation of information involves both internal and external considerations, external representation being the presentation of information at the user interface, and internal the organisation of information in machine storage; this latter point is discussed later. The most common forms of information associated with user interfaces are text and graphics. Less obvious, yet nevertheless common, are audible forms. To appreciate this point consider the operating system interfaces of many modern personal computers. These depend on a combination of visual (e. g., icons), textual (e. g., messages) and auditory prompts (usually in the form of beeping noises) to interact with the user.

Beyond the representation of information lies the manipulation of that information. This is commonly achieved by text-based editors/command processors, mixed initiative interactions, and even graphical manipulation. Yet before any external representation or manipulation of information is performed, the information must be retrieved. A particular problem exists when recovering information from large text bases. The texts in question are information rich to human beings who are versed in reading and writing. Yet for machines, whose natural language understanding abilities remain lamentably limited, the representation and organisation of this information in a manner that is convenient for recovery presents a considerable challenge. It was to deal with such aspects as these that the area of IR was developed.

2.3. Information in linguistics

Although communication is fundamental to linguistics, there has been some doubt as to the scope of communication theories in this field. In particular, concern has been shown towards Shannon's model in that it is not a linguistic theory *per se*, relating more to syntactic structure than to semantic content (Sperber – Wilson 1986). Much of this concern stems from the role of information in Information Theory. Here, communication tends to be viewed as an engineering problem focusing more on the means of communication rather than on its content. Information content is only of interest for encoding and transmission purposes. This is in contrast to linguistic communication that also attempts to pass information, but is concerned less with the carriage of messages and more with the meaning conveyed.

In conclusion, the notion of information in linguistics must take into account semantic considerations. This observation can be related to the needs of Information Processing whose roles include, as well as the storage and manipulation of information, the retrieval and communication of information with respect to meaning. In particular, the following study on the application of IR to corpora demonstrates the need for considering the semantics of information in developing intelligent intermediaries for information recovery.

3. Information retrieval

The aim of IR is to recover material (usually textual) which is relevant to a user's information need. The user's need relates to some topic of interest and is expressed formally as a query. In a classical IR system, textual material is arranged in the form of predefined documents, each document being treated as a homogeneous, indivisible entity. Thus, a typical system retrieves references to whole documents, some of which will subsequently be acquired and perused by the user.

Beyond this primary goal, IR systems are concerned with efficient organisation of information, rapid search and retrieval procedures, effective methods for disseminating retrieved items and for interacting with users. The following sections expand on these points, exploring important aspects of IR philosophies.

3.1. Overview of an information retrieval system

Conceptually, an IR system is very simple, being made up of the following components:
1) A collection of information items (documents), arranged either in full-text form else indexed via abstracts or key words.
2) A user interface, where queries are specified and retrieved items displayed.
3) A query handler, responsible for searching and retrieving information.

The crux of IR is mapping the input query onto the relevant information items. There is not necessarily a correct way of doing this, especially in more sophisticated systems that attempt to overcome the difficulties presented by linguistic features such as synonyms. A good IR system is considered one that addresses a query, retrieving as many relevant items as are required and as few irrelevant items as possible (Thompson – Croft 1989).

3.2. Organisation of information

Typical written forms of information include letters, newspaper articles, books, research articles, abstracts, and so on. A common feature amongst these is an emphasis on narrative structure; thus, IR systems must demonstrate the ability for representing topics which are inherently fuzzy in nature and can be represented in a virtually unlimited variety of natural language forms. This requirement is fundamental to their basic characteristics and distinguishes it from other related information-based domains, such as databases. Typically, the types of information handled by databases don't form coherent wholes, but instead consist of discrete items of information that for representation purposes can be categorised by imposing a predictable and uniform structure. As a direct consequence, access to the contents of a database is reasonably unproblematic. The information is arranged according to indivisible, homogeneous classes, and the imposed structure provides a convenient indexing mechanism for retrieval. It is not that simple in IR due to the nature of the information handled. Not only does this information display little inherent structure of use in information organisation, other than essential linear and rhetorical properties, but the emphasis on narrative structure makes it hard to devise and impose a suitable structure. As a result, this lack of relevant structure means that it often proves difficult to formulate precise information requests and this can result in the retrieval of inappropriate candidate documents.

3.3. Search and retrieval

For the purpose of searching for and retrieving documents, the act of addressing user requests can be re-interpreted as procedures for analysing the narrative. This involves determining the information content of documents, assessing the roles of constituents. Probably the most common scheme by which this can be achieved involves the use of an index. The role of an index is two-fold. The first, a matter of implementation convenience, provides a vehicle for information organisation through which retrieval can be carried out. The second, and perhaps most important, confronts the difficulties that acrue due to the nature of information, as previously described, by way of vocabulary control. This, in turn, improves the quality of topic representation effectively reducing "noise", in terms of inappropriate documents recovered.

Indexing schemes involve the declaration of an indexing language. For the purposes of mapping, documents are assumed to be represented by lists of elements from the indexing language. Measures for constraining mapping and search involve either fully controlled vocabularies where only listed preferred terms may be used, or partially controlled where (under a variety of arrangements) both preferred and "free" terms may be used. In general, introducing vocabulary control helps reduce the search space and thus is an effective way of reducing the scope of the search, but unfortunately can increase the number of candidates for retrieval. In contrast, uncontrolled vocabularies inherit difficulties due to the open-endedness of language.

Other useful facilities include the use of thesauri in an attempt to reduce the effects of multiplicity in language, ranked output achieved by incorporating measures of query/document similarity into the search, and recursive refinement search procedures that allow repeated query re-specification on the same candidate list, so reducing the number of retrieved documents to manageable quantities.

Of all the possible retrieval procedures, perhaps the most appropriate two, and therefore of greatest interest, are the classes of Boolean and linguistic retrieval. Boolean retrieval is based on Boolean logic. Queries are constructed using Boolean operators (e. g., AND, OR, NOT) to describe relationships between query terms. In many respects, this is akin to the principles underlying database access facilities and also relates to current access facilities for corpora, which are discussed later. Linguistic retrieval supports less restricted query specification and consequently uses sophisticated phrase extraction procedures. These have not proved too successful for general texts, but hold good potential for restricted or predictable domains.

3.4. Human-computer interface

The role of the human-computer interface is in interaction with the user. Important activities include input and output; specifying the query and displaying information recovered. User information requests must be specified according to a format recognized by the system. Such formalisms usually reflect the nature of the retrieval procedure used, in particular they often relate to the terminology of any indexing scheme employed.

In order to formulate a successful query the user must have a fairly clear idea about the type of information of interest. To facilitate more casual searching, however, less directed search facilities such as browsers are important. Browsing texts has long been possible with the use of text editors and the like, but is less convenient for the inexperienced user. Potential for the development of more specialised facilities to aid browsing exist, and are discussed in detail later.

In summary of the aspects of IR philosophies explored, there have been many attempts at developing full-text retrieval systems, spanning as far back the 1960s, one such early attempt being the BIRD system (Smith – Devine 1989). More recent developments have provided improved interfacing in the form of natural language querying and intelligent search assistants. Such advances encompass the use of thesauri, knowledge bases and user models to assist query formulation.

Full-text retrieval systems have been described in Schanze (1989) as the backbone of a new medium of electronic texts, and although research has been conducted in this area, there has been little aimed specifically at handling corpora, taking into account the nature of information stored, the kind of retrieval desired and the background of their potential users.

This crucial observation promotes an investigation into the retrieval facilities of machine readable corpora and an assessment of the applicability of IR to corpora. Such an IR application seeks to provide more powerful and convenient tools for information access than those currently available. By critically reviewing what facilities are already on offer in order to illuminate their inadequacies, and with knowledge of IR philosophies, it is possible to prescribe measures for overcoming their deficiencies and to hypothesize on what features one might expect from retrieval tools in the future.

4. The information retrieval paradigm in corpora

Before suggesting ways in which IR can benefit accessing corpora, it is important to establish their mutual compatibility. Also it is necessary to examine current facilities for information access in corpora, in order to identify any inadequacies that can be rectified.

4.1. The applicability of information retrieval to corpora

A comparison of the nature and purpose of information access in corpora with those of IR offers evidence that a good deal of common ground exists between the them. At the most basic level, there is not necessarily any distinction in content between corpora and IR text collections, other than their intended uses. This is especially true of unannotated texts where, to all intents and purposes, classical IR systems retrieve whole documents whereas with corpora the emphasis is on feature-based retrieval, focusing on finer portions of text (e. g., paragraph, sentence, line, etc.). Hence the area of contention between corpus retrieval and IR lies not at the level of the data, but at the level of operations on that data.

Even at this level of operations a clear overlap exists. A corpus has many uses, for instance, a linguist or computational linguist may wish to search for particular examples in order to formulate processing rules, to generate frequency information or to test and refine rules which distinguish between superficially similar constructs. While such tasks lie outside the mainstream of IR applications, there are a couple of points worth noting. The type of search task performed during corpus retrieval is a feature-based one which falls within the ambit of linguistic retrieval in IR. Secondly, it could be argued that the search task tended towards topic-based retrieval if semantic features are the focus of the corpus. Hence, although not immediately obvious at the functional level, corpus-based retrieval and IR are very similar both in terms of what is being searched and how that search is performed.

Next, consider the applicability of IR to corpora by examining the assertion that IR is of fundamental importance to corpora. Corpora can be viewed as large sources of information, most commonly comprising textual narratives ("pure" or "unannotated" corpora) and optionally augmented in various forms ("annotated" corpora). Whether used as archives, knowledge bases, or for more specific language sampling purposes, they can be considered useless if it is not possible to view, access or recover items from them in any way. Further, the primary motive for arranging corpora in machine readable form is to introduce an element of automation, which cannot be realised unless an efficient retrieval system is available. These requirements establish that IR, in an informal sense, is fundamental to applications of corpora in general.

At a more detailed level, consider the kind of information a typical corpus may contain. Textual narratives represent the sort of information processed by conventional IR systems, while textual annotation provides an even richer and attractive area for IR. By the imposition of a formal series of meta-textual tags upon any information source, a formal marking scheme is introduced which may be addressed by any query system. To elucidate, consider a query of the form, "find a document containing elephant used as a noun". With non-tagged text the query system would require an extensive ability to grammatically analyse text. However, for a tagged corpus the query system need only perform a string search for the appropriate tag and match it to the required string. Hence it can be seen that by enriching the corpus with a formal series of meta-textual tags it is possible to increase the scope of addressable queries by any IR system.

At a more technical level, as noted in Salton – McGill (1983), of all the operations required in IR, the most crucial and probably the most difficult one is the assigning of the appropriate terms and identifiers capable of representing the information content of items. These difficulties are potentially eased in the context of corpora if again one considers the nature of information they contain. It is possible to view annotated corpora as already having identifiers assigned, these reflect the type of information that is likely to be requested and retrieved. However, whether or not these identifiers can be considered compatible with the requirements of IR systems is an interesting point that needs further attention.

In general, the quantity and complexity of information stored has a significant bearing on both the role and performance of an IR system. Current trends are towards both larger and more complex corpora, made possible by increased storage capabilities, spurring interest into this relatively new medium of "electronic texts". These characteristics of corpora highlight the need for appropriate retrieval mechanisms.

Finally, an IR approach to corpora focuses on the need for information access in a manner that is primarily convenient to the user. Secondary considerations include computational efficiency and retrieval techniques appropriate for the type of information involved. This section has discussed the compatibility of IR with corpora and suggested that primitive forms of IR are already available for corpora, but more importantly hinted that IR has not yet been fully exploited, and its true potential not yet realised. The next section summarizes what facilities exist for accessing corpora.

4.2. Existing facilities for corpus retrieval

Current access facilities that serve in retrieving information from corpora, and that can be "loosely" classed as IR techniques, are concordance programs. These represent, almost entirely, the scope of purpose-designed tools that are available for interrogating corpora.

The type of concordance program used is largely determined by the corpus material. However, whilst there are many variations of concordance programs, most are designed for handling specific forms of annotated text bases. Unfortunately, it is not within the scope of the objectives to study in depth any of the current concordance tools other than to gain an insight into the sorts of facilities that are available. Thus, it suffices simply to outline some of the more common and fairly representative features boasted.

The first and unquestionably the most important is the ability to specify a query, based on information requirements. Whilst this statement is undeclarative as to the type query mechanism employed or the method of search adopted, its significance is supported by the fact that it removes the need for exhaustive, manual searching. This does not, however, claim that a query specification mechanism is always desirable. There are times when more freedom, in the form of casual browsing, is appropriate.

In line with the role of corpora, it is usually the case that portions of text are required, if not requested. This is accommodated by displaying the item satisfying the query in a prespecified amount of context. For example, an information request for occurrences of a particular word can be expressed as a query that retrieves the surrounding sentence or even paragraph.

A query need not always be definitive and explicit in terms of the text it is designed to match against. This can be realised by the metacharacter feature that allows for unspecific string matching of query terms against text. This is important for several reason. For instance, more flexible string matching can economize the need to specify multiple queries, and is also able to satisfy the need to express structure rather than content. One further benefit afforded by this is the ability to specify position-relative query constructs. Thus, it is possible not only to include wildcard matches, but also to take into account the positions of query terms relative to one another.

An important advance in the search capabilities is offered by the inclusion of logic operations. These allow more than one search string to be specified along with the Boolean relationship between them. These mean that complicated search strings can be specified detailing contextual relations between arguments, further enhanced by the metacharacter facility. A typical search string used on grammatically annotated text might have the effect of finding instances of either *not* or *n't*, followed not necessarily immediately by a word ending in *ed*. A further example for use on grammatically annotated text might search for all cases where infinitival *to* is not followed immediately or otherwise by a base form of a verb.

A more specialised facility can be found in use with certain forms of advanced annotated corpora, for example text augmented with grammatically parsed constituents. This example highlights firstly the potential richness of corpora as sources of information of varying types (e. g., syntax, semantics, etc.) and levels (e. g., itemised and higher-order constituents) and secondly, the need for sophisticated retrieval mechanisms. Such is the importance of graded information and its inclusion in the form of granular hierarchies in today's corpora, that these structures demand more complicated access facilities in order to be beneficial. Current facilities enable the user to express hierarchical relationships between arguments of the search string using hypertags that reflect the structure of information.

4.3. Inadequacies of current tools

In the light of what facilities exist for accessing the information in corpora it is appropriate to discuss ways in which they are inadequate, so that necessary modifications can be prescribed, and future directions outlined.

The concordance features outlined previously are fairly typical and representative of current facilities for information access on corpora. Whilst some of these features are useful, others can be considered deficient in some important respects. To restate the role of an IR system, its ultimate concern is in satisfying user requirements for information. However, this goal cannot be pursued blindly. Other important considerations include efficient organisation of information, rapid search and retrieval procedures, efficient and convenient user interfacing. While it is important to maintain the highest possible standards in each of these areas, the application of IR techniques to corpora presents other criteria that must also be taken into consideration; namely, the physical form of the information stored, the nature of information requests, and the backgrounds of potential users.

In general, current facilities appear sufficient for most practical retrieval requests on untagged texts. Such retrieval tasks involve little more than glorified string matching activities. Consequently, the critical review of this section principally focuses on the requirements of tagged corpora, although some of the criticisms can be extended to "pure" corpora.

A problem fundamental to successful retrieval of information is the need to reduce the number of items that are to be examined to a manageable size. This assertion highlights several weaknesses with current facilities. Firstly, it is clear that not all the information contained in today's corpora is in an appropriate form convenient for directed retrieval, resulting in poor performance in decision making, and secondly that current tools often do not support the necessary query-handling intermediaries essential for expressing requests in order that the search space can be reduced.

One of the most prominent weaknesses of the concordance programs is their inability to handle queries that contain implicit information requests. As a result only information that is explicitly represented can be retrieved, except for limited capability offered by metacharacters. This alone illuminates the rigidity of present query specification procedures.

Logic operators offer a precise and structured formalism for query expression, yet are not always appropriate for the retrieval task. They demand specialist knowledge of such mathematical formalisms which manifest as an assumption on behalf of the query specification procedure. Thus, consider the expression X AND Y OR Z. For a user unfamiliar with such expressions it is often difficult to appreciate the ambiguity entailed. In this case, two interpretations are possible, namely (X AND Y) OR Z and X AND (Y OR Z), where parentheses indicate priority evaluation. Thus, even if the user has clear intentions as to the information required, it is possible that an inappropriate query is formulated and unintended information received as a result.

One further observation concerning query specification relates to the nature of information held in any one corpus. The information tends to be of a specific type (e. g., semantic, syntactic), and queries reflect this fact. In general, system users will have appropriate domain specific knowledge, ranging from intermediate to expert levels. Consequently, it seems inconvenient that users should be constrained to specifying queries in an unfamiliar formalism, especially when the nature of queries is probably reasonably predictable given the type of information held, and that familiar language will probably allow more expression and be less prone to unintentional retrieval.

Finally, there is little emphasis on efficiency in current retrieval mechanisms. Since mapping and searching is fundamental to retrieval tasks, it seems sensible that the use of important resources, such as time and memory, should be minimised or at least sensibly balanced, in an effort to improve performance whilst making retrieval quicker and cheaper.

In conclusion, given the complexities of annotation typically found in today's corpora, more convenient, more efficient and more powerful access and retrieval facilities should be available. The next section seeks to suggest ways in which current tools can be modified, enhancing performance and "friendliness", by exploiting relatively new technologies emerging in IR domains.

5. Proposals for a corpus-information retrieval system

With continued interest and growth in IR, a wide range of new software strategies are becoming available. Recent work has seen developments not only on traditional techniques such as indexing (Zimin – White 1989), but also in areas such as artificial intelligence involving knowledge bases (Kennedy – Crear 1989), neural networks (Ford 1989) and natural language interfaces (Burton – Steward – Davenport 1989).

In light of such advances, its seems appropriate to consider ways in which emerging software technologies in IR could be used to support corpora and to outline future directions for the development of corpora-IR systems. This section discusses the application of expert and hypertext systems (Kennedy – Crear 1989; McEnery – Oakes 1989), and examines the potential benefits of such software tools. As part of this discussion a framework for query formulation is introduced.

5.1. Expert systems for accessing corpora

The role of the expert in IR is well known. Search intermediaries are trained human experts who search for information in a text base. An expert system for IR, as suggested in (Oakes 1990), seeks to replace the expert knowledge of the search intermediary with a system fulfilling, or at least seeking to fulfill, the same role. Indeed expert systems in general can be simply viewed as being software systems written to perform tasks for which some degree of knowledge-based expertise would normally be required from a human performing the same task.

In terms of corpora for linguistic research, the notion of replacing human expertise gives rise to differing types of expert system, as the corpora may be searched for information at many levels, from the pure string search, through syntactic, semantic and pragmatic knowledge. It is these latter knowledge-based searches that can benefit most. Further, this search may be facilitated within a tagged corpus by support at any

Table 1.

Expert System	Syntactic	Semantic	Pragmatic
Type 1	No	No	No
Type 2	No	No	Yes
Type 3	No	Yes	No
Type 4	No	Yes	Yes
Type 5	Yes	No	No
Type 6	Yes	No	Yes
Type 7	Yes	Yes	No
Type 8	Yes	Yes	Yes

or all of these levels. Thus the complexion of any expert system covering these three levels of linguistic knowledge would conform to one of the schemes shown in Table 1.

Table 1 is a generalisation designed to illuminate the possibilities available. Tagging in any of the fields covered by an expert system would be of use to that system, but would not necessarily remove the need for knowledge in that area. Tagging of corpora often tends to be of a specialised form. For example, in a semantically tagged corpus, only a particular aspect of the semantics of the words might be tagged. Hence while tagging in any of the levels of linguistic knowledge covered by an expert system may be of use, the system may still require knowledge in that area to deal with aspects of that knowledge type beyond the scope of the tagging.

Having outlined the role of an expert system in corpus-IR, it is appropriate to examine what they have to offer. This is done in the context of a description of a general rationale for querying an expert system.

The knowledge and user type involved in a query crucially determine the form a query should take. As already indicated, for an effective query to be formed by a user, it is vital that the user be allowed to specify queries in a formalism in which they are well versed. Hence, it seems inappropriate to ask a linguist to formulate a query as an abstract mathematical expression, which assumes a knowledge of mathematics, since it is unlikely that a linguist would be able to do this with a high degree of precision. Instead, query specification in some appropriate linguistic formalism would allow the linguist to be more precise and also reduce possible misconceptions as to the true meaning of the query. Given that the formalism underlying the query should be within the realm of the users expertise, it is important that the formalism itself is determined by the knowledge type under scrutiny. Hence it is clear that a different form of query term is appropriate given an information request concerned with semantics rather than one concerned with syntax. With this basic assertion made, it is worth considering the different types of query a linguist interrogating a corpus might need. Clearly, the optimal paradigm for interaction would be within a formal linguistic theory. Below are enumerated the basic levels of linguistic knowledge with a suggestion as to the form an optimal query term might take, dependent on the type of knowledge in question.

5.1.1. Syntactic retrieval using expert systems

Current tools are only able to address queries for information that are explicitly labelled in corpora. It is possible to extend this feature permitting the handling of certain forms of implicit information given that procedures exist for automatically analysing and annotating texts (Church 1988; Garside – Leech – Sampson 1987). From a syntactic perspective, building such capabilities into an expert system would allow syntax-oriented queries on plain text (pure corpora).

Beyond this, with tagged text as a working base, an expert system could attempt to parse out grammatical constituents to give a higher level of granularity to the grammatical constituents available for retrieval. Hence although any tagged system could deal with, say a query asking for all uses of the word *can* as a noun, an expert system could be introduced, a parser in effect, to further interpret these basic syntactic markings to enable queries of a type such as find all uses of the word *can* used as a noun within a subordinate clause. To sum up, an expert system primed with the appropriate knowledge of syntax could be queried by a linguist, via a syntactic formalism, in one of three ways. In the case of an untagged corpus, the text can be interpreted directly. A tagged corpus, however, offers two variations. Either the meta-textual tags in the corpus are sufficient to satisfy the query, or else it is necessary to interpret them as higher level of syntactic structures, in essence augmenting the tagged text.

5.1.2. Semantic and pragmatic retrieval using expert systems

Currently, a system of semantic tags can only be accessed from a syntactic (i. e., structural) perspective. Taking the philosophy for query formulation presented so far this too is an unattractive proposition. Instead, a query based on semantics should be specified within a suitable semantic formalism. To put the argument within the paradigm of Searle (1969) and other speech act theorists, the optimal query mechanism for an IR system dealing with semantics may be that of an illocutionary proposition. Hence the retrieval system could be presented with a sense and find fragments of the corpus with this sense. This form of query would fulfill the guidelines for a query system well suited to linguists where the query could be specified precisely within an existing and understood paradigm. Further, much of the ground work here is effectively complete since this rationale reflects the type of mechanism adopted by linguistic models of IR.

No facility for dealing with the pragmatics of language within existing IR systems exists. However, given the paradigm presented for semantic queries, it is possible to see that expressing query terms in the form of a perlocutionary proposition, i. e. forming query terms to match the force of an utterance, is an attractive way forward.

Given formalisms within which to express semantic and pragmatic meanings, in a fashion amenable to linguists, the role of expert systems in IR once again becomes apparent. Whether annotation is present or not, expert systems could be developed to search for given illocutionary and perlocutionary propositions within corpora. This aim would be highly problematic, as in essence wide scale text comprehension facilities would be required by any such system. But any advance that was made along these lines would be to the benefit of a user querying a corpus as it may alleviate a certain degree of manual searching. Further, the amount of querying needed via some level of knowledge not wholly appropriate, for example searching for semantics via a syntactic query system, may be lessened.

The previous discussion has been somewhat speculative. Yet given that intelligent knowledge-based tools for corpus retrieval are both feasible and viable propositions, the guidelines for the query interface presented provide a good basis for future research, as user-friendliness and precision are desirable elements within any IR system, as discussed. Further it is useful to note that tagged corpora already contain expert information, in some form. This provides a useful application area in which to develop expert systems, as a large part of the data to drive an inference engine is, in effect, already in place.

5.2. Hypertexts for corpus retrieval

Hypertext is a system of reading and writing that is designed to break the linear constraints inherent in text. By using the data processing capacities of the modern computer it is possible to respecify the operations of reading and writing to reflect the semantic superstructure, rather than the raw linear nature of texts. Even though complications exist in the application of this medium (McEnery – Oakes 1989; McEnery 1989), it is a field that still holds much potential. As such, it is worth considering what possible benefits hypertext has to offer the user of a corpus query system.

As a front-end to a corpus-IR system, hypertext can enhance the presentation of information to the user, and further, allow for greater ease of access to information. At this point two classes of user, not previously addressed, should be introduced: the naive user, and the browser. The naive user is unaware of how to use the interface system properly, whereas the browser, who also may be unfamiliar with the use of this mechanism, is actually searching through the text base with no particular information request in mind. No matter how precise the query language of an interface to a corpus, support is required to aid users in the navigation of the text base and to ease the use of the interface. A hypertext system can provide both.

To expand on these points, browsing has a serious consequence in that it is posssible for a browsing user to become lost within a text base by virtue of their rather random navigation. Browsing text bases is not a capricious act by an uncooperative user, rather it is a commonly employed strategy of some use, as noted by Cove and Walsh (1988) who called it "the art of not knowing what you want until you find it". Experiments with hypertext structures found that their provisions to ease the task of browsing and also to retain a map of the text base greatly facilitated navigation (Burgoine 1989).

Hypertexts allow for document presentation formed with respect to some specific system aim. To substantiate this assertion, consider a hypertext system using a semantic net representation. Such a system may prove appropriate for a text base analysed in terms of semantic constituents. The actual representation of the text itself would reflect the semantics of the text. Thus navigation of the system would, in essence, correspond to the formulation of a semantic query. Hence the process of querying the text base could be commuted to the process of navigating of the hypertext system itself.

In summary, the appeal of hypertext stems from its potential as a powerful yet convenient user interface, able to satisfy the needs of both the casual browser and naive user. The latter point proves to be especially important considering corpus users are primarily linguists. With such users a high degree of computer naivety may be expected, and hence the user-friendly aspect of the hypertext system as a retrieval interface, coupled with the guidelines to be suggested for query language formulation, should provide a sound basis, at least in philosophical terms, for the development of an effective corpus-IR system. Further, expert and hypertext systems are by no means incompatible since they have already been married in McEnery – Bench-Capon (1990); hence the use of expert systems in conjunction with hypertext systems remains a real possibility.

6. Conclusion

This paper has sought to introduce information and IR. Further, an outline has been presented of the components of IR software and their roles. Corpus-IR is concerned with satisfying user information requests on large bodies of tagged or untagged texts. Current tools facilitate these operations in a manner which is neither wholly suited to the perceived user nor to their potential application area. By specifying a philosophy for interface query language presentation this paper has sought to indicate the path along which the development of suitable IR tools for corpus linguistics may be developed. As part of this, software technologies such as expert and hypertext systems have been presented as possible solutions to the problems with current systems.

A general conclusion can be drawn that the field of IR is clearly relevant to the tasks of accessing and using machine readable corpora. For corpora to benefit from this observation, new intelligent retrieval mechanisms must be developed. Such tools, although speculative in nature, have a lot to offer over current facilities, and the benefits to be gained encourage their development.

References

Burgoine, M.
1989 Tools to support the browsing of a semantic net based hypertext system. [Unpublished Ms. C. thesis, University of Liverpool.]
Burton, A. – A. Steward – C. Davenport
1989 "An adaptive natural language interface to management information", *Proceedings of the BCS IR Colloquium* 11: 26–35.
Church, K.
1988 "A stochastic parts program and noun phrase parser for unrestricted text", *Proceedings of the 2nd Conference on Applied Natural Language Processing.* 136–143.
Cove, J. – B. Walsh
1988 "Online text retrieval via browsing", *Information Processing and Management* Vol. 24 Issue 1.
Ford, N.
1989 "Neural nets and information retrieval", *Proceedings of the BCS IR Colloquium*, 11: 228–229.
Garside, Roger – Geoffrey Leech – Geoffrey Sampson (eds.)
The computational analysis of English. London: Longman.
Kennedy, J. – M. Crear
1989 "The information retrieval facilities of generis, a knowledge base management system", *Proceedings of the BCS IR Colloquium*, 11: 16–26.
McEnery, A.
1989 *Aspects of text in hypertext*, CSCW Report Number 2, Department of Computer Science, Liverpool University.
McEnery, A. – T. Bench-Capon
1990 "WEB: An expert system to resolve pronoun reference", *Expert Systems For Information Management* Vol. 2 Issue 3.
McEnery, A. – M. Oakes
1989 "Defining hypertext with reference to medium and method", *Proceedings of the BCS IR Colloquium*, 11: 177–189.
Niemann, H. – M. Lang – G. Sagerer (eds.)
1988 *Recent advances in speech understanding and dialog systems.* (Springer-Verlag, NATO ASI Series, Vol. F46.) Berlin: Springer.
Oakes, M.
1990 *An intelligent front end to the ringdoc database.* Liverpool: Department of Computer Science, Liverpool University.
Salton, G. – M. McGill
1983 *Introduction to modern information retrieval.* New York: McGraw-Hill.
Salton, G.
1989 *Automatic text processing.* London: Addison-Wesley.
Schanze, H.
1989 "Introduction to the special section on full text retrieval systems", *Literary and Linguistic Computing*, Vol. 4 Issue 2.
Searle, John
1969 *Speech acts: An essay in the philosophy of language.* Cambridge: Cambridge University Press.

Shannon, C. – W. Weaver
1949 *The mathematical theory of communication.* Urbana: University of Illinois Press.

Smith, F. – K. Devine
1989 BIRD, QUILL and MicroBIRD: A successful family of text retrieval systems, *Literary and Linguistic Computing*, Vol. 4 Issue 2.

Sperber, Dan – Deirdrie Wilson
1986 *Relevance communication and cognition.* Oxford: Blackwell.

Thompson, R. – W. Croft
1989 "Support for browsing in an intelligent text retrieval system", *International Journal for Man-Machine Studies*, 30: 639–668.

Zimin, W. – J. White
1989 "A partial syntactic analysis based automatic indexing system for Chinese documents", *Proceedings of the BCS IR Colloquium*, 11: 139–153.

Part III
Corpora in language description

Relative infinitives in spoken and written English[1]

Christer Geisler

0. Introduction

The present paper will analyze textual properties of postmodifying infinitives that function semantically like relative clauses. For example, in a sentence such as (1), the infinitival clause can be paraphrased as a relative clause, with the noun phrase *the person* as antecedent.

(1) If that is so, then your doctor is *the person to guide you.* (LOB: F32 167)

I will concentrate on textual differences across speech and writing, i. e. differences between various genres or subgenres, and disregard grammatical or syntactic variation.

The antecedent noun phrase of the relative infinitive can have various syntactic functions in the infinitival clause, such as subject in (1), verb complement in (2), adverbial in (3) and (4).

(2) ... and the TV gives them *something to look at.*" (LOB: J26 36)

(3) it's |reckoned :January 'February M/arch #
|are *the :times to :see . !black 'grouse* on the l/ek # (LLC: 10.8.368)

(4) ... make the world *a far happier place*
for people of all races to live in... (LOB: F10 64)

I will briefly discuss the question of modality in the infinitival clause below, i. e. the fact that the infinitival clause in (1) *the person to guide you* means something like *the person who should/could guide you* (cf. Kjellmer 1975, Quirk *et al.* 1985: 1269). It should be noted that some relative infinitives are impossible to distinguish from adverbial clauses of purpose (see Mair 1990: 74, 120, 210, 216–217).

The set of syntactic features considered is based on grammatical features that have been mentioned as important in previous studies on relative infinitives, such as superlative and comparative adjectives, preposed prepositions, etc. In addition, features were included that appeared to be of interest for the study such as definiteness versus indefiniteness in the antecedent, and classification of antecedents according to the semantic characteristics of the noun. That is to say, an example such as (5) has head nouns in *time* expressing a temporal concept.

(5) There is no *time* to examine the victim,
no *time* to loosen clothing or clear the airway (LOB: J16 146–147)

1. Methodology

The investigation is based on the two computerized corpora of British English, the Lancaster-Oslo-Bergen Corpus of Written British English (1 million words running text, henceforth LOB) and the London-Lund Corpus of Spoken British English (circa 435,000 words running text, henceforth LLC). Instances of relative infinitives were excerpted from KWIC-printouts, and the excerpted material was also saved in computer files for subsequent tagging.

Frequent antecedent nouns such as *thing* have their own tag. Other tags include coordinators, presence of *for*-subjects, prepositions, as well as personal pronouns and proper nouns in the antecedent. Furthermore, each example in the material was tagged for a number of categorical parameters such as passive infinitival verb phrase, preposed versus post-posed preposition, the syntactic function of the antecedent in the infinitive (according to the types exemplified in [1]–[4] above), and the function of the relative complex in the matrix clause.

It could be argued that this is a rather item-based approach. However, individual features, or tags, will be discussed in a wider context in terms of their contribution to a differentiation of text types with regard to relative infinitives. Compare Biber: "...it is claimed that a cluster of features cooccur frequently in texts because they are serving some common function in those texts" (1988: 91).

The computer programs were written in Pascal and the quantitative analyses were carried out by the statistical system SAS. Figures reported represent percentages of a particular feature in a given sample. For example, the highest proportion of passive relative infinitives in the spoken material occurs in nondialogue texts, where 11 out of 51 instances have passive verb phrases, that is 21.6% (cf. section 2.3 and an example such as [15]). In the present study I have only included features that have a Chi-square value with an associated probability of 5 percent or less (i. e. $p < 0.05$). In 2×2 tables with very low frequencies, Fisher's Exact Test (two-tailed) was used instead of Chi-square.

2. A comparison of relative infinitives in the LOB and LLC corpora

There are no great differences between spoken and written English in terms of frequency of relative infinitives. In the LOB corpus there are 836 instances. There are 371 instances in the LLC corpus, which corresponds to a relative frequency of 852 per one million words.

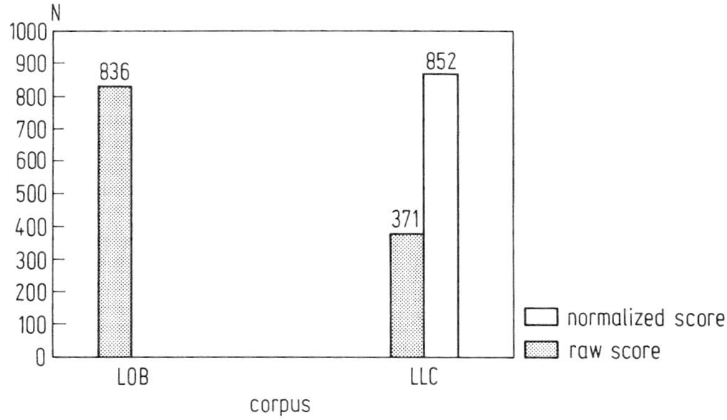

Figure 1. Distribution of relative infinitives in the LOB and LLC corpora

2.1. Variation across genres in the LOB corpus

Certain syntactic features in the relative infinitives are more frequent in some text types in the LOB corpus than others. For example, the proportion of passives in scientific writing (text category J) is significantly higher compared with the other text types, as is the proportion of compound pronouns ending in *-thing, -body*, and *-one* as antecedents in romantic fiction (text category P, cf. example (6)). See Table 1 below.

Table 1.

	J texts	non-J texts
Passives	37.0%	16.0%
	P texts	non-P texts
Compound pronouns	30.5%	14.6%

(6) "No," he replied, "there is *nothing to be anxious about*... (LOB: P17 193)

No interesting patterns of variation between the 15 text types could be discerned. However, if the material was divided into fiction and nonfiction, i. e. informational versus noninformational prose, several patterns emerged. The frequencies of relative infinitives in the two groups are roughly identical. Nonfiction texts constitute approximately 68% of the LOB corpus, fiction about 32%. The proportion of relative infinitives occurring in nonfiction is about 72% (or 599 out of 836 instances), and 28% of the material are in fictional texts (237/836).

There is a noticeable difference between fiction and nonfiction in the infinitival verb phrase, with features such as passives and preposed prepositions being favoured in nonfiction. Thus, example (7) has a passive infinitival verb phrase with the agent in a *by*-phrase.

(7) It was, I think, *the first night-club to be frequented by Royalty.* [Genre: Belle lettres] (LOB: G30 154)

Among the features in the antecedent NP, some are more frequent in nonfiction, such as ordinary nouns, premodifying adjectives, prepositional phrases other than *for*-subjects, and coordinating conjunctions. See example (8), which is from Press reportage:

(8) *THE next White Paper on defence, to be published in March*, is likely to contain a five-year... [Genre: Press reportage] (LOB: A05 7)

In Fiction, on the other hand, compound pronouns ending in *-thing, -body,* and *-one*, and adverbial antecedents of time, are more common, as well as the noun *thing*.

(9) a legend and a symbol, *someone for Grandmother to pin her prayers on,* ... [Genre: General fiction] (LOB: K17 149)

In (9) the antecedent is a compound pronoun in *-one* with human reference and the subject occurs in a *for*-phrase. In addition, fictional categories have more adverbs in the NP, and proper nouns in *for*-subject phrases.

The distribution of the various proportions is summarized in Table 2, and shown graphically in Figure 2.

We thus find two different patterns of cooccurrence of features in the LOB corpus (see Figure 2). One set of cooccurring features includes larger proportions of nouns, premodifying adjectives, passives, prepositional phrases, and coordinating conjunctions. Compare examples (10) and (11).

(10) ...this is *the only rocket and launcher in Europe to have reached a sufficient stage of development...* (LOB: A03 178)

(11) *The most obvious comment to make* is that there are remarkably few animals ... that feed exclusively on one item of diet. (LOB: F40 168)

This is a group of texts made up of text categories A-J, the informational prose genres. Such texts have a high information load or density in construction, and they favour phrasal coordination.

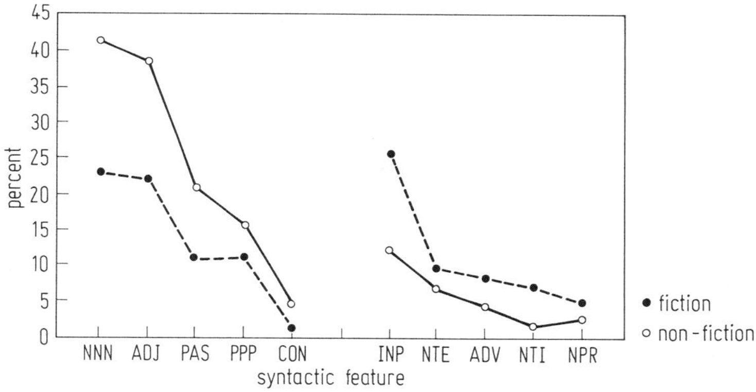

NNN = common nouns; the data for nouns have been halved to fit in better
ADJ = adjectives
PAS = passive verb
PPP = preposition
CON = coordinator
INP = compound pronoun
NTE = temporal antecedents
ADV = adverbs
NTI = the head noun *thing*
NPR = proper nouns

Figure 2. Distribution of features in the LOB corpus across nonfiction and fiction

Table 2.

	FICTION	NONFICTION
Common nouns	45.6%	82.6%
Adjectives	21.9%	38.4%
Passives	4.4%	21.6%
Prepositions	11.0%	15.5%
Coordinators	4.7%	13.7%
Compound pronouns	25.5%	11.9%
Temporal nouns	9.3%	6.5%
Adverbs	8.0%	4.0%
Head non *thing*	6.8%	1.3%
Proper nouns	4.6%	2.3%
N:	237	599

The other set consists of compound pronouns, temporal antecedents, a higher proportion of premodifying adverbs, the antecedent head *thing(s)*, and proper nouns in the *for*-subject constructions, as in (12) and (13).

(12) There was *nothing else for Joyce to do* but step inside and sit down in her corner again. (LOB: N17 118)

(13) I could have wished for *a more suitable moment to digest such confidences*. (LOB: K16 164)

This is a group of texts with a more interactive, personal style. It is made up of text categories K through R, the fictional style. It is made up of text categories K through R, the fictional genres. Thus, these patterns show that various genres within each of the two textual groups are more similar to each other, and that individual texts in these groups have syntactic features in common.

2.2. Variation across genres in the LLC corpus

My aim is to search for ways in which we can maximally account for cooccurring patterns of syntactic features in the LLC corpus. But the data in the LLC corpus are in many respects more difficult to interpret and classify than the data in the LOB corpus, as they do not show the same clear patterns as the written data. The question is thus what cross-classifications should be used to account for the textual variation of relative infinitives in spoken English. Part of the problem is that there is a smaller range of antecedent structures in the spoken material, and that several features have very low frequencies.

However, data can be reclassified in order to account for qualitative or categorical differences in a sample. Thus, Dillon – Goldstein (1984: 307) point out that if we restrict an investigation to pairwise comparisons of variables, we avoid the problem of small cell values. I made an attempt to find characteristic patterns of distribution of features in the LLC corpus. I first reduced the text categories to four main groups: face-to-face conversation (text categories 1 – 6), telephone (7 – 9), radio commentary (10), and oration (11 – 12), but this classification of text types in the LLC corpus yielded few interesting patterns. Therefore, a second set of investigations were carried out in which the text types were regrouped according to a set of binary distinctions made in Svartvik *et al.*

Table 3. Regrouping of LLC texts according to Svartvik *et al.* (1982: 20)

		DIAL	FACE	PRIV	SURR	RADIO
Face-to-face conversation	A	+	+	+	+	–
	B	+	+	+	–	–
Telephone conversation	C	+	–	+	+	–
Discourse, interviews	D	+	+	–	–	+
Public unprepared oration, demonstration	E	+	+	–	–	–
	F	–	+	–	–	+
	G	–	–	–	–	+
Prepared oration	H	–	+	–	–	–
Number of texts +/–		71/16	70/17	56/31	44/43	21/66
N of rel infs +/–		320/51	321/50	234/137	191/180	96/275

Texts included in each subgroup
A 1.1 – 14, 2.1 – 14, 3.1 – 6
B 4.1 – 7, 5.8 – 11, 6.2
C 7.1 – 3, 8.1 – 4, 9.1 – 3
D 5.1 – 7, 6.1, 6.3 – 5, 10.8
E 11.1, 11.4 – 5
F 6.6, 11.3
G 10.1 – 7
H 11.2, 12.1 – 6

(1982: 20–21): Dialogue, face-to-face conversation, private conversation, surreptitious conversation, and radio broadcasts. The starting point was to regroup each example into the following dimensions: +/– dialogue (DIAL), +/– face-to-face conversation (FACE), +/– private conversation (PRIV), +/– surreptitious recording (SURR), and +/– radio broadcasts (RADIO); see Table 3. In this way, the twelve original text categories, which represent eight text types (subgroups A–H in Table 3), were replaced by a binary system of oppositions. The frequencies were then recalculated using these dichotomies instead. Each binary opposition thus forms a dimension.

2.3. Dialogue

Dialogue texts include all texts except 6.6, 10.1–7, 11.2–3, 12.1–6 (i. e. subgroups F through H). The monologue material is made up of prepared and unprepared oration. The opposition between dialogue and monologue corresponds to the "participation" dimension in Crystal–Davy (1969: 69–71).

Dialogue has high scores on premodifiers. Premodifiers are a cover term for all types of premodifiers, e. g. adjectives, comparatives, superlatives, and the common adjective *only*. Biber (1988: 137–140) suggests that texts with high proportions of adjectives are descriptive or argumentative, but nonnarrative. Thus, dialogic conversation (+DIAL) would be less concerned with narrative than, for instance, speeches (–DIAL).

Nondialogue texts have the largest proportion of passive infinitival VPs compared with all other dimensions (as shown in Table 4 below). Compare examples (14) and (15).

(14) It was *a |m/atter#*
be . to |be dis!c/ussed# .
[ə] with . |mutual l/ove#
and |under!st\anding# – – –[Prepared oration] (LLC: 12.3.910)

(15) ((and)) |n=ow# .
|here is *the l\atest . /one to be built#* –
the |heir of a !long 'long trad\i:tion# [Radio commentary] (LLC: 10.7.62-64)

Negative determiners in *no* in the antecedent NP form another feature that dominates in the non-dialogue texts. Biber (1988: 109) following

Tottie (1983) suggests that synthetic negation is typical of narrative texts with denials and rejections. Compare (16) and (17), as well as example (22) below with an antecedent head in *reason.*

(16) and so there was |*no s\uper'vision* to 'do #
so they *|stayed* for a :nice 'long t/ime # (2.14.923)

(17) Los "|\Angeles #
is |*no place* to :go to # – (2.1.1358)

In addition, nondialogue texts have more numerals in the relative infinitives, as shown by Table 4 and figure 3. Numerals in the antecedent NP are further discussed in the following section; see example (25) below.

Table 4.

	+ DIAL	– DIAL
Common nouns	51.6%	37.3%
Premodifiers	42.5%	29.4%
Quantifiers	7.8%	2.0%
Passives	4.4%	21.6%
Numerals	4.7%	13.7%
Comparatives	5.0%	0
Possessives NPs	1.9%	0
N:	320	51

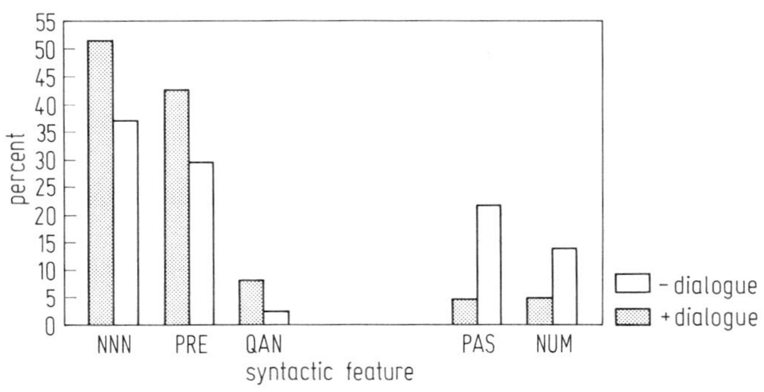

NNN = common nouns
PRE = premodifiers
QAN = quantifiers
PAS = passive verb
NUM = numerals

Figure 3. Distribution of features in the LLC corpus across dialogue and nondialogue texts

In general, the status of zero frequencies in the present study is interesting. There is a distinction in statistics between structural zeroes and sampling zeroes. The former involve a situation where it is theoretically impossible to find an occurrence, the latter is a zero frequency that is due to the size of the sample. Here I will discuss the occurrence of sampling zeroes in some of the dimensions. I will argue that the sampling zeroes are of special importance, since we can explain the absence of a feature rather than its presence. These zero frequencies involve otherwise common features. For instance, on the face-to-face dimension, a total of 24 adverbs occur exclusively in +FACE texts. Furthermore, in the dialogue dimension all 16 instances of comparative adjectives occur in the +DIAL texts (as in examples (18)–(19) below), whereas the monologue material has no instances.

(18) |there are there |are *!better* 'ways to 'go a:b\out it# [Spontaneous conversation] (2.8.539)

(19) that the |h\/ousewife# –
has a |*smaller* r\ange#
from |which to ch/oose# – [Radio interview] (6.1.1107)

Premodification in the form of a comparative adjective in (18)–(19) can be looked upon as a means to express subjective emphasis. Thus, the function of comparatives in the relative complexes is to strengthen an argument. We would then expect to find it in texts of an argumentative nature.

2.4. Face-to-face conversation

On the face-to-face dimension, –FACE is made up of texts categories 7–9, and texts 10.1–7 (i. e. subgroups C and G in Table 3). These include telephone conversation and a subset of the radio texts.

Continuing our discussion of sampling zeroes, all possessives, personal pronouns, and premodifying adverbs in the antecedent NP occur in +FACE texts. It is not surprising that both +FACE and +DIAL texts have all possessives (*her, my* and genitives) as well as personal pronouns (*me, him,* etc. in *for*-subject phrases), as in (20) and (21).

(20) [ɜ:m] and |has . |has *his !\own* internal
{|p\olitics to (({w|orry ab\out#}#))}# [Conversation] 1.2.255

(21) there's |nothing for '*me* to – to sup"!p\ort *him* 'with# in |this resp/ect# [Conversation] (6.5.1057)

Here the interactional character of such texts is reflected in personal pronouns indicating shared knowledge or situation-dependent reference. In addition, all adverbial antecedents of cause, headed by the noun *reason* (cf. Quirk *et al.* 1985: 1103–1106, 1255), are found in face-to-face conversation. This type of adverbial antecedent is entirely absent in -FACE texts, as in example (22).

(22) there's |abso'lutely :no *r\eason* # .
to |qu\estion # –
the sub|p/ort # . [Spontaneous oration] (11.4.618)

Adverbs in the relative infinitive complex signal syntactic elaboration of adjectival phrases, since the adverbs function as premodifiers of adjectives, as in (23)-(24).

(23) ⟨B⟩ it |may ((...)) |may sound a :*very* pe:culiar
⟨?⟩ *(– coughs)*
⟨(B)⟩ :point to m\/ake #
but if the |pr\emises {them|s\elves #}
{were im|pr\oved #} # – [Spontaneous conversation]
(3.3.498–500)

(24) |are we !free\ee [ə:] 'to [ə:] #
|draw up a *:rather* . ex!\iguous 'list # –
of |people to :\inter'view # – – [Spontaneous conversation]
(2.6.446–448)

It was suggested above that comparative adjectives in dialogue could be used for argumentative/persuasive purposes. Similarly, with adverbs in face-to-face conversation one could argue that a speaker has an option to elaborate an NP with either a comparative adjective, or an adjective phrase premodified by an amplifying adverb. Both options would serve related functions in discourse. Biber (1986b: 12) suggests that general adverbs not only tell us about facts but also about the interlocutor's attitudes. Thus, premodifying adverbs in the antecedent NP, as well as adverbial antecedents of cause ending in *reason* on the ±FACE dimension do not mark the +FACE texts as overly persuasive. Instead, it is rather the case that the zero frequencies of these two features in –FACE texts signal the nonpersuasive character of non-face-to-face conversation.

Texts marked –FACE have a larger frequency of numerals than +FACE. Lexical items marked as numerals do not include ordinals, since the latter have been tagged as superlatives (e. g. *first, last*, etc.) in line with Kjellmer (1975) and Quirk *et al.*'s "restrictive markers" (1985: 1269). Numerals seem to signal speech situations where more technical or abstract topics are discussed, as in sentence (25) below.

(25) setting 'up . !not /one # .
but |*tw*/*o* # –
|*two* !new f # etters # .
to be |placed up'on 'Scottish \ministry # . [Spontaneous oration] (11.5.229–232)

In addition, examples from –FACE include emphasizing expressions such as superlatives, as in (26).

(26) he'd |be the *!f**irst* 'man to to . to
|sort of . be:ware of :b\/ullshitting # [Telephone conversation] (7.2.552)

It is interesting to note that –FACE texts, which are partly made up of telephone conversations, have more locative antecedents; of (27) and (28).

Table 5.

	+ FACE	– FACE
Common nouns	51.7%	36.0%
Locative nouns	10.9%	22.0%
Numerals	4.0%	18.0%
Superlatives	3.7%	12.0%
Adverbials	7.5%	0
Possessives NPs	1.9%	0
N:	321	50

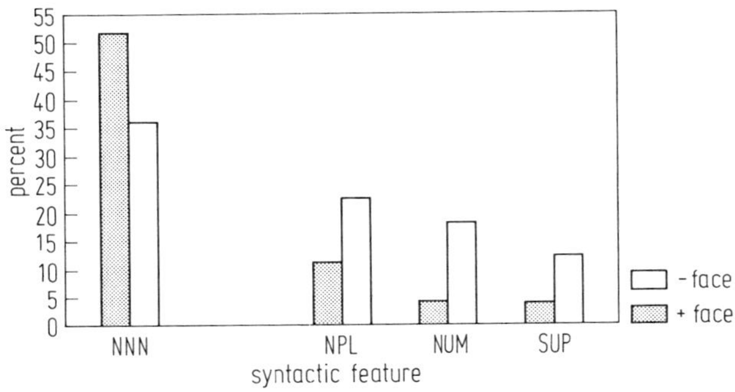

NNN = common nouns
NPL = locative antecedents
NUM = numerals
SUP = superlatives

Figure 4. Distribution of features in the LLC corpus across face-to-face and non-face-to-face texts

(27) it's |probably . [?] as [?] as !*good a 'place to 'meet* as: \/anywhere 'actually # [Telephone conversation] (7.3.1369)

(28) [? j] you |have my 'home addr/ess #
|that'd be *the 'place to s\end it* # [Telephone conversation] (8.3.856)

2.5. Private versus nonprivate conversation

Private texts consist of text categories 1 through 4, 5.8–11, text 6.2, and categories 7 though 9 (i. e. subgroups A to C in Table 3). Nonprivate texts include interviews, discussion, and oration. In Crystal and Davy's framework, the "status" dimension refers to levels of intimacy and formality (1969: 73–74). Nonprivate instances have more compound pronouns and passives. The higher proportion of compound pronouns which

Table 6.

	+ PRIV	– PRIV
Adjectives	33.8%	24.8%
Locative nouns	14.5%	8.8%
Compound pronouns	17.1%	28.5%
Passives	4.3%	10.9%
N:	234	137

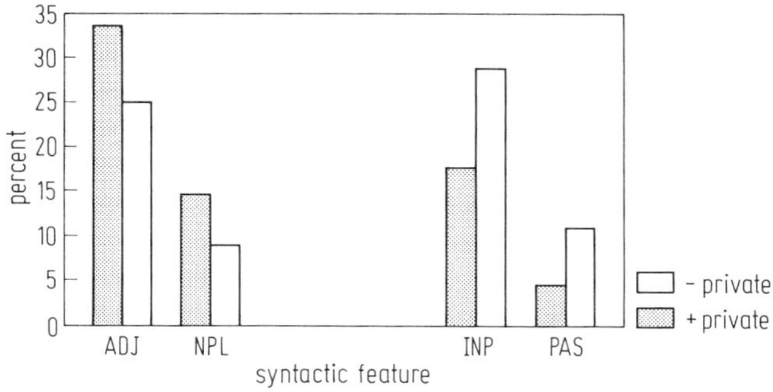

ADJ = adjectives
NPL = locative antecedents
INP = compound pronouns
PAS = passives

Figure 5. Distribution of features in the LLC corpus across private and nonprivate texts

are indefinite and inanimate expressions might signal narrative concerns. This would then imply that nonnarrative genres have more nouns with explicit reference. The private texts have more locative antecedents than nonprivate texts, which is a property that private texts share with -FACE texts.

In this connection I will also briefly discuss the surreptitious dimension. The surreptitious dimension is difficult to interpret. The surreptitious texts have more quantifiers and superlatives, whereas the nonsurreptitious texts have more compound pronouns as antecedents, as well as passives and *for*-subjects. However, it is practically identical to the ±private dimension, since the texts in subgroup B are only partially surreptitious (cf. Svartvik *et al.* 1982: 21, footnote 1). It is hard to find any special traits that mark this dimension as distinct from the private/nonprivate dimension.

2.6. Radio broadcasts

The texts included in radio commentary comprise text category 5, as well as 6.1, 6.3–6, all of text category 10, and 11.3 (i. e. subgroups D, and F to G in Table 3). This is a combination of Crystal and Davy's "modality" dimension (which deals with the purpose of a particular text) and "province" (the activity associated with a text) (1969: 71–75). The radio dimension is the only binary opposition where the "+" texts form a separate register (cf. Ferguson 1983, 1985).

Radio broadcasts, which include sports commentary, had high scores on compound pronouns. In this category we find all instances of relative infinitives with preposed prepositions followed by an overt *wh*-relativizer (cf. Kjellmer 1988), as in (29) and (30).

(29) and the |world 'therefore will :gradually be'come a :better place *in 'which* to l\ive# – [Radio broadcast] (5.7.918)

(30) we've got |two minutes l\eft *in which* to answer this :qu/estion# |Victor M\ishoon# [Radio broadcast] (5.4.1309)

Ferguson (1983) notes that in sports commentary infinitives function as syntactic markers of that register. In particular, he found adverbial infinitive clauses of result to be very common (cf. discussion of resultative infinitives in Quirk *et al.* 1985: 1079, Jespersen 1940: 256–258, Curme 1931: 307, and Mair 1990: 95, 203). Such adverbial clauses are also found in the LLC, and some of them are indistinguishable from relative infinitives, as in (31).

(31) and |so it's *a 'throw – to be 'taken by 'Willy M\organ#* [Sports commentary] (10.2.143)

Nonradio texts are marked by more adjectival premodification, and higher proportions of the topicalizing head noun *thing*, and manner adverbials in *way(s)*. It was suggested above that adverbs and comparatives in the antecedent could have persuasive functions in discourse. Relative infinitives with the topicalizing head noun *thing* could also be used in a similar way. In (32) the sentence with *the thing* allows an alternative to the pseudo-cleft construction, in that marked focus is on the subject complement (cf. Quirk *et al.* 1985: 1388-9).

(32) ⟨b⟩ *because* it's |just 'not
⟨a⟩ *|[=m]#*
⟨(b)⟩ *the :thing to !d\o#*
it's |not ac"!c\eptable# – [Conversation] (5.10.936)

Table 7.

	+ RADIO	– RADIO
Compound pronouns	29.2%	18.5%
Adjectives	24.0%	32.7%
Head noun *thing*	7.3%	13.5%
N:	96	275

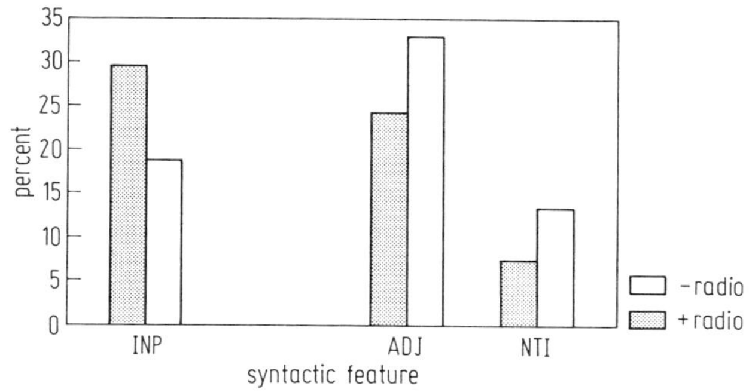

INP = compound pronouns
ADJ = adjectives
NTI = the head noun *thing*

Figure 6. Distribution of syntactic features in the LLC corpus across radio and nonradio texts

Here the phrase *the thing to do* means something like *the thing we/you/they should do*, with the modal expressing an obligational sense or desirability (cf. Quirk *et al.* 1985: 227). In (33)–(34) the adverbial relative infinitives in *way* express a speaker's attitudes toward an action.

(33) and |they say well !this was *the :qu\/ickest 'way {to dis|tr/ibute 'things#}#* [Spontaneous oration] (11.3.985)

(34) ⟨a⟩ which is *a ri"|d\iculous* *{|w\ay#}#
to ((sort of)) |start a 'conver!!s\ation#*
⟨b⟩ *|y\es#
((|quite#)) [Dialogue] (5.9.101)

If we accept the persuasive character of relative infinitives with the topicalizing noun *thing*, it makes perfect sense that radio texts have significantly lower proportions of this feature. This is confirmed by Biber (1988: 151), who found text types such as broadcasts to be markedly nonpersuasive and other spoken genres to be neutral as to this parameter.

The most striking property of the radio dimension is how stylistically unmarked it is; thus most features distribute evenly across this dimension. One would expect this genre to represent a relatively formal speech situation. The only indication that this is the case can be seen in the instances of preposed prepositions, as in (29)–(30) above.

3. Discussion

In the discussion of relative infinitives in writing I showed that compounds pronouns ending in *-body, -thing*, and *-one* are more frequent in fiction than in nonfiction. Thus, one would expect less formal speech events to have somewhat more compound pronouns than more formal speech. However, this is not the case. Instead, text samples that show the highest proportion of compound pronouns are classes marked by –PRIV and +RADIO, i. e. public oration and radio broadcasts. In other words, formal speech situations have more compound pronouns. Thus, although the nonfictional genres in writing are characterized by density of information reflected in higher number of nouns, the more formal genres in the spoken material do not pattern in the same way. It seems likely that it is narrative aspects of public oration and radio broadcasts that account for this difference.

As can be seen in example (10) above, the antecedents of relative infinitives in writing can be long and complex. There can be both premodifying phrases and postmodification in the form of prepositional phrases. In speech, however, we tend to find premodification and postmodification in more or less complementary distribution.

I also argued that samples having zero frequencies of a particular feature could be regarded as being of special interest. Two frequent syntactic features were absent in some dimensions. These were comparative adjectives in the monologue material, and premodifying adverbs in non-face-to-face conversation. In both cases it was possible to find a tentative explanation for the loading of a feature on just one dimension. I argued that these two syntactic features, together with the topicalizing noun *thing*, have argumentative/persuasive functions in discourse. We find further support for this hypothesis when we note that many relative infinitives can be given modal interpretations. Indeed, Biber (1988) found that argumentative texts with high scores on modals also had high scores on infinitives, i. e. modals and infinitives are correlated. Consequently, what we see here is another set of features having "overt expression of persuasion" (Biber 1988) and also how this set varies across textual dichotomies.

Note

1. The research was supported by generous grants from Uppsala University. I would like to thank Ingegerd Bäcklund, Gunnel Tottie, and Mats Rydén for helpful comments on previous versions of this paper.

References

Aarts, Jan – Willem Meijs (eds.)
1986 *Corpus linguistics II.* Amsterdam: Rodopi.

Biber, Douglas
1986 a "Spoken and written textual dimensions in English: Resolving the contradictory findings", *Language* 62: 384–414.
1986 b "On the investigation of spoken/written differences", *Studia Linguistica* 40: 1–21.
1988 *Variation across speech and writing.* Cambridge: Cambridge University Press.

Biber, Douglas – Edward Finegan
1986 "An initial typology of English text types", in: Jan Aarts – Willem Meijs (eds.), 19–46.

Curme, George C.
1931 *A grammar of the English language. Vol III: Syntax.* Boston: Heath.

Crystal, David — Derek Davy
1969 *Investigating English style*. London: Longman.
Dillon, William R. — Matthew Goldstein
1984 *Multivariate analysis. Methods and applications*. New York: Wiley.
Ferguson, Charles A.
1983 "Sports announcer talk: Syntactic aspects of register variation", *Language and Society* 12: 153—172.
1985 "Editor's introduction", *Discourse Processes* 8: 391—394.
Jespersen, Otto
1940 *A modern English grammar on historical principles. Part V*. Copenhagen: Eijnar Munksgaard.
Kjellmer, Göran
1975 "Are relative infinitives modal?", *Studia Neophilologica* 47: 323—332.
1988 "'What a night on which to die!' On symmetry in English relative clauses", *English Studies* 69: 559—568.
Mair, Christian
1990 *Infinitival complement clauses in English*. Cambridge: Cambridge University Press.
Quirk, Randolph — Sidney Greenbaum — Geoffrey Leech — Jan Svartvik
1985 *A comprehensive grammar of the English language*. London: Longman.
Svartvik, Jan — Mats Eeg-Olofsson — Oscar Forsheden — Bengt Oreström
1982 *Survey of spoken English. Report on research 1975—81*. (Lund studies in English 63.) Lund: Gleerup.
Tottie, Gunnel
1983 *Much about 'not' and 'nothing'. A study of the variation between analytic and synthetic negation in comtemporary American English*. (Scripta Minora 1983—1984: 1.) Lund: CWK Gleerup.

Who(m)? Case marking of wh-pronouns in written British and American English[1]

Edgar W. Schneider

1. Introduction

The variability of the case marking patterns of English wh-pronouns, i. e. the use of *who* for *whom* and the choice between *whose* and *of which*, poses a variety of interesting questions. Diachronically, the replacement of *whom* by the uninflected form *who* is in line with the proposed development of English from a largely synthetic to a predominantly analytic language (Sapir 1921). Synchronically, the result of this process is a relatively unstable situation, a modern usage problem under the impact of prescriptivism. Similarly, in the genitive synthetic *whose* and analytic *of which* are in paradigmatic relationship, with the choice of either form being governed by a number of constraints that have not been fully investigated as yet.

What makes the feature of the case marking of wh-pronouns so interesting from a variationist point of view is that there is a certain amount of variation and one can observe change to have occurred, and possibly to be still going on. The replacement of *whom* by uninflected *who* began at the beginning of the Early Modern English period and has been progressing for several centuries. Sapir (1921: 167) predicted the disappearance of *whom* "within a couple of hundred years", and indeed, the form is marginalized today, restricted to certain conditions both structurally and stylistically. In the case of the genitive, it is not even clear whether any change is going on, and if so, in which direction. *Whose* clearly is the original form which began to be replaced by analytic *of which* in the EModE period, which corresponds to the other developments from synthetic to analytic. However, for the recent period the feeling is that *whose* has been gaining ground again, especially if it is referring to nonhuman antecedents.[2]

The present paper adds a further dimension to the study of variation and change in the English wh-pronouns. It investigates whether or to what extent the two major national varieties of the language, British

English and American English, might differ in their uses of these forms. It will be suggested that although there is of course a solid "common core" of the grammar of English slight differences do exist under very specific conditions.

2. Variability in the system of wh-pronouns

To lay the foundation, here is a brief look at what modern grammars have to say on the use of *whom/who* and *whose/of which*. It is interesting that there are very few categorical statements; indeed, descriptors of vagueness such as "tendency", "often", or "preferred" are commonly used to describe the situation. As to the *whom/who* distinction, there are two things on which there seems to be general agreement. First, both forms are clearly distinguished stylistically, with *whom* being the formal and/or written variant and *who* its colloquial and spoken counterpart (although grammars disagree as to which of these forms is to be regarded as the more "fundamental" or normal one).[3] Second, a preposition that governs and immediately precedes the wh-form demands inflected *whom* almost invariably,[4] yet this construction is quite formal and usually replaced in spoken English by a stranded preposition in clause-final position, in which case both forms of the wh-word are possible (although the inflected form is said to be rare, presumably due to the informal character of the syntactic construction). Swan (1980: 135) believes that the replacement of *whom* by *who* occurs "especially in questions", with *whom* being infrequent in relative clauses anyway (due to the preference of zero or *that*) but the required form if the clause is "non-identifying", something, however, which constitutes an uncommon clause type in informal English. In the case of *whose/of which*, it is stated that *whose* may have both personal and nonpersonal antecedents, although for the latter group "there is a certain reluctance to use *whose*" (Quirk *et al.* 1985: 366). It can be avoided by using *of which*, yet this "involves stylistic difficulty", because this construction is "stiffly formal and cumbersome" (1985: 1249).[5] The competition between both constructions is restricted to those cases in which the function to be expressed is that of a possessive determiner, for *whose* cannot be used as a non-possessive equivalent of *of* + NP.

The paradigmatic relationship between *who* and *whom* in nonsubject function is a usage problem affected by a discrepancy between prescriptivist traditions and actual linguistic practice, and many native speakers are well aware of this tension.[6] Sarah Thomason, herself a distinguished linguist and the editor of the journal *Language*, recalls that her personal usage changed consciously: She "grew up (either from birth or from early schooling) with a fully internalized rule of *who/whom* usage that matched the literary standard rule: *who* as subject only, *whom* as object or oblique case, regardless of its position in the sentence", but by "the age of thirty, the spreading colloquial usage of sentence-initial *who* regardless of case ... began to interfere with her original rule", and ultimately "she dropped sentence-initial *whom* altogether in speaking and now conforms consistently to the colloquial usage except in formal prose." (Thomason – Kaufman 1988: 44 – 45).

The use of wh-pronouns is certainly not one of the areas in which British English (BrE) and American English (AmE) usage have been found to be different; nor is there even suspicion that this might be the case. Standard sources and grammars do not point out any such disparity. Kirchner (1970) mentions the frequent use of what he calls "accusative *who*" in AmE, both in interrogative (page 310) and in relative clauses (page 312); in the latter case, he adds the remark that "Die Objektform *who* wird AE häufiger verwendet als BE, bes. in der Umgangssprache." As to *whose*, he states that it is "im gesprochenen AE sehr selten" (page 314), especially in relative clauses and less so in interrogatives. John Algeo, who has recently been undertaking a comprehensive comparison of BrE and AmE, does not list any wh-forms in his recent publications (e. g. in Algeo 1988) but has pointed out that usage differences can be of a very subtle and, as he calls it, "unobtrusive" (Algeo 1989: 162) nature.

3. Methodological procedure of the present study

My point of departure and the original motivation for selecting this topic for study was a fairly accidental observation, namely the fact that there is a statistically significant frequency difference of *whom* in the Brown and LOB corpora, as given in the word frequency list by Hofland – Johansson (1982: 541). According to this source, *whom* occurs 219 times in LOB and 146 times in Brown, something which yields a difference coefficient in favor of BrE of 0.20[7] and an extremely high significance level of .001. In the case of *whose*, the ratio is 301 to 252, with a difference coefficient of 0.09 and significance at the 5% level. Therefore, it seemed worth trying to find out what this difference is based on: Are there any particular conditions under which BrE uses the inflected form more frequently, or is there any indication that BrE exhibits a generally more conservative character in this respect? The study is in line with various others that compare BrE and AmE as represented by Brown and LOB in various ways, e. g. Jahr (1981) on the nominal genitive, Krogvig — Johansson (1981) on *shall/will* usage, Meijs (1984) on elliptic structures, Johansson — Norheim (1988) on the subjunctive, Schneider (1988, especially vol. 2: 377 — 380) on mental verbs, Mindt — Weber (1989) on prepositions, etc.

Methodologically, the procedure employed can be regarded as a form of "problem-oriented tagging" (de Haan 1984). All occurrences of the forms *whom*, *who* (in other than subject functions), *whose*, and *of which* (in functions that are equivalent to possessive/genitive *whose*, i. e. not in partitive constructions and not in other chance combinations of *of* and *which*)[8] from the Brown and LOB corpora have been coded for a number of potentially influential factors that may contribute to the choice of either form in either of the paradigmatic pairs. The database management system R:BASE for DOS was used to store this information in a table with the following text columns: form; corpus; source of citation; genre; clause type (interrogative or relative); clause subtype (main/subordinate if interrogative, defining or nondefining if relative); syntactic function of wh-form within its clause (for *who/whom* only: direct object or prepositional complement; for *whose/of which*, this column was used to store information concerning whether the position of the wh-form was pre- or postnominal); preposition (if PrepC); placement of preposition (if PrepC: before or after wh-NP); and category of reference noun (human or nonhuman). For the analysis, I first used the respective commands provided by R:BASE to produce counts and crosstabulations of various categories. Second, contingency tables produced by the CROSSTAB command were submitted to the chi-square test for independence of the two factors involved.[9] Third, if possible, I used appropriate R:BASE commands (in particular, PROJECT and CHANGE) to transform sections of the database to the data input format required by the sociolinguistic program package VARBRUL, and ran a VARBRUL analysis of the data (for an introduction to this program, see Montgomery 1990). This program has the advantage of performing a regression analysis that calculates the extent to which any individual factor contributes toward the observed data structure, i. e. the distribution of the variants of a dependent variable. However, knockout factors must be excluded in this program, and absolute frequencies should not be too low, so in the given context a VARBRUL analysis could only be carried out for *whose* vs. *of which* and a limited set of two factors.

4. *Who* vs. *whom*

4.1. General constraints

With the given materials, the study of the relationship between *who* and *whom* suffers from a major problem, namely the fact that the corpora consist only of written and even printed texts. This results in a surprisingly low number of occurrences of uninflected *who*. With only two occurrences in Brown and only eight in LOB, absolute frequencies are too low for a detailed analysis of the use of nonsubject *who*.

Table 1 summarizes the factors that might have some influence on the choice of *whom* or *who*. No significant regional preference for either form could be found. Not surprisingly, the only constraint whose impact can be clearly proven is the different stylistic quality. With an error chance of less than .1 per cent, *who* comes up more regularly in the fictional text types (K – R), as opposed to the stylistically superordinate information-centered genres (A – J, though it does occur in these as well). Clause type clearly plays a major role, although the calculation of chi-square is blocked by Cochran's restrictions on low expected frequencies. Uninflected *who* is promoted by interrogative clauses, especially if they are subordinate rather than main clauses. The syntactic role of the wh-form within its clause as a direct object or a prepositional complement cannot be shown to have any impact upon the choice of either form, but if the wh-word is a prepositional complement it is clear that the stranding of the preposition is the factor which most strongly leads to the uninflected form *who*, while an immediately preceding preposition categorically demands case marking.

Table 1. Constraints on the use of *who* or *whom*

	who	*whom*	total	chi-sq (sig.)
corpus				
Brown	2 (1%)	144 (99%)	146	
LOB	8 (4%)	219 (96%)	227	0.86 (ns)
genre				
A–J	3 (1%)	300 (99%)	303	
K–R	7 (10%)	63 (90%)	70	14.41 (***)
clause type				
int	8 (32%)	17 (68%)	25	
rel	2 (1%)	346 (99%)	348	X
subtype (int)				
main	3 (21%)	11 (79%)	14	
sub	5 (45%)	6 (55%)	11	X
syntactic function				
Odir	5 (4%)	120 (96%)	125	
PrepC	5 (2%)	243 (98%)	248	0.61 (ns)
position of prep.				
before wh	0 (0%)	239 (100%)	239	
stranded	5 (56%)	4 (44%)	9	X
total	10 (3%)	363 (97%)	373	

4.2. Regional influences on the use of *whom*

Tables 2 and 3 display the results of an investigation to establish whether the possibility of any regional preference for the form *whom* in restricted conditions exists, i. e. the individual crosstabs test the assumption of statistical independence between the two corpora on one axis of the matrix and the options of various constraints on the other.

Table 2 discloses surprisingly strong regional preferences of the form *whom* in just a few specific genres. The chi-square values for individual genres are based upon a juxtaposition of the respective genre with the sum total of all the others. Only two of these distributions are statistically significant, but these associations are extremely strong: in AmE *whom* is the dominant choice in religious writing (genre D), while in BrE it is typically favored in category H, which consists mostly of government documents. The correlation between genre G (belles lettres, biography, essays) and BrE fails the conventional five-per-cent level of significance by only a narrow margin and would be significant with an accepted ten

Table 2. Use of *whom* by corpus and genre

	Brown	LOB	total	chi-sq (sig.)
A	8 (42%)	11 (58%)	19	0.00 (ns)
B	9 (50%)	9 (50%)	18	0.45 (ns)
C	7 (29%)	17 (71%)	24	0.73 (ns)
D	11 (100%)	0 (0%)	11	14.75 (***)
E	2 (50%)	2 (50%)	4	X
F	17 (38%)	28 (62%)	45	0.01 (ns)
G	51 (47%)	58 (53%)	109	2.89 (ns/*)
H	3 (10%)	26 (90%)	29	10.03 (**)
J	13 (32%)	28 (68%)	41	0.88 (ns)
K	8 (44%)	10 (56%)	18	0.03 (ns)
L	3 (30%)	7 (70%)	10	0.09 (ns)
M	2 (50%)	2 (50%)	4	X
N	1 (20%)	4 (80%)	5	X
P	5 (31%)	11 (69%)	16	0.20 (ns)
R	4 (40%)	6 (60%)	10	0.09 (ns)
total	144 (40%)	219 (60%)	363	28.10 (*)

per cent error likelihood. All other genre distributions are apparently haphazard, but the impact of these constraints is strong enough to render the overall patterning of genres by corpora significant at the 5-per-cent level (chi-square = 28.10, at 14 degrees of freedom). It is interesting to observe, however, that these regional preferences are obviously restricted to the individual text genres, for there is no difference in the overall stylistic marking. The distributions are clearly insignificant if corpora are calculated by category groups as established by Hofland–Johansson (1982: 12), with A–C, D–H, J, and K–R summarized (chi-square = 1.45 at 3 df), and also for corpora by general text types (A–J vs. K–R; chi-square = 0.17).

Table 3 discloses a strongly significant regional correlation for clause types. In particular, occurrences of *whom* in interrogative clauses tend to be in the AmE corpus; also, its frequency in relative clauses in BrE is slightly above average. Tendencies as to subtype preferences can also be established. Main interrogative clauses are more common in Brown and subordinate ones in LOB (but the low overall frequency does not permit the calculation of chi-square), and there is a prevalence of defining relative clauses in LOB, as opposed to nondefining ones in Brown (but the likelihood that this distribution is due to chance is 10 per cent).

Table 3. Use of *whom* by corpus and clause type

	Brown	LOB	total	chi-sq (sig.)
clause type				
int	13 (76%)	4 (24%)	17	
rel	131 (38%)	215 (62%)	346	8.54 (**)
subtype (int)				
main	9 (82%)	2 (18%)	11	
sub	4 (67%)	2 (33%)	6	X
subtype (rel)				
def	58 (33%)	119 (67%)	177	
nondef	73 (43%)	96 (57%)	169	3.56 (ns/*)

The other factors do not display any regional distribution. The syntactic functions of direct object and prepositional complement are evenly distributed in Brown and LOB (chi-square = 0.00; ns), as are prepositional positions, with two stranded ones in each corpus (and chi-square being impossible to calculate). The occurrences of individual prepositions with a total of at least five attestations have also been tabulated, and a few observations can be made. With *for, from, in, of, with,* and the remaining group of all others taken together, the distributions as cross-tabulated by the two corpora are insignificant, chi-squares varying between 0.11 and 0.99. The frequencies of *among, by* and *on* are too low for the calculation of chi-square, but their distributions are inconspicuous. There is only one preposition that behaves strangely, namely *to*. Out of the total set of its occurrences, 29 per cent (n = 14) are in Brown but 71 per cent (35) appear in LOB, as opposed to the 40 to 60 per cent ratio of prepositions with *whom* overall (97–146), implying that *to* is more common in collocation with *whom* in BrE, with a probability of 10 per cent of this being a chance outcome, i. e. somewhat too high to accept the result as convincing proof.

5. *Whose* vs. *of which*

5.1. General constraints

In the case of the *whose* vs. *of which* relationship (see Table 4), there are two so-called knockout constraints, i. e. environments in which one variant is not found at all, but statistical evaluation shows them to be of unequal status. Human antecedents require *whose* without exception, and of course this distribution is highly significant. In the corpora, *of which* is also not found in interrogative clauses, which is an obvious syntactic constraint, but the low number of such clauses does not permit this restriction to be fully established with the required degree of statistical significance. Similarly, there is a slight correlation between *whose* and defining relative clauses and *of which* and nondefining ones, respectively, but it fails to reach the conventional significance level. The same degree of almost-but-not-quite significance can be found with some genre associations, with informative prose (D – H) selecting *of which* but fiction (K – R), especially adventures (N) and love stories (P), having *whose* at rates above the average.

5.2. Regional influences on the use of *whose* and *of which*

The conditioning of *whose* and *of which* by corpora and clause subtype was the only area in this study where a VARBRUL regressional analysis could be sensibly carried out. The program selects subtype as the primary and only significant factor, with nondefining clauses promoting the "application value", the form *of which*, at a rate of .54 (which may vary between zero and 1; "defining" has .46, i. e. it slightly disfavors this form). Among the two corpora, LOB influences *of which* with .53, whereas Brown slightly inhibits it at a rate of .47, but this factor is rated insignificant. This evaluation corresponds to the first section of Table 4, the crosstabulation of the two forms by the two corpora, which also rates the relationship between both sides as such that the null hypothesis of independence cannot be rejected.

Thus, it will not come as a surprise that the individual studies of the two forms for regional preferences under specific conditions have not yielded significant results. Still, there are a few patterns that are noteworthy and come fairly close to the level of statistical confirmation. As

Table 4. Constraints on the use of *whose* or *of which*

	whose	*of which*	total	chi-sq (sig.)
corpus				
Brown	252 (76%)	78 (24%)	330	
LOB	301 (71%)	122 (29%)	423	2.32 (ns)
clause type				
int	12 (100%)	0 (0%)	12	
rel	541 (73%)	200 (27%)	741	3.14 (ns/*)
subtype (rel)				
def	237 (77%)	71 (23%)	308	
nondef	304 (70%)	129 (30%)	433	3.81 (ns/*)
category of referent				
human	360 (100%)	0 (0%)	360	
nonhuman	193 (49%)	200 (51%)	393	246.86 (***)
selected genres				
N	13 (100%)	0 (0%)	13	3.50 (ns/*)
P	19 (95%)	1 (5%)	20	3.83 (ns/*)
category groups				
A–C	111 (78%)	31 (22%)	142	
D–H	263 (69%)	117 (31%)	380	
J	98 (77%)	30 (23%)	128	
K–R	81 (79%)	22 (21%)	103	6.33 (ns/*)
total	553 (73%)	200 (27%)	753	

Table 5 indicates, *whose* is more common in genres E (skills, trades, and hobbies) and R (humor) in AmE, and N (adventure and western fiction) in BrE. However, it does not show regional preferences as to text type in general, clause type, subtype of relative clause, or category of referent – in these respects, BrE and AmE behave quite identically. Equally, in the case of *of which* (see Table 6), the difference between the two leading national varieties of English does not play a role with respect to text type identification, nor to its syntactic positioning before or after its head noun – in this regard, the percentage distributions are identical. There are two distributions, however, that in nine out of ten cases cannot be considered to be chance patterns, namely the prevalence of *of which* in genre K in Brown and in defining relative clauses in AmE but nondefining ones in BrE.

Table 5. Use of *whose* by corpus and various other factors

	Brown	LOB	total	chi-sq (sig.)
selected genres				
D	9 (33%)	18 (67%)	27	1.23 (ns)
E	14 (67%)	7 (33%)	21	3.08 (ns/*)
F	32 (54%)	27 (46%)	59	1.63 (ns)
G	60 (52%)	55 (48%)	115	2.22 (ns)
H	14 (34%)	27 (66%)	41	1.86 (ns)
J	39 (40%)	59 (60%)	98	1.33 (ns)
N	2 (15%)	11 (85%)	13	3.72 (ns/*)
R	8 (80%)	2 (20%)	10	3.56 (ns/*)
text type				
A–J	218 (46%)	254 (54%)	472	
K–R	34 (42%)	47 (58%)	81	0.30 (ns)
clause type				
int	4 (33%)	8 (67%)	12	
rel	248 (46%)	293 (54%)	541	0.32 (ns)
subtype (rel)				
def	104 (44%)	133 (56%)	237	
nondef	144 (47%)	160 (53%)	304	0.52 (ns)
category of referent				
human	158 (44%)	202 (56%)	360	
nonhuman	94 (49%)	99 (51%)	193	0.99 (ns)
total	252 (46%)	301 (54%)	553	

Table 6. Use of *of which* by corpus and various other factors

	Brown	LOB	total	chi-sq (sig.)
selected genres				
G	16 (33%)	33 (67%)	49	0.77 (ns)
J	13 (43%)	17 (57%)	30	0.11 (ns)
K	7 (70%)	3 (30%)	10	2.99 (ns/*)
R	3 (60%)	2 (40%)	5	X
text type				
A–J	68 (38%)	110 (62%)	178	
K–R	10 (45%)	12 (55%)	22	0.18 (ns)
clause subtype (rel)				
def	34 (48%)	37 (52%)	71	
nondef	44 (34%)	85 (66%)	129	3.10 (ns/*)
syntactic function				
attr	38 (39%)	59 (61%)	97	
post-N	40 (39%)	63 (61%)	103	0.00 (ns)
total	78 (39%)	122 (61%)	200	

6. Conclusion

The results can be summarized as follows. The uninflected form *who* comes up significantly more frequently in the fictional text types (K – R) than in the information-centered ones (A – J), and is also clearly promoted by preposition stranding and by interrogative clauses, especially if they are subordinate. Regionally, the form *whom* is significantly more common in Brown than in LOB in religious writing (genre D), and, reversely, is significantly favored by category H in the British corpus. Regional preferences of *whom* in particular clause types include a tendency to occur more regularly in interrogative clauses, especially if they are main clauses, in AmE and in relative clauses in BrE, especially when they are defining. Among the genitive forms, *of which*, as opposed to *whose*, is of course blocked with human antecedents, practically restricted to relative clauses, and more common in nondefining clauses. It is favored by informative prose (genres D – H) but disfavored by fiction texts (K – R, esp. N and P). Regional preferences for the use of *whose* or *of which* are slight. They include an association of *whose* with genres E (skills, trades and hobbies) and R (humor) in AmE but N (adventure) in BrE; an association of *of which* with K (general fiction) in Brown; and raised frequencies of *of which* in defining relative clauses in AmE as opposed to nondefining relative clauses in BrE.

Thus, I feel that what started out as an isolated observation of a figure in the book by Hofland – Johansson and turned into a kind of fishing in the mud for emerging correlations has ended with at least a few small fish on my hook. In many, in fact most respects of this fairly subtle area of grammar, British and American English behave identically, of course. The point is, however, that the conventional belief in a supranationally uniform grammatical core of English, to which the wh-forms certainly belong, should entail that no differences at all are to be found in this respect – but then there are a few regional preferences even in small corners where no one would have expected them to be hiding. That is not to say that differences between BrE and AmE should be exaggerated; the majority of tests have not shown any difference and thus confirmed the far-reaching homogeneity of the language. The very fact that some such differences have been disclosed, however, is noteworthy, because it is clearly unexpected. Extrapolating from Algeo's (1989) observations, it can be stated that the diversity of the two major varieties of English appears to be further-reaching in scope but subtler in kind than might have been suspected.

Notes

1. The present paper is part of a more comprehensive project with the aim of studying variation and change in the loss of the case marking of wh-pronouns. A comparable analysis for the initial stages of this process has been carried out in Schneider (forthc.).
2. See, for example, Lamprecht (1984: 144): "Zunehmend wird *whose* auch (besonders im Schrift-Engl.) in bezug auf Sachen verwendet, um das gewöhnlich schwerfällige *of which* zu vermeiden".
3. See Quirk – Greenbaum (1973: 106, 379) and Lamprecht (1984: 135 – 137).
4. According to Quirk *et al.* (1985: 368), "The further theoretical possibility does not occur, namely *who* following the preposition." The form *to who* is marked as ungrammatical by an asterisk, the "stylistic incompatibility" between the formality of the construction and the informality of the form being given as the reason for this (similarly page 1249).
5. In addition, "in some fields of discourse such as mathematics, no evasion is felt to be necessary: ... a triangle *whose sides*..." (Quirk *et al.* 1985: 1250).
6. Quirk *et al.* (1985: 14) actually cite this problem as the model case when discussing the issue of prescriptivism and its practical consequences. Walsh – Walsh (1989) attempt to explain the variability of *who/whom* as interference between a "prescriptive rule" and a "descriptive rule".
7. This coefficient is calculated by the difference of both raw frequencies of a word (LOB – Brown) divided by the sum of their frequencies, and varies between +1 and –1.
8. As in *a car ... out of which stepped...* (LOB K08, 16) or *Many another poem could I speak of which sang itself into my heart* (LOB G22, 126).
9. In the tables below, significance levels are conventionally indicated as follows:
   ns: "not significant at $p < 0.05$";
   ns/*: "not significant; sig. at $p < 0.1$";
   *: "significant at $p < 0.05$";
   **: "significant at $p < 0.01$";
   ***: "significant at $p < 0.001$";
   X: "chi-square must not be calculated because of Cochran's restrictions".
   Chi-square was calculated with Yate's correction. The calculation and use of the chi-square statistic is explained in most statistics handbooks and introductions: see, for example, Woods – Fletcher – Hughes (1986: 132 ff.).

References

Aarts, Jan – Willem Meijs (eds.)
1984 *Corpus linguistics. Recent developments in the use of computer corpora in English language research.* Amsterdam: Rodopi.

Algeo, John
1988 "British and American grammatical differences", *International Journal of Lexicography* 1: 1 – 31.

1989 "Queueing and other idiosyncracies", *World Englishes* 8: 157–163.

Haan, Pieter de
1984 "Problem-oriented tagging of English corpus data", in: Jan Aarts – Willem Meijs (eds.), 123–139.

Hofland, Knut – Stig Johansson
1982 *Word frequencies in British and American English.* Bergen: The Norwegian Computing Centre for the Humanities.

Jahr, Mette-Cathrine
1981 "The *s*-genitive with non-personal nouns in present-day British and American English", *ICAME News* 5: 14–31.

Johansson, Stig – Else Helene Norheim
1988 "The subjunctive in British and American English", *ICAME Journal* 12: 27–36.

Kirchner, Gustav
1970 *Die syntaktischen Eigentümlichkeiten des amerikanischen Englisch.* 2 vols. München: Hueber.

Kretzschmar, William A., Jr. – Edgar W. Schneider – Ellen Johnson (eds.)
1990 *Computer methods in dialectology.* (*Journal of English Linguistics*, Special Issue 22.1.) Athens, Georgia.

Krogvig, Inger – Stig Johansson
1981 "*Shall, will, should* and *would* in British and American English", *ICAME News* 5: 32–56.

Lamprecht, Adolf
1984 *Grammatik der englischen Sprache.* (5th edition.) Berlin: Verlag Volk und Wissen.

Meijs, Willem
1984 "'You can do so if you want to' – Some elliptic structures in Brown and LOB and their syntactic description", in: Jan Aarts – Willem Meijs (eds.), 141–162.

Mindt, Dieter – Christel Weber
1989 "Prepositions in American and British English", *World Englishes* 8: 229–238.

Montgomery, Michael
1990 "Introduction to variable rule analysis", in: William A. Kretzschmar, Jr. – Edgar W. Schneider – Ellen Johnson (eds.), 111–118.

Quirk, Randolph – Sidney Greenbaum
1973 *A University Grammar of English.* London: Longman.

Quirk, Randolph – Sidney Greenbaum – Geoffrey Leech – Jan Svartvik
1985 *A comprehensive grammar of English.* London–New York: Longman.

Sapir, Edward
1921 *Language. An introduction to the study of speech.* New York: Harcourt, Brace Jovanovich.

Schneider, Edgar W.
1988 *Variabilität, Polysemie und Unschärfe der Wortbedeutung.* Vol. I: *Theoretische und methodologische Grundlagen.* Vol. II: *Studien zur lexikalischen Semantik der mentalen Verben des Englischen.* Tübingen: Niemeyer.
forthc. "Who(m)? Constraints on the loss of case marking of wh-pronouns in the English of Shakespeare and other poets of the Early Modern English period",

to appear in: Matti Rissannen *et al.* (eds.), *English Historical Linguistics Papers from the Sixth International Conference, Helsinki, May 1990*. Berlin: Mouton de Gruyter.

Swan, Michael
1980 *Practical English Usage*. Oxford: University Press.

Thomason, Sarah Grey – Terrence Kaufman
1988 *Language contact, creolization, and genetic linguistics*. Berkeley: University of California Press.

Walsh, Thomas – Natasha Walsh
1989 "Patterns of *who/whom* usage", *American Speech* 64: 284–286.

Woods, Anthony – Paul Fletcher – Arthur Hughes
1986 *Statistics in language studies*. Cambridge: Cambridge University Press.

Discourse category and text type classification: Procedural discourse in the Brown and the LOB corpora[1]

Kay Wikberg

1. Introduction

1.1. Text classification: general remarks

Text selection and text classification are major problems in corpus linguistics. The reasons for this are obvious. On the one hand, the textual universe is infinite, on the other hand, there are numerous ways of classifying texts.

When the Brown Corpus was put together in the early 1960s, text theory was not even in its infancy. Since then, however, research in text linguistics and discourse analysis has given us a body of knowledge which throws new light on text classification. Such knowledge can be useful if one wants to compile new corpora, or it may help to understand how available corpora are composed.

For this paper I shall have to make a shortcut through the enormous literature on text types. This is simply necessary in order to get down to examining actual texts and specific data, which is what is primarily needed in corpus linguistics. Even so, I hope to be able to demonstrate that it may be worth while paying more attention to text classification when compiling corpora.

Dimter (1985: 224) makes the point that "A scientific classification is only justified in that it enables and stimulates further generalizations about the individual classes." Theoretically one could define a text type as a group of texts which share a cluster of linguistic features which occur with a significantly different frequency compared with some other group of texts. An example of such a text-internal approach to discourse is Biber's observation that the past tense clusters significantly with perfect aspect and 3rd person pronouns in narrative texts (Biber 1988: 135). But he also demonstrates that one may need to use quite a number of linguistic features in order to arrive at a safe classification of "textual dimensions".

In this paper a distinction will be made between "discourse category" and "text type". "Discourse category" (German "Texttyp") will be used as a superordinate concept to include descriptive, narrative, expository, argumentative, and procedural (or instructive), all of which refer to the function of the text and which therefore also imply an implicit addressee. The term "text type" (German "Textsorte") will be used to refer to concrete manifestations of such discourse, such as novel, editorial, manual, letter, recipe, sermon, and so forth.

1.2. Text classification in the Brown and the LOB corpora

As everybody knows, the selection of the categories in the Brown and the LOB corpora was made by stratified random sampling from bibliographical sources (cf. Francis – Kučera 1979). Because of the relatively large number of texts this ensured coverage of a wide range of text types. It is not surprising that in the two major machine-readable corpora available, the categories represent a number of different selection principles.

The term "text category" as used in Brown and LOB is intermediate between "discourse category" and "text type" as used here. Thus, if you examine the "text categories" in Brown and LOB, the following fictional genres are traditionally looked upon as narrative

K	General fiction
L	Mystery and detective fiction
M	Science fiction
N	Adventure and western fiction
P	Romance and love story

Press reportage (category A) would also be narrative although it differs from fiction in dealing with actual events. By comparison, B (press editorials) and C (press reviews) would primarily be argumentative whereas G (belles lettres, biography, essay), J (learned and scientific writings) and D (religion) would be expository, in part argumentative.

However, such crude labelling is not much help unless supplemented with specific linguistic and situational criteria, which allow us to do multi-feature and multi-dimensional analysis. The most interesting linguistic analysis along these lines so far is Biber (1988). A combination of linguistic and situational parameters has been proposed as a way of classifying texts for the International Corpus of English (cf. Leitner 1990).

What then is the relation between "genre", "discourse category" and "text type"«? Genres are traditional categories rooted in the study of literature. When using the term "genre", it is important to distinguish it from "text type". Brown – Yule (1983), for example, use "genre" throughout to stand for any text type whereas Biber (1988: 70) reserves the term "genre" for "categorizations assigned on the basis of external criteria" such as "the relation between the communicative participants, the relation of the participants to the external context, and the relation of the participants to the text itself". By contrast, "text type" would then "refer to groupings of texts that are similar with respect to their linguistic form, irrespective of genre categories".

If one looks at the contribution of various situational and contextual parameters to text classification, discourse topic is not particularly useful as a criterion. If the aim is to go beyond the recording of lexical items, discourse topic hardly qualifies as a serious candidate for scientific classification on its own. It is usually combined with purpose and with setting (cf. Biber 1988: 32), which is some guarantee that the text is put in a pragmatic perspective. We shall come back to Category E (skills, trades and hobbies) below to say more about its standing as "procedural discourse".

The problem of cross-classification arises with most texts in a number of ways. It is clear that Category E is made up of a number of different text types such as manuals and guide books. It also contains editorials, the main difference in relation to Category B being the discourse topic (such as farming in LOB-E37 and LOB-E38).

Finally, purpose stands out as an important situational criterion for classification. It relates to the five traditional discourse categories already mentioned, and seems to be particularly relevant for procedural discourse. Smith (1985: 242) uses the term "discourse framework" to refer to "the composite of a writer's attitudes and purpose with respect to his or her topic and audience, as well as the particular situation (linguistic and extralinguistic) in which the text is produced". According to Smith (1985: 245), it is in relation to such a framework that one should interpret the significance of particular linguistic features. Although procedural discourse often overlaps with descriptive or even expository discourse in terms of discourse topic, the discourse framework can be used to explain how it relates to the situational context.

2. Category E in the Brown and the LOB corpora

The best known text categories in the Brown and the LOB corpora are probably Category J ("learned and scientific writings") and the imaginative prose categories (K – R). By comparison, a category which has not attracted much attention in corpus studies is Category E, "skills, trades, and hobbies".[2] Hofland & Johansson (1982) demonstrate that there is a very high rank correlation between Category J and Category E as far as the 89 most frequent words are concerned.

Browsing in the texts of Category E, I noted that the texts left quite a mixed impression, which made me decide to have a closer look at Category E to find out how representative it is as a discourse category. Procedural discourse is growing in importance, not least because of developments in technology and the need to instruct ordinary human beings how to do complex things. However, it is worth pointing out that handbooks and other instructive texts have a long tradition in English, which can be seen in the Helsinki Corpus (cf. Rissanen 1989: 18).

In relation to Category E my purpose was to find out to what extent procedural discourse is represented in it since there are clear indications in the manuals that it does contain such texts (cp "Step by Step through Istanbul", "What You Should Know About Air Conditioning for New Homes" [from *How-to-Do-It-Encyclopedia*], "Instructions for Making Child's High Chair"). I would like to point out that I have not searched the whole of the Brown and the LOB corpora for procedural discourse. Bits and pieces of procedural discourse would no doubt be found elsewhere in Brown and LOB, but as I will demonstrate later, there is linguistic evidence that it is exactly in Category E that it is possible to single out this particular subcategory.

2.1. The textual composition of Category E

Category E (LOB):

E1 – E5	Homecraft, handiman
E6 – 10	Hobbies
E11 – 13	Music, dance
E14	Pets
E15 – 18	Sport

E19–20	Food, wine
E21–22	Travel
E23–26	Miscellaneous
E27–35	Trade, professional journals
E36–38	Farming

(cf. Johansson – Leech – Goodluck 1978: 5)

This list allows a text linguist to make a number of observations. Although it is apparent that the list represents subject areas and activities which involve human skills or expertise, it is by no means obvious that this is sufficient, from a text-linguistic point of view, to justify the inclusion of all these texts under the same category. I shall come back later to some examples of texts which, I think, could have been placed elsewhere with advantage.

Now, the whole concept of "text type" or "discourse category" is obviously based on the assumption that ideally there exist homogeneous texts, or at least, that it is possible to assign a given concrete text to a type or category by virtue of linguistic and/or contextual criteria. However, actual discourse is often much more varied than text typologies suggest. Virtanen (1988) makes a distinction between "unitype" and "multitype" texts. A good example of a unitype text is LOB-E20 ("Time is of the Essence"), which consists of recipes all through, i. e. it is a prototype example of procedural discourse. Another example is Brown-E13 ("Step by Step Through Istanbul"), a travel guide text.

A striking example of a "multitype" or mixed text is LOB-E09 ("Stamps of Lebanon's Dog River," *Philatelic Magazine*) which combines the description of stamps with a visit to Lebanon, interspersed with snatches of history. Another example is LOB-E23, which begins with the history of quilting, but continues with an account of how to make the most of the spring flowers (shift of subject matter).

Sometimes, the inclusion of a specific text in Category E may be questioned. Thus Brown-E26, "Oersted and the Discovery of Electromagnetism", is a historical account of the Danish scientist Oersted. Although the discovery of electromagnetism was a great human achievement there does not seem to be anything in the language of this text that justifies its place in Category E. The text clearly belongs to "Biography", which is part of Category G.

From the point of view of discourse theory, the most dubious subcategory for inclusion in Category E is the one called "Trading". Thus most of LOB-E28 is an argumentative text dealing with marketing management.

LOB-E29 among other things contains detailed technical descriptions of a harvester and some tractors. It seems justified to make a distinction between texts which primarily describe technical devices, on the one hand, like this one, and such as are meant to inform the addressee on how to use such technical devices, on the other hand. A combination of the two goals is of course another possibility.

Some of the problems of assigning texts to Category E are described in the LOB manual. For textual analysis the multitype character of certain texts in the two corpora forces you to decide whether they should indeed belong to E. If a corpus text sample is mixed and thus made up of specimens of entirely different discourse categories, it has been regarded as procedural in this investigation, provided that the procedural passages amount to more than 50 per cent of the text or that the dominant purpose is clearly instructive.

3. What is procedural discourse?

Two scholars who have described procedural or instructive discourse are Werlich and Longacre. Werlich first subclassifies what he calls "instructive text forms" into (a) "subjective" (= *instructions*), and (b) "objective":

> When communicating about the planning of future behaviour, the encoder can choose between the text form of *instructions*, which are instruction from a subjective point of view..., and the text form of variants of *directions, rules, regulations* and *statutes*, which are instruction from an objective point of view. (Werlich 1976: 121)

The terminology he uses is not particularly fortunate since the term "direction" is often used as a synonym for "instruction". However, the distinction is important even so. The latter type of "instructive" discourse is further divided into *practical*, which "can be subclassified as ... work directions, technical instructions, recommendations, precepts, prescriptions, recipes, motions, guides, manuals, etc." (Werlich 1976: 131) and *statutory* (e. g. rules of games, contracts, laws, etc.). While in the latter the addressee's future behaviour must conform to what is said in the text, the text user will in many cases have more freedom in instructions. This is also why practical instructions are more interesting in the way they reflect writer-reader interaction than strict rules, regulations and statutes.

Since the procedural texts in the Brown and LOB corpora consist of practical instructions, we shall focus on this subcategory of procedural discourse.

Longacre (1976: 200) establishes the further linguistic features of narrative and procedural texts in the following way:

NARRATIVE	PROCEDURAL
1. First/Third person	1. Nonspecific person
2. Agent oriented	2. Patient oriented
3. Accomplished time	3. Projected time
4. Chronological linkage	4. Chronological linkage

(1) "Nonspecific person" is typically manifested as *you*, but since procedural discourse is patient-oriented (2), one can expect a relatively high frequency of passive clauses with patient subjects. An exception to this is Brown-E02, which reports on how the writer, writing in the first person, looks after her garden, thus providing the reader with a model. This sample, then, is a procedural text written as a description. Another exception is Brown-E13, a report on the writer's past visit to Istanbul.

(3) Projected time is manifested as present tense, modals (including *will*) + infinitive, and imperatives. Finally, narrative and procedural discourse share the feature of chronological time (4). However, according to Virtanen (1988: 291), "A fundamental aspect of instructive, or procedural, texts is their strict conformity to experiential iconicity, which makes explicit markers of time, in their primary function, unnecessary."[3] Consequently, the coherence of procedural discourse is to a great extent seen in relation to how the described procedure conforms with how the actions are actually performed.

When describing his textual dimensions, Biber (1988: 140) makes a distinction between "procedural" and "expository" discourse:

> Procedural discourse differs from expository discourse in that it is event-driven and concrete rather than conceptual and abstract, but with respect to Dimension 2 these two types of discourse [descriptive + procedural] are similar in that they frequently use non-past verbal forms and attributive adjectives rather than past tense forms, third person animate referents, etc.

By " dimension 2" Biber refers to "discourse with non-narrative purposes (expository, descriptive, or other)" (1988: 115). What he says about attributive adjectives may be purely accidental and probably has to do with his choice of text (Brown-E07 on interlocking frames). It would therefore hardly apply to procedural discourse in general.

While Longacre and Werlich describe some of the typical linguistic properties of procedural discourse, I would like to capture its main pragmatic characteristics in the formula

X PRESCRIBE HOW Y DO Z

where	X	=	the knowledgeable text producer
	HOW	=	goal-oriented strategies
	Y	=	the knowledge-seeking addressee (identical with the potential actor)
	DO	=	a compound act
	Z	=	the goal

According to Longacre (1983: 12), the notional structure of procedural discourse is characterized by the performative verb PRESCRIBE.[4] I prefer to look at this rather as a macro-act of the directive type, which in turn has a number of subordinate micro-acts like ADVISE, CAUTION, RECOMMEND, and SUGGEST.

Compared with such illocutionary acts as ORDER, COMMAND, and even REQUEST, the listed micro-acts are all rather low on the directive scale in illocutionary force. In prototype procedural discourse, it is as if the text producer had in mind the following:

> if you want to do Z, then the best way to do so is to follow these steps.

Thus there is an element of manner implied in PRESCRIBE, which is necessary since the act is compound and sometimes very complex as well, as in many technical procedures.

Once you are involved with directive discourse there is the possibility of expressing yourself along the scale of directness. Many of the differences between procedural texts are connected with this parameter. In pedagogical contexts, for example, it will be an advantage if the discourse contains signals of indirectness so as not to put the reader off. But indirectness may also be inherent in the discourse topic. For example, the addressee has much more freedom when choosing wines for different parts of the year (LOB-E19) or breeding budgerigars in a flat (LOB-E14) than when making quilts (LOB-E23).

4. Some linguistic properties of procedural discourse in Category E

4.1. Structure words and some lexical words

Comparison between the Brown and the LOB corpora shows that Category E in each contains the same number (21) of what I have considered to be procedural texts.

To begin with, it may be instructive to have a look at a frequency list of what I assume to be the procedural (P) and non-procedural (N) parts of Category E in Brown and LOB.[5] If the two subcorpora represent different discourse categories, this can be expected to show up in the distribution of certain linguistic features, particularly function words (Table 1). There are at least three types of function words that deserve to be mentioned, i. e., some personal and possessive pronouns, the most common modals, and the subordinators *if* and *when*. *Mine* and *yours* are excluded because there are only one or two instances of each. For the same reason, the differences between interrogative (9 instances in Brown and 4 in LOB) and conditional *if* and interrogative and temporal *when* are ignored.

Table 1. Frequencies of specific structure words in the corpora (P = the procedural part of Category E, N = the nonprocedural part of Category E).

	BROWN			LOB		
Corpora	P	N	Brown	P	N	LOB
Number of texts	21	15	500	21	17	500
Words						
I, me, my	95	123	7,718	275	172	10,973
you, your	565	148	4,204	244	54	4,942
he, him, his	117	382	19,130	64	306	17,566
can	211	65	1,771	180	86	2,147
may	94	49	1,399	84	33	1,338
should	55	19	887	101	45	1,301

In spite of the striking differences in the frequency of the 1st person pronouns in Brown and LOB, their absolute frequency is lower than the expected frequency in all the four subcorpora, i. e. Brown/P, Brown/N, LOB/P and LOB/N. This applies even more to the third person singular

Table 2. Distribution of contingency clauses in P and N

	LOB		BROWN	
	Observed frequency	Expected frequency	Observed frequency	Expected frequency
if				
P	136 (75%)	92 (58%)	151 (74%)	93 (55%)
N	45 (25%)	66 (42%)	54 (26%)	75 (45%)
when				
P	127 (70%)	107 (59%)	113 (69%)	98 (58%)
N	90 (30%)	87 (41%)	51 (31%)	70 (42%)

he, *him* and *his*. This is simply evidence that there is no strong need to refer either to the text producer or to the 3rd person in Category E. There remain the 2nd person pronouns, mentioned in chapter 3 as a potential feature of procedural discourse. Their frequency in P in both Brown and LOB is significantly higher than in the N subcorpora. This is also true of all the other structure words in the table.

The high frequency of epistemic *can* and *may* expressing possibility, and *should* expressing advice or suggestion, in the P subcorpora, conforms with the predictions made in chapter 3. There is also a strong tendency for passive constructions in combination with *can* and *may*, as in

(1) The design of a mechanical interlocking frame is much like a mechanical puzzle, but once understood, the principles *can be applied* to any track and signal arrangement. (Brown-E7: 1 – 3)

(2) It *may be incorporated* into cattle creep feeds in levels from 1.0 to 1.5 milligrams of diethylstilbestrol per pound of feed. (Brown-E27: 49 – 50)

Finally, the contingency subordinators *if* and *when* are used in procedural discourse to convey conditions and circumstances for the action (cp Wikberg, forthcoming). In both Brown/P and LOB/P there is a marked preference for contingency clauses (*if*- and *when*-clauses) as compared with the non-procedural subcorpora, as in

(3) *If* your garage is damp, play safe and keep the drill in the house when not in use, for damp is one of the worst enemies of an electric motor. (LOB-E3: 61 – 62)

(4) *If* you want something really strong, with a high alcoholic content, Yugoslavia produces Dinjac, but it is not a wine for weak heads! (LOB-E19: 23 – 24)

(5) It may be useful to remember that there will be less splashing *when* joints are cooked longer, at a lower temperature; *when* the meat is covered with foil; *when* a container is well filled; and that the oven floor can be protected from spilt juice *if* a tray is put under pies or tarts. (LOB-E25: 66–69)

(6) *When* the oven does get dirty, it should be wiped out while it is still warm before the dirt has time to stick. (LOB-E25: 70–71)

Next we shall look at some content words. The verb *use* seems to be some kind of prototype verb in procedural discourse, as in

(7) Roll clay to thickness indicated in individual instructions. Whenever possible, *use* the wooden mold as a pattern for cutting clay. When mold has more than one design cavity, make the individual paper patterns. Place mold or paper pattern on rolled clay and cut clay by holding knife in vertical position... (Brown-E15: 12–16)

Since semantically there is little difference between the verb and the noun, the two have here been collapsed into a superlexeme $\mathrm{USE}_{N/V}$, including *use, uses, used* and *using*. It is interesting to note the strong tendency for more frequent use of these items in the procedural subcorpora (Table 3).

Table 3. Distribution of $\mathrm{USE}_{N/V}$ in the subcorpora.

	BROWN		LOB	
	Observed frequency	Expected frequency	Observed frequency	Expected frequency
P	175 (77%)	59	163 (76%)	55
N	53 (23%)	42	51 (24%)	44

The superordinate act which DO Z implies in the formula given in section 3 usually corresponds to what Vendler (1957) calls "accomplishments", such as *build a house, make a chair, make an omelet*. Apart from such texts on how-to-make-it, there are texts on how-to-do-it and how-to-use-it. Thus travel guides, which are how-to-do-it texts, form a subtype of procedural discourse where the verb is not causative but rather made up of intransitive verbs of movement.

Start and *finish* mark the opening and the end of a procedure. Although their overall frequency is not strikingly high, their importance in procedural texts is reflected in their distribution in the subcorpora. Thus in Brown, Category E, there are 28 instances of $start_{n/v}$, 25 in P and 3 in N. In LOB the corresponding figures are 10 (P) and 6 (N). For $finish_{n/v}$, the figures are in Brown 10 (P) and 2 (N), and in LOB 5 (P) and 3 (N).

Predicates in indirect procedural discourse can be subordinated to such predicates as *avoid* (both instances in Brown occur in Category E), *make/ be sure* (*make sure:* Brown/P: 8, N: 2; LOB/P 3), *remember*, and so forth. Note that these are all features that relate to the purpose of instructional discourse and the author's message to the reader rather than what Category E stands for thematically. Such predicates indicating the text producer's concern would be less appropriate in highly formalized step-by-step instructions, and would be out of place in strict rules and regulations.

What is it, then, that makes up the coherence of procedural discourse apart from experiential iconicity? The continuity seems to be found less in coreferential noun phrases than in sequences of actions and the uniform utilitarian purpose that applies to such sequences.

4.2. Textual and organisational features

Not all information on text type can be obtained by focusing on syntactical and lexical phenomena in texts. At some point or other there arises the need to consider organisational factors as well, such as paragraph structure, the use of predictors and other global textual markers, which are less easy to get at by means of the computer simply because they may span long chunks of text.

One textual feature of procedural discourse is numbered steps. Although this is not very common in Category E, there are some examples such as in LOB-E01 (on lace-making), LOB-E13 (on dancing), and Brown-E01 (on body-building). This feature is more common in more recent types of procedural texts, as in technical instructions like computer manuals. In the investigated subcorpora, recipes (as in LOB-E20) have at least an implicit numbering of steps, and so do the instructions on the building of a child's high chair (LOB-E04).

Travel guides, like LOB-E21, are built on a different principle. E21 is rich in detail and describes Rhodes and Minorca. Ordinary travel guide discourse takes you through space, characteristically with a paragraph-initial place adverb or a noun phrase indicating place, as in

(8) Of the third ancient city, Ialyssos, about 10 miles south-west of Rhodes, little that is visible remains. (LOB-E21: 76–77)

By contrast, LOB-E22 was written for travel advisers who in turn are going to advise prospective tourists. This makes it a much more general text, but one which contains a large number of evaluative sentences which often make up the topic sentence in a paragraph, as in

(9) Her motor coaches are among the most attractive in the world with unusual touches in colouring, shape and seating. (LOB-E22: 136–137)

On this basis LOB-E22 hardly qualifies as a travel guide text or as procedured discourse at all. Instructive texts can be seen as a subcategory of informative texts, to use a term adopted by the editors of Brown and LOB.

Obviously, listing is also found in nonprocedural discourse, such as LOB-E35 (which contains a list of "four good attributes" typical of successful salesmen and saleswomen) and the enumeration of objectives in LOB-E38. Neither of these is intended as a list of sequenced procedures. The most conspicuous global text strategies used in any of the procedural texts is the sustained use of questions in Brown-E30: 1–99 and the repeated use of imperatives in Brown-E35: 1–32 (plus the subsequent list of reasons, lines 33–46).

5. Conclusions

For this study the division of Category E into procedural and nonprocedural discourse was first made intuitively on the basis of reading the separate texts. Another approach would have been to start out from a ready-made set of features characteristic of procedural discourse to find out where the text samples could be placed along the procedural "dimension". It would no doubt have been hard to adopt such a method at the present state of knowledge.

The comparison of the distribution of high-frequency words and some textual features in the subcorpora has proved that there are considerable differences between the two subtypes. It has been demonstrated that over 50% of Category E in both corpora is made up of procedural discourse, which I do not hesitate to label a major discourse category with a long tradition in English going back at least to Middle English. It has also been shown that Category E contains a relatively large proportion of texts which cannot be categorized as procedural discourse by the criteria used here.

An important point that I have been trying to make is that in the future we need to pay more attention to text theory when compiling corpora. For users of the Brown and the LOB corpora, and possibly other machine-readable texts as well, it is also worth noting the multitype character of certain text categories. If you simply search the texts using various computer programs for retrieval of lexical and grammatical information, you may fail to see that there are important textual and organisational properties concealed in them. Finally, it should be noted that instructions can also be given in terms of description and narration, which is once more proof of the importance of purpose for the assessment of discourse category.

Notes

1. I am grateful to Norges allmennvitenskapelige forskningsråd and the H. W. Donner Foundation at Åbo Akademi for enabling me to do this research.
2. Biber (1988) includes 14 texts from Category E (LOB).
3. On iconicity, see Enkvist (1981).
4. In *Collins Cobuild English Language Dictionary prescribe* is defined as "to lay down as a rule or directive", not to be mixed up with *proscribe*, "to condemn or prohibit".
5. Procedural texts in the Brown Corpus: E01 – 03, E07 – 08, E12 – 17, E19 – 21, E24 – 25, E27, E30, E33, E35 – 36. Procedural texts in the LOB Corpus: E01 – 05, E07 – 08, E10, E13 – 14, E19 – 21, E23 – 27, E33 – 34, E37.

References

Biber, D.
1988 *Variation across speech and writing.* Cambridge: Cambridge University Press.

Dimter, M.
1985 "On text classification", in: T. A. van Dijk (ed.), *Discourse and literature.* Amsterdam – Philadelphia: John Benjamins, 215 – 230.

Enkvist, N. E.
1981 "Experiential iconicism in text strategy", *Text* 1(1): 97 – 111.

Francis, W. N. – H. Kucera
1964 *Manual of information to accompany a standard corpus of present-day edited American English, for use with digital computers.* Providence, Rhode Island: Department of Linguistics, Brown University.

Hofland K. – S. Johansson (eds.)
1982 *Word frequencies in British and American English.* Bergen: The Norwegian Computing Centre for the Humanities.

Johansson, S. – G. N. Leech – H. Goodluck
1978 *Manual of information to accompany the Lancaster-Oslo / Bergen corpus of British English, for use with digital computers.* Oslo: Department of English.

Leitner, G.
1990 "*International corpus of English:* Corpus design – problems and suggested solutions". *CCE Newsletter* 4 (1/2), 25 – 49.

Longacre, R.
1976 *An anatomy of speech notions.* Lisse: Peter de Ridder Press.

Longacre, R.
1983 *The grammar of discourse.* New York — London: Plenum.
Rissanen, M.
1989 "Three problems connected with the use of diachronic corpora", *ICAME Journal* 13: 16 — 19.
Sinclair, John (ed.)
1987 *Collins COBUILD English language dictionary.* London — Glasgow: Collins.
Smith, E. L., Jr.
1985 "Text type and discourse framework", *Text* 5 (3): 229 — 247.
Vendler, Z.
1957 "Verbs and times", *Philosophical Review* 56: 143 — 160.
Virtanen, T.
1988 Discourse functions of adverbial placement in English: Clause-initial adverbials of time and place in narratives and procedural place descriptions (Licentiate Thesis), University of Turku, Turku.
Werlich, E.
1976 *A text grammar of English.* Heidelberg: Quelle and Meyer.
Wikberg, K.
in press Diversifying procedural discourse, in: Enkvist, N. E. — A.-C. Lindeberg — K. Wikberg (eds.), *Nordic research in text linguistics and discourse analysis*, Vol. 2.

Opaque and transparent features of Indian English

S. V. Shastri

1. Introduction

The phonological features of Indian English (IE hereafter) particularly spoken IE or IEs are the most obvious transparent features of IE. The moment an Indian opens his mouth he announces himself as not only an Indian but perhaps as a Madrasi, Gujarati, Punjabi and so on. This is about the average educated Indian. But what about the English-educated speaker? The near-native speaker? or the native speaker himself? Which variety or sub-variety of speech does he use? The fact is that he adjusts himself to his audience, unconsciously but surely, if he has to achieve successful communication. We know that the native speaker has to speak in Butler English[1] if wants his bread and butter for sure. Some of us, the English-educated teachers of English, use many different sub-varieties when we speak to speakers of other sub-varieties, very often not merely for successful communication but as an indicator of informality and intimacy and so on. However, I must hasten to add that we all have our standard dialects – Gujarati English, Marathi English some near-native English and so on. Authentic and comprehensive descriptions of Spoken Indian English(es) are yet to be accomplished. The ICE project[2], when completed, will provide at least authentic materials for such descriptions.

2. Transparent features

Since my own research has so far been confined to written edited and printed IE material let me turn to the features of written IE – both transparent and opaque. Elsewhere I have made some sweeping generalizations about the nature of written IE. I have said that it does not differ substantially from its Anglo-American counterpart at least as far as syntax is concerned and I have also said that the real IE features are to be found in its lexis (Shastri 1981, 1983). Let me take up these issues. Let me modify the statement and say that written edited and published IE does not differ substantially in its syntax (for that matter even lexis) from its Anglo-American counterparts as far as the opaque features are concerned. There are obvious differences as far as the transparent features are concerned. What are these transparent features?

2.1. Code-mixing

Code-mixing at all levels of IE language structure – single lexical items, hybrid expressions, phrases, sentences and even whole chunks of text – is transparent. One can see clearly that this is IE. In my paper on "Code-mixing in the process of Indianization of English: a corpus based study" I have elaborated on this phenomenon in some detail (Shastri 1988 b). For the present purpose let me cite a few examples of Indian lexical items that occur in IE.

(1) Indian items used where (near) equivalents are available in the English language, e. g. *achari* 'cook', *azadi* 'freedom', *bhook* 'hunger', *cutcheri* 'concert', *film-otsav* 'film festival', *hartal* 'strike', *jhompadpatti* 'shanties', *kala* 'art', *kisan* 'farmer', *malik 'landlord/proprietor/master', mandir* 'temple', *mela* 'fair', *natak* 'play', *sammelan* 'conference'. The main motivation for this kind of mixing seems to be a deliberate attempt at asserting the Indian identity. However, their use as a strategy for mass communication cannot be ruled out. Some of them are stylistically marked or emotionally loaded.

(2) Indian items referring to peculiarly Indian concepts, institutions, flora and fauna for which exact English equivalents are not available. Very often no equivalents are available at all. These are by far the largest in number. They may be classified according to register as follows:

A. Religion and Philosophy (exact equivalents not available): *advaita* 'non-dualist', *atman* 'soul', *dharmic* 'religious'.

B. Fine Arts (no equivalents available):

(a) Music: *abhanga, alapa, bhava, karnatik, dholki, dhrut, gharana, Hindustani, halagi, khayal, lalit, matra, quawali, rasa, sarod, shruti, sitar, sutra, sarangi, sangeet, taal, thumri, tabla, veena.*

(b) Dance and Drama: *Bharatnatyam, chawka, odissi, kathak(ali), natak, natya.*

(c) Folk Art and Mythology: *apsara, bailata, gopi, Gokul, Gokulasthami, mohini, lavani, nautanki, tamasha, yakshagana.*

C. Administration (mixed): *challan, gauda, daphtary, lokpal, parishad, prabandhak, panchayat, rajya, samiti, swaraj, taluka, tehsil.*
D. Flora and Fauna (no equivalents available): *hangul, markher, palak.*
E. Society (mixed): *arrack, bhakri, bhoodan, bandh, bhopa, brahmin, crore, chappals, chit, Diwali, dalit, dharna, Doordarshan, goonda, ghat, harijan, Holi, hamal, jatra, jat, khadi, khandsari, lakh, mahout, maidan, mela, matka, peria, paisa, paan, satta, sari, satyagraha, vanaspati, shri, shrimati.*

It appears that the extent of code-mixing depends on the genre of writing. I have posited elsewhere (Shastri 1988 b) a cline of Indianness of IE, and I have also suggested that IE lies along a cline with the heavily Indian at one end and the hardly Indian at the other. The heavily Indian writings would include those on religion, philosophy, fine arts, as well as the hardly Indian scientific and technical writings. Between the two lie the other genres of writing. The extent of code-mixing might also depend on the writer and/or the audience.

Code-mixing may be argued to be a typical phenomenon in a language contact situation. But it must be acknowledged that there are many conditions that give rise to the phenomenon. The mixing of Indian items where English equivalents are available is a transparent IE feature, albeit an attitudinal marker. But consider the following passage:

> Two long walls of matting connected by a back wall and roof of the same material constituted the dining hall. Each person, about thirty in all including children, had a thin straw mat under him and a brass tray in front of him. Gandhi sat on a cushion. Male and female members of the ashram, moving noiselessly on bare feet, deposited food on the trays, and pots and pans at Gandhi's legs. He handed me a bronze bowl filled with vegetable mush in which I thought I discerned spinach leaves and pieces of squash. A woman poured some salt on my tray, another gave me a metal tumbler with warm water and a second metal tumbler with warm milk. Then I got two little boiled potatoes in jackets and several soft, flat circular wheatcakes. Gandhi – I was sitting one removed from him – handed me one hard paper-thin wheatcake from a metal container in front of him.

The writer has laboriously described many common Indian items such as *thali* 'brass tray', *phulkas* 'soft, circular wheatcakes' and *papad* 'hard paper-thin wheatcake' instead of straightaway borrowing the Indian words. The word *ashram* has no equivalent in English, and mercifully the writer has not tried to render it in literal translation. Even *mush spinach* and *squash* are alien to IE. Why does he use these? The reason may be that either he is ignorant of these words or he is writing for a larger Western or International audience. The author is Louis Fischer. (1954) The transparent features of non-IE are obvious.

It would be interesting to speculate on another allied phenomenon: Had Louis Fischer used these Indian words, what kind of English would that have been? I suggest that it would qualify to be called Indian English, only written (deliberately) by a non-Indian, a native speaker. Such a variety of English, often known as Anglo-Indian in literary parlours, was indeed extensively used by English writers in/about India. The best-known examples are Kipling and E. M. Forster.

3. Opaque features

3.1. Syntax

Let me now turn to the opaque features. Our own corpus-based work in the Department of English, Shivaji University has revealed that there is little difference between the native varieties and IE as far as syntax is concerned although the area probed so far is very restricted indeed. A study of the meanings of the modals in IE produced some hypotheses. The nine basic modal auxiliaries studied conformed in their usage largely to the Anglo-American standards. But it was noticed that in the case of conditional constructions and indirect speech the use of modals in IE threw up inconsistencies as compared to the Anglo-American usage (Katikar 1984). Taking a cue from this, a small M. Phil project investigated the *If*-constructions in IE and discovered that the choice between present and past forms of modals was inconsistent in such constructions (Patil 1986). This area – conditional constructions including the subjunctive – is being further investigated by a Ph. D. student.

Another area of syntax investigated is "Complementation in IE", restricted to certain items (Shastri, forthcoming). This study sets out to investigate Baumgardner's (1987) findings that Pakistani English differs from Anglo-American usage in respect of *to*+inf and prep+*-ing* complementation and his hypothesis that this may be the case with IE as well, arguing from available published works (Nihalani – Tongue – Hosali 1979 and Whitworth 1907).

In all, 29 items – verbs, adjectives, and nouns corresponding to some of them – dealt with by Baumgardner were analysed. It was discovered that out of the 29 items only 14 were found to display deviant features of complementation. One broad conclusion that was drawn from this is that not all the verbs, adjectives and nouns under investigation display the same behaviour in IE as in Pakistani English.

The second and more interesting observation that was made from this analysis is that even in the case of the 14 items which were found to display deviant features, very few are statistically significant. This means that statements like "In Indian English complementation, the adjective is frequently followed by a *to*+infinitive instead of the preposition and participle clause", lose much of their force because they cannot be said to be relatively frequent.

Perhaps *suggest* is the only verb which displays significant deviation because it is quantitatively significant (12.94%) and represents a variety of deviations.

An attempt was made to find out if some of the so-called deviant complementation types noticed in the Kolhapur Corpus[3] of Indian English also occurred in a native variety corpus. An investigation was carried out using the LOB corpus of British English. The fourteen cases of complementation types found to display deviant featues in IE were investigated, and it was discovered that in four, the LOB corpus threw up almost parallel instances. They are the following:

1. The verb *prevent* followed by *-ing* clause without the preposition instead of of prep+*-ing* clause. There is one instance of this type in the LOB Corpus.

My urgent duty now was to *prevent* it *doing* what, if left to itself, it would do. (R09 177)

2. The verb *like* followed by prep+*-ing* clause instead of *to*+inf. There are as many as 9 instances of this type in the LOB Corpus as against 4 in the IE material. e. g.

a) Among those who *like talking* politics... (B26 168)
b) They consciously enjoy their work. They *like selling*. (E35 158)
c) I won't *like going* to Italy. (P10 28)

The verbs that occur in the *-ing* form are: *talk, do, sell, wear, burden, stay,* and *be*.

3. The verb *hesitate* followed by prep+-*ing* clause instead of *to*+inf: there is one instance of this type in the LOB Corpus.

> He told us that people seem to think nothing of spending to light the way to their doorsteps, but will *hesitate at spending* the same amount for indoor lighting. (E05 118)

4. The verb *suggest* followed by -*ing* clause instead of *that*-clause. There is one instance of this type in the LOB Corpus.

> But Piers remained aloof, and when Beryl *suggested having* a second party, the following week, he poured cold water on the project. (P02 41)

Why do certain deviations or errors keep occurring in language use irrespective of whether it is natively or nonnatively used? The explanation, it was suggested, is to be sought in the descriptions of psycholinguistic processes in learning – language development.

But what is important to note is that such "deviations", which are claimed to be variety features on impressionistic basis, are, if truly variety features, opaque.

The major area of syntax in which IE is suspected to differ is in the use of articles and tense forms. Professor Leitner is investigating the perfective Vs present in IE.[4] His initial claim is that comparing "forms" is misleading. He seems to be convinced that Kachru's (1990) hypothesis about New Englishes is the key to discovering variety features, especially those of nonnative varieties of English. He suggests that we compare "notions" and how they are realized in texts. To me it appears that notions and how they are realized belong not only to the area of syntax but also to the domain of style and "creativity" in language. And I believe that native speakers can be as guilty of creativity as they can be of "deviation" – as guilty of both as their Indian counterparts can be. But let us wait for the results of further investigation. All that we may say at the moment is that the use of tenses in IE is partly an opaque feature, partly because the user is unaware of it, and so long as it is acceptable in the sense that the expression is within the creative mechanism of the genius of the language it is not "deviant", but stylistically different. It is Indian English.

My pre-corpus overtures on IE were made in a paper I gave at Lund (Sweden) on "The Structure of Non-Native EST – A New Hypothesis" (Shastri 1981). In that paper I listed a number of deviations I had identified in a project report by an Indian scientist on the effects of salinity on plant life (Joshi 1976). There were several native speakers of English among the audience and they did not apparently see many "deviations". According to them many of the so-called deviations were perfectly acceptable to them; only some of them felt that they would not themselves use those expressions. That was a point of "revelation". The concept of opaque features in IE took birth on that day.

3.2. Lexis

Earlier on I had done a semantic study of six lexical items in IE – *keep/put*; *dark/black* and *sick/ill* – and shown that the differences in the semantic coverage of *keep/put* in IE were due to the interference of Indian languages in the course of learning. In the case of *sick* and *ill* the archaic (now also American) features were found in IE. And the *dark/black* distinction was the result of sociocultural setting into which English has been transplanted (Shastri 1978, 1983).

In that study "no differences were observed between the British and American varieties in the meaning of the pair *put/keep* (restricted to those senses of the word which were studied). However, the Indian variety was observed to show a tendency to suppressing the feature +DURATIVE and introducing the feature ⟨BY MOVEMENT⟩ in *keep* in contexts in which the native varieties would not display these features." The following are some of the examples:

Keep
1. Congressmen must take a pledge to *keep* service above self.
2. "Dear, where did you *keep* my keys?"

put
3. "Sister if for the thorny pit the illusioned fall into you *put* the foreign govt!... and for the soul that searches for liberation you *put* Indian everything is clear."

Black/dark. It was found that there is no difference between the American and British varieties in the meaning of *black/dark*. But a significant difference was observed in their meaning in IE.

(a) *black* has acquired an additional component +INDIAN (caste marker) which is defined by the universe of discourse belonging to low caste;

(b) *dark* has acquired an additional component −NORM (Indian) as applied to complexion; and
(c) *black* contrasts systematically with *white* (and not with *grey*) when used to describe the colour of the hair, as the following examples illustrate:

4. And those five mainly from among the *black* untouchables.
5. Wish you luck with your future and your Winston, will he be *white*, black or khaki?
6. She was a young woman, whose plain features belied her *white* hair.

Ill/sick. A difference between the sense of the words *ill/sick* was clearly observed. The feature +NAUSEA in the word *sick* has become optional in all syntatic contexts in American English whereas in British English +NAUSEA is obligatory in a predicative complement construction. The Indian variety agrees with the American rather than with the British. This may be traced to the usual tendency of language not to change in a transplant situation. Many items in American English display this phenomenon. The following is an example from AE:

...eighteen weeks in which he was *sick* for a month. 1140 E1 G64.

An IE example:

The provision of medical services to the obviously *sick*...

The important point is that the differences are not apparent; they are opaque. Nihalani, Tongue and Hosali (1979) have not noted them, nor has any earlier scholar up to Whitworth (1907). The germs of the concept were already there only to be realized later.

3.3. Form and function

Several other studies based on the corpus have pointed to this same phenomenon. The Ph. D. thesis on "The Meanings of the Modals in IE" (Katikar 1984) has come up with the conclusion that there is no substantial difference in the use of the basic modals in IE, however, noting that this may be due to the polysemous nature of the English modals. Professor Leitner (forthcoming) has questioned this conclusion and maybe he will come out with a statement that, when an Indian uses a modal, he does not use it in the same sense in which his Anglo-American counterpart does. That would be another opaque feature – at the lexical level. Smaller M. Phil projects on the use of *some/any* (Ramtirthakar 1987) and on verb-particle constructions in IE (Patil 1986) have the same story to tell.

3.4. Style

This could also be true of other syntactic/stylistic features – the order of constitutents in a phrase, clause and sentence. It is alleged that the order of elements of structure in IE is different from that of its Anglo-American counterpart. Also, it is alleged that Indians use long, complex, and even cumbersome sentence structures. On an impressionistic basis from my experience of working with the three corpora[5] these claims seem to have some truth about them. My submission at the moment is that this can also be true of the native speakers' use of English.

This impression is based on an experience of academic leg-pulling (was it?). Once a literature friend of mine, an eminent scholar[6] widely travelled and acknowledged master of English literature wanted to test if I could tell between a native piece of English writing and a piece of Indian writing in English. He gave me five short passages concealing the names of the authors and asked me to find out by analysis or whatever process, which is which. I was also asked to mention the characteristic features on the basis of which I had made my decision. Out of the five passages, I put down three to Indian writers and two to natives. One of the criteria I had used was long involved cumbersome constructions and highly condensed phrases. It turned out that one of the passages I had identified as Indian was in fact by F. R. Leavis! Such stylistic features may be variety features or idiolect features as it happened to be in this case. In order to determine the distinction we have to have recourse to statistics. But all the same they are essentially opaque features.

So much for the opaque features in IE in general. Now let me turn to the last section which emerged from an attempt to locate differences within scientific writing by IE writers meant for different consumers.

3.5. Register

An attempt was made to compare two pieces of writing by the same author one, a semi-popular writing – the Presidential Address at a Science Congress – and another purely scientific paper meant for well-informed scientists. Obviously, a narrow area within this had to be chosen. A limited survey of the use of reporting verbs, in the sense of reporting scientific research, some instances of the use of the peculiar *having*-genitive and one of tenses, simple Vs perfective, was made.

No perceptible differences were discovered between the two types of text in the use of these items. However, it was noticed that what we have been calling opaque features seemed to be in evidence in both types of text. The following are some of the phenomena found in Yedekar – Powar (1986):

1. Reporting Verbs
(a) Non-technical verbs like *believe* and *consider* seem to be freely used when reporting scientific findings, e.g. (emphasis mine):

> While Heim and Gansser (1939), Valdiya (1980) and others *believe* that North Almora Thrust represents a thrust plane dipping southwards at a moderate angle, others like... Agarwal and Kumar (1980) *consider* it to be a vertical to highly dipping fault.

(b) Certain technical reporting verbs like *describe, evaluate* and *suggest* seem to be used in the technical sense, e. g.

> Various aspects of the geology of this area have been *described* by Heim and Gansser (1939)... The stratigraphy of the two tectonic units as *evaluated* by us is summarised in table 1. On the basis of lithological considerations,... we *suggest* that the our [*sic*] Chaukhutia Formation be equated with the Deobans... and correlated with the Chandpur Nagthat Formation...

(c) On the other hand certain reporting verbs like *recognize, see* and *show* seem to be used loosely, e. g.

> Photogeological studies and field work had enabled the recognition of [*sic*] a number of dislocations... A number of bedding-plane dislocations have been *recognized* [?identified/found/located]. At Khapwani the granitic gneisses have been mylonilised... and a 'fluxion structure' is very well *seen* [?discernible]... Augen mylonites are *seen* [?evident] at Bitna. The Rocks of the North Almora Zone *show* [?display] varying degrees of cataclasis... The rocks of Almora Crystalline Mass *show* [?indicate] relatively more intense cataclasis in a belt 1.0 to 1.5 km wide...

(d) Lastly certain "synonymous" reporting verbs seem to be used in an attempt to relieve monotony of style; e. g.

> Following Reed (1964) the structureless rocks... are *referred to* as brecciated rocks, mortared rocks, and cataclasites. The banded rocks... are *called* protomylonites, augen mylonites... Like-wise banded rocks showing both cataclastic and crystalloblastic textures are *designated* as blastomylonite and gneiss-mylonite. The fine-grained foliated rocks... are, following Knopf (1931) *referred to* as phyllonites.

2. Peculiar "*having*"-genitives

> X having a thickness of 15 m.
> X(range) rocks having stretched and ribbon-shaped quarty grains.

Genitive meanings in these contexts are perhaps conveyed in the native variety by a prepositional construction using *with*:

> with a thickness of 15 m.
>
> with stretched and ribbon shaped quartz grains.

3. Tense forms simple Vs perfective/passive

> The metasediments of the Almore Crystalline Mass *have been tightly folded* with the fold axes of the macroscopic folds...
>
> The lithological units... of the Badolisera-Pithoragarh Zone *are* likewise *folded* on axes...
>
> A variety of ... structures *are developed* in this area [=?have developed].

Thus it seems that a good deal of evidence is emerging to support the hypothesis that IE features are often opaque. And many of them may well be a matter of mere style differences.

4. Conclusions

I have tried to argue in this paper that variety features may be either opaque or transparent. Transparent features, especially of a nonnative variety, such as IE are, so obvious that we need not labour the point. However, as far as the identification and description of these features is concerned serious research has yet to begin in respect of spoken IE. In the case of written IE, work done so far indicates that the most obvious transparent feature of IE is code-mixing.

Opaque features, on the other hand, are elusive and the claims regarding many features found in Indian writing as peculiar to IE are either based on impressionistic judgement or on available/*ad hoc* data and when measured against standard databases turn out to be statistically nonsignificant. What is worse, some of these features are also found in native variety samples. And, finally, native speaker judgements on such IE features belie many a hypothesis. All this points towards the need for systematic quantitative studies based on large databases before we can say anything decisive about variety features. And that does not seem to be sufficient either: as it is perhaps not the "form" that is at variance but the "function". The identification of variant functions of the same forms in IE is the immediate task before us.

Notes

1. Butler English is a variety of pidgin English which was well established among the Indian domestic servants serving the British officials during the colonial times. It still survives in some Anglicized family environments in India.
2. ICE, International Corpus of English, a multi-million word database of over fifteen national varieties of English both spoken and written is currently being assembled by various teams of researches. The project is being coordinated by Professor Greenbaum, University College, London. The Indian component is being assembled by the present author in collaboration with Professor Leitner of the Free University of Berlin and Professor Kachru of the University of Illinois at Champaign-Urbana.
3. The Kolhapur Corpus of Indian English was built by the present author during the eighties and is available to researchers from the Norwegian Computing Centre for the Humanities, Bergen, Norway.
4. Personal communication.
5. The Brown Corpus of American English (Francis – Kucera 1964), the LOB Corpus of British English (Johansson – Leech – Goodluck 1978) and the Kolhapur Corpus of Indian English (Shastri *et al.* 1986)
6. Dr. S. V. Pradhan, Professor of Literature, Central Institute of English and Foreign Languages, Hyderabad 500007.

References

Baumgardner, Robert J.
1987 "Utilizing Pakistani newspaper English to teach grammar", *World Englishes* 6(3): 241 – 252.

Fischer, Louis
1954 *Gandhi, his life and message for the world* (A signet book). New York: The New American Library of World Literature Inc.

Francis, W. N. – Henry Kučera
1964 *Manual of information to accompany a standard corpus of present-day edited American English for use with digital computers.* Providence R. I.: Department of Linguistics, Brown University.

Johansson, Stig – Geoffrey. N. Leech – Helen Goodluck
1978 *Manual of information to accompany the Lancaster-Oslo/Bergen corpus of British English for use with digital computers.* Oslo: Department of English, Oslo University.

Joshi, G. V.
1976 *Studies in photosynthesis under saline conditions.* Kolhapur: Shivaji University.

Kachru, Braj B.
1983 *The Indianization of English: The English language in India.* New Delhi: OUP.

Kachru, Braj B.
1990 "World Englishes and applied linguistics, *World Englishes* 9(1): 3–20.

Katikar, Pratibha B.
1984 The Meanings of the Modals in Indian English. [Unpublished Ph. D. dissertation, Shivaji University. Kolhapur.

Nihalani, Paroo – R. K. Tongue – Priya Hosali
1979 *Indian and British English: A handbook of usage and pronunciation.* New Delhi: Oxford University Press.

Patil, B. N.
1986 *If*-conditionals in Indian English. [Unpublished M. Phil dissertation, Shivaji University. Kolhapur.

Ramtirthakar, Sheela
1987 A study of 'some' and 'any' in Indian English. [Unpublished M. Phil dissertation, Shivaji University. Kolhapur.

Shastri, S. V.
1978 English word meanings and their American and Indian variants: A study of six lexical items. [Unpublished M. A. thesis.] Lancaster.
1981 "The structure of non-native EST – A new hypothesis", (Hyderabad): *CIEFL Bulletin* 17(2): 25–34.
1983 "Towards a definition of Indian English", *CIEFL Newsletter* (Hyderabad) 18(3/4): 1–8.
1985 "Word frequencies in Indian English: A preliminary study", *ICAME News* 9: 38–44.
1988 a "The Kolhapur Corpus of Indian English and work done on its basis so far", *ICAME Journal* 12: 15–26.
1988 b "Code-mixing as a process in the Indianization of English", *Indian Linguistics* (Poona) 49: 34–53.
forthc. "Using computer corpora in the description of language with special reference to complementation in Indian English", in: *Proceedings of the First International Conference on English in South Asia.*

Shastri, S. V. – C. T. Patil-Kulkarni – Geeta Shastri
1986 *Manual of information to accompany the Kolhapur corpus of Indian English for use with digital computers.* Kolhapur: Department of English, Shivaji University.

Whitworth, George Clifford
1907 *Indian English.* New Delhi: Bahri Publications.

Yedekar, D. B. – K. B. Powar
1986 "A study of the North Almora Thrust Zone in the Chaukhutia-Dwarahat-Someshwar area, Kumaun Lesser Himalaya, *Current Trends in Geology* 9: 41–69.

Computer analysis of spelling variants in Chaucer's *Canterbury Tales*

Geoff Barnbrook

1. Introduction

1.1. Background

Anyone who has ever tried to use a spelling checker or a concordance program on a Middle English text, or who has translated such texts using a glossary, will probably understand why I began this research. Using a computer to handle Middle English texts made me acutely aware of some of the problems caused by variant spellings and of the inability of standard text manipulation software to deal with them. This paper describes a modest attempt to do something about this.

The research was carried out in the School of English at Birmingham under the supervision of Tim Johns. For program development I used Turbo Pascal version 4 running on an IBM-compatible PC. Apart from the general advantages of Pascal as a programming language, the program development environment provided by Turbo Pascal facilitated the testing of individual algorithms and allowed simple text analysis to be performed as needed.

The text of *Canterbury Tales* was obtained from the Oxford Text Archive on magnetic tape and transferred onto the PC with the help of Birmingham University Computer Centre.

1.2. Approach

1.2.1. Text selection

To begin the exploration I needed a text with a reasonably consistent and well known set of variations. Chaucer's work meets this requirement reasonably well, and *Canterbury Tales* provides a sufficiently large body of text in a single work. Robinson's edition, based on the Ellesmere manuscript, despite some textual shortcomings, provided a perfectly acceptable set of spelling variations for the program to work on, with the added advantage of being the text on which most earlier comments on spelling are based. Further, while Robinson's editorial principles necessarily involve some alterations to spellings, his approach seems to have left the bulk of the scribe's original spelling system intact.

1.2.2. Basic method

There are two main approaches possible in developing a program capable of recognising spelling variations in word lists. The spelling rules can be formulated by the researcher and incorporated into a word-matching program, and any errors found as the program is tested can be adjusted so that it is gradually tuned to the text's characteristics. The alternative approach, the one adopted for my exploration, makes the program discover the rules for itself. A training routine is needed to enable it to learn from tests carried out on the text, storing the results and converting this stored information into its own set of rules.

The training routine in the method I have developed began by selecting word pairs which seemed likely to be spelling variations of each other. I then examined selected pairs to check the words' relationship to each other and the program stored this information, gradually building up the data needed to formulate its own rules.

2. Development

2.1. Training routines

2.1.1. Selection of potential matches

The training program needed a list of potential spelling variants from which it could begin to learn the rules. I chose a very simple selection basis to eliminate all unnecessary sources of complication. The selection program read a word list produced from the entire text of *Canterbury Tales* and listed all word pairs differing by only one letter. The enormous number of comparisons needed for this meant that the program ran for over 30 hours, producing a list of 17,912 pairs.

Once this list had been constructed it became possible to identify and organise the differences between words. A set of sorting and summarising routines was used to produce a list of substitutions in frequency order. This revealed the main types of single letter differences found in the word list. In order to arrive at a manageable sample for training seven categories of difference were chosen:

addition of a final letter
addition of an initial letter
doubling of an existing letter
insertion of another letter in the body of the word
substitution of one vowel for another
substitution of one consonant for another
substitution of a vowel for a consonant

The ten most frequent letter pairs within each category were then selected for examination by the program, using a random sample of up to 30 word pairs.

2.1.2. Training

The training program presented each word pair on the screen together with a menu from which the appropriate decision could be selected. To enable me to make the decision correctly the program had a built-in concordance routine which allowed every line in the original text in which the word occurred to be displayed on the screen. This routine could be used as often as needed for both words before the decision was made.

As training progressed the decisions were recorded. Each letter pair had an associated training record, built up as the session proceeded, which recorded running totals of the results obtained from word pairs examined so far. If the two words were spelling variants the match total was increased by one, otherwise the non-match total was increased. Once ten word pairs had been examined the program checked these totals to see if a conclusive result had been reached. The level set for the program was a probability greater than 0.8 of a particular result. In other words, at the end of the first ten word pairs nine of the results must have been consistent. If consistency was not achieved after ten word pairs training continued until the results became conclusive or until the sample was exhausted.

By the end of the session a training record had been written for each of the seventy letter pairs. The information in these records formed the basis of the word matching carried out to test the rules.

2.2. Matching

The information contained in the training records was used to produce a file containing the totals of matches and non-matches encountered for each letter pair. These totals were then read into the computer's memory and used to predict matches between words.

The two possible approaches to matching could perhaps be described as the analytical and the generative method. The analytical method examines two words and assesses the probability that they are spelling variants of the same word. The generative version examines one word, performs all the possible letter changes on it and generates a list of words to check against the complete word list. The matching program produced to test the rules used the generative approach and examined a sample file of 300 words selected at random from the word list for the whole text.

The list of variants generated by the matching program was checked against the word list for the whole text and any variants found in the list were reported.

3. Results

3.1. Training

3.1.1. Letter Pairs

The list of word pairs differing by one letter contained 17,912 items. Once these had been sorted and summarised they resolved themselves into 365 different letter pairs. The letter pairs with a frequency greater than 200 were:

Final E	783
Final S	696
Final N	610
Final D	464
I : Y	410
D : N	310
A : E	285
Inserted U	289
Inserted R	250

E : O	210
Inserted E	207
Double E	201

The four most common items are all final letters, but only final E generally produced matches in the sample examined, while the other three generally produced morphological variations. I and Y are almost perfect equivalents for each other, while A and E and E and O are more erratic in their results and do not normally substitute for each other. D and N often produce morphological variations at the ends of words, linked to the final N and final D results already commented on. Inserted U is a very consistent source of spelling variations, while insertion of R and E generally produce words with no links. Double E generally produces matches.

Four of the twelve most frequent letter pairs, then, consistently give rise to spelling variations, and another three produce morphological differences. This in itself provides some justification for the selection technique adopted.

Choosing the ten most frequent examples within each substitution type produced the following list of 70 letter pairs:

Final letters:	E, S, N, D, T, R, Y, L, K, O
Initial letters:	S, Y, A, W, T, B, C, P, F, H
Inserted letters:	U, R, E, L, N, T, H, Y, D, S
Doubled letters:	E, O, L, A, T, D, C, R, N, P
Vowel substitution:	I for Y, A for E, E for O, E for Y, E for I, A for O, A for Y, O for Y, A for I, I for O
Consonant substitution:	D for N, N for S, D for S, L for R, N for R, L for S, S for T, D for L, D for T, R for S
Vowel for consonant substitution:	E for T, E for N, E for S, T for Y, S for Y, N for Y, D for E, D for Y, L for Y, R for Y

In each case a maximum of 30 word pairs was selected at random and used to train the program.

3.1.2. Word Pairs

Of the total of 1,992 word pairs made available to the training program only 880 were actually presented by the computer for my consideration. I have already mentioned the checking mechanism built into the training program which assessed the consistency of the information obtained after ten word pairs had been examined. Once this information seemed conclusive the program moved on to the next letter pair.

3.2. Matching

3.2.1. Probabilities

The totals of matches and non-matches were used to calculate a probability for each letter pair. This measures the likelihood, on the basis of the data obtained, that that letter pair difference will result in a spelling variation. The matching program only used probabilities above 0.6, a level which I chose arbitrarily. The letter pairs which met this criterion, and which were used in generating the list of possible variants, were:

I for Y	1.0000
Double A	0.9000
Double C	0.9000
Inserted U	0.9000
Double E	0.8095
Final E	0.8077
Double O	0.7667
Double T	0.6667

The substitution of Y for I where the surrounding minims demand a clarification is a generally accepted feature of manuscripts like the Ellesmere. It would be interesting to examine the circumstances of this substitution in more detail to determine whether this is the only rule affecting it, and indeed to see if it works.

The list shows a massive preponderance of doubled letters, with only one each of substitution, insertion and addition of a final letter. It is, perhaps, hardly surprising that the doubling of existing letters should appear to cause the least disturbance in a word. It would be interesting to examine the examples in more detail to see if any phonological implications of the doubling become apparent.

Addition of initial letters only just appears on the complete list of nonzero probabilities, and the highest score for the addition of a final letter (excluding final E) is O, with a probability of 0.32. These manipulations obviously both represent a fairly extreme form of disturbance in the form of the word.

The insertion of U may seem a little strange in view of the general point about disturbance. In practice this insertion is restricted to a limited range of preceding letter contexts, and according to Sandved (1985: 27) often represents an alternative spelling of a diphthong which can also be spelt with the single letter O.

A comparison of the main spelling variations with the descriptions given by Sandved (1985: 13–27) shows two main omissions from the test results: the substitutions of O and U and of U and W. Sandved claims that the O : U substitution has a similar distribution to that for I and Y. An examination of the original summary of letter pair differences shows that only 60 cases of O and U substitution were found, and this relatively low frequency meant that this pair was not selected for the training exercise. Similar considerations apply to the U : W substitution, also said by Sandved to be a common variation. It may be that both these variations are more widespread than these figures would suggest, but that they do not normally form the only difference between words. It would be interesting to explore this area further.

3.2.2. Word variants

The matching exercise produced the following results:

Number of words selected	300
Number of variants reported	98
Number of correct variants	78
Number of incorrect variants	20

The number of incorrect variants represents the number of variants produced which were not matches for the original word. The other type of error, in which a match which exists in the text has not been identified by the program, cannot easily be quantified.

As an overall result this suggests that the exercise, crude though it is, has succeeded to some extent. The errors that have been made show the need for a more precise discriminatory mechanism than a simple list of substitutions, and the program could easily be extended by analysing the training results to cover immediate letter context, word length and position of substitution or insertion.

4. Further developments

4.1. The analysis of multiple differences

Single-letter differences between words have obvious limitations as a full guide to spelling variation. Certain word differences may more commonly occur in conjunction with others, or may never appear completely in isolation. Because of this it might be useful to develop a second version of the comparison program which could select single-letter differences which occur in addition to the spelling variations already identified. This could provide more accurate evidence of the distribution of less common letter differences and a basis for testing and refining the simple spelling rules generated from the initial model.

4.2. Refinement of the training algorithms

The training results give a very crude measure of the likelihood of a substitution causing a spelling variation. Some of the letter pairs selected for the training process produced overall results which concealed important details.

For example, the A : E substitution produced an overall probability of 0.3 and so was not used for the matching routines. Within the 30 word pairs examined for this substitution 9 represented spelling variations. Two of these, *prayeres, preyeres* and *soverayn, sovereyn*, show variant spellings of the same diphthong. Sandved identifies its possible spellings as AI, AY, EI and EY, and the program results do not reflect these possibilities because the training algorithm does not discriminate A and E followed by I or Y from other cases.

An examination of the results for inserted U demonstrates another aspect of this principle. All of the cases examined involve an insertion immediately after O or A. The matching algorithm does not take this into account and creates potential variants by inserting U into every possible position in the word. Because this is applied to all the variants produced by adjusting for double letters, substitutions and final E any reduction in the number of positions tried would significantly improve the efficiency of the program.

As a simple refinement of the technique the program could explore the context of letter substitutions, with training records which could store details of previous and next letter context, word lengths and the position of substitutions within words.

5. Other applications

5.1. Text language analysis

Letter pair lists for single letter differences between words could be generated for each of the fragments of the text of *Canterbury Tales* on the same basis as those produced for the work as a whole. These could then be examined to identify any significant differences between text groups and to consider possible implications.

A similar comparison of the results from *Canterbury Tales* with those from other Chaucer texts or contemporary manuscripts of works by other authors could provide further evidence on classification schemes or scribal attributions.

5.2. Recognition of word variants

5.2.1. Reorganising word lists

The ability to recognise equivalent word forms would make it possible to produce more useful word lists which gathered together different spellings of the same word. This could be particularly valuable in glossary production, one of the problems which originally encouraged me to carry out this investigation.

5.2.2. Generating alternative spellings for word searches

Any applications which search texts for specific character strings, such as concordance programs, would be enhanced by an ability to generate and search for alternative spellings. The cut-off point for the generation of suggested alternatives could be adjustable by the user to optimise the efficiency of the program.

5.3. Lemmatisation

Single letter differences are only likely to identify a small range of morphological forms. To carry out a full analysis of the language in the text and to achieve any degree of automatic lemmatisation a more complex approach would be needed, but the existing programs could provide a starting-point.

This new approach could use the same basis but would need to define the type of variation being sought for rather differently. Words with the same stem could be extracted and the character strings causing the variations could be identified and analysed in a similar way to the technique used for the letter pair differences in the present program. This in itself would provide an interesting summary of the nature of the language used and might lead to the creation of an algorithm capable of recognising such differences and classifying them correctly. For this to work spelling normalisation routines would need to be incorporated into the comparison.

As an example, the words *acord, acorded, acorden, acordeth* and *acordynge* could not be associated with their alternative spellings *accord* etc., in which the c is doubled, without a preliminary normalisation using the spelling variations already discovered.

Once this process has been carried out it might be possible to identify stems of words on the basis of common elements, using a similar training process to that used for spelling, but one which allowed for the input and storage of more complex information. Possible affixes could be identified by the program on the basis of differences between words with common stems. Using the examples provided by the lemmas of *accord* quoted above, it would be possible to identify *-ed, -en, -eth* and *-ynge* as potential suffixes and to explore them on the same basis as the spelling variations.

Varying amounts of operator input could be involved, ranging from a technique which required the program to work its way backwards or forwards through the word until common elements were reached, to one which required the operator to give the necessary information. Both could be useful in exploring the rules of Middle English morphology, and both could produce practical results. The second approach might prove more efficient, but could be more heavily influenced by operator bias. Similar techniques could be applied to modern English and other languages.

5.4. Language learning

This is another situation in which spelling variation can occur. The analysis techniques provided by these programs could be used on texts produced by a learner to accumulate data relating to common spelling errors. This in turn could be used both to recognise variant spellings, so that a teaching program might be able to offer specific spelling advice based on the learner's known characteristics, and to analyse the reasons for those variations. Both applications could improve language teaching techniques and could shed more light on written language acquisition problems.

6. Conclusions

The results of this research perhaps reveal more about the nature of computer analysis of language than about Chaucer and the spelling habits of his scribes, but this is inevitable in view of the limited scope of the project. There is, though, some confirmation of the regularity of the Ellesmere scribe's spelling system, and of the detailed elements of that system described in the standard analyses of the text's language. Further investigations using developments from the basic approach might be able to reveal more fundamental aspects of the nature of spelling variation in Middle English or other suitable texts.

References

Robinson, F. N. (ed.)
1957 *Canterbury Tales*, in: *The works of Geoffrey Chaucer*, (2nd. edition). Oxford: Oxford University Press.

Sandved, A. O.
1985 *Introduction to Chaucerian English*. Cambridge: Brewer.

Pitch contours and tones in the Lancaster/IBM spoken English corpus

Gerry Knowles

1. Introduction

The Lancaster/IBM Spoken English Corpus,[1] collected 1984–1987, is now being used to raise interesting questions about the spoken language. In many cases this involves going beyond the kind of information contained in conventional orthographic transcripts, and getting to grips with the prosody. It may seem to the nonspecialist that phoneticians have long since learnt to transcribe prosodic patterns, and that studying the distribution of prosodic patterns in a corpus, or tracing their connection with more familiar text structures, is simply an extension of established procedures. In reality, a corpus throws up completely new problems, and it is far from clear how to categorize and make use of the mass of prosodic information.

To illustrate the point, consider the apparently familiar problem of the relative clause, and in particular the way in which the distinction between restrictive and nonrestrictive clauses is signalled in speech. According to Quirk *et al.* (1985), the nonrestrictive type is "usually" marked off with tone group boundaries – much as it is marked off with commas in writing – whereas the restrictive type is "usually" not. It is also sometimes claimed that in the nonrestrictive type, there is tone harmony or concord between the clause and its antecedent. But nowhere in these discussions is any clear idea given of what is meant by a tone group boundary, and how harmony should be defined. Altenberg (1987) finds that nonrestrictive clauses are marked off in 100% of cases, but so are 69% of restrictive clauses. These figures of course depend on the kind of discontinuity recognized by the transcribers as a tone group boundary. Nor is it self-evident what constitutes harmony: it presumably does not entail an exact copying of F0 values and durations: we need a rule to define what is an acceptable match.

Consider now the following example from text G01:

(1) The great rock | the big boys had swum through | rose sheer out of the white sand | …

where the relative clause *the big boys had swum through* is clearly of the restrictive type. Taking the transcription at its face value, we find against expectation that there is a tone group boundary before the clause; but since there is a fall on *rock* and a fall-rise on *swum*, the nuclei themselves do conform to expectation. But if instead of making a purely auditory analysis, we use a waveform editor,[2] we get a much more detailed picture. Whereas the boundary after *through* corresponds to a clear pause, the one after *rock* is less well defined, corresponding only to a pitch discontinuity, and an audible release of the /k/. If we allowed any discontinuity to count as a boundary for the purpose of the rule, we would have to say that this patterns like a nonrestrictive clause, and that its status is perhaps indicated by the mismatch between the nuclei. In fact (although this cannot yet be proved statistically) the boundary after *rock* is one that typically separates a noun phrase from a long postmodifier.

A self-evident prerequisite for the success of any mapping rules is that the domain and codomain must be characterized correctly. Just because relative clause is a familiar label in syntax does not mean that this is a relevant structure for prosody. *Postmodifier* – and *parenthesis* in the case of nonrestrictive clauses – is possibly a more useful category. We also have to describe correctly the prosodic patterns on to which these text structures map. The prosodic categories marked in a conventional intonation transcription of the kind developed by O'Connor–Arnold (1973) – a modified version of which was used for the transcription of the Spoken English Corpus – provides the phonetician's best guess at what these categories are like. Just as we take for granted that the best guesses of grammarians have to be revised after the study of a corpus, so intonation categories have to be checked against a corpus, and not just assumed to be correct.

Current work on the corpus involves going behind the transcription, combining the auditory impression with a visual inspection of the waveform. The first stage was to examine tone group boundaries in detail, and this has been reported elsewhere (Knowles 1991), and the present stage has included a preliminary study of the tones themselves.

Briefly, the findings on tone group boundary were that the simple distinction between major and minor boundaries was insufficient. There are in fact at least five different kinds of boundary:

0 Zero: Nothing measurable; in some cases one tone group pattern follows another without any embellishment of the join between them.
1 Segmental: This includes the audible release of stops, and a glottal onset to vowels.

2 Pitch discontinuity: A falling contour is followed by a jump up, or a rising contour is followed by a jump down.
3 Breathy pause: Breathing is audible during the pause.
4 Silent pause: No audible breathing.

For the speaker studied, a major tone group boundary was usually a long silent pause, with a duration of more than about 700msec. The examples in this paper were produced by that same speaker.

2. The status of tones

The labels conventionally applied to tones suggest that they are patterns which can be defined close to the physical level. Thus corresponding to

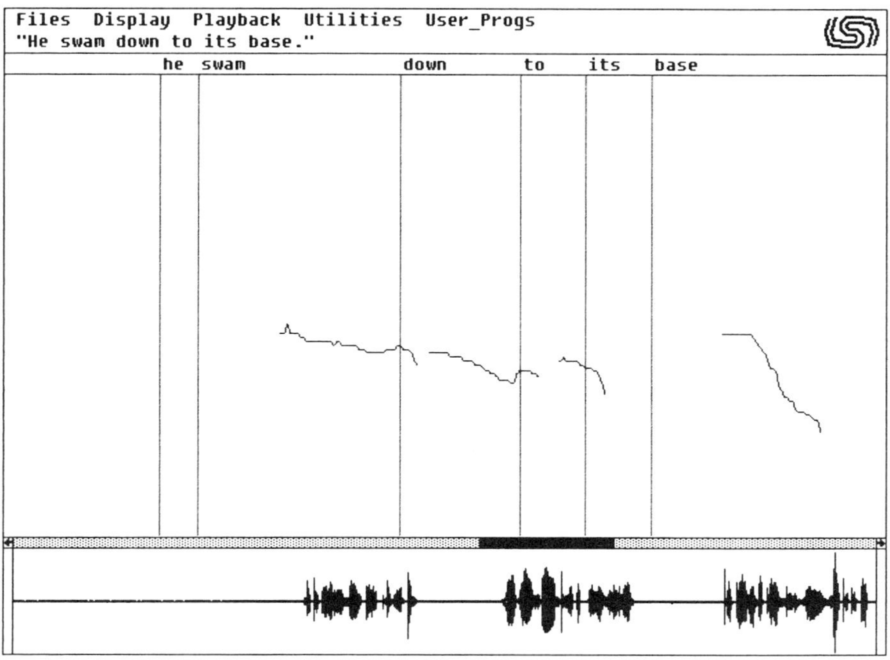

Figure 1.

a falling tone we can expect a fall in the fundamental frequency (F0), and for a rise there is a corresponding rise. The problem is the case of the "level" tone, for which one might expect an F0 pattern more or less level, or slightly falling with declination.

Some levels are of this kind, e. g. *swam* in the example

(2) He swam down to its base.

Figure 1 shows the annotated F0 contour, with the vertical lines positioned at the beginning of the accented syllables *swam* and *base*.
A rather different kind of "level" is found on *glimpse* in

(3) ...and caught a glimpse as he retreated of...

As shown in Figure 2, the F0 peaks on the accented syllable, which is thus out of line with neighbouring syllables. After the F0 drops back, it falls gradually until it reaches the second syllable of *retreated*, where it falls sharply. Note that the syllable *caught*, classed by the transcribers

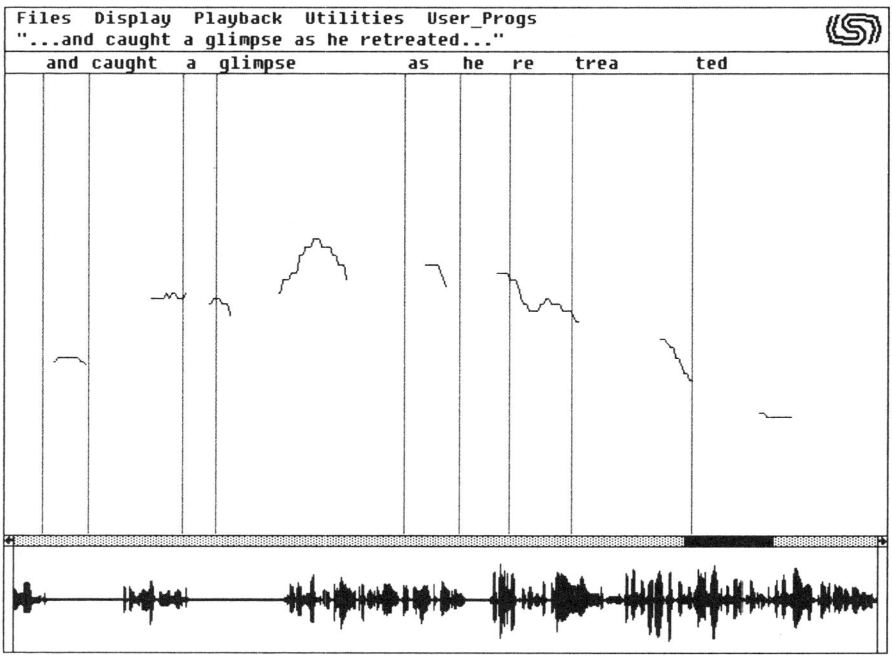

Figure 2.

not as having a level tone but as a "stressed but not accented" syllable, jumps up to a fairly level F0 contour.

The third common type of "level" occurs in the following example:

(4) The great rock

In the transcription, *great* is marked with a level, and *rock* with a fall. As can be seen in Figure 3, the F0 rises sharply for the "level" tone, and then falls back.

The patterns found in this extract from text G01 and marked as "level" tones varied from falls to rises to rise-falls: there were some level stretches, but these were marked in the transcription in some other way, e. g. "stressed but not accented".

Now unless the marks used by the transcribers are entirely arbitrary, there is an interesting phonological problem here. There is certainly no 1 : 1 relationship between prosodic categories and F0 events. In view of what has long been known about vowel and consonant phonemes, this is not surprising. Although we might define /d/ as a voiced alveolar stop

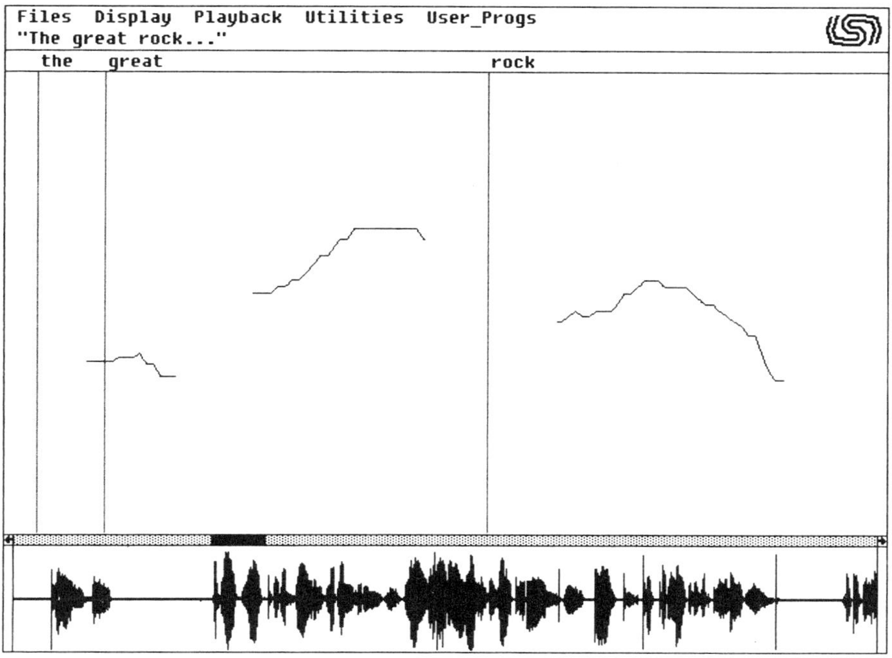

Figure 3.

– using a set of labels which seem to be close to the physical level – a particular instance of /d/ may not be voiced, need not be alveolar, and need not be made with a complete blocking of the air flow. Nor do individual features relate in a simple way to the physical level: voicing, for instance, does not depend on vocal fold vibration alone, but also involves voice onset time, and the effect on the duration of preceding segments. *Mutatis mutandis*, just because we use the label "level" to define a tone, that does not mean it has to be physically level in F0. Despite the phonetic terms used to label them, tones must be regarded as abstract phonological categories. And like vowel and consonant phonemes the rules for their phonetic realization are likely to be complex.

3. The accent point

An important feature of the phonetic realization of tones concerns the alignment of the F0 contour with vowels and consonants. Although the effect of a tone might be to highlight a whole word or phrase, its focus is on a single syllable. Within the syllable it focuses on the vowel, and if the vowel is a diphthong, on one of the elements of the diphthong. Ultimately within the relevant vowel there is a single point which appears to be the focus of accentuation. Since the term *focus* is already used in other senses, I shall call this point the *accent point*.

The accent point is implicitly used in the terminology used for tones. The auditory impression created by falls and fall-rises is that the accent point coincides with a peak in the pitch contour, while for rises it coincides with a trough. In the case of high and low levels, the pitch appears to jump to a higher or lower level and stay there. At the acoustic level, we find corresponding to the accent point local maxima (peaks) and minima (troughs) in the F0 contour. What we call a "fall" often corresponds to a hump-shaped contour, with an initial pitch transition to the accent point, while a "rise" corresponds to a trough, with an initial drop in F0 to the accent point. These initial pitch movements are disregarded in the terminology: it is not clear at this stage whether they are significant, or whether they should be regarded as the prosodic equivalents of allophonic variants. In the rise-fall the rise comes after the accent point, and in the fall-rise the fall follows the accent point. These complex tones may have an initial fall and rise respectively.

While it is relatively easy to measure peaks and troughs in any particular case, it is more difficult to find general patterns to account for the auditory impression of tones, or specify the kind of rule that determines where the speaker puts the peaks that give rise to the sensations of rise, level and fall. The peak corresponding to the accent point can come close to the beginning of the vowel, the end, or somewhere in the middle. In the illustrations above, *great* has a late peak, and *rock* an early one.

There are several forms such a rule could take. Among the more likely ones are:

(i) Put the peak x msec into the vowel.
(ii) Put the peak x msec from the end of the vowel.
(iii) Put the peak x% into the vowel.

In order to measure the peak position, we have to take the time at the beginning (B) and end (E) of the vowel, and the time of the peak (P) itself. The position can then be expressed as an elapsed time from the beginning (P-B) or the end (E-P), or as a proportion of the way into the vowel expressed as a percentage:

$$(((P-B)/(E-B)) \times 100).$$

Elapsed time rules are unlikely to be operating in view of the phenomena of *undershoot* and *overshoot*. The peak is not always found on the vowel at all, and can occur on a preceding or following voiced nonobstruent. Thus in *brick* early peak can occur on /r/, and in *banned* late peak can occur on /n/; *grand* can have the peak on the vowel, the /r/ or the /n/. If the position is expressed as a percentage, peaks on the vowel are in the range 0–100%, while cases of undershoot have a negative value, and those of overshoot a value of over 100%.

A study of the distribution of peak positions expressed as a percentage showed no evidence of clustering. There is no clustering round the mean as one would expect if the distribution were normal; nor is there any evidence of a bimodal distribution as one might expect if there were two phonological categories (say, "early peak" and "late peak"). In fact, a chi-square test indicated that the distribution could have arisen by chance. Peak position would seem to be a continuous variable.

At the extremes of the distribution, a few scores are much below zero or much above 100%, when the peak jumps a syllable, or even two syllables. These divergences cannot satisfactorily be explained by undershoot and overshoot. If the peak jumps to the syllable after the accented one, we can still measure its position relative to the vowel of that syllable.

We have here an independent variable which has a default value of zero, but can take on negative values (when the peak jumps to preceding syllables) or positive values (when the peak jumps to following syllables). This has long been recognized in the special case of the rise-fall, in which the peak jumps to the right.

The peak position was not explicitly considered when the transcription system was designed. But if it is an important feature of tones, it is at least possible that it might have been intuitively taken into account by the transcribers: if so, there could be interesting connections between tone type and peak position. Looking at the scores for tones for both transcribers, it emerges that the high level tends to peak at the end of the vowel, and at the other extreme the low fall just before the beginning of the vowel. This latter finding is not too surprising given that the low fall is often approached from a higher pitch.

The high level is of course the tone that occurs at the beginning of a tone group, and the low fall is the "final" tone *par excellence*, tending to complete a major tone group. It is possible that behind the phonological contrast of tone there is a functional contrast between an "initial" marker and a "final" marker. Looking at all final tones before different kinds of boundary, it was found that the greater the boundary the earlier the peak, with the earliest peaks preceding the silent pauses forming a major tone group boundary. The position with regard to initial position is not so clear: the latest peaks follow breathy pauses – i. e. those within a major tone group – followed by those following pitch discontinuities. Tones at the beginning of a major tone group are neither early nor late.

If instead of looking at all tones, we examine specifically initial high levels and final low falls, this association with minor tone groups rather than major tone groups becomes clearer. High levels peak latest after pitch discontinuity, often with overshoot and even peaking one or two syllables to the right; they peak earlier before pauses. Low falls peak earliest (often with undershoot) before breathy pause, and later and on the vowel elsewhere.

This connection with boundaries opens up the question of the phonology of the tone system. In the British approach, the tone as a whole is assumed to give pitch prominence to the accented syllable, and simultaneously to carry out its other meaningful functions. However, it might be possible to factor out the boundary features, leaving a simpler system for pitch prominence. This idea is not of course new: there is a long American tradition – going back at least to Trager–Smith (1951) and reappearing in Pierrehumbert (1980) – recognizing a *terminal juncture* or *boundary tone*.

4. Conclusion

One of the major questions which the linguist working on a spoken corpus will want to raise is how prosody relates to other aspects of linguistic structure, such as the relative clause types discussed at the beginning of this paper. Although a conventional transcription can give a useful first approximation, we really need to go beyond it, and measure prosodic parameters at the acoustic level. In doing this, we do not find direct acoustic correlates of perceived categories, and it is necessary to revise the theory on which the original transcription is based. There is no simple phonetic entity which can be identified as a tone group boundary at the acoustic level; nor are there stretches of unchanging F0 corresponding to "level tones". The findings so far must be regarded as tentative: they do relate after all only to one speaker in one text. Even so, they have some interesting implications.

First, the fact that the peak need not coincide with the accented syllable calls into question the definition of accent as stress with pitch prominence. If the pitch can peak (and thus give prominence) to the left or the right, we need some other definition of the accent itself. It is not possible to study what we think of as tones by examining F0 alone: we also need to take account of other factors such as duration, vowel quality and intensity (see Beckman 1986). Secondly, the possibility of factoring out boundary features from accentual features suggests quite a different model for this area of prosody. Instead of accent contours marked by a variety of tones, we have a single hump-shaped contour peaking and troughing in different ways relative to the accent point. Conventional tones are seen as members of paradigmatic system: for any accent the speaker selects one from the inventory of tones. Peak position is by contrast syntagmatic: every accent contour has a peak, and the question is where it comes. Tones are assumed to have a contrastive function, so that the "meaning" associated with a fall is distinctively different from that associated with a rise. Since tones do not in English distinguish lexical items from each other, these meanings must belong to some other part of the language system; but the theory of tones does not give any indications where they might be found. Peak position on the other hand is part of the linear organization of the text, and its function is closely related to that of prosodic boundaries. Any analysis of meaning in this area has to be firmly anchored in text organization.

Two categories which are of special interest for future research are low levels and rises. In the first place, the accent point for these coincides with the trough in the F0 contour, which is difficult to reconcile with pitch prominence. But in addition, any peak in the neighbourhood of the syllable perceived as accented is actually associated with the preceding accent, the following tone group boundary, or even the onset of the following tone group. It is anticipated at this stage that prosodic patterns which have in the past assumed to be part of the accentual system are more properly interpreted as part of the boundary system.

Notes

1. The Lancaster/IBM Spoken English Corpus was collected in a collaborative venture by the Unit for Computer Research on the English Language at the University of Lancaster, and IBM (UK) Scientific Centre. It consists of about 52,000 words in several versions, including standard orthographic text and prosodic transcription. The texts are divided into categories A through M; the examples in this paper are taken from category G, which consists of stories read aloud. Copies of the recordings are available from IBM (UK) Scientific Centre, St Clement Street, Winchester, Hants. Copies of the machine-readable versions are available from ICAME.
2. A waveform editor enables the user to see the waveform, a spectrogram and possibly the extracted F0 contour, as well as playing back any segment of the waveform. The package referred to above is the LSI Speech Workstation, made by Loughborough Sound Images.

References

Altenberg, Bengt
1987 *Prosodic patterns in spoken English. Studies in the correlation between prosody and grammar for text-to-speech conversion.* (Lund studies in English 76.) Lund: Lund University Press.

Beckman, Mary E.
1986 *Stress and non-stress accent.* Dordrecht: Foris Publications.

Johansson, Stig – Anna-Brita Stenström (eds.)
1991 *English computer corpora. Selected papers and research guide.* (Topics in English Linguistics 3.) Berlin: Mouton de Gruyter.

Knowles, Gerald
1991 "Prosodic labelling: The problem of tone group boundaries", in: Johansson–Stenström (eds.), 149–163.

O'Connor, J. D. – G. F. Arnold
1973 *Intonation of colloquial English.* London: Longman.

Pierrehumbert, J. Breckenridge
1980 The phonology and phonetics of English Intonation. (Unpublished PhD thesis, MIT.)

Quirk, Randolph – Sidney Greenbaum – Geoffrey Leech – Jan Svartvik
1985 *A comprehensive grammar of the English language*. London: Longman.
Trager, George – Henry L. Smith
1951 *An outline of English structure*. Washington: American Council of Learned Societies.

What do you think of that: A pilot study of the phraseology of the core words of English

Antoinette Renouf

1. Background

There is a continuing need in the field of applied linguistics, and particularly in language teaching and the hybrid area of text processing software development, for reliable criteria for assigning priorities in the selection of lexis. Corpus-based research points to frequency of word occurrence as an important factor, since a frequency profile of the lexicon of a text of any kind indicates that a small minority of words, unchanging at the very core, make the major contribution in text creation.

In 1984, as one of the advocates of a lexically-based language syllabus that took frequency into account (Sinclair – Renouf 1988: 140 – 160), I worked with a team within the Cobuild Project to identify the central features of the top 650 word forms in the Birmingham Corpus, for inclusion in such a syllabus (Renouf 1987: 167 – 178).

The lexical environments of those words were observed to include low frequency items; high-frequency words do not, of course, combine exclusively with each other. Linguists such as Lyons (1969) have pointed out that they are low in information content; and so they alternate with less common and semantically richer items, forming "collocational frameworks" (Renouf – Sinclair 1991: 128 – 143) to support them.

Since the 1984 study, the phenomenon of alternation between common and less common words, which I term "oscillation", has remained a matter of personal curiosity. In particular, I have wondered about the effect of reducing the degree of oscillation; or, to put it another way, what the nature is of the exclusively high-frequency language environment.

2. Aim

In this paper, we are therefore seeking to report on a study of what native speakers do with the language in the higher range; what the recycling of highly-frequent words produces; and, from a pedagogic point of view, what the learner of English can do with just the core words at his or her disposal.

We shall look briefly at the nature of the longest strings that are produced, then move on to study in some detail the semantics and grammar of shorter, more recurrent strings.

3. Data

3.1. The corpora

The data for the study consisted of an 18 million word written corpus and a 1.3 million word spoken corpus, the two components of the Birmingham Corpus. In this report, we shall refer to them as "corpora" rather than "sub-corpora". From these two corpora were drawn lists of the top 150 word forms, subdivided into the top 50, 100 and 150 respectively.

3.2. The word lists

In creating the word lists, a number of measures were taken in the interests of simplicity. Orthographic representations of nonverbal elements, such as *er* and *um* were removed, because they generally function as interpolations within otherwise unbroken lexical strings. A number of single characters, representing a range of functions, were also removed. They chiefly represent markers of participant change, but include the word *p* for the monetary denomination. On the other hand, contracted forms such as *don't* and *there's* were allowed, since these are single graphic forms. No attempt was made at homographic separation.

The resultant word lists are shown in Table 1.

Table 1. Top 150 word forms in the Birmingham Corpus

Written Component (18 m)			Spoken Component (1.3 m)		
1–50	51–100	101–150	1–50	51–100	101–150
the	up	made	the	don't	than
of	out	too	and	an	course
and	more	before	of	got	good
to	who	such	a	just	into
a	me	many	to	by	there's
in	them	us	I	them	should
that	about	through	that	when	only
was	has	little	in	get	did
it	will	also	you	that's	could
I	into	don't	it	then	fact
is	can	go	is	see	where
he	some	still	have	has	want
for	could	should	this	oh	its
with	like	own	yes	say	they're
as	do	years	we	going	over
on	then	good	they	were	work
had	only	must	but	some	here
be	time	never	was	more	make
you	now	those	for	out	you're
his	than	being	on	who	lot
at	other	make	think	been	first
but	its	come	be	up	actually
not	your	long	are	had	come
they	very	off	as	mean	down
by	over	work	what	other	us
have	two	day	well	go	back
this	even	think	it's	really	take
from	people	old	so	me	rather
are	any	again	one	much	those
or	our	world	at	will	does
she	these	between	do	their	years
her	down	it's	with	your	being
were	first	here	very	time	you've
all	most	right	not	I'm	most
which	just	take	or	my	her
we	back	life	there	how	put
one	after	say	if	she	many
an	way	might	about	thing	look
there	because	another	which	these	I've
their	did	come	all	any	question

continued overleaf

Table 1. continued

Written Component (18 m)			Spoken Component (1.3 m)		
1 – 50	51 – 100	101 – 150	1 – 50	51 – 100	101 – 150
would	much	thought	know	sort	same
so	how	going	he	things	find
if	know	away	no	way	year
said	may	great	can	right	also
been	new	got	people	quite	kind
my	man	went	because	said	we're
him	see	men	now	something	point
when	well	same	would	two	must
what	where	children	like	our	can't
no	too	while	from	his	may

The definition of high-frequency item includes, as can be seen in Table 1, not just items traditionally thought of as grammatical but also lexical words, notably core verbs.

The commoner a word is in these lists, the more likely it is to dominate the word strings that it and the other words enter into. For this reason, an anticipatory look was taken at the top 50 in each case, to see what they suggested in relation to language use.

The top 50 written words contain the pronouns *that, it, I, he, you, his, they, this, she, her, which, we, one, their, my, him* and *what*, that play a range of grammatical roles. There is a very sparse selection of verbs: simply *was, is, had, be, have, are, were, would, said* and *been*. Of these, *said* is the only lexical verb. This would suggest that the writers will be concerned with the fact or possibility of someone being or doing something, and on reporting what others said.

The top 50 spoken words include fewer pronouns, only *I, that, you, it* (*it's*), *this, we, they,* and *he*, in that order. Together with *people*, and in most cases the multi-class *all, what* and *which*, these can all occupy a grammatical subject position. There are few verbs available: *is, have, was, think, be, are, do, know, can, would* and *like*. The indications are that the 50 words will combine to facilitate interaction between speakers. Expression of opinion, and requesting of opinion and information are suggested. The words *yes* and *well* will allow agreement or qualification and, together with *but*, hedging and polite disagreement.

4. Methodology

Strings (string tokens) made up of the two word lists were extracted from the different corpus components. They were sorted into string types in order of length, beginning with the longest. The longest strings inevitably subsumed shorter ones, but the frequency count given to shorter string types was not modified to take that into account, and so understates somewhat their significance. This was not felt important for a preliminary study.

The strings were studied in isolation and in context, and the following findings emerged.

5. Findings

5.1. The longest word strings

We were interested to see just how long language users can go on stringing high-frequency words together, and what these strings consist of. Altenberg (1991: 1–26) observes that "the longer, less common [combinations] have a higher-incidence of open-class items", but this will not be the case where open-class words are largely prohibited. The results are shown in Tables 2 and 3.

From Table 2, we can see that the writer of English occasionally keeps going surprisingly long on a small vocabulary. We also see that this propensity increases with a greater lexical range. Strings are longer still, however, in the spoken data, as can be seen in Table 3.

The strings in Tables 2 and 3 are statistically interesting, but they are not of overwhelming interest to the linguist. One can observe that they are nonce formations. Whilst incomplete, they are largely regular in grammatical terms, made up of a series of linked or overlapping units. Their length is partly attributable to lexical reiteration. This is expected in speech (10, 15), but is perhaps surprisingly evident in the written examples, (1–6). The strings are largely lacking in idioms, but (4) is a (mis)quotation of the Lincoln aphorism beginning: "You can fool all the people some of the time and some of the people all the time...".

Table 2. Longest word strings in the written corpus

No.	Word Rank	No. of Words	
(1)	1–50	12	he was and what he was and he was not to be
(2)		12	it not to be there but it was there and when the
(3)		12	it was for you it was all for you you said I
(4)	51–100	19	all of the people some of the time and some of the people all the time but could not
(5)		19	if we can have two one for me and one for you like I said and we can have
(6)		18	that you know it and when you do not to know that you do not know that is
(7)	101–150	21	for a way to get through it I would think only about where I was I thought not what I was
(8)		21	it was for the little man that he should do so he had to get him out of the way at
(9)		21	that it was not for me even if it was or might have been for her even if it was her

Table 3. Longest word strings in the spoken corpus

No.	Word Rank	No. of Words	
(10)	1–50	18	and then I think she said that she will do it but I mean I don't know how
(11)		18	you know you know you know if there was some way if there was some way that we
(12)	51–100	22	in there and say you know right this is what you have to say and and this is what you have to
(13)		19	I know but I mean some people are I think I got my I think I got quite a
(14)	101–150	24	really want to take them I said to her well I don't know what to do and she said well if I were you
(15)		23	I mean I think you can there are I mean I think it's good to go into that sort of thing with the

Predictions as to the effect of the top 50 items in each corpus are not borne out by these data. We had anticipated that the presence of forms of the lexeme *be* in the written corpus would lead to existential statements, as in (1, 2), but in these strings we see that *be* is also used in phrasal combinations such as (3), (8) and (9). We thought that *said* would characterise the written strings, in introducing quotation; in fact, it is more influential in the spoken extracts. However, these discrepancies may be explicable in terms of the singular nature of very long strings.

Two observations of particular interest emerged from the data in Tables 2 and 3. The first is that the longest of the restricted word strings in the written corpus consist of written representations of speech from novels, such as (3); while, as intimated in the last paragraph, the longest strings of spoken words consist of quotation, of self and others, as in (10), (12) and (14).

The second observation is that these long and grammatically regular strings do not inspire one to internal investigation, but rather to speculation about their lexical completion. Two examples, (1) and (12) will be shown in their original contexts by way of illustration:

for (1) "He liked *where he was and what he was and he was not to be* lured into any associations that might compromise him."

for (12) "No I mean, really, er I I'm going to prime people before I go *in there and say, you know, "Right, this is what you have to say and this is what you have to* ask.""

The second of these contexts is notable in that, with the exception of the rarer word *prime*, a slight relaxation in lexical restriction would have allowed it to qualify as a single string.

5.2. The most recurrent word strings

The longer a word string, the more likely it is to be a single occurrence. The real interest comes when the phrases become recurrent. *Bona fide* dual instances of strings begin to occur, though sparsely, at around 7 words in both the written and the spoken corpora. They become established, along with multiple occurrences, at six words.

In Tables 4 and 5, the 30 most frequent six-word strings are provided, again made up of the top 150 words of each of the two corpora. The frequency count for each string in the particular corpus is provided (as it will be in all subsequent tables).

There are fewer instances of each phrase type among the spoken strings in Table 5 than among the written in Table 4. This is because the spoken corpus is approximately fourteen times smaller. The difference should be borne in mind when comparing the two batches; rank is probably a more reliable indicator of significance.

Table 4. Top 30 six-word strings in the written corpus

48	in such a way as to	10	and at the same time the
25	at the same time as the	9	to be one of the most
24	what you do and what you	9	it was going to be a
19	all you have to do is	9	for the first time in their
18	in the same way as the	9	at the same time he was
17	had it not been for the	8	the first of these is the
16	on the first day of the	8	it was one of the most
15	in such a way that the	8	it is one of the most
13	what are you going to do	8	in the same way that the
12	this is not to say that	8	I don't know what to do
12	in much the same way as	8	for the first time on the
11	for the first time in years	8	but it was not to be
11	and at the same time to	7	when we got back to the
10	of the way in which the	7	when I got back to the
10	for the first time in the	7	what do you think of the

Table 5. Top 30 six-word strings in the spoken corpus

6	what do you think of the	3	in a way but you see
6	can we have our first question	3	I think it would be an
5	what do you think about the	3	I think it would be a
5	may we have our first question	3	I do not think that the
4	to me to be a very	3	and I think that's a very
4	if you're going to be a	3	and I think one of the
4	if you see what I mean	3	and I think it is very
4	at the same time as the	3	and all that sort of thing
4	and this is one of the	2	yes I think the question is
4	and one of the things that	2	yes I think it's a very
4	and all this sort of thing	2	yes I think it was a
4	and all that kind of thing	2	with the question of how the
3	to me that one of the	2	which I think does to some
3	this is the first of a	2	what do you want to say
3	there are quite a lot of	2	what do you think of that

The strings shown are interesting in ways that the long strings are not. They are fairly heavily recurrent, which makes them more representative of the language as a whole. They are also less grammatically predictable from their parts, on the whole, so are worthy of internal investigation; we shall examine the idiomatic nature of these strings in more detail in table 11.

They also reveal recurrent semantic features. A tentative semantic regrouping of the two batches might be as shown in Tables 6 (written) and Table 7 (spoken).

Table 6. Semantic groupings in top 30 six-word strings, written corpus

Placing Things in Time/Order[i]	
25	at the same time as the
16	on the first day of the
11	for the first time in years
11	and at the same time to
10	for the first time in the
10	and at the same time the
9	for the first time in their
9	at the same time he was
8	the first of these is the
8	for the first time on the
7	when we got back to the
7	when I got back to the
Complete/Interactive Phrases	
19	all you have to do is
13	what are you going to do
8	I don't know what to do
7	what do you think of the
Indicating Manner	
48	in such a way as to
15	in such a way that the
10	of the way in which the
Making Comparisons	
18	in the same way as the
12	in much the same way as
8	in the same way that the
Placing Things in Importance/Specifying	
9	to be one of the most
8	it was one of the most
8	it is one of the most
Making Contrasts	
17	had it not been for the
12	this is not to say that
Prefacing/Concluding	
9	it was going to be a
8	but it was not to be
Fragments	
24	what you do and what you

[i] Some instances of the string-types containing *at the same time* may not express notions of time, but belong in the "contrasts" group.

Table 7. Semantic groupings in top 30 six-word strings, spoken corpus

Expressing Opinion	
3	I think it would be an
3	I think it would be a
3	I do not think that the
3	and I think that's a very
3	and I think one of the
3	and I think it is very
2	yes I think the question is
2	yes I think it's a very
2	yes I think it was a
2	which I think does to some
Complete/Interactive phrases	
6	can we have our first question
5	may we have our first question
2	what do you want to say
Requesting Opinion[i]	
6	what do you think of the
5	what do you think about the
2	what do you think of that
Generalising/Being Vague	
4	and all this sort of thing
4	and all that kind of thing
3	there are quite a lot of
3	and all that sort of thing
Specifying	
4	and this is one of the
4	and one of the things that
Placing Things in Time/Order	
4	at the same time as the
3	this is the first of a
Requesting Agreement	
4	if you see what I mean
Fragments[ii]	
4	to me to be a very
4	if you're going to be a
3	to me that one of the
3	in a way but you see
2	with the question of how the

[i] The third type in the "requesting opinion" group is a complete phrase, and so belongs also in the "complete/interactive" group

[ii] These fragments are suggestive of the semantics of other groups, but not interpretable without further context.

The semantic groupings in Tables 6 and 7 are of necessity provisional, but they serve to indicate that certain functions of language are characteristic among the high-frequency words, at least in the Birmingham Corpus. The most recurrent function within the written strings is the placing of a thing or event in time or order. Within the spoken strings, it is the expression of opinion; and four of the fragmentary spoken string types are also redolent of this pragmatic area.

There is some correspondence between the two corpora, particularly in the groups of "complete and/or interactive phrases". This may be attributable to the written representations of speech in the written corpus. But the similarity is only in the lexical content; in discourse terms, three of the written phrase types are "problem-solution" signals (Hoey, 1983 [1991: passim]), whilst this function is absent in the spoken types. There is one identically-worded string in the two groups – *what do you think of the* – which might or might not be significant. Svartvik (1991: passim) says, of multi-word items, that "most types do not appear to be characteristic of either the spoken or written varieties"; this is not borne out by the recurrent string types that we have looked at, but they are, after all, a particular subset of the totality of language.

They are nevertheless important for what they do show, which is that strings of common words bring meaning to the text. In speech, they are not just a product of the interaction; they create it.

5.3. Phrasal contexts

It will be apparent even from the limited data in Tables 4 and 5 that longer strings are in turn made up of shorter, more recurrent strings. If we extract these, within their longer contexts, we shall gain an insight into the context of phrases. Tables 8 and 9 show some patterns that emerge. Table 8 looks within six-word strings; Table 9 looks outside them.

As we see in Table 9, the lexical restriction imposed in our study allows us access only to recurrent contexts that are short and largely abbreviated. Nevertheless, these short contexts are worthy of consideration. What we see within each string type in Table 8 are the beginnings of collocational sets that represent the potential for internal variation in those strings. But it may be necessary to turn to unrestricted context outside these string types, if we are to reveal more about the relationship between the lexical variation and the semantics of these strings; this might, for example, show when *and all that sort of thing* is synonymous with *and all that kind of thing*, and when not.

Surrounding each phrase in Table 9, rather than within it, are the rudiments of grammatical units or, lexically speaking, phrases; in other words, we see colligational information as to the use of each phrase. In some cases, the context is complete, as in *in years* or in the incipient collocational set, *in his/her life*.

These preliminary findings point a way forward in relation to how we may look at phraseology. If progressively greater oscillation, or lexical range, is allowed, we shall be able to monitor accurately the manner in which collocational sets, of both single words and phrases, accumulate at each stage, or in each frequency band, within and around the phrase.

Altenberg (1987: 133–143) created a diagrammatic representation of high-frequency combinations in the London-Lund Corpus (LLC) to indicate their functional distribution in text. The presentation was similar to that of Tables 8 and 9, although we have not attempted to apply the

Table 8. Patterns of internal variation in six-word strings

(prep) the same (X)

25		at	the	same	time	as	the
11	and	at	the	same	time		to
10	and	at	the	same	time		the
9		at	the	same	time		he was
18		in	the	same	way	as	the
8		in	the	same	way	that	the

in such a way (X)

48	in	such	a	way	as	to
15	in	such	a	way	that	the

and all (det) (X) of thing

4	and	all	this	sort	of	thing
3	and	all	that	sort	of	thing
4	and	all	that	kind	of	thing

I think (pron) (be) (det)

3		I	think	it	would be	an	
3		I	think	it	would be	a	
3	and	I	think	that	's	a	very
3	and	I	think	it	is	a	very
2	yes	I	think	it	's	a	very
2	yes	I	think	it	was	a	

Table 9. Patterns of variation in the context of strings

for the first time in								
38		for	the	first	time	in		
11		for	the	first	time	in		years
10		for	the	first	time	in	the	
9		for	the	first	time	in	their	
6		for	the	first	time	in	a	
6		for	the	first	time	in	his	life
4		for	the	first	time	in	my	life
4		for	the	first	time	in	its	
7	and	for	the	first	time	I		
4	and	for	the	first	time	he		
3	to me	for	the	first	time			
what do you think								
7	what	do	you	think				
6	what	do	you	think	of	the		
5	what	do	you	think	about	the		
3	what	do	you	think	you			
2	what	do	you	think	about			
2	what	do	you	think	of		that	
could do with								
6		I	could	do	with	a		
4		you	could	do	with	a		
4			could	do	with	a		
1	and	he	could	do	with	more of it but this		

functional type of analysis to our data in any formal way at this stage. The LLC Corpus is relatively small, so yielded few instances of each phrase, on average. The Birmingham Corpus is larger and inevitably generates more instances of each phrase type, as shown in Tables 4 and 5, and would be an appropriate test-bed for Altenberg's (inspired by Halliday 1985: Chapter 3) analysis of functional position.

5.4. Lexicalising tendency of high-frequency word forms

Pawley and Syder (1983: 191–225) use the term "lexicalised" of units "of clause length or longer whose grammatical form and lexical content is wholely or largely fixed". We apply it somewhat differently; to the phenomenon of high-frequency words taking on a lower-frequency function of one kind or another.

When the degree of oscillation within word strings is limited, we note that the lexicalising phenomenon becomes more pronounced. It manifests itself in different ways, which we shall identify and illustrate with reference to our written corpus data.

5.4.1. Lexicalisation of grammatical words

Some of the grammatical items among the top 150 words take on a rarer lexical role, as shown in Table 10.

Table 10. Lexicalised grammatical words

he (pronoun to noun)	
1	that this he was not only a he but a he in the
in (preposition to adjective)	
3	with the in (breath)

5.4.2. Lexicalisation of high-frequency verbs

On a previous occasion (Sinclair – Renouf 1988: 153), we have talked of high-frequency verbs as being "delexical", of having the tendency to relinquish their independent meaning and enter into shared meaning with lower-frequency words. An example would be make in the lexical unit *make an arrangement*, where it cooperates with *arrangement* to mean *arrange*; and *arrangement* is the main contributor of meaning.

In our realm of restricted lexis, we find evidence of an opposing tendency. The very common verb is seen to shift role on occasion, and become a less frequent noun. This act of grammatical transformation is accompanied by a move into an idiomatic unit. Given the lexical restriction, we find the transformed item itself being the main contributor of meaning to the idiom. Some examples, taken from the written corpus, are presented in Table 11.

The important point demonstrated by Table 11 is that we have uncovered a grammatical shift that is a feature of everyday, educated English. It is one of the means by which speakers ring the stylistic changes whilst not shifting out of a high-frequency register; it allows variety.

A rarer lexicalised alternative is also an insurance against potential ambiguity. The unmarked *I know* is pressed into service very regularly and to many different semantic and pragmatic ends. To convey that one is a member of a small elite who knows something that others don't, there is always *I know* as a potential realisation, but it only conveys this meaning when pronounced in a particular way. The marked *I am in the know* is unambiguous.

Table 11. Grammatical transformation from high-frequency verb to low-frequency noun in the written corpus

in the know – (extract)	
4	in the know
2	in the know and
1	are in the know
1	in the know that
1	is in the know
1	those in the know
1	all in the know of
1	by those in the know
1	not in the know the
1	of those in the know
know how	
2	the know how of
1	have the know how to
1	on the know how of
1	but the know how of the
1	for the know how they will
1	through the know how of old
1	to see but the know how had also been
(be) a must	
4	is a must
1	a must if your
1	are a must for
1	as a must before
1	is a must a
1	is a must for
1	which is a must
1	is a must in our
1	to be is a must
1	it is a must for any
on the make	
3	on the make
1	men on the make
1	he was on the make had long
1	people on the make but I just then was
(while/if/when) the going (be) good	
2	while the going was good
1	while the going is good a
1	if the going is good he will
1	him when the going was good and he had

The further significance of this finding is that it indicates a move towards nominalised structures. This is a trend that is conventionally associated with writing in technical domains, and formal and academic registers (although we prefer to see it in relation to discourse purpose). Here we have found nominalisation in everyday speech and in nontechnical writing.

6. Conclusion

This was a preliminary study, intended to reveal the phraseological relationships entered into by just the commonest 150 words. We have discovered that at this level of restriction, there is relatively little which can be expressed fully. To this extent, we have not yet hit the most fruitful vein, which would support a categorical statement about the language, nor are we yet in a position to offer any comprehensive data or advice to language learners.

Nevertheless, we have been able to observe what can be achieved at this level. The recurrent strings that occur are seen to be anticipating and setting up the conditions for different sorts of discourse activity, such as the requesting and giving of opinions, or the narration of events. They also manage to create some complete utterances, albeit short ones.

Looked at from a lexico-grammatical point of view, such strings reveal the beginnings of high-frequency collocational sets as part of their internal variation. The external context of recurrent strings has also been examined, and found to contain rudimentary colligational information about the use of phrases, rather than just words.

Finally, we have been able to uncover a tendency among the high-frequency words, both grammatical and lexical, to take on new roles as lexical items in low-frequency idioms.

The natural next step will be to increase the lexical range of our study. We have a strong suspicion, based on inspection of the data during this study, that with even a minor addition to the word lists, say of another 50 or 100 words, the strings will become significantly longer before hitting the oscillation barrier, and more often phraseologically complete.

The less restricted lexicon will also bring us a clearer view of phrasal contexts; fuller collocational sets will emerge within and around phrases.

The sets will still not be complete, at this high-level range, but they will begin to reveal more about the interchangeability of high-frequency items, such as the modals and other verbs.

References

Aarts Jan – Willem Meijs (eds.)
1990 *Theory and practice in corpus linguistics.* Amsterdam: Rodopi.

Karin Aijmer – Bengt Altenberg (eds.)
1991 *English corpus linguistics: In honour of Jan Svartvik.* London: Longman.

Altenberg, Bengt
1987 "Speech as linear composition", in: Graham Caie *et al.* (eds.), 133–143.

Altenberg, Bengt – Mats Eeg-Olofsson
1991 "Phraseology in spoken English: Presentation of a project", in: Jan Aarts – Willem Meijs (eds.), 1–26.

Caie, Graham – Kirsten Haarstrup – Arnt Lykke Jakobsen – Jorgen Erik Nielsen – Jorgen Sevaldsen – Henrik Specht – Arne Zettersten (eds.)
1990 *Proceedings from the Fourth Nordic Conference for English Studies* (Elsinore 11th–14th May 1989). Copenhagen: University of Copenhagen, Department of English.

Carter, Ron – Michael McCarthy
1988 *Vocabulary and language teaching.* London: Longman.

Halliday, Michael A. K.
1985 *An introduction to functional grammar.* London: Edward Arnold.

Hoey, Michael
1983 *On the surface of discourse.* (Reprinted 1991, University of Nottingham.) London: George Allen and Unwin.

Lyons, John
1969 *Introduction to theoretical linguistics.* Cambridge: Cambridge University Press.

Pawley, Andrew – Frances Hodges Syder
1983 "Two puzzles for linguistic theory: Native-like selection and native-like fluency", in: Jack C. Richards – Richard W. Schmidt (eds.), 191–225.

Renouf, Antoinette
1987 "Moving on", in: John Sinclair (ed.), 167–178.

Renouf, Antoinette – John Sinclair
1991 "Collocational frameworks", in: Karin Aijmer – Bengt Altenberg (eds.), 128–143.

Richards, Jack C. – Richard W. Schmidt (eds.)
1983 *Language and communication.* London: Longman.

Sinclair, John (ed.)
1987 *Looking up: An account of the COBUILD project in lexical computing and the development of the Collins COBUILD English Language Dictionary.* London: Collins.

Sinclair, John – Antoinette Renouf
1988 "A lexical syllabus for language learning", in: Ron Carter – Michael McCarthy, 140–160.

Svartvik, Jan
1991 "What can real spoken data teach teachers of English?". [Paper read at the Georgetown University Round Table on Languages and Linguistics, April 1–4, 1991.]

Sequences of spatial and temporal adverbials in spoken and written English

Hilde Hasselgård

1. Introduction

This study is aimed at investigating some aspects of the distribution and the organisation of adverbial sequences in speech and writing. Before I go to the main part of the investigation some definitions and delimitations may be in order.

The term "adverbial sequence" will be taken to denote two or more adverbials which belong to the same clause and thus relate to the same verb phrase. For this study I am examining adverbial sequences containing two or more spatial and/or temporal adverbials.

At this stage of my investigation the material collected imposes one very important limitation on the analysis: so far written language is represented only by newspaper language (taken from the news pages of 15 British newspapers), and spoken language only by conversation (eight 5000-word texts from Svartvik – Quirk 1979).

The focus of interest in this study, then, is the organisation of adverbials in sequences. In which order do they occur? What determines their placement? Are there any rules or regularities? And most importantly for this particular study: Are there any differences to be found between spoken and written adverbial sequences?

The most frequent position of spatial and temporal adverbials is at the end of the clause, after obligatory clause elements (e. g. Quirk *et al.* 1985: 499). It is, however, often possible to have these adverbials in other positions as well; their freedom of position is relatively great.

There are several angles from which the placement of adverbials may be viewed. Syntax certainly plays an important part. Some adverbials are obligatory, others are optional. I analyse as obligatory those adverbials which are required in order to make the clause grammatically acceptable. These adverbials are regularly placed in End position (after the Predicator), and it is very hard to move them to other positions. Most optional adverbials have a greater "transportability range" (cf. Enkvist 1976b: 63).[1]

The placement of an adverbial may be an indicator of its syntactic function or semantic role:

(1) He *still* works here. (time adjunct)
(2) *Still* he works here. (conjunct)[2]

In example (1) *still* functions as a temporal adverbial, whereas in (2) its initial position strongly favours an interpretation of it as a conjunct adverbial.

The position of an adverbial can also determine its semantic scope. See below for further discussion.

2. Types of adverbial sequence

In my analysis I distinguish two main types of adverbial sequence. A sequence of adverbials which occur in the same position is termed a "cluster". Spatial/temporal adverbials in a cluster are normally adjacent, but may be separated by some other optional constituent. Examples of clusters:

(3) *Out in the road between the two main hospital buildings* the noise was deafening. (*Daily Mail*, 4. 2. 88: 9)
(4) Teaching seems to come *to an end* you know *after about six weeks.* (S.1.4.632)[3]

The other type of sequence is called a "combination". Combinations are sequences where two (or more) adverbial slots have been filled.

(5) *On the 6th* winds gusted to 90 mph *at Mumbles in South Wales.* (DT 1.2.88: 18)
(6) ...because there *still* seems to be some *in the box.* (S.1.7.86)

There are several reasons why I have made this distinction. One is that the two types differ in frequency, cf. Table 1.

The number of sequences analysed thus totals 736, of which 561 (76.2%) are clusters, and 175 (23.8%) are combinations. This suggests that when adverbials of time/space occur in the same clause, they tend to be attracted to each other. Clusters can thus tentatively be viewed as more basic than combinations. It has even been suggested by Taglicht

Table 1. The distribution of clusters and combinations in the written and in the spoken material

	newspapers		*conversation*	
2A cluster[4]	334	67.9%	158	64.8%
3A cluster	49	10.0%	10	4.1%
4A cluster	9	1.8%	1	0.4%
2A combination	77	15.7%	61	25.0%
3A combination	19	3.9%	11	4.5%
4A combination	4	0.8%	2	0.8%
5A combination	–	–	1	0.4%
Total	492	100.0%	244	100.0%

(1984: 21) that a sequence of adjacent adverbials should be treated as one constituent, as a kind of "quasi-appositional structure". When several adverbial expressions are piled up on top of each other, it may indeed be difficult to determine which ones function on their own as separate adverbials, and which ones should be analysed in terms of appositional or postmodifying structures, related to an NP in the preceding adverbial expression.

(7) Do you remember when Harry McLair, *about a year ago* showed some *in his shed in a cold spell at Christmas about this time of the year before that party*? (S.1.7.1033)

This sentence contains maximally six adverbials. It is however possible to analyse both *at Christmas* and *about this time of the year* as postmodifiers to *cold spell*, in which case we have reduced the number of adverbials to four. The criterion I have used for giving a phrase the status of a separate adverbial in such structures, is that it should be able to function as such on its own, without the support of any other (adverbial) phrase.

A difference in frequency is of course not sufficient reason for establishing two categories of sequences. However, there is also a difference in the internal organisation of clusters and combinations.

In clusters, especially in End position (where most of the clusters occur) there is a marked tendency for the adverbials to follow a certain order, the main principle being that spatial adverbials precede temporal ones (Hasselgård 1988: 96). In combinations, on the other hand, no such order can be detected. There is even some evidence that combinations are used when the speaker/writer wants to use a sequence of adverbials that cannot be realised as a cluster, or which is very rarely realised as such (1988: 141). The order of adverbials in a cluster is also largely dependent on the semantic scope of each adverbial. There is a clear tendency for predicational adverbials (whose scope is the predicate) to precede sentential adverbials (whose scope is the whole clause). This is the prevailing ordering principle in the following much quoted example from Quirk *et al.* (1985: 512) where the first adverbial is predicational, the second sentential. The order of these adverbials could not have been reversed, and only the second one could have been moved to initial position.

(8) She kissed her mother *on the cheek on the platform.*

Table 2 gives some figures which show clearly that combinations and clusters are differently structured. (The total number of examples is lower

Table 2. The internal structure of adverbial sequences containing both a spatial and a temporal adverbial.

	Clusters		*Combinations*	
Space + Time	325	87.8%	15	12.5%
Time + Space	45	12.2%	105	87.5%
Total	370	100.0%	120	100.0%

in this table than in Table 1, because all the sequences containing just one type of adverbial – either space or time – have been disregarded.) This difference in structure is partly due to the relatively greater mobility of temporal adverbials as compared to spatial adverbials. This means that whereas spatial adverbials tend to be placed in End position, temporal adverbials are more apt to occupy other positions as well.

An interesting point is that the structure as well as the use of combinations seems to be governed by factors which reside outside the clause to a fairly great extent. Thus it is often possible to detect some reason why a combination has been chosen in preference to a cluster, which in many respects seems to be a more "basic" way of organising an adverbial sequence. Such reasons may be clarity (i. e. making the sentence comprehensible), sentence balance (end weight), information structure, and cohesion.

(9) *Before the debate* a "Yes to merger" pamphlet, written by seven leading social democrats will be sent *to every delegate.* (*Guardian*, 27.1.88: 3)

In this example the temporal adverbial has been placed in initial position. In a cluster in End position it would in all probability have occurred clause-finally, i. e. after the spatial adverbial, due to the "basic order" found in clusters in End position (see above and Hasselgård 1988: 96). Such an order would, however, make the spatial adverbial less prominent in the information structure than it appears in clause-final position. A reason for having the first adverbial in initial position may thus be to get it out of clause-final position, so that end focus may be assigned to the spatial adverbial. Besides, the temporal adverbial contains a definite NP, which marks it as given information. The sentence thus displays a nice progression from given to new information. *The debate* has been mentioned earlier, so that the placing of it in initial position serves as a cohesive tie.

Medial position does not readily accept clusters, and so a combination may be chosen instead. Example (10), in which the speaker corrects himself, shows this very clearly. (The example was found in the files of the Survey of English Usage.)

(10) And as I *often* had *previously* made – m – (as I) made plain to the house – *on previous occasions*. (SEU.s.11. 4.56)

Adverbial placement can also function as a text-structuring device. Example (11) displays what Enkvist (1976 a: 11) calls "iconic cohesion", namely "the repetition of patterns which leads to isomorphism between different constituents of a clause or sentence". The fact that all the sentences start with a spatial adverbial contributes strongly to the unity of the text.

(11) *In the Irish Republic* a woman was hit by a farm gate and pinned against a wall at Casteisland, Co Kerry, and *in Devon* a woman died at Mary Tavy when a tree was blown on to her car. *In Ireland* winds reached 107 mph and touched 96 mph in Wales. [...] *In Cornwall* hundreds of homes were without electricity after power lines were cut. (*The Independent*, 11.2.88: 3)

Another important ordering principle here is what Virtanen (1988: 238) calls "the principle of crucial information first". In (11) all the different actions take place in different settings, so it is crucial for an adequate interpretation of each clause that the setting should be indicated before the action is described. This enables the reader to keep track of the events, and to make sense of the text.

According to Virtanen (1988) a text tends to be dominated by some *text-strategic continuity*, defined (1988: 94) as "a thematic or topical uniform text-structuring orientation or unity chosen to attain [...] a maximally profitable text organisation". The text-strategic continuity is manifest in the text as linguistic elements, often placed towards the beginning of the clause. One such type of continuity is *continuity of place*, where a series of references to a spatial frame structures and creates unity in the text. Within this framework, then, the text from which (11) has been taken clearly exhibits continuity of place as its main principle of organisation.

3. Differences between spoken and written English

Table 1 above shows that there is a difference between the spoken and the written material investigated as regards the distribution of clusters and combinations. Although the material is as yet too small for any firm conclusions to be drawn from it, there are strong indications that adverbial sequences are realised as combinations more often in the spoken than in the written material, as shown in Table 3 (a simplified version of Table 1).

Table 3. The distribution of clusters and combinations over the spoken and written material.

	newspapers	*conversation*
clusters	79.7%	69.3%
combinations	20.4%	30.7%
Total	100.0%	100.0%

A closer look at the structure of the combinations found in both types of material helps to explain the difference in frequency. We find that the "spoken combinations" with one adverbial in initial position and one in medial or end position constitute a fairly homogeneous group. Their most frequent pattern is the one shown in (13–16), with an anaphoric Time relationship adverbial in initial position.

(13) And *then* you clambered *up on the platform.* (S.1.3.526)
(14) And *then* I shan't get any scripts *from the assistants before about ... the eighth.* (S.1.1.185)
(15) and *then* we all sat *this long table...* (S.1.3.657)

(16) *after that* I shall have another week – pretty hard – *about the seventh to the fourteenth of August*. (S.1.1.148)

This type of combination typically occurs in relatively lengthy, narrative-like contributions to the conversation. The initial adverbial functions as a marker of cohesion. Thus it also signals coherence, showing that an action follows chronologically after the previously described action. The initial adverbial at the same time serves as an overt marker of a topic shift, as in (15), which is the opening sentence of a description of a formal dinner.

A preliminary count shows that over half of the initially placed adverbials in combinations are realized by *then*. Other deictic or anaphoric adverbial expressions are also fairly frequent. They structure the text by making explicit a *temporal continuity* typical of narrative texts (Virtanen 1988: 113). At the same time they serve as convenient sentence-openers; since a temporal *then* can often be inferred in a narrative, it is relatively unimportant in the information structure, and can prepare the ground for the new or more important information which is to come.

In written combinations, too, cohesion is an important reason for having an adverbial in initial position. However, in the written material initial position seems to be exploited for other reasons as well much more often than in the spoken material. The point where I find the most marked difference, is in the use of initial position as a focal point. It seems that the principle referred to above as "the principle of crucial information first" applies above all to written texts. In written combinations it is not unusual to place an informationally heavy adverbial as a marked theme in initial position, whereas this occurs very rarely in the conversation material. Examples of marked theme:

(17) *Thirteen years after he was said to have shot dead a London policeman*, an Irish American *yesterday* stood trial for murder *at the Old Bailey*. (*The Independent*, 11.2.88: 3)

(18) *In Spain after the settlement of the key obstacle in the shape of the agreement to remove the 72 F-16 fighters*, Washington *now* hopes that the way is clear for a new defence pact. (*The Independent* 5.2.88: 10)

In (17) it is interesting to observe that three different adverbial slots have been filled. The initial adverbial is long, and the information it contains is not known. Rather it functions as a necessary background for the interpretation of what follows.

In (18) the initially placed adverbial cluster has been raised from the embedded *that*-clause. Again its most important function must be to mark the setting (and perhaps also to reserve end focus for the last constituent).

It is worth mentioning that as far as combinations are concerned, spoken language shows far less variation than written language. This may have to do with the amount of preplanning involved in the two media. A writer has more time to plan his sentences than a speaker. It is also possible in writing to change things (like word order) before the text is exposed to a text-receiver. The writer may thus exploit word order to achieve some special effect. In speech, intonation can serve the same purpose; see (19–21) below.

In the internal organisation of clusters, too, spoken language displays a greater regularity, as well as a greater degree of conformity to what is normally said in grammars about the order of adjacent adverbials, namely space before time. (See e. g. Close 1975: 285.) Table 4 shows that clusters where the temporal adverbial precedes the spatial one are slightly less frequent in the spoken than in the written material. ("Mixed pattern" could be the order S+T+S or T+S+T.)

Table 4. Internal organisation of clusters in End position containing both spatial and temporal adverbials

	newspapers		*conversation*	
S + T clusters	208	80.9%	112	91.1%
T + S clusters	34	13.2%	11	8.9%
Mixed pattern	15	5.8%	–	–
Total	257	100.0%	123	100.0%

In all the examples of time+space clusters in the conversation material, the space adverbial consists of, or contains, a word with nuclear stress.

(19) I have only seen her *once since I HEARD*[5] *this news* I think *in … the REFECTORY*. (S.1.4.1077)

(20) …cos it draws your EYE *all the time* draws your eye *AWAY from the [pi] OUT of the picture*. (S.1.8.715)

(21) This letter came *LAST week from HER*. (S.1.6.125)

In (19) the spatial adverbial is added as a kind of final specification, nearly an afterthought. (20) is not a straightforward cluster since the predicate is repeated, but still the time adverbial is given before the space adverbial. Here the temporal adverbial seems to function as a kind of pause-filler, while the speaker is thinking of how to express herself next. This impression is of course also due to the fact that the spatial adverbial contains a false start and a correction.

(21) would probably have been unacceptable if the last adverbial, which is predicational, had not constituted a separate tone unit. It is, however, highly unusual to assign nuclear stress to an anaphoric pronoun. The first adverbial is sentential, so the sequence is unusual as regards the ordering of adverbials with different semantic scope, too. The reason for adding the second adverbial must be that the speaker wants to be more specific, although *her* is anaphoric and thus marked as given information.

4. Some concluding remarks

The above discussion will have shown that the distinction between clusters and combinations is relevant and practicable in an investigation of the factors determining adverbial placement. It is also useful in the comparison between different text types, here exemplified by newspaper language and conversation. Note finally that this small study does not pretend to say anything decisive about differences between speech and writing in general. A future study will be based on a much larger sample of material. Several types of text will be analysed along the same lines, and attention will be paid to more aspects of the organisation of adverbial sequences.

Notes

1. David Crystal (1980) also establishes a category of *semantically obligatory* adverbials, i. e. adverbials which are not strictly necessary to make the clause grammatical, but which are crucial in making the message complete. It is not difficult to see why such a category may be desirable, since it is often hard to distinguish between the adverbials required by the syntax and those required by the semantics of the clause. I think, however, that it would be even more problematic to draw a line between adverbials which are needed in order to make the message complete and those which are not.
2. The terminology has been adopted from Quirk *et al.* (1985).
3. The reference is to Svartvik – Quirk (1979).
4. 2A, 3A, 4A denote how many adverbials there are in each sequence.
5. The capital letters serve to mark words carrying nuclear stress.

References

Close, R. A.
1975 *A reference grammar for students of English.* London: Longman.
Crystal, David
1980 "Neglected grammatical factors in conversational English", in: Greenbaum *et al.*, 153–166.
Enkvist, Nils Erik
1976a "Prolegomena to a symposium on 'the interaction of parameters affecting word order' ", in: Enkvist–Kohonen (eds.), 5–13.
1976b "Notes on valency, semantic scope and thematic perspective as parameters of adverbial placement in English", in: Enkvist–Kohonen (eds.), 51–73.
1980 "Motives for topicalisation", in: Thelwall (ed.), 1–15.
Enkvist, Nils Erik – Viljo Kohonen (eds.)
1976 *Reports on text linguistics: Approaches to word order.* Åbo: Åbo Akademi.
Greenbaum, Sidney
1969 *Studies in English adverbial usage.* London: Longman.
Greenbaum, Sidney – Geoffrey Leech – Jan Svartvik, (eds.)
1980 *Studies in English linguistics for Randolph Quirk.* London: Longman.
Hasselgård, Hilde
1988 On position and function of spatial and temporal adverbials. (Unpublished thesis: University of Oslo.)
Horova, Eva
1976 "On position and function of English local and temporal adverbials", *Brno Studies in English, Vol. 12*: 93–123.
Jacobson, Sven
1964 *Adverbial positions in English.* Stockholm: Studentbok.
Quirk, Randolph – Sidney Greenbaum – Geoffrey Leech – Jan Svartvik
1985 *A comprehensive grammar of the English language.* London: Longman.
Taglicht, Josef
1984 *Message and emphasis.* London: Longman.
Thelwall, Robert (ed.)
1980 *Linguistic studies in honour of Paul Christophersen.* (Occasional Papers in Linguistics and Language Learning, No 7.) Ulster: The New University of Ulster.
Virtanen, Tuija
1988 Discourse functions of adverbial placement in English: clause-initial adverbials of time and place in narratives and procedural place descriptions. (Unpublished thesis, Åbo University.)

Sources of data

Svartvik, Jan – Randolph Quirk
1980 *A corpus of English conversation.* Lund: C. W. K. Gleerup.

British newspapers from January/February 1988

Grammatical or nativelike?[1]

Göran Kjellmer

In an influential paper published some years ago, A. Pawley and F. H. Syder (1983: 191–226) showed that although the application of grammatical rules to language material will produce grammatical sentences, such rules cannot be relied on to define the actual usage of native speakers. The rules will allow forms and constructions that are not used by native speakers:

> It is a characteristic error of the language learner to assume that an element in the expression may be varied according to a phrase structure or transformational rule of some generality, when in fact the variation (if any) allowed in nativelike usage is much more restricted. The result, very often, is an utterance that is grammatical but unidiomatic e. g. *You are pulling my legs* (in the sense of deceiving me).

Pawley and Syder suggest that many grammatically possible sequences never occur, and that learners of English as a foreign language often make the mistake of using phrases which are theoretically possible but nevertheless totally un-English. It may reasonably be assumed that the corresponding phenomenon holds for learners of all languages.

Against this background it would be interesting and possibly rewarding to investigate the actual occurrence of "grammatical variation" of a few very basic patterns in a corpus of modern English. The question that should be asked is not, of course, whether the variation in question is represented in the corpus at all – in a reasonably large and representative corpus it is bound to be. The question is rather if the variants are distributed over the items where, according to a grammatical rule "of some generality", it should be found, in the proportions which could be expected, given the overall frequencies of the lexical items. If items belonging to the same rule-defined group differ significantly or very significantly with respect to the incidence of the pattern(s) allowed by the rule, this could be taken as an indication of the existence of lexically-based restrictions that operate within the rule-defined field. Such restrictions could then be seen as instrumental in selecting nativelike sequences from among merely grammatically possible ones.

In the present paper a few grammatically possible patterns and variations will be discussed from this point of view. The basis for the investigation is the Brown Corpus. Although the Corpus is on the small side for the proposed exercise, it might be possible to find indications of general tendencies in the material contained in it.

The first type of variation concerns verb tenses. English verbs are regularly used in both present-tense and past-tense forms. The question that arises in this connexion is to what extent the verbs differ in their distribution of present-tense and past-tense forms, and also which verbs are particularly present-tense prone and which particularly past-tense prone.

Since the Corpus has been tagged,[2] it is convenient to use the tagging for comparative purposes. The tagging distinguishes present-tense third person singular forms, tagged VBZ, and past-tense forms, tagged VBD. It is therefore possible to compare the frequencies of those forms for each verb by computer. At the same time it is obvious that the VBZ category may not contain all the present-tense forms of a given verb: the ones that are formally identical with the infinitive are tagged VB, base form. We could then compare the frequencies of VBZ and VBD, in which case the present tense would be under-represented, or we could compare the frequencies of VB+VBZ and VBD, in which case the present tense would be over-represented. Neither procedure is hence satisfactory on its own. However, a combination of them might be a better solution. We could carry out both comparisons and in either case rank the verbs in the corpus according to their "present-tense" proportions. If we then select the verbs that get top rankings in *both* ranking lists, the resulting collection could be assumed to be a more representative "present-tense" group in the sense that different types of present-tense forms would be more adequately represented (although those forms would still be under-represented as a group). Analogously, we could then select the verbs that are found near the bottom of both ranking lists and regard them as "past-tense" verbs.

For the "present-tense verbs" the following principles were adopted. The verbs with the highest present-tense ratings from the VBZ/VBD ranking list were compared with those with the highest present-tense ratings from the VB+VBZ/VBD ranking list. The number of verbs differed slightly between the lists as it was not possible to use the same cut-off point in both lists, some verbs having the same present-tense proportions. First, from the group of verbs where past-tense forms did not occur at all, those were considered where the number of VBZ (in the first list) and of VB+VBZ (in the second list) was 20 or more. None occurred in both lists, so none qualified for inclusion. Secondly, out of the 39 top "present-tense verbs" in the first list, 16 occur among the 44 top verbs in the second. Those 16 will henceforth be referred to as the present-tense verbs. The verbs, which are arranged in a falling order of "present-tenseness", are shown in Table 1.

Table 1. Present-tense verbs

	VB	VBZ	VBD	VBZ / VBD (a)	(VB+VBZ) / VBD (b)	Rank (a)	Rank (b)	(a)+(b)
amount	30	20	2	10	25	1	2	3
illustrate	17	7	1	7	24	3	4	7
derive	13	9	1	9	22	2	6	8
define	19	5	1	5	24	5.5	4	9.5
distinguish	19	5	1	5	24	5.5	4	9.5
promote	32	4	1	4	36	10.5	1	11.5
conform	10	5	1	5	15	5.5	10	15.5
exceed	18	10	2	5	14	5.5	12.5	18
strengthen	16	4	1	4	20	10.5	8	18.5
influence	18	3	1	3	21	14.5	7	21.5
affect	33	18	4	4.5	12.75	8	15	23
reinforce	10	4	1	4	14	10.5	12.5	23
utilize	10	4	1	4	14	10.5	12.5	23
hurt	15	3	1	3	18	14.5	9	23.5
aid	22	6	2	3	14	14.5	12.5	27
induce	9	3	1	3	12	14.5	16	30.5

Similar principles were applied to the "past-tense verbs". This time the verbs to be considered for inclusion were taken from the bottom of the ranking lists.[3] Altogether 78 verbs were selected in this way from either list; of those, 19 occur in both lists. Those 19 will henceforth be referred to as the past-tense verbs. The verbs, which are again arranged in a falling order of "present-tenseness" and hence in a rising order of "past-tenseness", are presented in Table 2.

A comparison of the two lists (Tables 1 and 2) is revealing. From a semantic point of view it is obvious, both that each list contains verbs that are closely related, and that the two groups are widely separated from each other. The present-tense verbs might be described as verbs of organisation or abstract relations, the common semantic element being less pronounced in the three bottom ones. The present-tense verbs characteristically occur with abstract subjects in expository or discursive types

Table 2. Past-tense verbs

	VB	VBZ	VBD	VBZ / VBD (a)	(VB+VBZ) / VBD (b)	Rank (a)	Rank (b)	(a)+(b)
exclaim	1	1	14	0.071	0.143	1	11	12
pause	5	1	25	0.040	0.240	8	4	12
peer	2	1	19	0.053	0.158	5	9	14
mutter	1	1	16	0.063	0.125	2	13	15
smile	10	3	68	0.044	0.191	7	8	15
lean	7	1	37	0.027	0.216	9	6	15
laugh	9	1	46	0.022	0.217	10	5	15
toss	6	0	22	0.000	0.273	15	1	16
climb	11	0	41	0.000	0.268	15	2	17
roar	1	1	18	0.056	0.111	3.5	14	17.5
swing	11	0	43	0.000	0.256	15	3	18
stumble	1	1	18	0.056	0.111	3.5	15	18.5
flee	1	1	22	0.045	0.091	6	16	22
whisper	4	0	20	0.000	0.200	15	7	22
stare	9	0	58	0.000	0.155	15	10	25
yell	3	0	21	0.000	0.143	15	12	27
nod	4	0	49	0.000	0.082	15	17	32
sigh	1	0	22	0.000	0.045	15	18	33
grin	1	0	29	0.000	0.034	15	19	34

of text. This squares with Johansson's observation (1978: 24) that "the present tense seems to be comparatively more frequent with many verbs [in learned and scientific English]. A natural explanation of this could be that definitions as well as scientific discussion and argument in general are normally expressed in the present tense." The past-tense verbs, on the other hand, could be called verbs of physical action or expression and occur almost exclusively with human subjects. Their proper stylistic sphere would seem to be a narrative style.

So with regard to the choice of tenses it is obvious that different English verbs have different preferences. At the same time, however, it seems possible to derive those preferences from a common guiding semantic or stylistic principle.

The second pattern to be looked into is simply that represented by *to* + infinitive. In principle, every infinitive can be preceded by *to*, its "infinitive marker", given suitable conditions. This is taken so much for granted that no grammar-book and no dictionary to my knowledge tries to specify, in their descriptions of the use of the infinitive marker *to*, any verbs that are especially likely to be preceded by *to*. We shall therefore attempt to find out whether there are any indications in the corpus material that some infinitives are predominantly *to*-infinitives and some predominantly bare infinitives.

We shall again put the tagging to good use. Unfortunately there is no tag for "infinitive" among the verbal tags; as we have just seen, there is, however, the tag VB, which stands for "verb, base form" (Francis—Kucera 1982: 9), and which hence includes the infinitive, but also finite present-tense, imperative and subjunctive forms.

If the verbs in the Corpus are sorted according to the ratio (*to* + VB)/VB, computed for each verb, the top of the list should include the verbs whose infinitives are most disposed and the bottom those whose infinitives are least disposed to take *to*. Only the verbs with a VB frequency of 10 or more were included. The top part of the list is shown in Table 3 and the bottom part in Table 4.

Table 3. Verbs often cooccurring with *to*

	to + VB	VB	% *to* + VB
purchase	11	11	100.00
secede	10	10	100.00
minimize	15	16	93.75
clear	13	14	92.86
free	10	11	90.91
recover	10	11	90.91
swing	10	11	90.91
review	9	10	90.00

There are several reasons why the verbs in the bottom part of the list seem to take *to* only rarely or not at all. No common underlying factor seems to be involved. First, a great many of the verbs are often or regularly followed by *to* : *amount, intend, seem, want, tend, need, wish, like*. It is likely that the combination *to* + VB + *to* is avoided if other ways of expression are available.[4] Secondly, some of the verbs are of the type discussed above, verbs of organisation or abstract relations: *differ, deduct, range, comprise, commute* (in the mathematical sense). Such verbs favour the present tense, as we have seen, so for these verbs more than for other verbs the figure for VB can be suspected of representing instances of the present tense rather than of the infinitive. This assumption

Table 4. Verbs seldom cooccurring with *to*

	to + VB	VB	% *to* + VB
hope	4	68	5.88
mean	9	158	5.70
figure	1	20	5.00
like	9	210	4.29
wish	3	87	3.45
need	5	160	3.13
mind	1	38	2.63
tend	1	43	2.33
want	5	318	1.57
seem	3	229	1.31
owe	0	10	0.00
damn	0	10	0.00
commute	0	10	0.00
comprise	0	11	0.00
beg	0	11	0.00
range	0	12	0.00
deduct	0	12	0.00
intend	0	14	0.00
differ	0	18	0.00
even	0	28	0.00
amount	0	30	0.00

turns out to be well-founded: infinitives make up only a small proportion of the VB forms of the verbs concerned, smaller than for other verbs.[5] Thirdly, a few verbs occur almost exclusively in a very limited number of constructions, none of which is *to* + infinitive: *mind, figure* and *damn*. The predominant patterns of *mind* are AUX (+ NEG) + *mind* (*don't mind*) and the set phrase *never mind*, and in a similar way the predominant pattern of *figure* is AUX (+ NEG) + *figure* (*can't figure out*). *Damn*, finally, occurs exclusively as a subjunctive in the Corpus (*damn it, damn the consequences*), so here VB does not represent a single infinitive.

The verbs in the top part of the list are more difficult to account for. There seems to be no obvious reason why those particular verbs should favour the *to*-infinitive.[6] With a corpus as small as the Brown Corpus, marked random variations are of course to be expected. However, chance fluctuation is hardly the sole explanation, since those verbs that are frequent enough to be considered show similar tendencies in the LOB Corpus.[7] So with regard to the occurrence of the *to*-infinitive, it seems we can predict, in a very approximate fashion, the behaviour of some but by no means all verbs.

A third area that may be of interest here is that of "passivity". English transitive verbs can generally occur in the active or passive voice. Nevertheless, certain constraints operate in this field, constraints that will make a passive transform of an active verb less likely or altogether impossible. "Although it is the general rule that transitive verb sentences can be either active or passive, there are a number of exceptions where the active (transitive) and passive sentences are not in systematic correspondence" (Quirk *et al.* 1985: 3.67). In the present context it is therefore tempting to look into quantitative aspects of the active-passive relation. To do so, we shall again make use of the tagged Brown Corpus.

A computer program was devised that related the frequency of the past participle (VBN) of a given verb immediately preceded by a form of *be*[8] to the overall frequency[9] of that verb in the Corpus. The ratio could be seen as a rough measure of the tendency of any verb in the Corpus to be used in the passive voice. Since the majority of the verbs occurred so infrequently in the Corpus that the ratio had very low reliability, it was decided to include only those verbs that had a frequency of 10 or more. The program then sorted the verbs according to their "passive tendency".

Before we consider the outcome of the operation, a few reservations should be made and a few points should be considered. Some of the *be* + VBN combinations are passives only in a loose sense of the word. Granger (1983: 109–111) refers to such forms as adjectival or verbal pseudopassives, as in

the tsarina *was devoted* to Russia (adjectival pseudopassive), or
as far as I *am concerned* (verbal pseudopassive).

In our statistics they will hence be regarded as passives.

Further, the formula used captures the normal type of passive, i. e. the *be*-passive, but not the *get*-passive (as in *get caught*). The latter "is avoided in formal style, and even in informal English it is far less frequent than the *be*-passive" (Quirk *et al.* 1985: 366).[10] Nor are *become*-passives, *grow*-passives, *stand*-passives or *rest*-passives included (cf. Svartvik 1966: 92–93).

What may be more serious is that the mechanical application of our formula excludes from the passive group examples with interventions between the *be* form and the past participle. Thus, what seemed to be the only case of non-passive *baptize* in the Corpus turned out to be "has been badly baptized".

Finally, it is obvious that passivity as such is not adequately covered by our formula. Passivity can be expressed by past participles on their own in nonfinite clauses, as in

The chief, annoyed by these questions, knocks Voltaire down...

There are, for example, 24 occurrences of the verb *subject* in the Corpus, 22 of which are past participles. 16 of the 22 are immediately preceded by a form of *be*, which thus produces a passivity rate of 16/24 = 66.67%, but none of the remaining six participles are of the active type ("has subjected"), all six being either mediately preceded by *be* ("are thereupon subjected") or else the passive verb of nonfinite clauses ("didn't want them subjected").

The combined effect of the last few factors is therefore that the degree of passivity in the verbs is underrepresented in the statistics based on our formula.

For each verb the incidence of passive forms, defined as above, was given as a percentage. With the reservations just mentioned, this percentage could be seen as the degree of passivity of the verbs. The number of verbs exhibiting different degrees of passivity is shown in Figure 1.

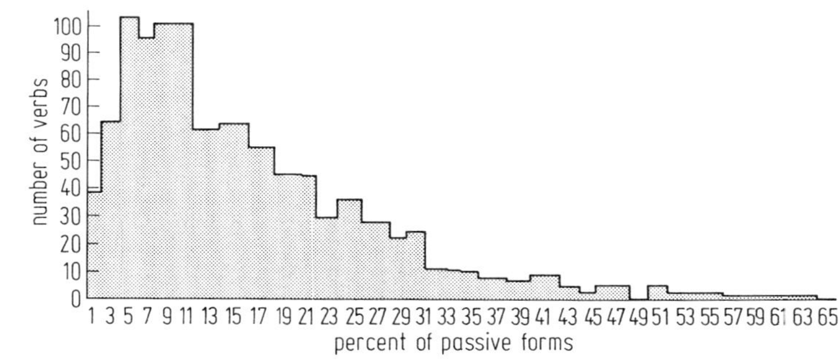

Figure 1. Ratio of passivity of transitive verbs in the Brown Corpus

The diagram represents the distribution of the 996 verbs with a frequency of 10 or more in the Brown Corpus which have at least one occurrence as VBN in the formula *be* + VBN. The last proviso was intended to restrict the verbs to transitive ones. There is a heavy concentration of the verbs to the left half of the diagram. The average degree of passivity of the verbs is 14.78%. The great bulk are used in passive forms in less than a third of their manifestations. (Those with over 33% passive forms account for only 6.2% [62/996].) Here it is essential that the reservations made above should be borne in mind. We can thus take it for granted that the passivity rate is higher than is indicated by these figures.

From our present point of view, both ends of the diagram are interesting. The right-hand part represents the transitive verbs with an exceptionally high proportion of passive forms, and the extreme left represents those with an exceptionally low proportion of such forms. What verbs are they?

Table 5. Verbs with a high passivity rate

Verb	BE + VBN	Total occurrence	Passivity rate (%)
baptize	11	12	91.67
subject	16	24	66.67
situate	12	19	63.16
tempt	11	18	61.11
retrieve	7	12	58.33
institute	8	14	57.14
deposit	6	11	54.55
wage	6	11	54.55
oblige	11	21	52.38
mail	12	23	52.17
transform	19	37	51.35
award	11	22	50
compound	8	16	50
nominate	6	12	50
doom	5	10	50
confine	10	21	47.62
transfer	18	38	47.37
launch	14	30	46.67
affix	7	15	46.67
schedule	19	41	46.34
base	58	130	44.62
arrest	12	27	44.44
credit	7	16	43.75
compute	16	37	43.24
incline	9	21	42.86
amaze	6	14	42.86
punish	6	14	42.86
bury	10	24	41.67
derive	27	65	41.54
bear	82	200	41

If we select the top 30 verbs, those with a high passivity rate, and the bottom 30, those with a low passivity rate, altogether 60 verbs from the

996 in the list, we should be able to compare the two types of verbs. They are listed in Tables 5 and 6.

Table 6. Verbs with a low passivity rate

Verb	BE + VBN	Total occurrence	Passivity rate (%)
eat	2	118	1.69
expand	1	63	1.59
enjoy	2	128	1.56
gather	1	65	1.54
acquire	1	66	1.52
hate	1	66	1.52
grow	4	298	1.34
swing	1	77	1.3
look	11	901	1.22
begin	7	583	1.2
help	4	347	1.15
laugh	1	88	1.14
stare	1	95	1.05
stay	2	192	1.04
watch	2	209	0.96
tend	1	104	0.96
contribute	1	108	0.93
care	1	107	0.93
run	4	433	0.92
suffer	1	110	0.91
live	4	462	0.87
wonder	1	119	0.84
talk	2	276	0.72
love	1	141	0.71
like	2	292	0.68
wish	1	161	0.62
want	2	623	0.32
let	1	412	0.24
get	2	1466	0.14
come	1	1542	0.06

The verbs range from a passivity rate of 91.67% for *baptize* (which, as we saw, would have been 100% with a less mechanical selection criterion) to one of far below 1%.[11] One factor that distinguishes the two types of verbs is immediately obvious, viz. their rate of occurrence in the Corpus. On average the verbs in the high-passivity group occur 31.83 times, while those in the low-passivity group occur 321.73 times, more than 10 times as frequently. The difference might be explained in this way.

It has been shown that there is a high correlation between the frequency of a word and its semantic diversity.[12] Frequent words can be expected to carry more senses and be used in more constructions than infrequent ones. Generally speaking, it is therefore natural that infrequent transitive verbs should show a pronounced tendency to occur in either, but not both, of the two theoretically possible constructions, while frequent transitive verbs should alternate more freely between them. We may therefore expect some infrequent verbs to predominate among the transitive verbs with the highest passivity rate and other infrequent verbs to predominate among those with the lowest passivity rate, the lowest passivity rate being 0. This hypothesis seems to be borne out by the material. The verbs with a passivity rate of 0 are not represented in the table since they of course include the intransitive verbs, which are *a priori* incapable of forming passive transforms, but as it turns out that the verbs with a passivity rate of 0 also represent a substantial proportion of transitive verbs. We shall presently return to them.

If it is natural to expect infrequent transitive verbs to stick to either the passive or the active voice, the question arises what makes those listed under "High Passivity Rate" in the table prefer passivity. Several factors seem to be involved. The action described by the verb may be such that our attention is naturally focused more on the object of the action than on the agent. Such verbs are typically *bear, baptize, bury* and also many of the others: *arrest, punish, doom, confine, tempt, amaze*. A related case is that exemplified by Granger's pseudopassives where the *be* + VBN form "is used in a nonagentive way, i. e. no agent is thought of" (1983: 111): *situate, compound, schedule* in most of their uses. A stylistic factor may also be at work. The passive voice, particularly in the present tense, is a characteristic of "specialized and scientific texts" (Krámsky 1969: 114 ff.). The fact that the verbs *retrieve, subject, deposit, transform* and *compute* have a high passivity rate could therefore be explained by their concentration to scientific texts.

At the other end of the scale we should first discount a largish group of verbs that are primarily intransitive but which become transitive as prepositional or phrasal verbs. They are *talk (away, to), wonder (at), live (in)*,[13] *care (for), stare (at), laugh (off)*, and *look (at/after/into/over/to/up/upon)*. The percentage given for those verbs is misleading in that it does not represent the relation between the passive forms and the forms of the corresponding transitive verb (*be talked to:* TALK TO) but rather the relation between the passive forms and all forms of the verb, most of which are intransitive (*be talked to:* TALK); they will therefore be disregarded in this context. With the exception of *come*, the remaining verbs are ordinarily used, or at least capable of being used, transitively.[14] Unlike other verbs where the passive transform is possible they thus show a marked reluctance to appear in the passive form. Although it is possible to explain the tendency of some verbs not to occur in the passive – thus both *grow* and *run* are primarily used intransitively and hence have little scope for a passive transform – it is difficult to provide a generally valid explanation to account for this reluctance. It may therefore be natural to conclude that there is a strong idiosyncratic, non-rule-bound element in some of these verbs.

The verbs whose passivity rate is 0 fall into several groups. The first group comprises the genuinely intransitive verbs where consequently no passive forms can be expected. They are verbs like *happen, wait, remain* and *exist*, which do not take an object. The second group is made up of verbs that are used both transitively and intransitively (*fail, ride, fly*, etc.). In this group might be included the normally intransitive verbs that occasionally take an object (*stand* something on its head, *walk* one's girlfriend home, *shine* a light on something), which could be of the "cognate object" type (*smile* a happy smile, *die* a peaceful death). Lastly, there is a third group of verbs like *like, suspect, deserve* and *grab*, which regularly or invariably take an object and where we therefore *can* expect passive forms to occur. It is primarily the third group that is of interest in this connexion. Verbs which occur 30 times or more in the Corpus and which belong to this group are listed below.
A few of these verbs, such as *lack*, could be regarded as belonging to a separate class of verbs, sometimes referred to as "middle verbs", stative relational verbs normally occurring only in the active (Quirk et al. 1985: 1014). Other such verbs are *possess, have, suit, become, fit* and *equal* (as in "Five times six equals thirty"). However, while these verbs are not conceivable in the passive (cf. *"A life insurance policy isn't possessed by Jack," Quirk et al. 1985: 1014), many of those in the table above are marginally or definitely possible in the passive.

Finally, in addition to the exclusively transitive verbs, the ones which are used both transitively and intransitively are also of some interest, particularly those which are predominantly transitive. Out of the predominantly transitive verbs, i. e. those most of whose occurrences are transitive in the Corpus, the following are not found in the *be* + VBN

Table 7. Transitive verbs with no passive forms (1)

Verb	BE + VBN	Total occurrence	Passivity rate (%)
demand	0	92	0
lack	0	69	0
survive	0	61	0
favor	0	49	0
suspect	0	47	0
earn	0	44	0
thank	0	44	0
deserve	0	40	0
command	0	38	0
grab	0	38	0
insure	0	37	0
attain	0	35	0
undergo	0	34	0

Table 8. Transitive verbs with no passive forms (2)

Verb	BE + VBN	Total occurrence	Passivity rate (%)
drink	0	85	0
back	0	55	0
cook	0	50	0
advertise	0	47	0
search	0	41	0
score	0	35	0
kiss	0	31	0
wave	0	30	0

formula and consequently have a passivity rate of 0. (Only those verbs are listed which occur 30 times or more.)
So even if "he kisses her" a great many times in the Corpus, "she is not kissed by him" even once!

It is sometimes clear why a verb figures in this list. *Drink* is there because, in the context *be + drunk, drunk* with reference to human beings is tagged JJ (adjective) and is hence not included among the *be* + VBN cases; moreover, the past participle *drunk* seems to be avoided even with reference to beverages, presumably beccause of unwanted associations.[15] It may also be unnatural to passivise active clauses whose objects are parts of the body or personal belongings (cf. ?*the man's shoulders were shrugged,* ?*his hair was scratched*, ?*her watch was looked at*); this would explain the 0 passivity rate of *wave*. But on the whole it is again obvious that many of the verbs of which no passive forms have been found are at least marginally possible in a passive construction.

So, to sum up this section, it seems clear that a number of English verbs which are theoretically capable of alternating between the active and the passive voice are markedly reluctant to do so, occurring as they do almost exclusively in one of the two voices. Although many of these extreme cases can be explained with reference to general principles, not all of them can. To describe them structurally as just transitive verbs with the implication that they are equally likely to occur in the active and in the passive voice does them less than justice.

Let us conclude. We have seen that there are indeed variations and exceptions within some rule-defined domains of the English verb, variations and exceptions which are partly due to chance fluctuations but which cannot all be accounted for by reference to some general principle. This circumstance should be particularly relevant to lexicographers but is also of importance to linguists in general. It is certainly an important task of linguists to find and define the rules and general principles that operate in a language or any language, but, almost as importantly, they must realise that their conclusions are open to modification by lexically based restrictions.

Notes

1. I am very grateful to Christian Sjögreen, who put his programming expertise at my disposal, and to Alvar Ellegård, who commented on an earlier version.
2. "...the rationale for the tagging is basically syntactic, though some morphological distinctions with little syntactic significance have been recognized" (Francis – Kucera 1982: 9).
3. From the first list those verbs were selected where the VBZ/VBD ratio was between 0.00 and 0.08 plus those with a VBZ/VBD ratio of 0.00 where the number of VBD was 20 or more. From the second list were selected the verbs with a VB+VBZ/VBD ratio of 0.00 – 0.273; there were no verbs in the second list with a ratio of 0.00 where the number of VBD was 20 or more.
4. It has been shown, for instance, that *help* is followed by the bare infinitive ("help me read") much more frequently than by the *to*-infinitive ("help me to read") if *help* is itself preceded by *to*. (Kjellmer 1985: 159 – 160.)
5. 3 out of 18 in *differ*, 4 out of 12 in *deduct*, 2 out of 12 in *range*, 2 out of 11 in *comprise* and 0 out of 10 in *commute*.
6. Thus 100% of the VB-forms of *purchase* are preceded by *to* (11/11), while for instance only 65.7% of the corresponding forms of *buy* (46/70) and 68.3% of those of *sell* (28/41) are *to*-infinitives.
7. In LOB, *to* + VB answers for 9 of the 11 VB cases of *purchase* (= 81.8%), 7 of the 13 VB cases of *clear* (= 53.9%) and 8 of the 17 VB cases of *recover* (= 47.1%), all of them well above average (which in the Brown Corpus is 40.0%).

8. *Be, being, been, am, -'m, is, -'s, was, were.*
9. I. e. the combined frequencies of the tag classes VB, VBZ, VBD, VBG and VBN.
10. In Granger's corpus of spoken English there are 53 *get* + VBN forms as against 1,157 *be* + VBN forms, i. e. an approximate proportion of 1 : 22 (Granger 1983: 193).
11. *Come* is clearly not a transitive verb. The one case of *come* in the *be* + VBN formula is "They that have turned the world upside down, are come hither also" (from G38). A handful of verbs (one of which is *come*) with an active meaning can be used with the *be*-construction in present-day English. See Rydén – Brorström 1987: 211 – 212.
12. See Kjellmer (1986), with references.
13. Two of the four passives of *live* occur with the "cognate subject" *life*: "my life was being lived", "life as it is lived".
14. *Come* is intransitive (see note 11), and *stay* occurs passively in two archaic-sounding sentences: "Thou wilt keep him in perfect peace, whose mind is stayed on thee" and "...let the hand of vengeance be stayed".
15. Cf. William Safire's column "On Language" in the *New York Times Magazine*, 22 April 1990:
"I can understand a liquor company not using the word *drunk* in an ad," writes Ernest M. Lorimer of Stamford, Conn., "but this sentence clanks and should have been rewritten."
The advertisement in question ... was for Gilbey's gin, and read in part: "Coincidentally, the martini has made a return as well. And it's still drank the same way it was sixty years ago."

References

Francis, W. Nelson – Henry Kucera
1982 *Frequency analysis of English usage: Lexicon and grammar.* Boston: Houghton Mifflin.

Granger, Sylviane
1983 *The BE + past participle construction in spoken English.* Amsterdam: North-Holland.

Johansson, Stig
1978 *Some aspects of the vocabulary of learned and scientific English.* (Gothenburg Studies in English 42.) Göteborg.

Kjellmer, Göran
1985 "*Help* to/ *help Ø* revisited". *English Studies* 66: 2.
1986 "Legible but not readable: On the semantics of English adjectives in *-ble.*" *Studia Neophilologica* 58: 11 – 38.

Krámsky, Jiri
1969 "Verb-form frequency in English". *Brno Studies in English* 8: 111 – 120.

Pawley, A. – F. H. Syder
1983 "Two puzzles for linguistic theory: Nativelike selection and nativelike fluency", in: Richards, J. C. – R. W. Schmidt (eds.), *Language and communication.* London: Longman, 191 – 226.

Quirk, Randolph et al.
1985 *A comprehensive grammar of the English language.* London – New York: Longman.

Rydén, Mats — Sverker Brorström
1987 *The* be/have *variation with intransitives in English.* Stockholm: Almqvist and Wiksell.

Svartvik, Jan
1966 *On voice in the English verb.* The Hague—Paris: Mouton.

Collocation and bilingual text

Jacques Noël

1. Introduction

Investigating collocation in bilingual texts and corpora, as is done in this paper, has become an increasingly popular pursuit in recent years, especially in the context of theoretical studies on translation and machine translation. It is with this objective in mind that Buro voor Systeemontwikkeling (BSO), an Utrecht-based Dutch firm active in MT research, developed, jointly with a Brigham Young University team under Allen Melby, what I will refer to as, the BSO corpus. This corpus contains some 2.5 MB of UN and EEC bilingual English-French machine-readable texts, produced by scanner and made available to us under a research contract with BSO. Recently, I received various unpublished papers on compound translation units by BSO's senior researcher Dr. Victor Sadler and by an ISSCO team in Geneva (Catizone – Russell – Warwick 1989).

Let me also mention:

a) a recent Langenscheidt French-German dictionary, aptly called *Kontextwörterbuch* (Ilgenfritz – Stephan-Gabinel – Schneider 1989): its introduction is centred on the notion of collocation. Despite its limitations (only nouns have entry status; only collocations involving nouns are given; some fixed phrases have been left out) it offers a rich spectrum of word combinations and examples. Its concentration on nouns is perhaps one of the most obvious testimonies to the merits of tagging in practical lexicography (see below).

b) BBI (Benson – Benson – Ilson 1986), the well-known monolingual English combinatory dictionary.

c) Johansson and Hofland's selective lists of collocations in the LOB corpus (1989; hereafter JH).

For translation purposes, however, and in particular for the English-French language pair, this paper starts from the finding that most monolingual and bilingual dictionaries fail to provide the kind of collocational data available in the BSO corpus and other bilingual texts. Using the BSO corpus with students in English and in translation, we (Jocelyne

Vanandroye, who was my assistant, and myself) also found that as teachers we performed poorly on collocations even in French, our mother tongue (in fact, no better or worse than in English), and that students were no better, either in monolingual production or bilingually. For example, *further attention* (not in BBI, not in JH) and *further* (adj) *progress* (in JH, not in BBI) are not easy to translate into French, or to retrieve from their French equivalents.

This paper, then, explores a computerized procedure for uncovering collocation data in bilingual texts. The procedure consists of three main steps, and, unlike the two papers just mentioned, does not postulate the use of any special formalism (the BSO system in the BSO paper) or of statistical techniques (as does the work of the Geneva group).

2. Step one: transforming bilingual text into parallel text

It is common knowledge that a text in one language is not the same length as its translation in the other language and, to limit myself to the English-French language pair (or F-E, no matter which one is prior), an English text is always shorter than the French translation. For translators this creates such practical problems as the costing of a translation job (do you base your tender on the length of the text in the source or in the target language, or both?) and various problems of typesetting and layout. The computational problem addressed in this paper is how to produce a given text and its translation that will run parallel, that is, in the words of the ISSCO authors, how to automatically establish correspondences between bilingual texts. Unlike Catizone – Graham – Warwick (1989), however, I do not attempt sentence-by-sentence alignment as such, because linguistically or for other reasons (such as adaptations for various groups of readers: see "Acid rain" in the appendix), translationally equivalent texts need not exhibit such parallelism. Rather, what I have developed is a semi-automatic procedure that results in parallelism or near parallelism for any given text in terms of the number of lines taken on the printed page. In other words, the method consists of determining a ratio that will serve to edit the French and the English versions of a text so as to produce the same number of lines in the two languages.

My first successful attempt was based on a 30/35 ratio; the 46/54 ratio worked almost as well for the same text, a *Scientific American* text on acid rain and its French translation (published in *Pour la science*). After removing the blank lines, I first formatted (Unix fmt) the English text with right AND left justification (-j), using 30 characters per line (-l 30), and did the same with the French text, but giving it 35 characters per line (-l 35); I then displayed the two in two columns (pr -mt x y). Note that the English is in upper case, in order to distinguish homographs such as *causes* and *CAUSES*; English is, of course, the obvious choice for such transliteration, as unlike French it does not rely heavily on accents.

The Unix (MKS) and CLAN instructions are displayed in the appendix, section one, 1.1 and the first lines of the resulting file are appended in 1.2. Section two shows the first lines of each text interspersed horizontally.

Note that the 30/35 ratio performs very well on this pairing task, as the divergence between English and French at the end is only ten lines in a bilingual text file of 2,711 lines. Unix left and right justification is crucial to obtain this result as it is language-independent, the interword spaces being entirely variable and computed by Unix for each line in accordance with the number-of-character-per-line parameter of the format (fmt) instruction.

Though it works well with a fair number of texts, it should be made clear that the 30/35 ratio is by no means a universal magic formula applying to all texts. As I found with other texts, in the BSO corpus, such ratios are text-specific and are therefore to be established empirically for each text. Rarely, however, did I find strong divergence from the 30/35 ratio, which can thus be seen as indicative of some average difference in length between the English and French versions of any given text.

Once the parallel texts have been produced, there are various pairing methods available, two under Unix or in the formalism of CLAN, and a third one which comes as a standard feature in some editors:

a) Either the texts are run parallel in columns vertically; part of the BSO corpus was provided to us ready-made in such a two-column layout for use under the WordCruncher text retrieval system (the rest of the corpus was unedited bilingual text of rather poor quality, which took quite a long time to edit); though I have not been able to reconstruct the method, manual or automatic, used to produce this layout, it may be useful to show a small sample of it in order to appreciate the difference in length between English and French even at sentence level (appendix, section three). A small extract from my WordCruncher version of the "Acid rain"/"Pluie acide" parallel texts is appended as section four.

b) Alternatively, as was shown in our second figure (section two), the text lines can be run in parallel across the page, using the "merge" option of CLAN's pair-instruction, or the equivalent *interspersing* facility in Unix. This horizontal mode seems to be less popular with some users, even if it has the obvious advantage of making it possible to edit the two texts at the same time and without upsetting the line records. Capitalizing the English is important not only for ease of perception and visualization but also for retrieval when working with a language pair with such misleading false friends and homographs as English and French.
c) A third possibility is to partition the screen horizontally into two windows, in which the two parallel texts can be edited and scrolled, as in various editors and wordprocessors, which enable you to swap windows. A facsimile of this is shown as section five.

3. Step two: marking up English collocations

After some hesitation I decided to begin by marking up collocations in a large set of English texts in the BSO corpus. This proved to be profitable for various reasons, and particularly because, for those of us who are nonnative speakers of English, collocations are easier to identify in English than in our mother tongue even though, as already noted, we have difficulty translating them into French. The interesting thing about parallel texts is that they greatly facilitate the identification of collocational and other equivalents in the other language.

Despite the possibility of using frequency to do at least part of the job of identifying collocations (the method followed by Johansson and Hofland), I decided to do it all by hand. My assistant was asked to mark up as "xyz" or "xy" all expressions of three or two words believed to be collocations, irrespective of their grammatical nature and function.

The xy and xyz strings were then deleted and the truncated texts, together with their integral French translation, were provided to our undergraduate students in English and to MA students in translation as slot-filling exercises, and as selective translation exercises. A sample of xyz-annotated text is given in section six of the appendix, and the opening lines of a parallel English-French version of the same text is given in section seven.

Because such marking up in half a megabyte of text is quite time-consuming, and based purely on intuition, it is open to various types of criticisms. One may argue that the illustrative passage is undercoded and that many more expressions could be considered to be collocations (for example, *my first real look at it*). One might also feel that there are some mark-ups (see section nine of the appendix) which most people would not call collocations in any commonly accepted sense of the term (even if they are clearly idiomatic: *X'beggar-my neighbour'X YapproachY to State aid*, for example).

Before giving more examples from our work with the BSO corpus, let me turn briefly to the problem of what is meant by collocation in this paper. Consider two examples:

– *provide information* (BBI, under *information*); we believe that this is rightly entered as a collocation and that *provide data* (BSO) should also be recorded.

– *isolated/rare case* (BBI, under *case*); similarly, *exceptional case* (BSO) should also be recorded as a collocation.

To define collocation (including BBI's notion of *lexical collocation*) we can best refer to the definition of LDOCE (Procter 1978; new edition): *a habitual combination of words which sounds natural* (for example, *strong coffee* vs. **powerful coffee*). But the definition is incomplete, as it relies on the example following; so what distinguishes lexical collocation from other idiomatic word combinations is that alternative combinations of equivalent or synonymous words (for more details on this aspect, see FJ Hausmann's introduction to *Langenscheidts Kontextwörterbuch* [Ilgenfritz – Stephan-Gabinel – Schneider 1989]) are less idiomatic (*find a job* vs. *land (oneself) a job/décrocher un emploi*) or even clearly inappropriate (**unhook a job*, a literal translation of the French idiom). Also, in contrast with most classic definitions of collocation I would stress the possibility of having several equivalent idiomatic word combinations: *give* (etc)/*pay* (vs. **invest*) *attention*.

Admittedly it is not easy to draw the line between collocation and compound translation units, even if this is a broader notion, as I wish to show in the next illustrations: see section eight of the appendix. 8.1 and 8.2 of the appendix give typical *translation units* and 8.3 is in addition intended to make the point, well-known to translators, that more often than not the literal translation is not idiomatic, and does not read well. Wherever this is the case, there is a strong likelihood of collocational restriction.

4. Step three: searching bilingual texts for collocations

To conclude, I would like to provide samples of three types of batch searches which turned out to be most productive and revealing. Computationally, these searches made use of a number of methods: the find-instruction of DOS, or the equivalent egrep in Unix; or the kwal instruction with its convenient windowing facility in CLAN. The main advantage of the Unix and CLAN batch searches over equivalent WordCruncher searches (not illustrated here: various French translations of *implement(ation)* found in Melby's BSO corpus, for example) is that such batch searches enable one to search the raw, unprepared text and that one can search for up to 500 words in a single search query, using the -i(nclude) option in CLAN or the -f(ile) option of egrep in Unix.
a) Section nine of the appendix gives an alphabetically sorted list of xyz expressions found by a search on xyz in our hand-coded BSO corpus. Despite possible criticisms, it is clear that such a list contains collocations not entered in our dictionaries.
b) Section ten of the appendix – a passage from Melby's BSO corpus in which xyz annotations were added for the two languages – is intended as a further plea for compiling fresh mono- and bilingual collocational facts.
c) Ideally, tagged bilingual corpora should be available for such compilations. What comes closest to this ideal is concentration on a given part of speech, such as nouns in the Langenscheidt dictionary I have referred to. Focussing on a noun which is a notorious false friend and homograph in the E-F language pair, namely *ATTENTION, attention*, sections eleven, twelve, and thirteen of the appendix give sample occurrences of these words in the hand-coded BSO corpus (12, 13) and in Melby's (15), illustrating the differences between the two languages.
d) Lastly, section fourteen of the appendix illustrates an interesting possibility offered by parallel texts, which remains to be investigated, namely the use of keywords in one language (here French) to uncover collocations in the other language. In this illustration, from Melby's BSO corpus, *draft declaration* was found, corresponding to *projet de déclaration*, using a keyword (the French word *projet* appearing in collocations discovered in the xyz hand-coded BSO corpus).

References

Benson, Morton – Evelyn Benson – Robert Ilson
1986 *The BBI combinatory dictionary of English. A guide to word combinations.* Amsterdam – Philadelphia: Benjamins.
Catizone, Robert – Russell Graham – Susan Warwick
1989 *Deriving translation data from bilingual texts.* Geneva: ISSCO.
CLAN
undated *Child Language Analysis Package.* Pittsburgh: Carnegie Mellon University.
Johansson, Stig – Knut Hofland
1989 *Frequency analysis of English vocabulary and grammar based on the LOB Corpus.* Volume 1: Tag frequencies and word frequencies. Volume 2: Tag combinations and word combinations. Oxford: Clarendon Press.
Ilgenfritz, Peter – Nicole Stephan-Gabinel – Gertraud Schneider
1989 *Langenscheidts Kontextwörterbuch,. Französisch-Deutsch. München: Langenscheidt.*
Mohnen, V.
1988 *The challenge of acid rain, Scientific American* 259 (2): 14–22.
1988 Le danger des pluies acides, *Pour la Science* 132: 54–62.
Procter, P.
1987 *Longman dictionary of contemporary English* (LDOCE). Harlow: Longman
MKS Unix Utilities
Waterloo, Ontario: Mortice Kern Systems, MKS.
Sadler, Victor
1989 a *Handling lexical divergence in machine translation.* Utrecht: Buro voor Systeemontwikkeling (BSO/Research).
1989 b *Translating with a simulated bilingual knowledge bank.* BKS.
1989 c *The bilingual knowledge bank: A new conceptual basis for MT.*

Appendix

Section One

1.1 Unix: fmt -j -l 30; fmt -j -l 35; pr -mt e f (OR pair e f, in CLAN)

1.2 THE CHALLENGE OF ACID RAIN ACID RAIN'S EFFECTS IN SOIL AND WATER LEAVE NO DOUBT ABOUT THE NEED TO CONTROL ITS CAUSES. NOW ADVANCES IN TECHNOLOGY HAVE YIELDED ENVIRONMENTALLY AND ECONOMICALLY ATTRACTIVE SOLUTIONS. THE ATMOSPHERE FUNCTIONS AS A	Le danger des pluies acides. Les pluies acides dégradent tant le sol et l'eau qu'il est urgent d'en maîtriser les causes. Les progrès scientifiques et techniques ont abouti à la mise au point de solutions économiquement et écologiquement intéressantes. L'atmosphère se comporte comme un réservoir où se produisent des

Section Two

THE CHALLENGE OF ACID RAIN
Le danger des pluies acides Les
ACID RAIN'S EFFECTS IN SOIL
pluies acides dégradent tant le
AND WATER LEAVE NO DOUBT
sol et l'eau qu'il est urgent d'en
ABOUT THE NEED TO CONTROL ITS
maîtriser les causes. Les progrès
CAUSES. NOW ADVANCES IN
scientifiques et techniques ont
TECHNOLOGY HAVE YIELDED
abouti à la mise au point de
ENVIRONMENTALLY AND
solutions économiquement et
ECONOMICALLY ATTRACTIVE
écologiquement intéressantes.
SOLUTIONS.
L'atmosphère se comporte comme un
THE ATMOSPHERE FUNCTIONS AS A
réservoir où se produisent des

Section Three

```
|U1|S0|L0                              /            +
|S0|L0                                 / —
|L1 @P1                                / @P1
|L2 ⟨u Chapter I ⟩u HISTORICAL         / ⟨u Chapitre I ⟩u HISTORIQUE
|L3 BACKGROUND OF THE WORLD            / DE L'ASSEMBLÉE MONDIALE SUR LE
|L4 ASSEMBLY ON AGING                  / VIEILLISSEMENT
|S1|L0                                 / —
|L1 1.  On various occasions           / 1.  Avant 1977 – et même dès
|L2 before 1977, and even as long      / 1948, année où l'Assemblée
|L3 ago as 1948 when the General       / générale a adopté la
|L4 Assembly adopted resolution        / résolution 213 (III) relative
|L5 213 (III) concerning a draft       / à un projet de déclaration des
|L6 declaration on the rights of       / droits des vieillards –, la
|L7 the elderly, the subject of        / question du statut social des
|L8 the position of the elderly or     / personnes âgées et des
|L9 aged or older persons in           / vieillards avait à plusieurs
|L10 society had received              / reprises et dans des contextes
|L11 incidental attention in the       / divers, bénéficié de
|L12 General Assembly of the United    / l'attention de l'Assemblée
L13 Nations and in the United          / générale des Nations Unies et
|L14 Nations bodies specially          / des organes des Nations Unies
|L15 concerned with social             / spécialisés dans les questions
```

|L16 questions. / sociales.
|S2|L0 / —
|L1 For example, in article 11 of / Ainsi, à l'article 11 de la

Section Four

|@ THE CHALLENGE OF ACID RAIN
2 ACID RAIN'S EFFECTS IN SOIL
3 AND WATER LEAVE NO DOUBT
4 ABOUT THE NEED TO CONTROL ITS
5 CAUSES. NOW ADVANCES IN
6 TECHNOLOGY HAVE YIELDED
7 ENVIRONMENTALLY AND
8 ECONOMICALLY ATTRACTIVE
9 SOLUTIONS.
|@ THE ATMOSPHERE FUNCTIONS AS A

Le danger des pluies acides Les
pluies acides dégradent tant le
sol et l'eau qu'il est urgent d'en
maîtriser les causes. Les progrès
scientifiques et techniques ont
abouti à la mise au point de
solutions économiquement et
écologiquement intéressantes.
L'atmosphère se comporte comme un
réservoir où se produisent des

Section Five (Facsimile)

THE CHALLENGE OF ACID RAIN ACID RAIN'S EFFECTS IN SOIL AND WATER LEAVE NO DOUBT ABOUT THE NEED TO CONTROL ITS CAUSES. NOW ADVANCES IN TECHNOLOGY HAVE YIELDED ENVIRONMENTALLY AND ECONOMICALLY ATTRACTIVE SOLUTIONS.
THE ATMOSPHERE FUNCTIONS AS A POOL AND CHEMICAL-REACTION VESSEL FOR A HOST OF SUBSTANCES. MANY OF THE MOST IMPORTANT ONES – OXYGEN, CARBON DIOXIDE AND NITROGEN AND SULFUR COMPOUNDS, FOR EXAMPLE – ARE RELEASED BY THE ACTIVITY OF ORGANISMS. OFTEN WITH THE HELP OF THE WATER CYCLE, THEY PASS THROUGH THE ATMOSPHERE AND ARE EVENTUALLY TAKEN UP AGAIN INTO SOIL, SURFACE WATER OR ORGANIC MATTER. THROUGH TECHNOLOGY, HUMAN BEINGS HAVE ADDED ENORMOUSLY TO THE ATMOSPHERIC BURDEN OF SOME OF THESE

Le danger des pluies acides Les pluies acides dégradent tant le sol et l'eau qu'il est urgent d'en maîtriser les causes. Les progrès scientifiques et techniques ont abouti à la mise au point de solutions économiquement et écologiquement intéressantes.
L'atmosphère se comporte comme un réservoir où se produisent des réactions chimiques entre de très nombreuses substances. Les plus importantes de ces substances – l'oxygène, le dioxyde de carbone, l'azote et les composés du soufre, par exemple – sont dégagées par les organismes. Entraînées, souvent par le cycle de l'eau, elles circulent dans l'atmosphère avant de se redéposer au sol, à la surface de l'eau ou dans la matière organique. Les industries ont tant surchargé l'atmosphère en certaines de ces substances que les répercussions

Section Six

My first contact with space and my first real look at it was, as for many others of the second generation, coincidental with the launch on 4 October 1957 of Sputnik-I, the first man-made object to have orbited the Earth. Of course, the fact that the Soviet Union had made this possible was as strong a XcauseX YofY ZastonishmentZ as the intrinsic value of the event itself. With no exceptions whatsoever, the front pages of the newspapers had titles several centimetres high and all celebrated the technical challenge. Without any information on how the event had been made possible, the most imaginative and exotic designs of the hypothetical launcher made up of many fancy shaped boosters and stages, were offered to our incredulous eyes and left the best comics of that time far behind. My own XimaginationX was YstruckY, but I did not realise how XprofoundX the YconsequencesY of the event would be on the orientation of my studies and on my own later life. At that time, I was a 20-year-old student at the University of Paris where I was studying physics with the intention of later teaching this subject myself. I was, as many others in the same situation, trying to XfindX my YwayY ZthroughZ the equations without any particularly well focused motivation. The 4 October event XopenedX

Section Seven

MY FIRST CONTACT WITH SPACE AND
MY FIRST REAL LOOK AT IT WAS,
AS FOR MANY OTHERS OF THE
SECOND GENERATION, COINCIDENTAL
WITH THE LAUNCH ON 4 OCTOBER
1957 OF SPUTNIK-I, THE FIRST
MAN-MADE OBJECT TO HAVE ORBITED
THE EARTH. OF COURSE, THE FACT
THAT THE SOVIET UNION HAD MADE
THIS POSSIBLE WAS AS STRONG A
XCAUSEX YOFY ZASTONISHMENTZ AS
THE INTRINSIC VALUE OF THE
EVENT ITSELF. WITH NO
EXCEPTIONS WHATSOEVER, THE
FRONT PAGES OF THE NEWSPAPERS
HAD TITLES SEVERAL CENTIMETRES
HIGH AND ALL CELEBRATED THE
TECHNICAL CHALLENGE. WITHOUT
ANY INFORMATION ON HOW THE
EVENT HAD BEEN MADE POSSIBLE,

Mon premier contact avec l'espace
et ma première vision de ce qu'il
était réellement, coïncidèrent,
comme pour bien d'autres de la
seconde génération, avec le
lancement, le 4 octobre 1957, de
Spoutnik-1, le premier objet
artificiel à tourner autour de la
Terre. Bien entendu, le fait que
l'Union Soviétique ait fait
l'exploit était une cause
d'étonnement au moins aussi grande
que la valeur intrinsèque de
l'événement lui-même. Sans aucune
exception, les premières pages des
journaux étalaient leurs titres
sur plusieurs centimètres de haut,
et toutes célébraient le défi
technique. Sans aucun détail sur
la façon dont l'événement avait

Section Eight

(1) (the system's) established status
(2) are not likely to succeed

solide implantation du système
seraient probablement vouées à
l'échecl&

(3) From file ⟨bsol1-3.byb⟩

*** File bsol-3.byb. Line 1464. Keyword: sincerely
|L4 task was to deal with the
|L5 problems of aging. Where
|L6 other, more general, issues
|L7 arose, no matter how
|L8 important, she sincerely hoped
|L9 that their political content
|L10 would not distract the
|L11 Assembly from this noble task
|L12 or prevent it from adopting

/ mémoire que leur tâche
/ primordiale était de s'occuper
/ des problèmes du
/ vieillissement. La Présidente
/ a vivement souhaité que si
/ d'autres problèmes à caractère
/ plus général, si importants
/ soient-ils, se posaient, leur
/ contenu politique ne distraie

Section Nine

X'beggar-my-neighbor'X YapproachY to State aid.
XAccordinglyX, in the last twenty
XAdoptionX YaboveY ZobjectiveZ
XAgainstX YdisquietingY ZbackgroundZ, the Commission
XAllX YinY ZallZ, the Japanese automobile industry has attained such a
XAllowingX YgreaterY ZsayZ
XAlongX YsameY ZlinesZ, perfection of an instant
XAnalysisX and
XAsX YaY ZresultZ, the amplitude and frequency of the
XAsX YregardsY ZcostZ, it is generally agreed the price of
XAsX YstatedY by the president of the Commission and the Member of the
XAssessX YitsY ZimpactZ
XAtX YallY ZeventsZ
XAtX YallY ZeventsZ
XAtX YanyY ZeventZ
XAtX YthisY ZstageZ, let us confine ourselves to an analysis of the
XAverageX YhourlyY ZearningsZ
XBasisX YwageY ZcalculationZ
XByX YjudiciousY ZuseZ
XCarefulX Yconsideration ZgivenZ
XCollectionX YofY ZdataZ
XConciliationX YbeY ZeffectedZ
XContactX YmadeY ZwithZ
XCooperationX YincreasedY through
XDeclarationX YissuedY on 15

Section Ten

|L4 ASSEMBLY ON AGING	/ VIEILLISSEMENT
|L4 Assembly adopted Xresolution	/ xrésolution 213 (III) yrelative
|L5 213 (III) Yconcerning a draft	/ à un projet de déclaration des
|L7 the elderly, the Xsubject of	/ xquestion du statut social des
|L8 the position of the elderly or	/ personnes âgées et des
|L9 aged or older persons in	/ vieillards avait z1à plusieurs
|L10 society and Yreceived	/ reprises et z2dans des contextes
|L11 Z1incidental Z2attention Z3in the	/ divers, ybénéficié de
|L12 General Assembly of the United	/ l'zattention de l'Assemblée
|L14 Nations Xbodies Yspecially	/ des xorganes des Nations Unies
|L15 Z1concerned Z2with social	/ y1spécialisés y2dans les zquestions
|L1 For example, in article 11 of	/ Ainsi, à l'article 11 de la
|L4 (resolution 2542 (XXIV) of 11	/ domaine social (résolution
|L5 December 1969, which also	/ 2542 (XXIV) du 11 décembre
|L9 Covenants on Human Rights) the	/ l'homme et aux pactes
|L10 XGeneral Assembly had Yreferred	/ internationaux relatifs aux
|L11 ⟨u inter alia ⟩u to the Zneed	/ droits de l'homme, l'xAssemblée
|L12 to protect the rights and	/ générale yévoquait notamment la
|L13 Xassure the Ywelfare of the	/ znécessité de protéger les
|L14 aged.	/ droits et d' xassurer le
|L15 +	/ ybien-être des personnes âgées.

Section Eleven

e04b01: as toxicity with particular attention
e04b01: cialX YattentionY should be ZpaidZ to fire
e04b01: XfurtherX YattentionY must be ZgivenZ.
e11b01: to the attention of the Council the need for a
e11b01: YadverselyY, and for XparticularX YattentionY to be
e11b01: XSpecialX YattentionY should be ZdevotedZ to this
e11b03: last October drew attention to the economic
e12b02: by drawing their attention to the result of
e13b01: XparticularX YattentionY should be ZdrawnZ to the ap-
e13b01: this context, XparticularX YattentionY must be ZpaidZ
e13b01: ensure that XeverX YcloserY ZattentionZ is paid to the
e13b01: world, XgivingX YspecialY ZattentionZ to the problems
e13b01: The Ten have continued to XpayX YcloseY ZattentionZ
e13b02: ZattentionZ of the XhostX YgovernmentY. In the absence
e13b02: mary drawing the attention of the Political
e13b02: which XattractedX YmuchY ZattentionZ, to play an
e17b02: the problems of space should XengageX YtheY ZattentionZ of scientists

Section Twelve

f04b01: utilisées. Une attention particulière devrait être accordée aux
f04b01: l'attention : Mise au point et essai de procédés visant à
f04b01: l'attention sur le nombre croissant d'accidents imputables au
f04b01: d'attirer l'attention sur les méthodes de travail au jour des
f04b02: aux répercussions du bruit. Notamment, une attention spé- ciale
f11b01: privilé- giant les régions défavorisées et une attention
f11b01: Il s'agit là d'un phénomène qui requiert une attention
f11b02: plus grande attention, notamment compte tenu de l'accroissement
f11b03: ces deux domaines doit en effet être examinée avec attention.
f13b01: sée entre les institutions. Une attention particu
f13b01: chant une attention particulière aux problèmes
f13b02: l'attention du gouvernement auprès duquel il
f13b02: l'attention du Comité politique sur les ques
f17b02: naturel que les questions spatiales attirent l'attention des

Section Thirteen

446 |S658|L0	/ —
447 |L1 Special attention is being	/ On accorde d'autre part un
448 |L2 paid to the difficult position	/ intérêt tout particulier à la
449 |L3 of girls. To persuade	/ position précaire des filles.
450 ————————————	
451 |L4 aspects of the vocational	/ branche. On se bornera à
452 |L5 training courses. We will	/ parler de l'alternance de
453 |L6 concentrate our attention in	/ l'enseignement à l'école et de
454 |L7 the following on the	/ l'enseignement pratique au
455 |L8 alternation of the training	/ cours de la formation et à
456 ————————————	

457 |L6 be seen from the survey / l'alternance de l'enseignement
458 |L7 contained in Fig. 3. The / à l'école avec l'enseignement
459 |L8 reader's attention is also / pratique. On se reportera pour
460 |L9 drawn to the laws referred to / plus de détails aux textes des
461 |L10 in this survey. / lois mentionnées dans ce
462 ————————————
463 |L27 this rule). Thus in terms of / faible, plus ses risques de
464 |L28 long-run employability, / chômage sont élevés (il semble
465 |L29 attention must be paid to the / toutefois que l'Italie fasse
466 |L30 training opportunities / exception à cette règle). Il
467 |L31 available to all young / convient par conséquent, si
468 |Done with file ⟨bso1-3.byb⟩

Section Fourteen

From file ⟨bso1 – 3.byb⟩

*** File bsol-3.byb. Line 10. Keyword: projet
|L3 ago as 1948 when the General / générale a adopté la
|L4 Assembly adopted resolution / résolution 213 (III) relative
|L5 213 (III) concerning a draft / à un projet de déclaration des
|L6 declaration on the rights of / droits des vieillards -, la
|L7 the elderly, the subject of / question du statut social des

---

*** File bsol-3.byb. Line 16. Keyword: attention
:IL9 aged or older persons in / vieillards avait à plusieurs
|L10 society had received / reprises et dans des contextes
|L11 incidental attention in the / divers, bénéficié de
|L12 General Assembly of the United / l'attention de l'Assemblée
|L13 Nations and in the United / générale des Nations Unies et

---

*** File bsol-3.byb. Line 24. Keyword: progrès
|S2|L0 / —
|L1 For example, in article 11 of / Ainsi, à l'article 11 de la
|L2 the Declaration on Social / Déclaration sur le progrès et

Key Word Index

Stig Johansson
Anna-Brita Stenström (Editors)

English Computer Corpora

Selected Papers and Research Guide

1991. VII, 402 pages. 75 illustrations. Cloth.
ISBN 3 11 012395 9
(Topics in English Linguistics 3)

The contributions in this collection show the wide range of current work on machine-readable texts in English language research. The contributors discuss grammar, syntax, lexis, speech, dialects, specialized corpora and software.

Most of the papers report on descriptive studies, but more general topics such as probabilistic grammar study and quantitative versus qualitative analysis are also covered.

The volume also contains a detailed survey of English machine-readable corpora and a full bibliography of publications drawing on some major computer corpora (primarily the Brown Corpus, the LOB Corpus and the London-Lund Corpus), and thus serves both as a research guide and a description of the state of the art in English corpus work.

mouton de gruyter

Berlin · New York

Dieter Kastovsky (Editor)

Historical English Syntax

1991. 23 x 15.5 cm. VIII, 510 pages. With 80 illustrations.
Cloth ISBN 3 11 01243190
(Topics in English Linguistics 2)

This volume presents historical English syntax as a field no longer limited to one or two topics. The collection presents discussions of such topics as modals, the typological status of Old English syntax, per-, post- or adpositions, reference, passives, valency, hypotaxis/parataxis, and negation as well as more commonly treated subjects such as word-order and *do*-periphrasis.

Table of contents:

J. Anderson, Should · *L. Breivik*, On the typological status of Old English · *F. Colman*, What positions fit in? · *A. Danchev*, Language change typology and some aspects of the SVO development in English · *H.-J. Diller*, Pronoun and reference in Old English poetry · *O. Fischer*, The rise of the passive infinitive in English · *U. Fries*, Question-answer sequences in Old English · *A. Jucker*, Between hypotaxis and parataxis. Clauses of reason in *Ancrene Wisse* · *V. Kniezsa*, Prepositional phrases expressing adverbs of time from Late Old English to Early Middle English · *M. Kytö*, *Can (Could)* vs. *may (might)*: regional variation in Early Modern English? · *A. Mukhin, N. Yulikova*, Locative valency of the English verb: a historical approach · *T. Nevalainen*, Motivated archaism: the use of affirmative periphrastic *do* in Early Modern English liturgical prose · *M. Rissanen*, Spoken language and the history of *do*-periphrasis · *M. Rydén*, The *be/have* variation with intransitives in its crucial phases · *D. Stein*, Semantic aspects of syntactic change · *R. Stockwell, D. Minkova*, Subordination and word order change in the history of English · *T. Swan*, Adverbial shifts: Evidence from Norwegian and English · *Gunnel Tottie*, Lexical diffusion in syntactic change: frequency as a determinant of linguistic conservatism in the development of negation in English · *S. Wright*, On the stylistic basis of syntactic change.

mouton de gruyter

Berlin · New York